T0032844

ALSO BY QUINN SLOBODIAN

*Globalists: The End of Empire and
the Birth of Neoliberalism*

*Foreign Front: Third World Politics in
Sixties West Germany*

CRACK-UP
CAPITALISM

CRACK-UP CAPITALISM

Market Radicals and the Dream of a World Without Democracy

QUINN SLOBODIAN

METROPOLITAN BOOKS

Henry Holt and Company

New York

Metropolitan Books
Henry Holt and Company
Publishers since 1866
120 Broadway
New York, New York 10271
www.henryholt.com

Metropolitan Books® and ▣® are registered trademarks of
Macmillan Publishing Group, LLC.

Library of Congress Cataloging-in-Publication data is available.

ISBN: 978-1-250-75389-2

Our books may be purchased in bulk for promotional, educational, or business use. Please
contact your local bookseller or the Macmillan Corporate and Premium Sales Department at
(800) 221-7945, extension 5442, or by email at MacmillanSpecialMarkets@macmillan.com.

First Edition 2023

Designed by Kelly S. Too
Maps by Marion Kadi

Printed in the United States of America

1   3   5   7   9   10   8   6   4   2

for my sister, Mayana

But early in the twenty-first century it became clear that the planet was incapable of sustaining everyone alive at Western levels, and at that point the richest pulled away into their fortress mansions, bought the governments or disabled them from action against them, and bolted their doors to wait it out until some poorly theorized better time, which really came down to just the remainder of their lives, and perhaps the lives of their children if they were feeling optimistic—beyond that, *après moi le déluge*.

Kim Stanley Robinson, *The Ministry for the Future*

CONTENTS

CRACK-UP
CAPITALISM

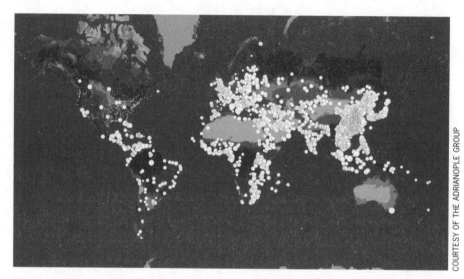

The world's special economic zones. The dot size corresponds to the area covered by each zone. For an interactive version of the map see openzonemap.com.

Shatter the Map

Without looking at your phone, how many countries are there in the world? Not sure? The answer is about two hundred, more or less. Now think ahead to the year 2150. How many will there be then? More than two hundred? Fewer? What if there are a thousand countries? Or only twenty? What about two? Or one? What kinds of futures would these maps suggest? What if everything depended on the answer?

The person posing this thought experiment in 2009 was the forty-one-year-old venture capitalist Peter Thiel.[1] Having made a small fortune by founding PayPal and investing early in Facebook, he had just taken a huge hit in the financial crisis the year before. He now had one thing on his mind: how to escape from the tax-collecting democratic state. "I no longer believe that freedom and democracy are compatible," he wrote. "The great task for libertarians is to find an escape from politics in all its forms."[2] The more countries there were, the more possible places to take your money, and the less likely any country would be to raise taxes for fear of spooking the goose that laid the golden eggs. "If we want to increase freedom," he said, "we want to increase the number of countries."[3]

Thiel cast the idea of a world of thousands of polities as the utopian dream of a future reality. What he didn't mention was that the future he was describing in many ways already existed.

A standard globe shows an uneven mosaic of colors, pixelated more densely in Europe and Africa, easing out to broader chromatic stretches across Asia and North America. This is a familiar vision of the world, the one that we have been taught since grade school, the one that Thiel was referring to: each patch of land with its own flag, its own anthem, its own national costume and cuisine. The opening parade of the Olympic Games performs this version of the globe every couple of years, reassurance that it's a small world after all.

But we make a mistake if we see the world only in this jigsaw of nations. In fact, as scholars remind us, the modern world is pockmarked, perforated, tattered and jagged, ripped up and pinpricked. Inside the containers of nations are unusual legal spaces, anomalous territories, and peculiar jurisdictions. There are city-states, havens, enclaves, free ports, high-tech parks, duty-free districts, and innovation hubs. The world of nations is riddled with *zones*—and they define the politics of the present in ways we are only starting to understand.[4]

What is a zone? At its most basic, it is an enclave carved out of a nation and freed from ordinary forms of regulation. The usual powers of taxation are often suspended within its borders, letting investors effectively dictate their own rules. The zones are quasi-extraterritorial, both of the host state and distinct from it. Zones come in a bewildering range of varieties—at least eighty-two, by one official reckoning.[5] Among the more prominent are the special economic zone, the export-processing zone, and the foreign-trade zone. At one end of the socioeconomic spectrum, zones can be nodes in the networks of cross-border manufacturing.[6] Often ringed by barbed wire, these are sites for low-wage production. At the other end, we can see a version of the zone in the tax havens where transnational corporations secrete away their earnings—what the economist Gabriel

Zucman calls "the hidden wealth of nations."[7] The flight of corporate profits to these low- or zero-tax jurisdictions costs the United States alone $70 billion a year in tax revenue, while offshore tax shelters hold an estimated $8.7 trillion of the world's wealth.[8] Some Caribbean islands count more registered companies than residents.[9] In his first run for office, candidate Barack Obama singled out Ugland House in the Cayman Islands, which contained twelve thousand corporations. "That's either the biggest building or the biggest tax scam on record," he said.[10] In fact, it was totally legal, a workaday fact of the global financial system.[11]

There are over 5,400 zones in the world, far more regimes than in Thiel's fantasy of a future world of a thousand countries. One thousand new zones have appeared in the last decade alone.[12] Some are no bigger than a factory or a warehouse, a switch-point in the logistical circuitry of the global market, or a site for storing, assembling, or refining a product to avoid tariffs.[13] Others are urban megaprojects— such as New Songdo City (Songdo International Business District), in South Korea; Neom, in Saudi Arabia; or the city of Fujisawa, in Japan—which run under their own rules like private city-states.[14] In 2021, lawmakers in Nevada floated a similar idea, suggesting they might let corporations that relocate to their state write their own laws—the return of the company town a century later, made over as the "innovation zone."[15] In the United Kingdom, the Conservative government made the creation of a chain of duty-free zones or free ports the centerpiece of a proposal to "level up" the deindustrialized North after Brexit. Its quixotic goal? To compete with Dubai's Jebel Ali Free Zone, founded in 1985, where corporations enjoy half-century tax holidays and have access to foreign laborers housed in dormitories and paid a fraction of a British living wage.[16]

I use the metaphor of perforation to describe how capitalism works by punching holes in the territory of the nation-state, creating zones of exception with different laws and often no democratic oversight. The philosopher Grégoire Chamayou adds another metaphor, likening projects of privatization to the technique of the longhorn beetle, gnawing away at the structure of society from inside.[17] We could reach for another metaphor and recall how a piece of lace is made by knotting threads together with gaps in between. What emerges gives the impression of a pattern by what is left out. The insider's term for this is *voided patterning*. To understand the world economy, we need to learn to see the voids.

Most of the world's zones are in Asia, Latin America, and Africa. China alone has almost half of them. Europe and North America combine for less than 10 percent.[18] Yet as we will see, zones have some of their most ardent supporters in the West, who hail them as experiments in what I call *micro-ordering*, or the creation of alternative political arrangements at a small scale. Champions of the zone suggest that free-market utopia might be reached through acts of secession and fragmentation, carving out liberated territory within and beyond nations, with both disciplining and demonstration effects for other states. "Localized freedom," the Heritage Foundation's Stuart Butler wrote in 1982, "can rot the foundations of the unfree state around it."[19] Promoters of perforation cast themselves melodramatically as guerrillas of the Right, reclaiming—and decomposing—the nation-state, zone by zone. Once capital flees to new low-tax, unregulated zones, the theory goes, nonconforming economies would be forced to emulate these anomalies. By starting small, the zone sets out to model a new end state for all.

This book tells the story of what I call *crack-up capitalism*. It is, at once, a description of the world that has come into being through the uncoordinated efforts of private actors seeking profit and economic security over the last forty years, enabled by willing governments, *and* the tale of a deliberate ideology. Crack-up capitalism is a label for both the way the world works and a way that specific people hope to continue to change the world. It is a way to describe a world that is both ever more interconnected and ever more fragmented. Crack-up capitalists spot signs of the mutation of the social contract and ask whether they could accelerate and profit from the dynamics of dissolution. They are students of what Lionel Shriver calls in her 2016

novel, *The Mandibles*, "the recently minted genre of apocalyptic economics."[20]

The zone is not only out there in the world. The zone begins at home.
For most, this does not mean outright secession or the creation of a
new state—not seizing the heights of power but the accretion of many
small acts of refusal. One market radical calls this *soft secession*.[21] We
can secede by removing children from state-run schools, converting
currency into gold or cryptocurrency, relocating to states with lower
taxes, obtaining a second passport, or expatriating to a tax haven.[22]
We can secede, and many have, by joining gated communities to create private governments in miniature. By the new millennium, about
half of all new developments in the American South and West were
gated and master-planned.[23] Gated enclaves are global, from Lagos to
Buenos Aires.[24] In India, gated communities began with the seizure of
public roads through the installation of steel barriers, before moving
on to blue-sky master-planned "colonies" clustered around special
economic zones.[25]

A venture capitalist who worked for Peter Thiel coined an ingenious term when he called this form of soft secession *underthrow*.[26]
For him, the best model of politics was the corporation. We opt in
and out as customers. If we don't like the product, we shop elsewhere.
Nobody demands anything of us and we feel obliged to nobody in
particular. We rely, in the classic dichotomy laid out by the economist
Albert Hirschman a half century ago, on exit rather than voice.[27]

Each act of soft secession—each corporation stashing away its
profits with a brass-plate company in Switzerland or the Caribbean;
each standoff over grazing rights with federal agents; each rent-a-cop,
contractor, or mercenary hired to patrol, jail, or raid—is another small
victory for the zone, another pinhole in the collective. We are being
encouraged to live in zones by those who profit most by our abdi-
cation from the shared set of responsibilities. A hundred years ago,
the robber barons built libraries. Today, they build spaceships. This
book is a history of the recent past and our troubled present, when
billionaires dream of escaping the state, and the idea of the public is

repellent. It tells the story of a decades-long effort to pierce holes in the social fabric, to opt out, secede, and defect from the collective.

To UNDERSTAND THE significance of crack-up capitalism, we need to step back and recall the big stories scholars have told about the last several decades. The fall of the Berlin Wall on November 9, 1989, inaugurated an era of globalization. In his novel *Islands in the Net*, Bruce Sterling conjured a vision of this hyperconnected earth "all netted together in a web over the world, a global nervous system, an octopus of data."[28] The dominant visualizations are of connection: blue lines of lasers linking the world's far-flung locations, a skein of exchange and mobility. The trend was toward interconnection: the World Trade Organization, the European Union, and the North American Free Trade Agreement were created within a few years of one another. But there was also an alternative timeline if you looked closely, one that was marked as much by fragmentation as unity. The two Germanys unified in 1990, but the Soviet Union splintered the following year. Yugoslavia dissolved as the European Union formed. Somalia descended into a civil war and would have no central state for over a decade.

New barricades replaced old ones as the Cold War ended. Goods and money were free to flow, but not people. Walls were built the world over. By one estimate, more than ten thousand miles of borders worldwide have been hardened with barriers.[29] In 1990, the United States planted its first stretch of border fence, south of San Diego. President Bill Clinton liberalized trade in North America while he authorized Operation Gatekeeper, further fortifying the southern border.[30] Two months after the Wall fell in Berlin, the BBC released a drama called *The March*, which follows a Sudanese man as he musters people displaced by war and poverty to march across North Africa to Europe. The final scene shows the caravan arriving in a resort town in southern Spain, climbing steps toward a wall of armed troops as a helicopter hovers overhead. An African teenage boy in a Miami

Dolphins cap is shot dead on the beach by the soldiers, an icon of cosmopolitanism's broken promise. Since 2014 alone, upwards of twenty-four thousand people have died at sea attempting to reach Europe.[31] Globalization has both centripetal and centrifugal force. It binds us together while it tears us apart.

This book homes in on the 1990s as an underrated period of political ferment and a crucible of national and post-national imagination. The story we tell of the decade—based on ever-broader integration and ever-larger economic unions—must be flipped to show the depth of the secessionist energy and zeal for experiments in micro-ordering. When the political scientist Francis Fukuyama speculated about "the end of history" in 1989, he meant the convergence of the world around the model of liberal democracy but also the uncontested reign of a particular model of arranging the earth: divided into bound, self-determining nation-states within a single global economy linked through public international law.[32] But the ongoing evolution of global capitalism has changed the picture. The end of empire and the end of communism birthed a bevy of new sovereign nation-states even as another political form was also coming into being. From the 1990s, and increasingly so through the present day, the nation-state has been joined by the new entity of the zone.

Zones help us rethink globalization as a fracturing of the map into what scholars call the "archipelago economy of offshore," with territories engaged in perpetual competition for roving clients, savers, and investors.[33] In the wake of the blockbuster research of Thomas Piketty and Emmanuel Saez, and the jaw-dropping revelations of the Panama and Paradise Papers, we are beginning to learn more about one particular kind of zone, the tax haven.[34] But to see the zone as a device of "wealth hoarders" is both true and not enough.[35] We must appreciate how, for market radicals, the zone was not merely the means to an economic end but an inspiration for the reorganization of global politics as a whole.

The zone serves many functions for the capitalist right. The specter of the zone and the attendant threat of capital flight serve to blackmail out of existence the remains of the social state in Western Europe and North America. The zone also showcases a second belief central to the shared imagination of the contemporary political right: a belief that capitalism can exist without democracy. When Germany reunified, the political philosopher Raymond Plant observed that "in the light of the collapse of communism in Eastern Europe, some may think the relationship between capitalism and democracy is obvious. Yet this is far from the case, and some of those who have been in the intellectual forefront of the debate about free markets are now rather worried about the relationship between markets and democracy." He pointed out that "according to this argument, democracy as it has grown up in Western societies may be inimical to the growth and maintenance of markets."[36] To some, longtime colonial holdouts like Hong Kong, homelands in apartheid South Africa, and the authoritarian enclaves of the Arabian Peninsula offered evidence that political freedom may actually corrode economic freedom.

The idea of capitalism without democracy circulates more broadly than we might think. One of President Donald Trump's chief economic advisors and nominees to the Federal Reserve Board, Stephen Moore, a longtime fellow of the Heritage Foundation and mainstream right-wing intellectual, stated frankly: "Capitalism is a lot more important than democracy. I'm not even a big believer in democracy."[37] Far from an idle joke or a slip of the tongue, this is a well-formulated position that has quietly been on the advance for the last fifty years, shaping our laws, institutions, and the horizon of our political aspirations.

The shattering of the world map has not happened spontaneously. It has had its champions. This book is about those who came before and after Thiel, the people who have seen a crack-up coming and cheered it on. After the Cold War's end, they proposed something surprising: maybe capitalism had secretly lost. Maybe social democratic superstates were picking up where communist ones left off, as state spending was only continuing to grow. Maybe for the true victory of capitalism, it was necessary to go further. What if the end of history was not the checkerboard of two-hundred-plus nation-states

existing under conditions of liberal democracy, but tens of thousands of jurisdictions of various political systems in constant competition? As one market radical put it, "What if the greatest political trend of the past two hundred years, namely the centralization of state power, reverses in the twenty-first century?"[38] What if society needed to be founded anew?

Beginning in the 1970s, the zone offered a sleek alternative to the messiness of mass democracy and the sprawl and bloat of unwieldy nation-states. Secessionism, not globalism, was the mantra of the thinkers at the core of this book. It follows this group of market radicals around the globe for half a century as they look for the ideal container for capitalism. The journey leads from Hong Kong to the London Docklands to the city-state of Singapore, from late apartheid South Africa to the neo-Confederate American South and the former frontier of the American West, from the war zones of the Horn of Africa to Dubai and the world's smallest islands, and finally to the virtual realm of the metaverse. The proponents of crack-up capitalism envisioned a new utopia: an agile, restlessly mobile fortress for capital, protected from the grasping hands of the populace seeking a more equitable present and future.

In his 2020 novel *Red Pill*, Hari Kunzru describes a man writing a manifesto in a hallucinatory state "about a system that would eventually find itself able to dispense with public politics altogether and put in its place the art of the deal: a black box, impossible to oversee, visible only to counterparties. There would be no checks and balances, no right of appeal against the decisions of the deal-makers, no 'rights' whatsoever, just the raw exercise of power."[39] This captures the world described in the pages of this book: a radical form of capitalism in a world without democracy.

PART I

ISLANDS

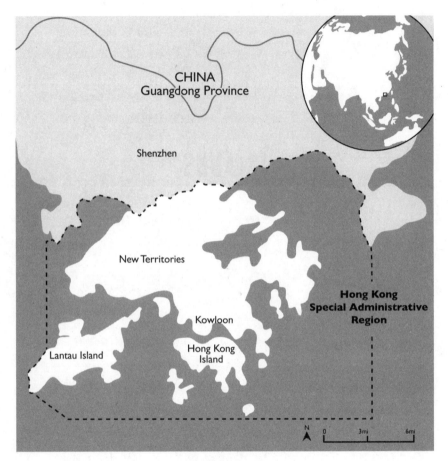

Hong Kong

Two, Three, Many Hong Kongs

When Peter Thiel spoke of a world of a thousand nations, it was not speculation—it was a business plan. He was presenting at an event for an institute he funded that had the goal of drastically increasing the number of the world's territories. Details came from the man who joined him at the lectern, a Google software engineer in his early thirties. "So, the future," he began, and riffed on his plans for turning political sovereignty into a for-profit enterprise.[1] Since time immemorial, he wrote elsewhere, there had been only one way to create a new nation: break up an existing one, subdivide the land, and rename it. It was a hard business to get into. You often needed to fight a war. But what if you could make a polity where none existed before?[2] What if unclaimed space was out there somewhere, waiting? His proposal: repurpose offshore oil rig technology and set up settlements beyond the jurisdiction of terrestrial states, homesteading the high seas.[3] Beyond the "exclusive economic zone" that stretches two hundred miles out from every country's shore, the open ocean was free for private exploitation and political experimentation. "Seasteads" would escape the taxing and regulating state, declare independence, and spark what he dubbed a "Cambrian Explosion in government."[4] In the jargon of Silicon Valley, these would be *start-up nations*.

The man onstage was Patri Friedman. He had a famous grandfather, perhaps the century's most notorious economist, both lionized and reviled for his role in offering intellectual scaffolding for ever more radical forms of capitalism and for his sideline in advising dictators: Milton Friedman. The two shared a basic lack of commitment to democracy. "Democracy is not the answer," Patri wrote, it is merely "the current industry standard."[5] His ideal communities would be modeled on corporations. "You just get more effective products from corporations competing with each other for customers than you get from democratic systems," he said.[6] In the fortieth-anniversary edition of his bestselling *Capitalism and Freedom*, published in 2002, Milton agreed. "While economic freedom is a necessary condition for civil and political freedom," he wrote, "political freedom, desirable though it may be, is not a necessary condition for economic and civil freedom."[7]

Milton cited his favorite example: Hong Kong. More than anything, Hong Kong had persuaded him that capitalist freedom could be secured without the ballot box. Standing onstage, Patri echoed his grandfather, saying that what he wanted to see was a "floating Hong Kong."[8] The header for his blog included a slogan adapted from Mao Zedong—"Let a Thousand Nations Bloom"—but the image was of Hong Kong, and the logo looked suspiciously like a sinuous version of the bauhinia flower on Hong Kong's flag.[9] What was it about the territory that made it the perfect template? To understand the Friedmans' enthusiasm, we must travel decades earlier to when Milton fell for his colonial capitalist paradise.

1.

In late 1978, inflation was high and rising in the United States. Britain was entering its own "winter of discontent," a record-breaking number of labor actions helping to spawn a backlash that culminated with union-buster Margaret Thatcher's rise to power. Unrest rumbled in

Iran, where revolutionary leftist students joined with their no less revolutionary religious counterparts to overthrow the government, speaking in the name of God and the people with fists in the air. The three largest countries in South America languished under military rule. Vietnam invaded Cambodia, and China prepared to invade Vietnam. The world was in the grip of what a group of political scientists, including Samuel Huntington, described in an influential report as a "crisis of democracy." The authors wondered if the world had become "ungovernable," whether social life had become too complex and popular pressures too great for governments to adequately respond. They quoted the West German chancellor Willy Brandt's prediction that "Western Europe has only twenty or thirty more years of democracy left in it."[10] The cover of the report showed a national flag in a rifle's crosshairs.

Doom ruled the world, but the sun shone in Hong Kong. In late September 1978, Milton Friedman smiled as he gestured at the city spiked with white skyscrapers glittering in the South China Sea behind him. Here, he promised, was a solution to the crisis, a place far from the paroxysms of popular sovereignty. Perhaps this place, he suggested, might be the desirable end state for global capitalism. Perhaps the ideas of national self-determination; one man, one vote; and the power of the people were so many detours, cloverleafing roads to serfdom, and this impeccable vessel for commerce and finance— armored against the demands of the population but nimbly responsive to the demands of the market, a capitalist juggernaut at full throttle—was the future. What if we needed to short-circuit the chaos of democracy to ensure the success of the market? What if the flag in the crosshairs actually had to be shot to make the world governable again? What if the era when the nation-state dominated political aspirations, from the end of the First World War to the 1970s, was no more than a blip? "I believe a relatively free economy is a necessary condition for a democratic society," Friedman would say in an interview in 1988. "But I also believe there is evidence that a democratic society, once established, destroys a free economy."[11]

Hong Kong's origins tell a story about how Friedman's ideal state was created—at the barrel of a gun. The British claimed Hong Kong Island in perpetuity as the spoils of the First Opium War with the Treaty of Nanking in 1842. Blessed with a deep and wide harbor protected from typhoons by a mountain left over from a Mesozoic supervolcanic explosion, its city was named Victoria after the monarch and turned into an entrepôt free of customs duties with the economy driven by the drug trade—the through traffic of opium grown and processed in India and shipped on to Chinese consumers.

The British hoped that trade would unite the Chinese "in amicable intercourse" with "the more active and enterprising inhabitants of what we are accustomed to call the civilized world" (meaning themselves), but the intercourse was less than amicable and they were less than civilized.[12] Britain and France instigated the Second Opium War, which led to the British acquisition of Kowloon, across the harbor, in 1860. In 1898, the Japanese defeated China and took Taiwan as their booty. Smelling weakness, other European powers began a "scramble for concessions," turning the Chinese coast into a Swiss cheese of more than eighty treaty ports, concessions, and international settlements.[13]

Ceded to foreign powers on leases ranging from a quarter century to perpetuity, the coastal concessions were both of China and outside of it—states of exception, or zones. The foreigners inhabiting the zones were extraterritorial. Even on Chinese land, they were governed by their own laws, and their crimes were tried by their own courts.[14] Hong Kong itself was a mixed entity. While the island and Kowloon were possessions of the British, the agricultural hinterland of the New Territories was leased to Britain for ninety-nine years in 1898, expanding the colonial footprint tenfold. The broader Chinese economy was also forced open by law. While its sovereignty was left formally intact, treaties bound the government to a low tariff policy. The "most-favored-nation" principle meant that the privileges granted one power, say the United States, were immediately granted to the Russians, the Germans, the French, and so on.

These laws were remembered as the "unequal treaties"—the core of China's "century of humiliation." A leading Chinese diplomat referred to them in 1912 as secured "with the aid of the sword."[15] Less often observed is how the combination of violence, territory, and law helped set the template for the economic globalization in the century that would follow. Zones created patchworks of semi-sovereignty: container ports and military bases were ceded on long-term leases; trade organizations like the WTO worked on the most-favored-nation principle; and treaties allowed foreign investors to be governed by their own courts. Far from the relic of a sepia-tinted past, the constellation of enclaves was a preview of the future.

Hong Kong thrived in the new legal landscape. Beginning as a trading port, it accelerated into manufacturing for global markets after the 1949 victory of the Communist Red Army drove people into the city, to be funneled into the small workshops and factories popping up everywhere. Around one million refugees and migrants— more than the colony's total population when the British retook it from the Japanese in 1945—brought labor and capital, especially from the commercial center of Shanghai. Hong Kong's population quadrupled from 1945 to 1956.[16] Its factories were small, informally organized, and responsive to changes in consumer demand. Workshops would pop up and close down as needed with many located in six-story "flatted factories" built by the government to boost trade.[17] Hong Kong focused on the downstream end of the value chain, making cheap goods for export—consumer products for the postwar baby boom, from textiles and clothing to plastic flowers, dolls, and packaged foods.[18] By 1972, the colony was the world's biggest exporter of toys.[19] By the late 1970s, it was the world's top exporter of clothing.[20] A territory of less than five hundred square miles, it was the twentieth-largest global exporter, with its economy growing at 10 percent a year.[21] It had also gone from a manufacturing center to rapidly become the financial center of Asia.[22] The number of banks more than doubled in the 1970s and their assets grew by six times.[23]

This was the moment when Friedman touched down in Hong Kong.

Funded by conservative donors, including the Getty Oil company and the Sarah Scaife Foundation, he was there to film the first episode of what would be his wildly popular PBS series *Free to Choose*.[24] In his midsixties, Friedman was nearing the end of his academic career and reaching the height of his fame. His regular *Newsweek* column was already read in the homes of millions of Americans, and his star rose further when he won the Nobel Memorial Prize in Economics in 1976. The series would broadcast into homes all over the United States and eventually in Britain, accompanied by a book version, which spent an astounding fifty-one weeks on the *New York Times* bestseller list as the top-selling nonfiction book of 1980. For $4,800 (around $17,000 in today's money), you could enjoy videotapes of the man whom *Time* called Uncle Miltie at home or in the classroom.[25] "By now," one journalist wrote, "the cherubic countenance and gnome-like figure of economist Milton Friedman are standard features on the American intellectual landscape."[26]

In Friedman's Hong Kong scenes on-screen, the impish economist ambled past vegetable stalls and fishmongers, and the camera grazed over curbside tinkers and back-alley ivory ateliers. Transitioning from footage of New York's Chinatown, Friedman praised the sweatshop, reminiscing about his own mother's previous work under similar conditions. The libertarian magazine *Reason* celebrated the hire-and-fire model in Hong Kong: small factories would take on employees for a job as short as a month and terminate them thereafter.[27] In what one journalist called "Milton Friedman's dream world," "labor is obliged to go wherever capital directs it, for whatever it chooses to pay."[28] Friedman himself dubbed Hong Kong "an almost laboratory experiment in what happens when government is limited to its proper function": people know that when people fail, "they bear the cost."[29]

The episode was titled "The Power of the Market," but it was really about finding shackles for the state. How could one prevent governments from expanding welfare programs, extending social entitlements, and spending more on new areas like environmental protection, health care, public education, and energy conservation? It was these many demands, among others, that Friedman held responsible for the spike of inflation and unemployment in the 1970s. He saw Hong Kong as a breath of fresh air in a decade dragged to ruin by the demands of popular sovereignty in both the Global North and the Global South. People's choice to divorce, have children out of wedlock, or loll around on university campuses studying Herbert Marcuse and Karl Marx had strained government budgets.[30] There was no such mollycoddling in Hong Kong.

What made such discipline possible was first and foremost the absence of democracy. No labor unions or popular elections meant no leverage for workers or citizens. Hong Kong's financial secretary was more important than its colonial governor.[31] The British colony was run more like a "joint stock corporation" than a nation, as an admirer put it.[32] One of Friedman's colleagues at the conservative Hoover Institution, Alvin Rabushka, praised Hong Kong as an "approximation to the textbook model" of neoclassical economics "made possible by the absence of an electorate."[33] Policymakers were "free from the ever-present electoral pressures that prevail in economic decision-making in most democratic polities."[34] Rabushka celebrated Hong Kong's model of "administrative absolutism" and the "no-party administrative state."[35] It was the very "absence of politics," he wrote, that allowed for "economic freedom."[36] The result? Not always a comfortable or secure life but rather one where "working people here in Hong Kong accept the verdict of market forces."[37] Rabushka also noted that the free enterprise system depended upon "the fact of continued colonial status."[38] Hong Kong had been permitted by London to set its own trade and taxation policy since the late 1950s.[39] This decoupled it from the construction of the welfare state in postwar Britain while the disenfranchisement of the local population as subjects rather than citizens prevented disruptive moves to self-determination. The colonial governor kept taxes low and tariffs nonexistent. In 1978, the top rate of income tax in the UK was 83 percent and in the United States it was 70 percent. Meanwhile Hong Kong had no taxes on capital gains or inheritance and a flat income tax of 15 percent. The secret to making

Hong Kong "the last truly capitalist place on earth," as the director of the Hong Kong Chamber of Commerce called it, was that it succumbed to neither the siren song of decolonization nor democracy.[40]

Friedman filmed the scenes for *Free to Choose* while he was in Hong Kong for another occasion: the biennial general meeting of the Mont Pelerin Society. Founded by the Austrian-British economist Friedrich Hayek in 1947 to defend against the threat of creeping socialism and the welfare state, the MPS was a private club of intellectuals, politicians, think tankers, and journalists. (Friedman himself was a founding member and the society's president in the early 1970s.) Its members called themselves *neoliberals* into the 1950s.[41] Although the term has many definitions, this book uses *neoliberal* as a helpful shorthand for those associated with the MPS and its affiliated think tanks.

Within the neoliberal group, there were thinkers of different shades but they were united by the belief that capitalism had to be protected from democracy in the age of mass democracy. There were a few main groups of thinkers. Those that concern us most in this book would recognize themselves in the term *libertarian*. Although libertarianism contains many schools and tendencies, they are united by the belief that the state's role is to protect the market, not to own property, manage resources, direct companies, or deliver services like health care, housing, utilities, or infrastructure. Maintenance of inner and outer security, the protection of private property, and the sanctity of contract: these should be the main role of the government. The main difference, as we will see, is between those who believe in a minimal state (sometimes called minarchists) and those who believe in no state at all (known as anarcho-capitalists).[42]

It must have been easy to fall in love with Hong Kong when the society met there in 1978. The weather was balmy and the sky was not yet clouded by the haze from the coal furnaces of Shenzhen that would later become the norm. MPS conference attendees were housed at two of the city's most luxurious hotels, the Excelsior and the Mandarin.[43] A striking hexagon of over forty stories of beveled windows, the Excelsior was built on "Lot Number One"—the first plot of land auctioned off after the British took possession of the island. The Mandarin, meanwhile, was the city's first five-star hotel and the first in Asia to have bathtubs and direct-dial telephones in every room.[44] It was so iconic as a destination for the jet set that a journalist quipped later that you could "write an insider's London political column" from the lobby.[45]

Both hotels were owned by the British firm Jardine Matheson, also known as Jardines. One of the original Hong Kong merchant houses, it had made its start selling opium to the Chinese in the 1830s. Later it pivoted into retail, shipping, and hospitality, getting into China early (with joint ventures there in 1979) and getting out early too— switching its base of operations to Bermuda, where the tax rate hovered at an attractive zero percent.[46] A couple of years after the Mont Pelerin meeting, Jardines would become widely known under the alias Noble House, the company at the center of James Clavell's 1,200-page eponymous novel—a "four-pound love letter to Hong Kong"— which sold half a million hardcover copies in 1981 and sat atop the *New York Times* bestseller list for months. "Overcrowded, with everyone except the very rich living cheek by jowl, Hong Kong is a metaphor for the modern world," wrote one reviewer.[47] *National Review* declared the book an "*Atlas Shrugged* of the Eighties" and praised its glorification of capitalist competition and individualism.[48] Clavell would have been pleased—he sent a copy with a warm dedication to Ayn Rand, "the goddess of the market" herself.[49] NBC broadcast an adaptation of *Noble House* across four nights during sweeps week of 1988, starring Pierce Brosnan as a "supreme leader," or *taipan*, glowering at his corporate rivals from the penthouse of Jardine House. *Town & Country* called Hong Kong "this moment's most dazzling boom town."[50]

Visitors had a memorable arrival at Kai Tak Airport, a strip of reclaimed land that jutted out from the densely populated Kowloon Peninsula—the Brooklyn to Hong Kong Island's Manhattan. As their stomachs dropped on descent, passengers could peer into the windows of the multistory collections of flats and workshops that housed the city's ballooning population. Dealing with the influx of newcomers into squatter encampments (and placating social demands after violent protests in 1967) drove the government into the public housing business along with the public education and basic health service it already provided; state expenditure grew by half from 1970 to 1972.[51] By 1973, almost a third of Hong Kong's 4.2 million residents lived in government housing.[52] This was one of the many ways Hong Kong was in fact far less than a pure model of libertarianism. The syndicated columnist John Chamberlain wrote from Hong Kong in 1978 that "some of the Mont Pelerin purists were distressed to learn from a paper presented at their meeting that Hong Kong has rent control and a fair amount of government housing."[53]

Of greater concern, however, was Hong Kong's uncertain future. The ninety-nine-year lease on the New Territories was set to run out in 1997, less than twenty years from when the Mont Pelerinians met. Its status as a colony was becoming more of an anomaly from year to year. Over the previous century, Britain had devolved control to its overseas territories, starting with the "white dominions," such as Canada, Australia, and New Zealand. In India, the empire's crown jewel, many internal affairs were conducted by an elected national government by the 1920s. In 1947, India was let go altogether, followed by other countries in Asia and Africa. The number of new sovereign states swelled in the middle decades of the twentieth century. Most of Britain's Caribbean and African colonies gained their independence by the mid-1960s. By the late 1970s, Hong Kong had gone from being one star of many in the firmament of overseas European empires to one of the last lonely satellites in an era of postcolonial nationalism. Hong Kong was, as a common phrase went, "living on borrowed time in a borrowed place."[54]

The neoliberals were anxious. Would the heirs of Mao Zedong kill the goose that laid the golden eggs? China previewed its intentions already in 1971, when it had the United Nations remove Hong Kong

from its list of colonies.[55] The implication was that Hong Kong had always been Chinese sovereign territory and would become so again. Hong Kong was a place out of joint.[56] It was a colony in a time of nation-states and a tiny territory in the time of Great Powers. Yet the neoliberals saw it as a harbinger of the future. "Instead of being a 19th century anachronism," Chamberlain wrote from the conference, Hong Kong was "something to be cherished and extended."[57] But how to do so? Was it possible to extend the Hong Kong experiment in colonial capitalism in an era defined by the common sense of decolonization?

The Mont Pelerinians came to praise Hong Kong, but many were also there to smuggle its essence out in their luggage ahead of what they feared was its imminent demise. In the years and decades afterward, Friedman and his collaborators created a Portable Hong Kong, miniaturized and stripped of internal contradictions, complexity, and differences of class and culture. They turned it into a mobile template, untethered from place and freed for realization elsewhere. As a model zone, Hong Kong held out the prospect of an escape from the dilemmas and pressures of midcentury democracy. In 1967, at the high point of anti-colonial rebellion, when the nation was still the horizon of liberation, Che Guevara had called for "two, three, many Vietnams." In 1979, *Reason* winked and revised the slogan into one for national termination, calling for "two, three, many Hong Kongs."[58]

2.

In 1841, the British had taken control of Hong Kong as what one contemporary called "a commercial acquisition."[59] Since then, they had run it as much like a perfect form of capitalism as they could. The prospective end of empire was likewise considered a business deal. Some British politicians looked at their remaining colonies as a consultant would look at a distressed or bankrupt company, sniffing out the value of the asset and ferreting out the deadweight. There were voices in the government who felt that fiscal prudence meant letting the remaining territories go.[60] But others, like Thatcher herself, had both a sentimental and strategic attachment to empire. Her successful war to hold on to the distant Falkland Islands off the coast of Argentina had boosted her approval ratings, and Hong Kong was a high-performing outpost of the British brand. When she considered the future of the enclave in 1982, she emphasized that it remained a "great asset" to China.[61] What if they were to treat it like a firm and separate ownership from control?[62] If China regained sovereignty but Britain continued to administer the territory, then the Chinese Communist Party (CCP) would be akin to the shareholders and the UK to their CEO. The British would ensure "commercial confidence" while the Chinese would have the satisfaction of restoring national territorial integrity.[63] Thatcher hoped they might renew the lease on the New Territories. She recalled pointing out that "British administration had been so successful with the Chinese character, would they, as the landlord who has the freehold, give us another lease or give us a management contract for administration?"[64] Another option floated was also borrowed from business: a "leaseback" arrangement, in which Hong Kong would return to China but the UK would lease it again.[65]

The Chinese rejected these notions. One of the leadership's goals was to erase the historical stain of the loss of territory to imperialism.[66] Yet they were also aware they needed to do so without losing the utility of the colony. Economically, China had grown to depend on Hong Kong. Despite its placement in the "Second World" by Western observers, China had been estranged from the Soviet Union since the early 1960s and found its primary trading partners in the West. Much of that trade happened through Hong Kong.[67] It was important for the Chinese that capital and goods continue to flow in and out of the territory even after the handover, irrigating the People's Republic by a back channel. Hong Kong was China's air lock—its openness to the world economy meant that China could remain selectively protected from it. It had to remain that way once it returned to national control.

China's first challenge was how to calm the Hong Kong capitalists "nervously checking the exits."[68] For 150 years, the balancing act for the British colonial government was how to keep the business community happy and its demand for participation in government placated without opening the door for the masses to enter. This meant an informal system of bargains and unwritten entitlements but also the direct appointment of selected elites to the colony's rubber-stamp government—a group referred to fittingly as the "Unofficials."

One solution arrived at by China and the colonial authorities was to constitutionally enshrine as many capitalist freedoms as possible under the new management. Premier Zhao Ziyang gave early reassurances that China would keep the territory as a free port and international financial center.[69] In 1979, Deng Xiaoping clarified that Hong Kong would be ruled as a "special administrative region" (SAR) after it was folded into the People's Republic of China, free "to practice its capitalist system while we practice our socialist system."[70] The Sino-British Joint Declaration of 1984 put this in writing, as the Chinese agreed not to alter the system in Hong Kong for fifty years after the handover, setting the clock for full absorption into the mainland in 2047. The new leader would be called the chief executive, a term borrowed from the corporate board room. In a further sign of continuity, the Hongkong and Shanghai Banking Corporation—HSBC, known locally as "the Bank"—opened the doors of its new Norman Foster-designed headquarters in 1986. The fifty-six-story slab was described by one journalist as a "beached oil rig," but, more important, as "a commitment of one billion dollars immovably embedded at the heart of the financial district."[71]

Negotiations for the handover were made easier by the discovery that the CCP elite and the Hong Kong business community had something in common with Milton Friedman: a clear prioritizing of economic over political freedom. Business elites were the first targets for a "united front" strategy to smooth the transition, making up 70 percent of the drafting committee for Hong Kong's mini-constitution, or Basic Law.[72] Few people in the rooms that mattered were invested in expanding the possibilities of democracy.[73] One representative from business was quoted as saying that Hong Kong had "benefited over the years from the lack of democracy," crediting it with fending off demands for a minimum wage in the 1950s and 1960s.[74] Another business leader put the sentiment more bluntly when he called democracy "gone wrong" as a system where "the whole is equal to the *scum* of the parts."[75] Those who wanted to ensure a degree of local control were sidelined; as the journalist Louisa Lim put it, "the Hong Kong people were mere spectators to their own fate."[76]

What could be called the Hong Kong compact was at the heart of the Basic Law, a mutually beneficial arrangement between local tycoons and the incoming Chinese rulers that followed smoothly on the "rewarding alliance" with the colonial rulers that preceded it.[77] The point was brought home when the Basic Law passed in 1990. It included clauses to preserve features of the old Hong Kong by guaranteeing balanced budgets and low taxes. A Hong Kong lawyer was not far off when he observed that the clauses read "like an excerpt from Milton Friedman."[78] The drafters had cited the work of MPS members Buchanan and Rabushka directly.[79]

The Basic Law came as a revelation to neoliberal intellectuals.[80] They had worried that the Communist Party would destroy the foundations of economic freedom in the territory. Yet they found that the CCP and the Hong Kong businesspeople wanted the same thing: rule of law, bank privacy, weak labor laws, security of contract, and a stable currency. Rather than a threat to capitalist freedoms, the CCP looked like a bulwark. The Chinese were also innovating. Thatcher paid little heed when the Chinese premier mentioned that they were opening parts of the southern coast as "special areas" free to develop their own foreign trade yet the aside would be of great consequence.[81] They were about to teach the British about the changing nature of capitalism. China's rise to global economic power would happen, in part, by turning the country into a galaxy of miniature Hong Kongs.

3.

The Hong Kong of the Joint Declaration and Basic Law was a strange beast, coming close to a state within a state. An international lawyer trying to make sense of it noted that it had more autonomy than provinces or other federal units but less than fully fledged nation-states. He had to reach back in time for analogies, comparing it to free cities like Krakow created in the nineteenth century or the Swiss cantons before federation.[82] The legal curiosity of Hong Kong had internal self-rule but was externally dependent on Beijing. While defense was covered by China, Hong Kong had control over its own internal affairs, including currency, taxation, judges, police, and courts, as well as some external affairs, including its own visa and immigration procedures. Beijing collected no tax in Hong Kong, and the territory was legally slated to remain both a free port and international financial center, with a guarantee of the free movement of goods and capital. Under the title of Hong Kong, China, it could enter some international agreements independently, especially those related to the matters of trade, shipping, and aviation. Hong Kong became party to the General Agreement on Tariffs and Trade (GATT) in 1986, and joined the World Trade Organization years before China itself.[83] It had, in short, economic freedom and legal self-administration without the status of national independence.

"One country, two systems" is how Deng defined the arrangement, first in reference to Taiwan and then to Hong Kong.[84] Although the phrase has become familiar through repetition, it is worth noting how unusual it actually is. The Cold War frame that dominated world politics from the late 1940s to the 1990s was seen as a clash between two blocs, each with its own monolithic system. It was Capitalism versus Communism, and only one could triumph. The idea that a single economic system would be coterminous with national borders was self-evident, too obvious to even state. China was communist, America was capitalist. What could it mean for part of "Red" China

to shed its color and partially tolerate capitalism? Deng was propos-
ing a subdivision of the nation-state, which did not scan to contemporary minds.[85]

Few of the Mont Pelerin Society intellectuals hobnobbing at the
Mandarin and the Excelsior realized they were arriving at a world-
historical moment of flux as China realigned the energies of its one-
billion-strong population and huge latent productive force. While the
MPS members gathered for their political education and shopping
junket, Deng was preparing a plan for reform that came to be called
"crossing the river by feeling for the stones."[86] It could have been called
crossing the river by feeling for the zones. After he became paramount
leader in December 1978—and Time's Person of the Year—the first
four experimental special economic zones (SEZs) were created on the
Pearl River Delta, nestled up to Hong Kong on the South China Sea.
In contrast to the shock treatment meted out by Augusto Pinochet
to Chile after his 1973 coup, or the Big Bang overnight price reforms
carried out in postcommunist Russia and Eastern Europe, China
used a model of "experimental gradualism," opening up sluices and
locks to foreign investors and market-determined prices rather than
dynamiting the levee and letting it all flood in.[87]

The first opening for the experiment in capitalist hydraulics was
the district of Bao'an—on the other side of the Shenzhen River, which
divided the New Territories from China—fifteen miles from Central Hong Kong but a world away in terms of the standard of living
in the late 1970s. Visitors across the frontier described subsistence
farmers in simple houses, with none of the mass market comforts
enjoyed by even poorer Hong Kongers. In January 1979, the seam
between the two worlds was breached when a Hong Kong businessman pitched the idea of a zone for what would later be called Shenzhen. He brought with him the import from Hong Kong closest to
the neoliberals' heart: the 15 percent corporate tax rate.[88] By spring
of that year, Hong Kong businesspeople were invested in a couple of
hundred light industry projects on the Pearl River Delta, with many
more waiting. "Just as the Americans have taken advantage of the

underpaid, nimble-fingered factory girls of Hong Kong to cut costs by processing their goods here," one journalist wrote, "so Hong Kong capitalists involved in less sophisticated, labor-intensive industries are turning speculative eyes on the underpaid Communist workers."[89]

For many years, arriving in Shenzhen would have felt like entering a foreign country. It was ringed by barbed-wire fences, and even Chinese citizens needed visas to enter, "quarantining a space of economic experimentation."[90] Inside, a radical undertaking was underway. Local entrepreneurs were left to self-organize with little or no direction from Beijing, and government took the form of corporate management.[91] The zone welcomed a massive influx of foreign investment and hosted an epochal transformation: the rendering of Chinese land and labor back into commodities. Beginning in 1982, contracts were introduced for workers in Shenzhen, breaking with communist China's "iron rice bowl" tradition of permanent employment. They called it *ant theory*—attracting scout ants with sweetness, who would bring other investor ants in tow.[92] The model later spread to the whole country.[93] Since the revolution in 1949, land had been governed by the "three withouts": "allocated through administrative means without compensation, without specified tenure and without market transaction."[94] In Shenzhen in 1987, for the first time, a market in land was introduced under pressure from Hong Kong investors.[95]

The outcome was a deluge. What became known as *zone fever* gripped the nation, as huge amounts of land were sucked from rural usage and collective ownership and transformed into private property on long-term leaseholds, constituting one of the biggest transfers of public into private wealth in the modern age.[96] On paper, the success was staggering, one of the fastest episodes of economic growth in world history.[97] In 1980, officials had aimed to bring perhaps three hundred thousand people to Shenzhen by 2000.[98] The real number was ten million. By 2020, the population had doubled again, to twenty million, with a GDP greater than Singapore or Hong Kong. The template was set for a "China of enclaves," what some dubbed the country's "zonification."[99]

"If there were a single magic potion for a Chinese economic take-off," one scholar writes, "it was Hong Kong."[100] As the so-called big master for the zones, Hong Kong was a prototype, a place to study the limits of liberalization and the relative uses of freedom, as well as a template for experimentation and proof that huge volumes of money and goods could travel through a small conduit.[101] Two-thirds of foreign direct investment in China came through the "southern gate" of Hong Kong in the decades after opening up.[102] From their beginnings in the late 1970s, the SEZs multiplied from southern anomalies to further experiments up the coast, until they spread across the entire country.[103] They were joined by zone-like small-scale efforts of marketization, as "town and village enterprises" were permitted to produce and sell for the market.[104] The "decollectivization" of the countryside created a reserve army of migrant laborers who moved between the city and the countryside, offering their labor as the crucial input for the construction-led boom.[105]

When Western politicians fret about the Chinese aspirations to global economic dominance, they are looking, in part, at an adaptation of the Hong Kong model once removed—a network that allows for the channeling of investment and labor through a honeycomb of zones, with public accountability limited by outlawing direct elections above the local level. The imperfect way that Hong Kong fit into the usual boxes of sovereignty spoke to a change in the nature of sovereignty itself in an era of hypermobile capital and easily transferable sites of production.

As is the case in nature, what looks at first like an aberration is often actually a mutation adapted to the changed environment—a genetic freak ends up becoming dominant down the line. So it was with Hong Kong. The lack of a seat among the sovereign states in the General Assembly of the United Nations did not mean it did not have its impact on world history. In the end, there was a fitting symmetry between the image of Milton Friedman over the skyline of Hong Kong in *Free to Choose* and the famous billboard in Shenzhen showing Deng Xiaoping over its own skyline. Neither man over five feet tall, they loomed large as champions of the shared belief that a competitive edge could be gained in global markets by suspending the pressures of a voting public within a sequestered territory, allowing private market actors to act with the aid of a cooperative state and set of laws. In 1990, Friedman said that the right model for Eastern Europe after state socialism was not the United States, Great Britain, or Sweden. It was Hong Kong.[106] Capitalism did not need democracy to work, and the path to success led through the zone.[107]

4.

At the stroke of midnight on June 30, 1997, "God Save the Queen" played as the Union Jack and colonial flag were lowered slowly at the Hong Kong Convention and Exhibition Centre, to be replaced by the red flag and five yellow stars of the People's Republic just above the bauhinia flag of the Hong Kong Special Administrative Region. With this ended what Friedman called a "fifty-year experiment" in economic policy in which postwar Hong Kong's economic growth outpaced Israel, the United States, and the United Kingdom.[108] When describing the experiment, Friedman talked about the low tax rate, the protection of private property, the trustworthy courts, the light-touch regulation, the low barriers to trade—the pithy outline of the Portable Hong Kong. What he did not mention was its real, unrepeatable history: how Hong Kong's rise was seeded by the influx of Chinese refugee capital and labor, accelerated by its status as an entrepôt for essential goods for an isolated mainland, and later supercharged by coordinating investment for the SEZs. Nor did he mention the importance of language and kinship ties across the border that facilitated Hong Kong's role as the switchboard and front shop for the mainland factory, a cockpit for the Chinese boom.[109]

To give just one example of the diaspora in action, the Hong Konger who opened the first zone in the Pearl River Delta had been born in Bao'an himself and fought with the communists in the revolution. When he applied to open the zone, his request was forwarded on by his former military superior, who had become the Chinese minister of communications.[110] Hong Kong was no island adrift in the South China Sea. Even through the years of division, it remained knitted into the mainland's side.[111] Rather than attend to any of this complex history, Friedman opted instead, as he spoke to students at the University of Hong Kong, to remind them of the dangers of democracy. "Unfortunately, political democracy has elements which tend to destroy economic freedom," he told them.[112]

Happy to reduce the territory to caricature, the neoliberals shipped out versions of a Portable Hong Kong in their carry-on bags.

One was its 15 percent flat tax, which Rabushka promoted from the floors of Congress in the 1980s to postcommunist east-central Europe in the 1990s, often to great success. The flat tax was adopted in twenty-one countries of the former Soviet bloc over the course of only a few years; Rabushka's book *The Flat Tax*, inspired by Hong Kong, was described as the bible of tax reform.[113]

Another was the constitutional clause enforcing a balanced budget, which prevented Keynesian expansionary spending and put hard limits on state investment. Known in Germany as a debt brake, balanced budget amendments spread across Europe in the first decade of the twenty-first century.[114]

Yet another was the celebration of the possibility of economic freedom without political freedom, or what scholars call liberal authoritarianism. Rabushka, Friedman, and others believed the virtues of this model had been overshadowed by the overemphasis on democracy in the definition of the Free World in the Cold War. As Friedman put it, democracy was not an end in itself: "the believer in freedom has never counted noses."[115]

Taking the annual *Freedom in the World* rankings by the liberal NGO Freedom House as their template, Rabushka and Friedman convened a series of workshops in the late 1980s to devise what they called an *Economic Freedom of the World* index that self-consciously broke with what one of its drafters called "this fetish for democracy" and ranked the world's territories instead by their tax burden, openness of borders to trade, ease of doing business, along with other indicators.[116] Hong Kong took top spot, as it would for over two decades. The definition of freedom they used in their calculations meant that democracy was a moot point, monetary stability was paramount, and any expansion of social services meant a fall in the rankings. They declared the "'right' to food, clothing, medical services, housing or a minimal income level" as "'forced labor' requirements" and called redistribution "(slave) labor."[117] Taxation was theft, pure and simple. According to the authors, it did not matter "whether the theft takes place via the ballot box, or more directly as in the style of an armed robbery."[118] Hong Kong was followed closely by Singapore and other lesser-known low-tax territories like Mauritius at number five and Costa Rica at number nine.[119] More unlikely champions could be found elsewhere. The historical overview suggested that, in 1980, the dictatorship of Guatemala was among the top five freest economies in the world.[120] The economic freedom index was the map to a parallel universe to that of Freedom House measures of political liberty. This was a world of territories ranked by their level of porousness to the flow of what one participant in the workshops called "quicksilver capital."[121]

By color-coding nations, celebrating victors on glossy paper stock, and giving high-ranking countries a reason to celebrate at banquets and balls, the indexes helped perpetuate the idea that economics must be protected from the excesses of politics—to the point that an authoritarian government that protects free markets is preferable to a democratic one that redesigns them. Not content with mere economics, the think tank behind the index joined up with the Cato Institute to publish the first global index of "human freedom" in 2016. They included all the earlier indicators and supplemented them with numerical measurements of civil liberty, right to association, and free expression alongside dozens of others. The number of terrorist fatalities and the percentage of women who have undergone female genital mutilation made the list. Multiparty elections and universal suffrage did not. The authors noted specifically that they excluded political freedom and democracy from the index. Hong Kong topped the list again.[122] This was a redefinition of the Free World, where free elections were eclipsed by free markets, as understood as the inviolability of private property and ownership. We could call it a New Free World, where the idea of government was replaced by management, and the ideal of the elected leader by the CEO.

Reducing Hong Kong to the absence of democracy would take ever more repression from year to year, though. In 1990, 150,000 people had gathered in solidarity with the crushed protest at Tiananmen Square. The annual marches grew into the next decade, as more pushed on the phrase in the Basic Law, which though focused on business stability also included the ambiguous clause that government should be "constituted by elections . . . worked out in the light of the actual situation in Hong Kong and applied in a gradual and orderly way."[123] For years, pro-democrats tried to squeeze their demands through this narrow opening, disappointed time and again as a mishmash of direct and indirect elections by representatives of professional groups favored the existing powers in the business community. The dismal fact was that average Hong Kong residents did not have a vote in selecting their leader but, through their CEOs, top corporations did.[124] An early climax of the demands for self-determination came with the so-called Umbrella Movement in 2014. One person who channeled Friedman's logic then was Hong Kong's chief executive Leung Chun-ying, a former real estate developer. Asked why suffrage could not be expanded, he laid out the logic of restricted franchise in a matter-of-fact response. It was a "numbers game," he said. Expanding the vote would increase the power of the poor and lead to "the kind of politics" that favor the expansion of the welfare state instead of business-friendly policies.[125] For him, the trade-off between economic and political freedom was clear as day.

5.

Looking at the last century through Hong Kong disrupts three narratives we tell about the recent past. One is about the rising tide of democratization as a supposedly universal and natural phenomenon. If Samuel Huntington was diagnosing a terminal crisis for democracy in the 1970s, by the 1990s he was hailing democracy's revival.[126] Places like China in the process of "reform and opening" or postcommunist Russia were assumed to be in the midst of a movement to full democracy. *Transition* was the term of the moment. It even spawned an academic subfield: transitology. Yet by the following decade, the transition seemed to have stalled. It started to look like some places, including Hong Kong, despite the fervor of local demands, might simply stay in the "gray zone" forever.[127] China's success made it look like state capitalism without democracy might be a winning formula.

Another story is about the movement from a world of empires to a world of nation-states. This narrative relies on a vision of empires as blobs distended over the world's surface, being diced into the tidy containers of individual states as self-determination replaced alien rule. But empires were not blobs. They were complex, internally segmented organisms. They ruled diverse populations and territories differently.[128] At times, they annexed land and administered it directly, as in Hong Kong. At other times they established only a toehold, as in the treaty ports along the Chinese coast. Self-governing populations lived inside imperial bodies, sovereignties nested inside sovereignties. Empire, as the historian Lauren Benton puts it, was "lumpy," not smooth.[129] The age of the nation was too. New nations formed as empire ended but then they fractured further, divided into a dizzying array of zones, city-states, districts, havens, enclaves, gateways, and logistics corridors. The historian Vanessa Ogle has shown how this legal unevenness reproduced some of the earlier traits of empire.[130] Modern globalization has "jagged edges," and the familiar outline of national borders tells only part of the story.[131]

Some critics of Deng accused him of re-creating the nineteenth-century treaty ports by opening up coastal cities to foreign investment and trade.[132] In some ways, they were right. The CCP preferred the term *zone* because it was blank, symbolically delinking it from the toxic legacy of the treaty port it resembled.[133] At the same time, the character used, *qu* (区), could also mean "area," "district," and "region," allowing for the interpretation that these were not outside the national territory but administrative redivisions within it.[134] Rather than the monolith it is sometimes assumed to be by Western observers, China in the age of reform worked through "fragmented authoritarianism."[135] The global multiplication of zones has helped create a world of "one country, *many* systems." Looked at this way, the hybrid of Hong Kong was odd only in the sense that the future was odd, a testament to the fact that the passage from the age of empire to the age of the nation was not one-way.

A third story we tell is that capitalism, for all its faults, produces things that are useful to humans. But is this always true? Some of the features that did not appear on the *Economic Freedom of the World* index were improvements in productivity, nature of investment, level of unemployment, social security, welfare of the population, or economic equality—in short, all the things that make it possible for inhabitants of a territory to experience economic freedom in their daily lives. If they had measured these things, Hong Kong would have looked quite different.

Wealth is extraordinarily concentrated. The net worth of Hong Kong's top ten billionaires accounts for 35 percent of its GDP, as compared to 3 percent for the United States.[136] From its founding, Hong Kong was less a freewheeling market open to all entrants than an economy controlled by a handful of merchant houses—and later family conglomerates and tycoons—with a cozy relationship to the government.[137] Studies show "the ten largest families in Hong Kong controlled about a third of the corporate sector."[138] Less celebrated than the economic freedom index was the fact that Hong Kong topped the *Economist*'s "crony capitalism index."[139] This was a

capitalist paradise with little competition. The lack of inheritance tax means the wealth is dynastic and leaves little interest in challenging the status quo. Thomas Piketty and Li Yang found that the top 15 percent wealthiest in Hong Kong were the least likely to support moves to more democracy.[140]

In the end, the essence of the Hong Kong model was not an abstract idea of economic freedom. Rather it was the legal demarcation of a small territory with little or no democracy and close collusion between a tight club of business elites and the government to capitalize on the captive market through maximal economic openness and the rising value of scarce land.

It was precisely these features that would be brought home to the heart of the empire—turning London into Hong Kong's distant twin.

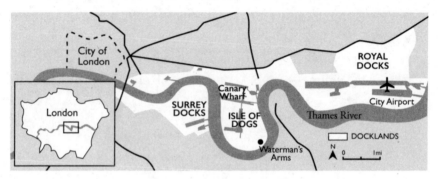

The London Docklands

City in Shards

Cities have long been legal islands in the ocean of the surrounding territory. In the Middle Ages, entering the city walls made you subject to a different code. For a time, serfs could flee their lords for a new life there, giving rise to a German saying: "City air makes you free." Medieval and early modern Europe was pockmarked by tens of thousands of different legal zones. The Holy Roman Empire of the eighteenth and nineteenth centuries alone had upward of a thousand independent entities.[1] The historian Fernand Braudel called early modern European cities "autonomous worlds" ringed by both real and "juridical ramparts."[2]

Though the march of the nation-state was well advanced by the twentieth century, one medieval enclave that survives to the present sits at the heart of modern London. The "Square Mile" of the financial district on the north bank of the Thames—known as the City—is not altogether part of its host country. When the Normans invaded, the City kept its property, its militia, and its own Lord Mayor. Its governing body, called simply the Corporation of London until recently, predates Parliament.[3] To this day, as the journalist Nicholas Shaxson reminds us, when the king or queen enters the City, he or she has to touch the mayor's sword.[4] The City is a primal zone, carved out from its surrounding political space and governed by different rules. Most notable is the fact that, in its elections, as in Hong Kong's, businesses have ballots too. Their thirty-two thousand votes outnumber those of the nine thousand humans.[5] One academic compares it to the early modern city-states of Genoa and Venice.[6] Another calls it "London's own Vatican"—a Vatican of capitalism.[7]

For centuries, the City has stood for a vision of the British economy rooted in finance and the power of money. Tensions between City and Crown existed over those centuries, but the two were locked in an embrace. The City needed the Crown for protection and the Crown needed the City to raise funds for war and empire. The City took on a new importance in the postwar decades as a place to hold dollars "offshore," meaning beyond the reach of US regulators. Individuals, foreign-owned banks, and later major oil-exporting states like Saudi Arabia, Libya, and the United Arab Emirates used the City of London as a place to deposit money and organize large loans. As Britain's overseas empire dissolved, a "Second British Empire" arose in its place as a collection of tax havens, including British dependent territories like the Cayman Islands and Bermuda and former colonies like Singapore, Ireland, and Dubai.[8] And the City was at the center of it all.

In 1938, Lewis Mumford compared capitalism to a cuckoo bird that laid its eggs in the walled city and crowded out the city's own native offspring.[9] After Margaret Thatcher deregulated financial services with the so-called Big Bang in 1986, the City burst out of its confines and spawned a double of itself downstream, in a grove of glass skyscrapers known as Canary Wharf. Dubbed Hong-Kong-on-Thames, Canary Wharf was more than just a new financial district: it was a prototype for a new form of zone, designed to capture the state for developers, cut loose from ground-level needs of the city's ordinary inhabitants.[10]

Like the Sacré-Coeur cathedral built on Paris's highest point after the destruction of the 1871 Paris Commune, Canary Wharf was also a monument to a defeated version of the city. Urban socialist projects of Red London were abandoned, eclipsed, and demolished to build investment vehicles for the ultrawealthy. The result was a city in shards.

1.

One place to begin the story of London's metamorphosis is with the 1980 gangland thriller *The Long Good Friday*. In the film's opening scene, local crime boss and would-be developer Harold Shand (played by Bob Hoskins) hovers over an architectural model on his yacht in a white pinstripe suit, cigarette and whiskey in hand. The location is the Docklands neighborhood a few miles east of the city center. Once the busiest in the world, the docks were in steep decline by the late 1970s, the workforce down to a couple of thousand.[11] The container ship had spelled the beginning of the end. Moving a standard-sized steel box from ship to railcar and trailer required a fraction of the labor needed to hoist goods by nets and pulleys.

Shand and his wife (played by Helen Mirren) sip Bloody Marys on deck with the rusting machinery of the decommissioned port in the background. Their yacht glides past empty warehouses and idled cranes lining the waterways like funeral statuary. "There used to be eighty or ninety ships in here at one time," Shand declaims in a speech from the prow framed by Tower Bridge. "Used to be the greatest dock in the world one time, this." Shand sees opportunity in the decay. His plan? Tap overseas investors to fund construction of a site for the future Olympic Games, greased by favors from crooked local politicians.

One of Shand's haunts is a smoky bar with red flocked wallpaper called the Waterman's Arms on the Isle of Dogs, a part of the Docklands that hangs like an uvula in the Thames. In the movie, Shand's overseas-investors scheme unravels. But by chance, just months before the film was shot, the very same bar witnessed the birth of a much more successful real-life analogue. Gathering at the pub, a clutch of Conservative politicians set out a proposal not so different from Shand's: parcel off chunks of London, free investors in those areas from taxes and regulations, and give them subsidies and grants on top of that, to make what had been formerly called corruption into the law of the land.[12] The areas would be called enterprise zones. In the Docklands, the zone would turn a working-class neighborhood into a second financial district.

The lead speaker at the Waterman's Arms was Geoffrey Howe, a career politician in his fifties with a ripple of gray hair and watery eyes behind rectangular tortoiseshell glasses—a gift to caricaturists. He was the shadow chancellor of the exchequer for Thatcher's Conservative Party, which would have its breakthrough victory the following year. The world economy was at an inflection point as he spoke. The tables of history seemed to be turning. For five centuries, ever since armed Portuguese and Dutch galleons entered the Indian Ocean, and Spanish conquistadors defeated Indigenous American empires, the part of the world known as the West had stood uncontested atop the global hierarchy. By the late 1970s, though, some saw its dominance teetering. The political scientist Ezra Vogel wrote a bestseller called *Japan Is Number One: Lessons for America*.[13] Britain's share of global manufacturing fell from one-quarter to a tenth in the first three postwar decades.[14] In 1976, the UK went hat in hand to the International Monetary Fund to borrow money—a measure usually reserved for developing countries. Some were projecting a grim future. A strategy document written by a neoliberal think tank wondered whether Britain would have to "start again as a low-wage second-world economy, trying to keep up with Taiwan, South Korea, Hong Kong and Singapore?"[15]

For Britain, swallowing the idea that one of its own colonies might have something to teach the mother country about capitalism was a bitter pill. But the surge in Hong Kong's standing as both a manufacturing center and a site for offshore financial services was undeniable.[16] In the second half of the 1970s, Hong Kong had annual GDP growth rates as high as 16.9 percent while the UK's GDP growth topped out at 4 percent and even went negative a couple of years later.[17] Howe pointed out the irony that Hong Kong, the "show-place of enterprise and self-discipline," was "the child of two parents, Britain and China, which were at almost the same moment plumbing the depths of national humiliation: the one as the 'sick man of Europe,' the other as victim of the Cultural Revolution."[18]

China was already emulating aspects of Hong Kong in its coastal experiments. Its special economic zones showed that you did not need to create new nations to have laboratories: you could just carve up old ones. At the pub, Howe began by sharing the radical proposal of the geographer Peter Hall to do just that. Hall contrasted the moribundity of British cities to the thriving hubs of Hong Kong, Singapore, Seoul, and São Paulo. He conceded that they practiced "an imperfect version of Western democracy," but perhaps this helped explain their success. He pitched a "non-plan": rather than determining in advance what should be built, a vacuum would be created where something new might arise. British politicians could sequester swaths of inner cities and make them into new "Crown colonies" without any control of the inflow and outflow of people, goods, or money. In his thought experiment, people who opted in would lose their national citizenship and protections but would be liberated to build, truck, and barter unimpeded by taxation or regulation of any kind. The zones would leave the European Economic Community and re-create Hong Kong "inside inner Liverpool or inner Glasgow."[19]

One of Thatcher's closest partners, Keith Joseph, was humming the same tune. Speaking at a neoliberal think tank in 1978, Joseph was asked whether he would agree to put socialism and liberalism to a head-to-head test by implementing socialism in one place, like the Isle of Wight off the South of England, and laissez-faire on another. He responded that the Conservatives had precisely the intention to designate areas "where the Queen's writ does not run": taxation, labor laws, and health and safety regulations would all be eliminated. Instead of offshore islands, though, they would use sites of "inner-city decay." The audience apparently broke into applause at the idea.[20]

The most ambitious aims for the zone were elaborated by the Heritage Foundation's Stuart Butler, who was also trying to bring zones to the United States to create what one magazine described as "Hong Kong on the Hudson."[21] Butler called the enterprise zone "a political animal."[22] The goal was to create a "frontier community in the heart of a major city" and kick-start a change in mentality in the era of big government.[23] Cut loose from the authorities, residents would be compelled to improvise their own solutions. The depth of inner-city poverty was a plus. "Crisis breeds entrepreneurs," Butler wrote.[24] The zone was an experiment in creativity crossbred with desperation. Policy entrepreneurs cast themselves melodramatically as guerrillas of the Right, occupying and decomposing cities zone by zone. One commentator called the enterprise zone a "dagger aimed at the heart of socialism."[25]

Eleven enterprise zones were rolled out in Thatcher's first budget.[26] All were exempted from requirements for local planning approval, freed from local taxes for ten years, and provided capital allowances for commercial buildings.[27] In the words of the historian Sam Wetherell, they "pierced holes in Britain's national economic fabric, briefly allowing aggressive free market capitalism and a regulatory social democratic economy to live literally streets apart."[28] Despite the hype, the results were disappointing and showed little evidence of new investment.[29] Business mostly shifted around, moving to zones to chase tax breaks while landlords jacked up rents to get a piece of the action and investors found ways to lower their tax bills.[30] BUY A BUILDING FOR FREE, read one headline wooing investors into the zone.[31] HOW TO BUILD A TAX HAVEN read another, and meant it like a good thing.[32] Thatcher's advisor Alan Walters (another Mont Pelerin Society member) said they'd like to turn Britain into "one big Enterprise Zone."[33] But if tax dollars were being drawn from one part of the economy to pay for the other, whom would that leave to pay the subsidies? The government's own consultants conceded that "only some areas can get priority."[34]

The zones seemed like window displays—Potemkin villages of

the free market.[35] But what if we took Butler's idea of the "political animal" seriously? One geographer proposed that the zones were experiments in statecraft more than economics.[36] The zone was not a non-plan at all. It was a plan of its own. The innovation was the way it short-circuited local government and handed control straight to developers. The facsimile of Hong Kong proposed first by Hall and Howe was one of grassroots commerce. What succeeded was argu-ably a more enduring version of the colony built on a close partner-ship between real estate developers and local government to create "landing strips for highly mobile financial capital."[37] The historian Perry Anderson recalls an episode at the World Bank when Walters praised Hong Kong as the "freest society in the world." When the eminent statistician Angus Maddison interjected that it "doesn't even have elections," Walters replied with a "beatific smile" and said, "Yes, that's just what I meant."[38]

2.

In 1985, the opening scene from *The Long Good Friday* came to life as maquettes were unveiled for a complex in London's Docklands atop the old West India Docks on the Isle of Dogs. Covering seventy-one acres, with ten million square feet of office space, the original plan included not one but three of the tallest skyscrapers in Europe and was billed as the largest real estate development in the world. The project brought together the starchitect studio of Skidmore, Owings & Merrill—which had built the Sears Tower in Chicago the decade before—with I. M. Pei, whose Bank of China Tower had just bro-ken ground in Hong Kong. It was called Canary Wharf after the warehouse that once held fruit shipped from the Canary Islands.[39] The architects claimed they were gesturing to the traditional urban fabric of London. Unlike Paris, Vienna, Budapest, or Madrid, with their grand boulevards climaxing in monuments, opera houses, and museums, London was more hivelike. It looked in toward squares and parklets.[40]

Others saw a different template. One critic saw a "virtual carbon copy" of Exchange Square, then still under construction in Hong Kong's Central District.[41] The megaprojects resembled one another as clusters of glass skyscrapers constructed around an open space, but the similarities reached indoors too. Exchange Square was built to accommodate the Hong Kong Stock Exchange's shift to electronic trading. The same shift was happening in London, driving people out of the cramped, historically protected buildings of the City of London. Built around central elevator shafts, those buildings could not accommodate the demand for the vast floors of monitors and cooling systems for the new age of "electronic banking."[42] The move to computer trading called instead for flexible layouts and raised floors for running cable and wiring workstations.[43] "Hong Kong Central today is exactly what Docklands is supposed to become in the third millennium," the critic wrote, "a new financial city; a bridgehead for American money in Europe just like the bridgehead for American finance half a world away."[44]

What he did not observe was the further similarity in the way the two complexes had come to be. In the Hong Kong model of "administrative absolutism," appointed officials and representatives of big business made the decisions with no input from ordinary residents. Canary Wharf built in a similar mechanism. Because it was an enterprise zone, an entity called the London Docklands Development Corporation, headed by figures from real estate, could bypass local government, forgo the usual planning permission, and ignore the housing needs of residents.[45] The corporation's first director was not coy about his contempt for what he called the "surplus population" of existing residents—and he didn't have to be.[46]

Developers were given deals too good to turn down: land at a sixth of market value as well as promises of state investment in infrastructure.[47] In 1986, the first flights landed at the newly constructed City Airport in the Docklands. A few years later, a new train line opened that would take you from the Docklands to the heart of the City in under ten minutes.

Canary Wharf laid down a marker on London's future. It was a symbol of the UK's drift away from where it had been since the Second World War, namely a country defined by manufacturing and even agricultural self-sufficiency. Before the war, Britain had been a trailblazer of globalized trade. At the start of the twentieth century, it imported almost all its food, right down to eggs.[48] After the war, there was a shift to more production for local consumption. London's Royal Docks closed down because of containerization, but also because grain silos weren't necessary when wheat was being grown at home.[49] This self-sufficiency faded in the 1980s, as the UK once again began to import more than it exported. The country that had been the "most manufacturing-intensive economy in the world" began to do other things.[50] Chief among those was the business of finance. By 1991, there were more people in office work than in manufacturing or agricultural production.[51] "The London that had traded things," one historian writes, "became the London that traded money."[52]

The zone may have been a dagger aimed at the heart of socialism, but socialism did not go down without a struggle. The strongest opposition came from the city government itself, the Greater London Council (GLC), which became the standard-bearer for a socialist vision of London after the election of left Labour politician Ken Livingstone in 1981. If Thatcher's government drew lessons from the economic dragons of the Far East, the "new urban left" of the GLC practiced a different kind of internationalism. They sought to create links between the recent immigrant communities in London with the older working class.[53] The GLC saw the neighborhood as a place where small versions of the future could be made, what are sometimes called prefigurative politics. An early success came on Coin Street, across the Thames from the financial district of the City, where they were able to block the plans of a developer and claim the land for a community trust, given to local residents to develop in their own interests.[54] The group organized clerical workers in the City of London and even mobilized to have the anachronistic medieval government that ruled the financial district abolished.[55]

The Docklands was another focus of their efforts. The GLC funded a People's Plan Center to gather alternative visions of reviving the docks beyond the plans of high-profile developers.[56] They used grassroots outreach, showing up at bingo sessions, toddler groups, and the few remaining factories to gather input for the plan. In 1984, the finished version was delivered to every household in the Docklands. The People's Plan expressed the hope that there be "more to our working lives, and our children's, than being porters and lavatory attendants for passing businessmen," imagining instead a way of restoring small-scale manufacturing and reviving the docks, a proposal seconded by an outside consulting firm.[57]

The alternative vision of London was a thorn in Thatcher's side.[58] Her response was to counterattack. At the Conservative Party conference in 1983, the Tories included a new demand in their manifesto: eliminate the GLC. Party chairman Norman Tebbit put the rationale in plain terms: the GLC stood for the "divisive version of socialism [that] must be defeated. So, we shall abolish the GLC."[59] Another MP was even more graphic. Saying the GLC had developed "into a monster," she added that "the only way of dealing with that monster was to slay it, to kill it."[60] Five metropolitan councils in other cities were abolished at the same time and a limit placed on the amount of revenue local government could raise through taxation.[61] Local government, and the platform it offered for the revival of the British tradition of municipal socialism, was deliberately hobbled. Usually synonymous with breaking unions, Thatcherism was also about breaking local government.

We often think of the 1980s in terms of the struggle between the state and the market. But this doesn't capture the dynamic at all. Thatcher's government and the GLC were both part of "the state." Where they differed was in their conception of what the state was for. The urban new left had their share of skepticism about the benevolent role of government; sometimes they referred to what they were doing as operating "in and against the state."[62] But what matters is where decisions are being made—and in whose interest they are being made. Thatcher's evaporation of the GLC removed the largest urban government in Europe at the stroke of a pen.[63] It was a coup from above. In its aftermath, the path was clear for a new vision of the city to be rolled out with less obstruction.

3.

By century's end, Red London was on its knees and finance was ascendant. Recovering from a stumble after the Black Monday stock market crash of 1987, by the mid-1990s Canary Wharf stood as the City's double, a glistening monument to the new metropole. Estimates suggested the developer had used the enterprise zone status to secure £1.3 billion in tax breaks and infrastructure for a supposed "paragon of free-market urban revitalization."[64] Its central structure was One Canada Square, a fifty-story skyscraper capped with a pyramid designed by another of the era's star architects, César Pelli. When Prime Minister Tony Blair hosted French president Jacques Chirac on the thirty-eighth floor of the building, they looked down on streets named after famous settlers of the Americas—Columbus Courtyard, Cabot Square—as well as on the site where Blair, like Shand, planned for the Olympic Games.[65]

If London had gone from trading things to trading money, now it started trading space, as real estate—and housing in particular— became a new global asset.[66] Homeownership became depersonalized and tradable, set adrift on waves of global supply, demand, and speculation. By the new millennium, there seemed to be no alternative but to surrender to the model of "municipal mercantilism," parceling off ever more parts of the city to offer ever more tax breaks and public subsidies for new towers.[67] The shift was evidenced by the fact that the leftist Ken Livingstone himself returned to government as the mayor of London and became a leading promoter of the private tower in the zone.

The world built skyward after the year 2000. In the first fifteen years of the new century, the number of buildings over two hundred meters globally more than tripled.[68] Part of the push came from money seeking a refuge. The 2003 invasion of Iraq by the United States and the UK helped drive oil prices upward, boosting profits for oil-producing states, which invested in real estate through massive sovereign wealth funds. By 2005, Russian oligarchs seeking places to park their wealth overseas earned Britain's capital the nickname Londongrad.[69] In a symbolic moment, the oligarch Roman Abramovich bought West London's Chelsea Football Club in 2003. China's precipitous rise also meant more money looking to get out. The 2008 global financial crisis—itself a product of overleveraged speculation in the housing market—deepened a sense of volatility and instability. With zero interest rates, money was cheap and it was seeking, as it does, high profits, low risk, and governments willing to make this happen.

Britain was eager to oblige. A small number of luxury districts came to be seen as unassailable "safe havens" for mobile wealth.[70] London was the "unrivalled king of the global property league for the super-rich."[71] From 2009 to 2011, £8 billion of London real estate was purchased through the British Virgin Islands alone; by 2015, an astonishing £100 billion had been purchased from offshore.[72] In 2012, scholars found, "85% of all high-end residential real estate in London and 50% in New York were bought by foreign buyers."[73] In many cases, this was housing in name only, as many practiced "buy to leave" with the units left empty. "We've been building the world's most expensive safety deposit boxes," one real estate consultant said in 2017. "You just put your valuables in and then never visit."[74] In 2015, a Labour MP condemned the "global superrich" for buying "London homes like they are gold bars as assets to appreciate, rather than homes in which to live."[75]

The zone had morphed from manufacturing to office space to three-dimensional bank accounts for the wealthy. A highly visible outcome was the spiking of the skylines of a small number of global metropolises. In New York, the towers were concentrated on Billionaires' Row, just south of Central Park. The form they took was borrowed from a style popular in Hong Kong in the 1980s: the pencil tower, with a small footprint supporting an impossibly narrow and tall residential skyscraper. The New York twist was that each floor hosted only one apartment. One of the first penthouses was sold to a hedge fund manager with no plans of moving there; he thought he might throw a few parties before he flipped it.[76] The penthouse of another building became the most expensive apartment in history when it sold to another hedge fund manager for $238 million in 2019.[77] He did not intend to live there either.[78] It was a gilded pied-à-terre.

In 1991, the sociologist Saskia Sassen wrote critically of the rise of what she called "Global Cities," a small number of "command-and-control centers" for the world economy, where a small number of people, mostly employed in financial services, relied on a large substratum of precarious and underpaid workers to iron their shirts, plate their entrées, mix their drinks, towel off their weight sets, drive their town cars, and clean their homes. She saw this as a new motor of inequality and a decoupling of metropolitan areas from abandoned postindustrial hinterlands, portending future political problems and economic disconnection.[79] By the following decade, though, the critique had been rinsed out of the term and Global City had become jargon for brokers' sales pitches.[80]

One of the most notable buildings in this brave new twenty-first-century world of "ultra-prime" real estate was the Shard, designed by Renzo Piano. Proposed in the mid-1990s and ushered into existence by Livingstone himself, the Shard was London's first "supertall" skyscraper, putting it in the league of Dubai's Burj Khalifa and the Shanghai World Financial Center.[81] The building's name did not begin as a marketing gimmick but as a slur: English Heritage described the building as tearing through "historic London like a shard of glass."[82] *Shard* is also a term for the shell of an insect, specifically the crusty bit of exoskeleton over a beetle's wing, and that definition fits as well. Buildings like the Shard were shells, often hollow repositories for mobile wealth, channeled in many cases through so-called shell companies.[83] In the 2010s, it became common for what one critic called "shardettes" to be purpose-built specifically for overseas buyers. Many were sold at real estate shows in China and Hong Kong before they had even been constructed.[84] One of two shows for the luxury Maine Tower on Canary Wharf was held in Hong Kong.[85] The two hundred units sold out in five hours.[86] The Qatari Investment Authority owned 95 percent of the Shard.[87]

Thatcher spoke in 1997 about China's "sinister and so far successful experiment in combining economic freedom with political servitude."[88] It was a grim irony that China and Qatar—two prime examples of capitalism without democracy—became the landlords of what was described as her "legacy," Canary Wharf.[89] The year Thatcher died, London mayor Boris Johnson traveled to Beijing to ink a deal with Chinese developers to build what he billed as "a third financial district in the capital" in the Royal Docks Enterprise Zone next to the Isle of Dogs.[90] Chinese private developers acquired thirty-five acres with plans for a $1 billion business park as a foreign investment push encouraged by Xi Jinping brought new money to London.[91] Johnson was trying to play back the Canary Wharf tape and run it one more time. "The U.K. is a very small country," said one Chinese developer, "if you didn't snatch up the opportunities early enough, there wouldn't be any opportunities left."[92]

At the beginning of the 1980s, market radicals had set out to turn London into a miniature Hong Kong. Thirty years later, this vision had been achieved to an extent they could never have dreamed of. Scholars call Hong Kong a "tycoon city" because the government is caught in a symbiotic relationship with the city's billionaires, almost half of whom made their fortunes in real estate.[93] The government retains ultimate control of the land in Hong Kong, but it auctions off long-term leaseholds, relying on continually rising property prices to finance its own operations through sales and fees.[94] In a bestselling book, Alice Poon described the Hong Kong model as "real estate hegemony"—an economic model built on speculation as property replaced other forms of production.[95] Likewise, in Britain's tycoon nation, one-quarter of the richest people have property as their main source of wealth.[96] The global cities of London, Hong Kong, and New

York all have two-tier labor markets where most of the gains accrue to a small number of people at the top. The state's primary role is in safeguarding rising property prices and granting whatever blandishments are necessary for mobile capital to call their city a temporary home.

In "the plutocratic city," urban governments see the presence of the super-wealthy as a sign of urban health.[97] The result is a city with forces moving in two opposite directions: the rich are sucked in, inflating property values, and the poor are expelled.[98] After soldiers returned from the trenches of the First World War, early social housing projects were called Homes for Heroes. In 2013, Boris Johnson called the superrich "Tax Heroes" and suggested the top ten richest should be given an automatic knighthood.[99] If the zone was a dagger aimed at the heart of socialism, it seems to have struck its target.

Another place where the original dream of the enterprise zone—a frictionless place for attracting investment—came to fruition was courtesy of "America's first developer president," Donald Trump.[100] Trump was an early devotee of the zone. As a developer, he put up buildings only if he received massive tax breaks. His breakthrough was the Grand Hyatt on Forty-Second Street in New York City, which opened in 1980, glittering with gold inside and out. Trump made use of the Urban Development Corporation, a New York agency similar to the London Docklands Development Corporation that controlled Canary Wharf. In his case, he nominally sold the property for one dollar to the state agency, which then leased the property on the cheap back to Trump. The arrangement cost the city more than $360 million in tax revenue.[101] And as in London, the corporation could glide over land use laws and building codes.[102] Three years later, Trump cut the ribbon on another golden pile named after himself: Trump Tower. He sued the city successfully to secure a tax break worth tens of millions more.[103]

In the 1990s, Trump bought an island off New Rochelle for $13 million, hoping to fill it with two thousand condominiums as a safe haven for Hong Kong millionaires fleeing the city before the colony's return to China.[104] Trump's island, sparkling with crystal towers whose residents would be shuttled to the financial district by hydrofoil, never materialized, but his debt to the zone was clear. A British journalist observed that the "central formula of his success" was the same one that Thatcher used in Britain's inner cities.[105]

As president, Trump remembered his fellow developers when he slipped something called "Opportunity Zones" into his massive tax cut in 2017. The zones were designed, like Thatcher's, to encourage investors to put their money into distressed areas long-term by eliminating taxes there. People who sold stocks or other investments and put their capital gains into designated zones could lower their taxes to what Trump called "a very big, fat, beautiful number of zero" if they left them there for ten years.[106] They were miniature tax havens, pockets of offshore territory.

Opportunity zones cut requirements for all oversight, approval, and reporting. Trump's own inner circle, including his former press secretary and his son-in-law, cashed in immediately. Zones were used to build luxury housing in Miami and condo towers in Westchester County complete with doggie spas.[107] A consultant active in designing the program and choosing the zones gave a grim verdict on them before Congress in 2021. The fact that zones were costing $1.6 billion in foregone tax revenue every year was bad, but even worse was what they represented: the final reneging on the role of government in community development. It was planning by tax break, development by profit-minded developers alone, a vacuum in the place of a vision.[108]

A New York councilor complaining of the state of affairs said that "billionaires shouldn't be able to buy the sky and cast the rest of the city in shadow."[109] But in the first decades of the new millennium, this was simply how things were done. When Amazon put out the call for a new headquarters in 2017, New York City offered $3 billion in tax breaks and government assistance. When Hudson Yards, the largest mixed-use private real estate venture in US history—a jumble of housing towers and office buildings, a 720,000-square-foot shopping mall, and a climbable sculpture nicknamed the Shawarma—opened on Manhattan's West Side two years later, it had received nearly $6 billion in tax breaks and other government assistance.[110]

The *New York Times* architecture critic called it a "neoliberal Zion" but it was also a novel spin on the neoliberal zone.[111] Although built in one of the most high-rent districts in the world, the complex was funded through a special program that sells visas to overseas investors who put money in economically distressed areas. To secure this funding, developers had traced a serpentine line of census tracts from genuinely economically depressed areas of Harlem south through Central Park to the edge of one of the most high-rent neighborhoods in the city.[112] There, Hudson Yards sprouted like "glass shards on top of a wall," as the *Times* put it.[113] A gerrymandered enterprise zone helped make it happen.

In London, the city in shards was given a far more gut-wrenching counter-icon in 2017. That June, a small fire turned into an inferno that engulfed Grenfell Tower, a social housing building in the middle of one of the city's "golden postal codes"—an area where 10 percent of properties were purchased through offshore "secrecy jurisdictions," and where the average salary was £123,000 but one-third of the inhabitants earned below £20,000.[114] The fire left seventy-two people dead. The council had ignored concerns from residents about the building's inexpensive cladding, which ended up acting as a vacuum, pulling up the flames through the gap between the material and the exterior walls. Sprinklers and other potentially lifesaving measures had been omitted because of a drive to reduce requirements for new buildings. The "bonfire of regulations" so often celebrated to lure in developers had led directly to the inferno.[115] The tower stood like a charred gravestone for a defunct version of the social contract.[116]

4.

In *The Long Good Friday*, Shand seems to meet his end at the hands of Irish guerrillas. The Docklands were the site of an IRA bombing in

1996, which killed two and caused over a hundred million pounds of damage. In its wake, a "mini ring of steel" was built around Canary Wharf, with controlled road access, closed-circuit cameras, and a police cordon.[117] Some of these features, like the cameras, would soon be familiar sights across the country. By 2015, there were a half million installed in London alone.[118] As a privately owned public space—a POP, in the jargon—Canary Wharf is not subject to the usual rights of assembly and free speech. The Transport and General Workers Union found this out when it sought to protest the low wages of cleaning staff and was stopped by a high court injunction.[119] There was a bitter irony to the exclusion. The union—once the largest in the world—had formed after a sequence of events beginning with a strike on those very docks in 1889.[120]

The journalist Anna Minton observes that the secured and surveilled spaces of Canary Wharf became a template for public and private building projects in the early twenty-first century.[121] Thatcher moved briefly into a gated community in South London, taking part in a piecemeal return of the walled city.[122] By the 2010s, there were gated communities in the sky. In what one geographer calls "vertical secession," people were retreating upward to "luxury cocoons of uber-wealth and fortressed security."[123] The popular "podium building" arrangement, pioneered in Vancouver, places a second-floor courtyard—featuring amenities such as artificial ponds and outdoor bars—above the ground floor, an ersatz street above the street.[124] When the Shard was completed as London's tallest building in 2011, the critic Owen Hatherley reflected on how impossible it was to imagine a "block of council housing or an NHS hospital as one of the pivotal objects on its skyline."[125] From a penthouse ninety floors up, the city is reduced to a backdrop.

The last forty years are often described as a time of capitalism unfettered or set free. It is common to speak of the inability to govern finance. It moves too fast to catch, we are told. The zone shows how this quality is built in by design, multiplied in business improvement districts and many other forms of land being given to developers outright, on the model of what some call "incentivized urbanization" and others call "geobribery."[126] As geographers have shown time and again, gentrification is not what happens when the market is set free. It happens when the state leads it by the hand.[127]

Canary Wharf is the most famous example of the use of the zone in the late twentieth century.[128] By 2012, it housed more bankers than the City of London.[129] To its champions, it tells the story of a stirring vision of untrammeled entry and experimentation—the seductive tale of economic freedom. But it cashed out as the concentration of power moved upward and outward. The enterprise zone and development corporation showed themselves not as features of an experimental free-for-all but as a one-way conveyor belt delivering British land to the balance sheets of the world's wealthiest oligarchs and sovereign wealth funds. One of Thatcher's greatest policy victories was her Right to Buy program, which sold council housing to tenants at a deep discount. When she came into office, about one-third of dwellings in Britain were publicly owned council housing. A few years into the twenty-first century, roughly half of that public housing stock— around 2.7 million homes—had been sold.[130] The goal of this massive transformation of public into private property was to expand a home-ownership society. Yet after peaking in 2003, homeownership actually began to decline.[131] Moving housing from state ownership into the market had helped turn homes into a speculative asset. The fable of small shareholder democracy turned into the reality of private capture of public wealth.

The limits of the state's power can be seen in the Canary Wharf of the 2020s, where new shards have stalled and Boris Johnson has watched his super-prime real estate knights ride away. The Royal Docks project, which had been one of the key triumphs of his mayoralty, has become a "ghost town," with foliage repossessing the fences.[132] Another of his putative victories was a Chinese-backed development on Canary Wharf with the lackluster nickname "the Spire" slated to be the tallest building in western Europe. Construction of the Spire was slowed by uncertainty after Brexit, the pandemic, and the Chinese crackdown on overleveraged real estate investment. The developer lobbied the council to purge the ninety-five affordable units from the plan to preserve its profit margin.[133] As of 2022, the Spire was a hole in the ground. After the Russian invasion of Ukraine, the moral quandary of being an offshore piggy bank for oligarchs also became more pressing. Abramovich sold Chelsea, and politicians tried to figure out how to untangle the rat's nest of blind trusts and blandly named offshore shell companies that effaced the identity of property owners—while wondering what the effect on the city's economy would be if they did.[134]

As the government went from seeing its role as facilitating an industrial or agricultural base to attracting mobile buyers, the city of shards appeared as a natural consequence—and so did the city of holes when the money dried up and the city of aliases when the money became too tainted. All the more reason to remember the defeated versions of an alternative city. Progressive proposals of recent years draw inspiration from the policies of the 1980s GLC. Programs like Health Emergency and the London Black Women's Health Action Project, focusing on preventive care and responding to community needs, as well as technology networks for "socially useful production" and efforts to discourage single-rider automobiles now look like cutting-edge ways of dealing with risks and opportunities in the modern city.[135] The revival of municipalism as well as ideas of community land trusts and the urban commons propose a different relationship between property, community, and the role of the state than the city of shards.[136]

In 1994, the geographer David Harvey described Canary Wharf as "floating like a lost ark downstream from the City on the tide of the Thames."[137] It is worth finishing the story with a counterimage. When a group called Democracy for Docklands was trying to figure out how to publicize their alternative plan for developing the area, one resident mentioned that he owned and operated a small barge. Local artists came up with a logo for the movement, a dragon whose sinuous body was in the shape of the river Thames running through the docks, and affixed a large red poster of it to the barge. In April 1984, with the barge at the head of a large procession of boats, a thousand people took part in the first People's Armada to Parliament. Copies of the People's Charter for the Docklands were delivered to every member of Parliament.[138] More armadas would take place over the following years. Their route to Parliament took a little more energy than the "lost ark" from the City imagined by Harvey. Unlike Canary Wharf, the people's fleet had to travel against the current.

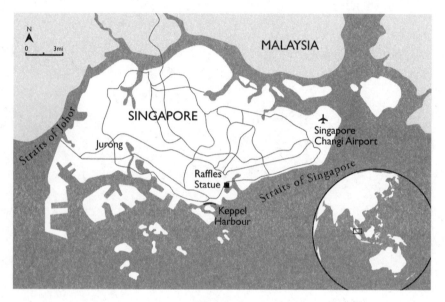

Singapore

The Singapore Solution

The drift of the Hong Kong model to London in the 1980s helped turn it into a tycoon city. But toward the end of the millennium, a different metropolis burned even brighter in the market's radical imagination. Margaret Thatcher wrote to a friend that she thought Britain should turn away from Europe to become "a kind of free-trade and non-interventionist 'Singapore.'"[1] A quarter century later, her acolytes did just that, leading the country out of the European Union after a successful vote for Brexit. "Let Singapore be our model," one wrote.[2] In parallel, China has also sought to "Learn from Singapore." Since 1990, over twenty thousand Chinese officials have made the pilgrimage to the city-state.[3] In 2012, Xi Jinping, then vice president, commissioned a ten-part television series on the lessons of Singapore for China.[4]

Singapore is, by any measure, an unusual place. It is a city-state, a form whose heyday was in the Middle Ages. It is about the size of Greater London—or less than 0.1 percent of China's landmass—yet it is fully independent, with a seat in the UN. What lessons could this tiny anomalous patch of political geography have for much larger, longer-standing powers? Citing the Singapore model only raises the question of which Singapore one means. Is it a welfare dictatorship? A laissez-faire wonderland? A node in the information economy? A triumph of state-led industrialization? A sustainable utopia of public housing and green space? A paranoid surveillance state? All of the above? The micronation of Singapore is a kaleidoscope—it looks different from every angle. Yet despite—or because of—this ambiguity, it remains the lodestar for projects of political economic reinvention from Kazakhstan to Brazil, from Beijing to Britain.

Singapore and Hong Kong sit together on top of the neoliberal indexes of economic freedom and can look like twins from a distance—but they are not identical. Unlike Hong Kong, Singapore enjoyed self-rule since 1959 and full national sovereignty since 1965. Milton Friedman, for one, did not love these offspring of the British Empire equally. On his first trip to Singapore in 1963, he sneered at the government's active role in guiding development. "When one looks at these models, plans, etc., it's sort of like something between children playing house and an artist molding a figure," he said. "It would be interesting to come back in about 20 years and see what happens."[5] Friedman was honest enough to eat his words when he returned in 1980 to a boomtown growing at a rate of 10 percent a year. But even then he bent the facts, arguing that the city-state had succeeded "despite extensive interventions of government."[6]

This got it backward. As one economist put it, it was the "long arm of state intervention" more than the "invisible hand of the free market" that explained Singapore's success.[7] While private interests shaped Hong Kong with the government in a supporting role, in Singapore, the state took center stage. The government built industrial estates and added hundreds of acres of new land to its coastline through massive land reclamation projects. Many of its biggest companies were owned by the state, and huge sovereign wealth funds invested Singaporean savings domestically and globally.[8]

The Singapore Solution meant using the power of government to find your niche in the world market. Foreign Affairs Minister S.

Rajaratnam laid out the strategy in 1972. By "plugging in" to multinational corporations, Singapore could leapfrog decades of development by bringing in more advanced technology from abroad. Singapore would no longer need a hinterland: "Our port makes the world our hinterland."[9] It would not need a domestic public sphere: "We can, via the satellite, see and hear on our television events in London, Tokyo or Djakarta a split second after they happen." Air travel meant it was easier to get from Singapore to Hong Kong than to a Malaysian town a couple of hundred miles away. "Through the tentacles of technology," he said, a small number of metropolises "form a chain of cities which today shape and direct, in varying degrees of importance, a world-wide system of economics."[10] Once, ideas of statehood had been premised on the idea of being able to feed and clothe your own citizens through the products of your own territory. Singapore turned the model on its head. It embraced global opportunity even at the price of global dependence. If you could tap into the world markets, then why would you need to have your own mines, your own farmland, and, especially, your own troublesome working class? Small was good. You could pivot more quickly when the winds of economic demand shifted.

An aspect of the Singapore Solution that Rajaratnam left out was the treatment of noncitizens. The city-state dealt with foreign workers the same way you would any other resources: turn the tap on when you need them and off when you don't. The prosperity of the national community depended on a bottomless reservoir of surplus labor. By the mid-1970s, there were up to two hundred thousand foreign workers in the city-state, about 10 percent of the population. By 2008, foreigners made up 22 percent of the population; by 2017, it was nearly 40 percent.[11] "Nonresidents" enjoy none of the privileges or rights of citizens. When the market slumps, they bear the brunt of the layoffs.[12] Being a Singaporean citizen means access to a range of services including a compulsory savings account that one could draw on for pension, health care, and to buy a home. Being a foreign worker means you are not just hire-and-fire but fire-and-deport.[13]

The Singapore Solution also meant a thin commitment to democracy. Elections in Singapore were multiparty but hardly free. The same party has been in power for the country's entire existence, and one man, Lee Kuan Yew, led the government from 1959 to 1991. Until recently, there was no freedom of protest, and opposition politicians were regularly sued into silence, imprisoned, or driven into exile.[14] Newspapers have to regularly renew their publication licenses, and those that step outside the space of allowable discourse are simply put out of business.[15] The most well-respected index of political freedom consistently ranks Singapore as only "partly free."[16] Central control is justified with the language of "pragmatism" but also by appeal to culturally specific "Confucian-communitarian" values in the majority-Chinese nation, which allegedly permit a degree of paternalistic rule in exchange for stability and order.[17]

Fukuyama has been invoked already for his pronouncement that liberal democracy was the last model left at the "end of History." But we might also direct attention to the piece he published right afterward, where he found "one potential competitor to Western liberal democracy" in what he called the "soft authoritarianism" of East and Southeast Asia.[18] Singapore was a prime example. Peering through the kaleidoscope of the Singapore Solution helps us understand the range of futures people see for the reform, reversion, or acceleration of global capitalism in an age when the tiny "start-up state," far from a mere geographic curiosity, has been an enduring object of emulation.

1.

The exceptional nature of Singapore begins with its location next to the Strait of Malacca, where the Indian Ocean meets the South China and Java Seas—an artery of long-distance trade for centuries linking the Middle East, North Africa, and South Asia to East Asia.[19] Before Christopher Columbus had sailed for the New World, the Chinese general Zheng He sailed ships four times as large as the *Niña*, *Pinta*, and *Santa María* past Singapore on an exploration and tribute mission that reached the coast of Africa.

This long past notwithstanding, the official history of Singapore begins with a more recent date—1819—when the British East India Company officer Stamford Raffles arrived to sign a treaty with the Malay sultan to use the harbor for trade. Raffles's statue still stands on the waterfront, arms crossed and head cocked upward in a pose of defiant ownership. Inscribed on its base is the official self-narration of how Raffles "with genius and perception changed the destiny of Singapore from an obscure fishing village to a great seaport and modern metropolis."[20] Raffles made Singapore a free port with no duties, drawing in Chinese merchants from around the South China Sea.[21] The opening of the Suez Canal in 1859 increased traffic. As a coaling station for the Royal Navy, Singapore joined a string of ports from Hong Kong to Aden to Nova Scotia that let the maritime force safeguard its supremacy of the seas, what a colonial official called "strategic points on the earth's surface."[22]

Military routes were also conduits of the drug and arms trade. Singapore's economy, like Hong Kong's, was built on opium, which accounted for between one-third and one-half of its revenue before 1900.[23] In the twentieth century, Southeast Asia supplied new products including the sap of the gutta-percha tree, used to insulate the telegraph cables laid on the seabed between continents, rubber for tires, tin for cans, and oil for the navy, which switched from coal before the First World War.[24] Another substance drawn from trees—rubber—was exported through the subsidiaries of early multinationals like Firestone and Goodyear. And after Royal Dutch Shell (which took its name from one of the original investors' importing of shells from East Asia to London) began drilling for oil on the Dutch colonial island of Sumatra, it built storage facilities in Singapore.[25]

Rubber, tin, and oil were essential ingredients for not only the consumer economy but also the war economy. Among the military planners who realized their dependency on the region's products were the

66 CRACK-UP CAPITALISM

Japanese fascists of the 1930s, who resented the British, American, and Dutch imperial stranglehold on the region.[26] Japan plunged into the Second World War, in no small part, to bring the region's raw materials under its control. The same day that bombs dropped on Pearl Harbor, they dropped on Singapore, Hong Kong, and Manila too.[27] When Singapore fell in 1942, the Japanese designated it as the capital of a new province in their Asian empire.

One of the goals of the international order designed by the United States after the war's end was to move away from the focus on colonial empire. It exited its own Southeast Asian possession of the Philippines in 1946 and pushed for access to Britain's colonies. After Singapore's move to self-rule in 1959, its first leader, Lee Kuan Yew, said the micronation had to do two things to survive: make itself a "poisonous shrimp" inedible to its larger neighbors and stay close to the larger fish.[28] The city-state built up its military, arming itself with fleets of tanks and armored vehicles.[29] It also clung to the old imperial master; the British navy stayed on as a major employer even after full independence in 1965. Singapore aided the new hegemon—the United States—with its war in Vietnam six hundred miles to the north. The war brought "collateral benefits" to his country, Lee said later, allowing it a chance to begin to catch up to the far more industrialized Japan.[30] The "Asian Miracles," one scholar quipped darkly, were built on "Asian Massacres."[31]

When the British announced the departure of their navy, a Dutch advisor from the United Nations, Albert Winsemius, offered two pieces of advice. The first was to crush the communists, which Lee had already begun by imprisoning opposition and outlawing parties and independent trade unions. Winsemius went further. "I am not interested in what you do with them," he summarized later. "You can throw them in jail, throw them out of the country, you can even kill them. As an economist it does not interest me, but I have to tell you, if you don't eliminate them in Government, in unions, in the streets, forget about economic development."[32] The second advice was to let Raffles remain standing. They should not repeat the error of

Indonesian freedom fighters who tore down a statue of the Dutch colonial officer who had massacred the Indigenous population in the conquest of the archipelago.[33] The Raffles statue would be testimony "that you accept the heritage of the British" and would serve as a beacon to Western companies.[34]

Singapore's leaders followed both recommendations. In 1972, they followed another one and became the second country in Asia (after Japan) to adapt their port for containers—the same technology that killed the London docks. Nearly overnight, Singapore became the fourth-busiest port in the world.[35] A visitor riding the newly installed cable car across the island in the 1970s would see cranes erecting tall white boxes of new buildings in the business district alongside the gantry cranes and forklifts of the new container port. Among the more impressive buildings was the fifty-nine-story OCBC Tower designed by the ubiquitous I. M. Pei, a brutalist slab looming over low-rise red tile roofs, moored fishing barges, and the statue of Raffles—now updated and enlarged in synthetic marble.

At independence, one of Singapore's models was the US island possession of Puerto Rico, a pioneer in export processing zones, which experienced a flurry of industrial activity after the Second World War by attracting investors to simple factories funded by tax breaks and filled largely with women sewing underwear and other garments.[36] By the 1980s, Singapore had moved up the value chain from textiles to high tech. Winsemius helped court electronics companies like Philips to the island in the early years.[37] By 1969, the world's largest producer of semiconductors, Texas Instruments, had opened a plant; Apple followed in 1981.[38]

Singapore also built up its financial sector by taking a page from the City of London. Winsemius recalled a financier holding a globe and pointing out the island's location halfway between the markets closing in San Francisco and opening in London.[39] Singapore became an offshore financial center, meaning banks could conduct their business and make loans in dollars after 1968. Controls on buying and selling foreign currencies were abolished altogether ten years later.[40]

For centuries, trade goods had passed through the Singapore Strait. Now they were joined by great volumes of money transacted at the stroke of a key.

2.

By the 1990s, Singapore's economy had been growing for decades at a rate unparalleled in the world. From one-third of the GDP per capita of its former colonial master at the time of independence, it surpassed it for the first time in 1994. What was the secret of its success? Already in 1977, in his PBS series that inspired *Free to Choose*, the economist John Kenneth Galbraith mused that it was "very unfashionable in our time to explain economic development by race or ethnic origin" but he would still "attribute much in Singapore to the excellent ethnic admixture."[41] He was ahead of the curve. Cultural essentialism became the preferred way to explain Singapore in the 1990s. Singapore was a multiracial city-state, with relatively steady ratios of 75 percent Chinese, 14 percent Malay, and 8 percent Indian population, but leadership in business and government was dominated by the Chinese.[42] They set the tone for what came to be called "Confucian capitalism."[43]

The trope of "Asian values" took traditional ideas of Orientalism and reversed them. The East was fundamentally different from the West—and that was a good thing. Long seen by Western scholars as a brake on Chinese capitalist development, Confucianism was redefined as its rocket fuel, promoting not only social peace but also diligence, loyalty to employers, and cooperation within the workplace.[44] The most vocal proponent of this thesis was Lee Kuan Yew. He turned to talk of tradition first in the 1970s in response to signs of Western-style counterculture in the city-state. Restrictions on rock music, long hair for men, and homosexual activity were accompanied by an insistence that hedonism and individualism contradicted Confucian family values. The turn was formalized when he consulted a group of scholars (ironically nearly all from US universities) and released a white paper on "Shared Values" in 1988.[45] According to Lee, Asian values focused not on the individual but on "the extended family, the clan, [which] has provided a kind of survival raft for the individual."[46] The nation was a collection of organically bound families rooted in tradition rather than the atomized individuals of the West.

Lee was an unlikely mouthpiece for cultural essences. Born in Singapore, he was of Chinese descent but only learned Chinese as a third language; he was raised speaking English and educated at the London School of Economics and then at Cambridge as a barrister. As a young man he professed to be baffled by "the peculiar workings of the Chinese mind."[47] Yet by middle age he held forth on the "Sinic" culture of Korea, Japan, China, and Vietnam. Why? One could say Asian values did double duty for Lee. They acted as the secret ingredient or nonreplicable variable of the Singapore model that made it something more than the "country run like a corporation," as it was often described.[48] They also offered a ready-made justification for the suppression of civil freedoms in the city-state. Lee complained that democracy was a system they were "caught in" because of the British zeal to "export [it] all over the place, hoping somewhere it will take root."[49] Government would go more smoothly if he could make the decisions himself. Years later, he said, "I believe what a country needs to develop is discipline more than democracy."[50]

The Singapore Solution combined economic openness with political control, a means to put the genie of capitalist globalization not back in the bottle but into a sturdy harness. In the wake of the global disruptions of the 1960s and 1970s led by youth movements and guerrilla insurrections, elites worldwide were seeking a way to assert such control. Perhaps nowhere was this more true than in the People's Republic of China, where a decade of the Great Proletarian Cultural Revolution unleashed by Mao Zedong after 1966 had encouraged the uprooting of all forms of authority, from the military down to the local mayor and middle-school principal.[51]

The opening of the economy from the late 1970s brought incremental prosperity but also turned in unwelcome directions, feeding a wave of enthusiasm for political liberalism among intellectuals that culminated with the occupation of Tiananmen Square by a group of students demanding political freedoms to match the newly granted economic freedoms. The violent suppression of the movement in 1989 solved half the problem but left the question of what new language the leadership could use to explain their vision of the good society. It had to be different from both the liberty of the United States and the glasnost of the Soviet Union, which looked to the reigning Chinese Communist Party like two versions of suicide. Singapore offered itself as a model.

"Growth must come before sharing," said Lee in 1974.[52] "Let some people get rich first" is how Deng Xiaoping phrased it a few years later. Both countries accepted medium-term inequality for long-term growth. Singapore seemed to have lessons about containing the potentially disruptive effects of this process. In 1992, Deng traveled to Singapore and praised its "good public order." "We should learn from its experience," he said, "and surpass it in this respect."[53] Hong Kong taught the idea of the segmentation of space (as adopted in Shenzhen) and the incentives of low taxes and privatization of land. Singapore was more about what Chinese intellectuals called "good governance."[54]

If Hong Kong produced "zone fever," Singapore fed "culture fever" as intellectuals discussed the relative merits of Western versus Chinese traditions.[55] The events of the 1990s buoyed the proponents of the latter. The Chinese watched American advice lead to the chaos of "shock therapy" privatization in the former Soviet Union.[56] The West was plagued by economic inequality, ecological disaster, voter apathy, and the elite capture of the democratic process.[57] NATO fought an air war in the Balkans in the name of human rights that included the bombing of the Chinese embassy in Belgrade. Given this dispiriting picture, why shouldn't "Sinic" Asia go its own way?

Four hundred Chinese delegations traveled to the city-state in 1992 alone as Singapore quickly became the dominant foreign model.[58] Singapore's approaches to management and planning were copied in experimental zones in China, from a Singapore-Sichuan Hi-Tech

Innovation Park in Chengdu and a Knowledge City in Guangzhou to a Food Zone in Jilin and, most significant, an industrial park in the southern city of Suzhou.[59] Planned to house six hundred thousand and employ three hundred thousand, the Suzhou Industrial Park was developed as what one scholar calls a "clone" of the Singapore industrial district of Jurong.[60] While Western depictions of Singapore recycle photographs of its skyline and project the image of a compact and cramped metropolis, Singapore—like Hong Kong and London—is in fact one of the greenest cities in the world, with nearly half its area devoted to green space. The Chinese version of the Singapore approach emphasized a managed balance between people and nature. The Suzhou Industrial Park built greenbelts and protected natural spaces and lakes.[61]

Implanted in China, mini-Singapores had their own sets of laws, regulations, and even welfare systems, consistent with the atmosphere of subnational experimentation that characterized the period of reform and opening up. Singapore offered a streamlined Asian capitalist modernity that mixed hospitality for multinational investors with a containment of any of the less desirable values that came along with them. It was a vision of slick real estate prospectuses, all lens flares, panes of glass, and hyperreal greenery against blue skies.

Following the Singapore model of Confucian capitalism finessed China's abandonment of socialism, making it appear to be the realization of something autochthonous rather than an import from beyond. It also added a cultural gloss to the strategy of fragmentation through special economic zones. Rather than merely miniatures of the Hong Kong Crown Colony or copycat export processing zones, these were presented as part of the localism of traditional Chinese villages, and an inheritance of a decentralized form of imperial rule. Confucian capitalism opened the possibility of what was called "multiple modernities," the idea that the world might not all be moving in the same direction toward a common goal—and that this might be for the best.[62]

In 1977, the international relations scholar Hedley Bull published a classic book called *The Anarchical Society* in which he called out the "tyranny of existing concepts."[63] The problem, he said, was that we had a narrow-minded idea of what states should look like. We had grown too comfortable with a small range of options for human political organization. We still thought in terms of a binary—either empires or nation-states—living in thrall to familiar categories even as the world eluded their confines. As one of only two city-states (along with Monaco) in the UN, Singapore broke with the tyranny of existing concepts. Imported into Deng's China, it was spawning flexible forms of the zone, variations of capitalism "with Chinese characteristics."

3.

In 1965, Gordon Moore, one of the founders of Fairchild Semiconductor, observed that the number of transistors that could fit on a microchip was doubling every two years. What became known as Moore's law meant that hardware was shrinking every year even as the amount of data it could handle ballooned. Singapore was at the vanguard— the perfect nation for the age of the microchip. The first place to call itself a "smart city," Singapore attempted to wire the country with broadband and put a computer in every home with the Intelligent Island initiative in the 1990s.[64] Not only did the country produce the literal hardware at its semiconductor foundries, but its laws, when exported to places like coastal China, were referred to as "software."[65] Singapore chimed with the idea of cut and paste, the notion that a government's operating system could be duplicated and realized elsewhere.

The microstate of Singapore seemed to be moving in the opposite direction of other economic trends. As technology scaled down, economic territories were scaling up. The North American Free Trade Agreement created a trade bloc out of Canada, the United States, and Mexico. The World Trade Organization made the global economy a new institutional reality. The Maastricht Treaty wove the European Union into an ever-closer common market for goods, services, and labor. Most observers saw these treaties as a victory for transnational capitalists and a boost for outsourcing production and increasing access to cheaper consumer goods. But a vocal minority on the Right saw them as Trojan horses of the Left, smuggling socialist and ecological policies into laws beyond the reach of nations.[66] For the so-called Euroskeptics in the British Conservative Party, Singapore became a talisman, representing the belief that smaller was better, and an even more radically capitalist world was possible.

The patron saint of the Euroskeptics was Margaret Thatcher, one of Singapore's biggest boosters. She praised the city-state continually through her years in power, comparing it time and again to the moribund Europe to which Britain was bound. She swallowed Lee's Asian values talk whole, referring to the Chinese as "natural capitalists" and "born traders."[67] To her, Singapore was a happy hybrid, having also profited from the values of the "Anglo-Saxon world."[68] "Tell me, what is the recipe for the colossal achievement you had?" she asked friends in Singapore. "But we learnt it all from you, all the lessons of free enterprise," she heard in response, "It is just that you have forgotten them and we have taken them on!"[69]

Singapore seemed to keep Victorian principles of self-help and toil alive. One Singaporean recounted that the message drilled in from a young age was that "the world doesn't owe you a living." Rather than socialized medicine, Singaporeans had compulsory personal savings accounts, which the Tories admired, from which they drew for health care, retirement, and real estate purchases. Legitimized by talk of Confucian filial duty, the government offloaded many responsibilities for care work onto families.[70] One book written by Thatcherites, including future prime minister Liz Truss, praised Singaporeans for working on average two hours and twenty minutes longer per day than the British.[71]

To Tory Euroskeptics, Singapore combined the old with the new— conservative social values with a willingness to contort into whatever new position the world economy demanded. As momentum built toward the 2016 Brexit referendum, the idea of Singapore-on-Thames became a buzzword to describe one vision of what Britain might look like outside the EU. The term was used both by critics and advocates. Along with opposition to socialized health care, it implied low taxes, deregulation, and the erosion of worker rights, a combination of the offshore tax haven and the sweatshop. It also alluded to the rapid rise of Singapore as an international finance center. The focus was often on how the City of London might have more opportunities after leaving the European Union. The *Economist* argued that London outside the EU could be "a sort of Singapore on steroids."[72] Some backers of Brexit embraced the term. One of the nation's highest-paid advertising executives praised the prospect of a "Singapore on steroids, a regulation-light, tax-light UK economy, open for business in a way we haven't seen before."[73]

For the globally minded wing of the Brexiteers, to invoke Singapore was to put stock in optimism. The metamorphosis of Singapore from what one called "a mosquito swamp into a gleaming city-state" was an inspirational tale about the combination of national sovereignty and a commitment to free trade.[74] One Conservative politician compared Brexit to Singapore's moment of independence, quoting Rajaratnam directly to say this was a chance that the UK, too, could plug into the "international economic grid."[75] Another wrote that, as with Singapore, the only variable was "boldness."[76] The chancellor promised a repetition of the Thatcherite moment of deregulation: a "Big Bang 2.0."[77]

In their emphasis on the virtues of exit, some of the Tory ideologues showed their debt to the fast-moving world of finance from which they came. In finance, you can indeed make money just by leaving. Exiting a position at the right moment was often the key to massive profits.[78] One Brexiteer had spent three years himself working in Singapore, making in the range of £3 million a year as Deutsche Bank's managing director. He boasted of reading a scene from Ayn Rand's *Fountainhead* biannually his entire adult life.[79] Another cut his teeth in Hong Kong and ran a hedge fund that operated out of Singapore and Dublin.[80]

Yet, as the Tories soon discovered, the Singapore Solution was less like an instantaneous bet on a stock than a decades-long process of grinding material into a new shape. In Boris Johnson's first speech as prime minister, he announced what the press dubbed "Singapore-style freeports" across the country.[81] The idea was to cordon off sections of the British coastline and lift the usual regulations, labor laws, and taxes to create offshore areas more attractive to foreign investment. The free ports followed the template of the Thatcher-era enterprise zones. In fact, some of the very same think tankers were involved.[82] "Freedoms transformed London's Docklands in the 1980s," declared Truss as international trade secretary, "and free ports will do the same for towns and cities across the UK."[83] Being out of the EU seemed like it would create new room for maneuver, but the government soon discovered that WTO law was just as restrictive.[84]

The political philosopher Isaiah Berlin made a famous distinction between negative and positive freedom. The error of the market radicals in the Brexit camp was to think of Singapore purely in terms of negative freedom. All that was necessary was less rather than more. But the Singapore Solution was not a project of negative freedom in the sense of removing taxes and regulations. (The two countries' corporate tax rate was within a few percentage points of each other by the time of Brexit.) It was an active project of positive freedom, producing security, health, and capacity. To Thatcher, the success of Singapore and other Asian tiger economies was "not the result of some grandiose state plan; they were the aggregate of hundreds of thousands of individuals and firms each trying, and superbly succeeding, to improve his lot."[85] Yet Singapore's success was precisely the result of a grandiose state plan. In 1963, a master plan for "Ring City Singapore" was developed with UN advice, a loop of transportation infrastructure around the island with evenly spaced high-rise new towns.[86] Later plans layered onto this one, adding industrial plants, recreation facilities, and expanded housing.[87] Far from the Thatcherite fantasy of the "non-plan" in the enterprise zone, these were meticulously laid through central command and control.

The Singapore Solution was not just about building an eye-catching skyline. It was also about cultivating popular legitimacy through the provision of housing and infrastructure that improve the lives of everyday people.[88] Inspired by massive projects of wartime mobilization and postwar nationalization, Singapore had expropriated almost every scrap of territory in the first year of independence. The land was used to move the population from their shophouses and thatched-roof villages (known as *kampong*, the origin of the English word *compound*) into high-rise apartment blocks.[89] By 1963, Singapore's "Housing for the People" program was building a new unit every forty-five minutes.[90] Newly issued currency featured serried ranks of modernist blocks, a testament to the care of the population.

By 1977, 60 percent of Singaporeans lived in public housing.[91] A quarter century later, it was 80 percent. Even as 90 percent owned their units as long-term leaseholds, the government remained the owner of the land, allowing it to take advantage of rising property prices, and intervene where necessary for its master plan.[92] Real estate was not shaped only by the market. Housing complexes were actively integrated both racially and socioeconomically—with quota systems for different races (also designed to mitigate ethnic mobilizations against the Singaporean state) and a mixture of different-sized apartments, a far cry from the racial and class segregation of British cities driven by private interests.

Britain after Brexit is suspended between two versions of Singapore. One is the free port—Raffles with his chin out—calling for the firm hand of leadership, low tariffs, and generous tax breaks. The other version of Singapore is that of the meticulous plan. This version has its fans too. The key strategist behind the Brexit campaign, Dominic Cummings, praises Singapore not for its small state but for its central control, meritocratic civil service, occasionally harsh law and order system, military preparedness, and application of research with state backing to find new niches for national economic growth.[93] He calls Singapore a "high performance startup government." He and others saw that the way to ameliorate regional inequality in

Britain—which is what voters wanted—would require Singapore-like state investment in infrastructure and other forms of industrial policy: positive not negative liberty.[94]

The argument over the meaning of Singapore is part of a larger argument over the future of capitalism. Will the race to the bottom based on low taxes, low wages, and light regulation continue or will it be replaced by a race to the top based on high wages and heavy investment? Either way, the vision is marred by blind spots. The first is the question of climate change. Looking at Singapore itself, it is clear that there is no exit from the earth. Not only is the city-state highly dependent on air-conditioning and imported water, but its projects of sucking up sand from poorer neighboring countries to build out artificial space for more real estate makes it a parable of the human denial of limits.[95] Its location at one degree above the equator, highly exposed to changing currents and extreme weather, puts it in the crosshairs of coming climate disaster.

Second is the question of people. Decades ago, the economist Paul Krugman delivered a devastating critique of the Singapore growth model when he argued that the economy was not necessarily any more efficient or productive than others. Like the briefly booming Soviet Union in the 1940s and 1950s, it was just inputting resources at a faster pace. It was not building a better engine. It was just throwing in more fuel so the flames grew higher.[96] That fuel was not just state funds or raw materials but also the injection of new people. In Singapore, these workers are drawn mostly from South Asia, China, Thailand, and Burma, with about half employed in construction, many of the rest as domestic workers, and a smaller number of professionals and executives.[97] Excluded from public housing over the years, manual workers are housed in dormitories segregated from the rest of the city by fences and accessible only by slip roads, shuttled from work to home to the enclave of Little India for shopping and recreation. It was in Little India that worker discontent spilled over in 2013 after the death of an Indian construction worker, leading to the first large-scale riot in Singapore in half a century.[98]

Labor is the sand in the machinery of globalization. As Britain was convulsed with immigration politics in the 2010s, Singapore was too. In 2011, the ruling party received its lowest election results ever over the steep rise in the number of noncitizens moving into the city. Similarly, what most of those who voted for Brexit wanted was reduced immigration.[99] The first slogan for the Vote Leave campaign was "Go global," but the slogan that won was "Take Back Control."[100] In the end, Britain cannot become like Singapore to solve its problems, because Singapore has similar problems. It is caught in the same demographic trap as the rest of the industrialized world. An aging population is keen on protecting its social entitlements even as it grows ever more critical of the influx of new workers necessary to keep the system going.

As a hero in the pantheon of crack-up capitalism, Singapore seems to teach the lesson that anything is possible with enough discipline, determination, and subordination to the forces of globalization. But it is also a showcase of capitalism's intractable contradictions: endless growth in defiance of limits, social security for some based on the growing number of excluded, and the difficulty of securing the consent of the governed as economic spoils are ever more unevenly divided. Among wealthy territories, its depth of inequality was second only to Hong Kong. The title of a bestselling book in Singapore was blunt in its assessment of the city-state: *This Is What Inequality Looks Like*.[101]

Singapore, in the end, is not an island—it's everywhere.

PART II

PHYLES

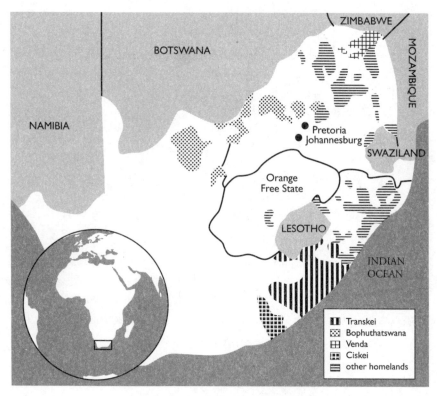

Late Apartheid–Era South Africa

4

Libertarian Bantustan

It has been said that a city is a mine turned upside down.[1] Places like Hong Kong, Canary Wharf, and Singapore depend on faraway sites of exploration and extractions of minerals to be refined and processed: iron for steel cladding, sand for glass curtain walls, copper for pipes, sandstone and marble for glistening lobbies. Global cities draw on a vast tracery of shipping lanes and highways stretched across the earth, and pits, shafts, and pumps descending into it. The human labor that makes them run, meanwhile, relies on reserves of calories and regimes of coercion.

If Hong Kong, London, and Singapore were at one end of the value chain in the 1980s, South Africa was at the other. There would seem to be few places more physically different. Hong Kong hugs a deep harbor at the base of a mountain covered in dense jungle. With building space so scarce, it is a vertical city, its skinny skyscrapers greedy for square footage. Canary Wharf likewise thrusts upward from the sprawl of Greater London, and Singapore out of blue-green straits crowded with ships and tankers.

The Eastern Cape of South Africa, by contrast, bent the axis of construction ninety degrees, bringing it back to earth. Its buildings were low-slung, made from cinder blocks patterned for ventilation, decoration, and economy. The few urban areas featured a smattering of multistory towers in reinforced concrete; halfhearted stretches of streetlights lined asphalt roads that vanished off into the yellowing grassland, thornbushes, and shrub-clumps of the veld. Dirt roads wound down to collections of rondavels, round mud huts topped with thatched roofs, or to rectangular dwellings capped with sheets of corrugated iron. Yet unlikely as it sounds, in the 1980s this place was just as much a site of neoliberal experimentation as Hong Kong, London, and Singapore. It was the hinterland and its workers, as much as the tax haven and its jet set, that symbolized capitalism's brave new future. Libertarians flocked to both. Just a few years after calling for "two, three, many Hong Kongs," *Reason* magazine asked: "How hard is it to get South African citizenship?" It made the eyebrow-raising pronouncement that "it is possible that in the past decade no country has moved further toward a libertarian society than South Africa."[2]

Speaking to an audience of two thousand at the University of Cape Town in 1976, Milton Friedman announced that democracy was overrated. The market was a much surer route to liberty, he said; voting by dollars was better than voting by ballots.[3] The key to freedom was not free elections but decentralization of state power itself. In the 1980s, South African libertarians followed this line—but in a direct betrayal of their own rhetoric, their version of radical capitalism was entirely dependent on the disciplining (and subsidizing) hand of the state. As an overlooked case of neoliberal ideas in action, the Black "homeland" of Ciskei in white-ruled South Africa shows how certain kinds of economic freedom depended on political disenfranchisement.

1.

Apartheid South Africa was in the midst of a legitimation crisis as Milton Friedman gave his lecture. Since the late 1950s, new flags had risen one by one across the continent. Where once flew Union Jacks and the blue-white-and-red of the French *Tricolore* now waved the Masai shield of Kenya, the crane of Uganda, and the black star of Ghana. When Portugal finally quit Africa in the late 1970s, Angola put a machete on its flag, and Mozambique chose another symbol of armed struggle: the AK-47. Rhodesia became Zimbabwe in 1978, making South Africa's white minority rule an even more striking aberration. Digging in at the southern end of the landmass, the apartheid establishment was alone and embattled.[4] As a solution, the government chose a version of what Friedman was recommending: decentralization instead of democracy. Creating a series of so-called homelands on the baseless notion (derived from colonial anthropology) that certain populations rightfully belonged in certain territories. Many homelands were noncontiguous, creating a fragmented landscape that led anti-apartheid activists to dub them Bantustans, combining the umbrella South African category for Africans with a suffix from the precedent of Pakistan, which was split by colonial powers into West and East Pakistan (later Bangladesh) on opposite sides of independent India.[5]

Extending the technique of "divide and rule," some Bantustans were even made into pseudo-independent nations, unrecognized by any other states. The first to gain this nominal independence was the Republic of Transkei in the Eastern Cape. In a pantomime of decolonization, the ceremony included speeches from the new head of state and a 101-gun salute to a sparse crowd in a newly built stadium. The only foreign dignitary in attendance was a general from the military dictatorship of Uruguay, an emissary from the Southern Cone's own version of capitalism without democracy.[6] Transkei was the first of four fake nations created in South Africa's effort to prove that it was following the trend toward self-determination and the end of empire.[7] It was followed by Bophuthatswana in 1977, Venda in 1979, and Ciskei in 1981. Under Bantustan policy, Black South Africans lost their South African citizenship and were made into citizens of homelands that many had never set foot in. Upwards of 3.5 million people were relocated by force, especially the elderly, women, the unemployed, and opponents of the regime.[8] The idea was to make South Africa itself progressively whiter while retaining access to an itinerant labor force concentrated in balkanized territories. It was a vision where only a minority of the population were citizens and the rest guest workers.[9] Critics rightly described the homelands as "dumping grounds."[10] The anti-apartheid activist Steve Biko called them "sophisticated concentration camps" and "the greatest single fraud ever invented by the white man."[11]

Like Transkei, the pseudo-nation of Ciskei was on the Eastern Cape, in the southeast of South Africa. It had its own airline and its own national stamps, showcasing handmade carpets, pineapple canneries, and bicycle factories. In a grimly symbolic episode, when its flagpole was raised on December 4, 1981, it broke and had to be held up by South African soldiers.[12] While Ciskei was known mostly as an open-air prison for South Africa's "surplus people," in the 1980s it also became the unlikely site of what neoliberals called a "laboratory experiment . . . designed with the help of a blueprint which was drawn up by economists who believe in the power of markets, prices and incentives."[13] Rather than replacing the Bantustan model, libertarians wanted to figure out how to make use of it while being less explicitly racist. They hoped that the homeland could work as a kind of zone, inviting in foreign capital while encouraging voluntary segregation from below instead of mandatory segregation from above.

South African libertarians were given their opening when Ciskei's leader for life, Chief Lennox Sebe, assembled a commission to give shape to the new homeland's economic policy. Written by what the *Financial Times* called "the supply siders of Ciskei," the report was a recipe for turning the homeland into "an African Hong Kong."[14] Its authors expressed optimism that the homeland could become the "banking haven" that Africa lacked.[15] Acting on its recommendations, Ciskei privatized traditional land and granted tax holidays to foreign investors.[16]

At the head of the commission was Leon Louw, a South African who had attended the Hong Kong meeting of the Mont Pelerin Society

on Friedrich Hayek's invitation.[17] Louw was born in 1948 into a conservative Afrikaner family in the mining town of Krugersdorp—a
town whose namesake, South African president Paul Kruger, also
graced the gold coin called the Krugerrand, an investor favorite.[18] In
1975, Louw helped found the Free Market Foundation, a think tank
that brought Friedman to the country. The FMF saw South Africa's
"tragedy" in the mismatch between its rhetoric of pro-capitalism and
anti-communism and the reality of what they saw as "creeping socialism."[19] To them, apartheid was just another taxpayer-funded social
program reliant on a high degree of intervention, incorporating
color bars in the labor market, welfare for the white population, and
state ownership of many companies.[20] Louw called himself an "abo-
litionist"—he believed that free markets would secure social order
and deliver prosperity better than the racial state-led capitalism that
apartheid represented.[21]

Louw hoped that Ciskei would be a showcase of a more open form
of capitalism to influence the rest of the nation, creating buy-in from
the Black community previously excluded from property ownership
and independent enterprise. A significant aspect of the commission's
report was its claim that private property was part of the traditional
model of land tenure in southern Africa.[22] It praised the suppressed
"free market spirit" of the Black community.[23] Yet what came into
existence bore little resemblance to the cultivation of an indigenous
entrepreneurial class. The homeland that sold itself as "Africa's Switzerland" was a caricature case of corporate welfare, overseen by union
breakers willing to murder.

The instrument used in Ciskei was the export processing zone, or
EPZ. An EPZ traced out a patch of territory that was legally designated
as outside the host country: an offshore space without leaving home
soil, with a different set of regulations, rules, and oversight, inevitably more favorable to investors. As scholars like Patrick Neveling have
shown, EPZs had several antecedents. One was foreign trade zones in
the United States, duty-free spaces created out of warehouses or factories. First seen in America in the 1930s, these took off in the 1980s,

especially for oil processing and automobile assembly.[24] Another fore-runner was the duty-free zone of Shannon Airport in the Republic of Ireland. Once a necessary stopover for transatlantic flights, Shannon adapted after aircraft range improved and rendered it redundant by becoming a trailblazer of tax-free manufacturing in 1958.[25] A third precursor was in Taiwan, which set up its first EPZ in the port of Kaohsiung in 1966. An American labor leader testified about seeing the Kaohsiung EPZ a few years later, separated from the city by a high fence and armed guards. He recounted his guide explaining "with obvious pleasure that by virtue of the fence and a few laws, the land we were standing on was no longer considered part of Taiwan." Companies operating inside the fence could avoid paying Taiwan's domestic taxes. He called the zones "fantasy islands for intensifying corporate profits."[26]

Libertarians aimed to construct such a fantasy island in Ciskei. In the 1980s, the South African government sent agents abroad to solicit foreign investors for what they euphemistically called "decentralization areas." The agents had their best luck in Taiwan and Hong Kong, promising to undercut what had formerly been low-wage zones that had themselves seen wages slowly rise into the middle-income tier.[27] By 1988, there were eighty small Taiwanese factories in Ciskei, producing "everything from doll heads to fishing rods."[28] One Taiwanese investor praised the situation. "This is like Taiwan 30 or 40 years ago," he said: "no competition, cheap labor."[29]

As in all EPZs, the workforce was mostly female. Reporting on the "bonanza" for Asian companies, the *Boston Globe* featured a picture of women in headscarves at Ciskei's China Garments.[30] Another textile factory was staffed entirely by women, who sat side by side on benches or sacks of fabric.[31] These were typical sweatshop scenes: low-ceilinged factories crowded with scores of workers in hairnets, laboring at sewing machines alongside piles of clothing under fluorescent lights.[32]

Reports hailed an "economic boom" of rapid industrialization and rising employment, but this relied on increasing aid flows from the South African government, with transfers of 120 million rand (about $20 million in today's dollars) in 1984 alone.[33] A rise in the price of gold—one of the nation's key exports—filled state coffers and allowed it to set up some of the best investor incentives in the world.[34] Ciskei wages were already artificially low, set at 50 percent of the wages in nearby East London, which were themselves 25 percent below the national average. On top of this, investors received a fifty-dollar monthly wage subsidy per worker out of the aid budget, meaning, as the *Wall Street Journal* reported, "It didn't take much to figure out that by paying workers less than $50 a month . . . investors could make money just by employing people."[35] Indeed, some businesses, including an American clothing company operating through a Hong Kong subsidiary, hired unnecessary workers just to collect the subsidies.[36] In the supposed "laboratory experiment" of free markets in Ciskei, investors were offered a deal too good to pass up, as the state paid the wages of their employees, subsidized 80 percent of the cost of their factory rentals, and billed them for no corporate taxes.[37]

While investors were lured to Ciskei by the carrots of state subsidies, they also profited from the apartheid state's liberal use of the stick—and the gun. The would-be libertarian utopia operated hand in glove with the South African security forces. These punished everyday civilian acts of resistance while actively enforcing the prohibition on trade unions. One activist, Priscilla Maxongo, described how women in the labor movement were routinely arrested, interrogated, and tortured. She recounted having a rubber tube tied around her neck to cut off her air supply until she divulged information about the groups organizing for workers' rights.[38]

In 1983, police killed fifteen protesters when they shot into crowds demonstrating against a 10 percent bus fare increase.[39] The *Times* called Ciskei an "ugly little police state."[40] Thozamile Gqweta, the secretary of the South African Allied Workers, had his house set on fire with the front door wired shut; his mother and uncle died when their houses were similarly set on fire; his girlfriend was shot by police as they left his mother's funeral; and he was himself detained for three months and tortured with electric shock.[41] In another incident of many that transpired in the year that *Reason* celebrated Ciskei as a "haven of prosperity and peace in South Africa's back yard," security forces entered a Ciskei church commemorating the tenth anniversary of the Soweto uprising and beat the congregation with whips made of rhinoceros hide, hospitalizing thirty-five and killing a fifteen-year-old boy.[42]

The tragedy of the partnership with the police state was starkest in 1987. That year, Louw traveled to Dakar to meet members of the African National Congress in exile. He hoped to persuade the socialist ANC that privatization was a better way to reform South Africa.[43] Months later, the Black civil rights lawyer who had organized the meeting was found in the back seat of his own car bound and beaten to death by the Ciskei security forces.[44] Louw's partners in building a libertarian utopia were actively exterminating the democratic anti-apartheid opposition.

Ciskei was a "Trojan horse to topple apartheid." So claimed a British neoliberal think tanker on the front page of the *Wall Street Journal*.[45] But it was no such thing. Rather, as a South African economist stated frankly, "If the ANC came into power in South Africa, they would conquer Ciskei and integrate it again into South Africa at large. So the continued success of Ciskei depends upon the continued survival of the South African government."[46] Another economist supported the sentiment, saying that the last thing South Africa needed was "the kind of government you are getting in the rest of Africa. Every citizen is better off with the current traditional regime firmly entrenched."[47] By "traditional," of course, he meant the tradition of white minority rule.

The libertarian Bantustan was not an expression of the popular longing of the South African people. It was not a lever to weaken the grip of the apartheid state. Rather, it served a role in the strategy of the apartheid state and it needed the apartheid state to live. Libertarians were not brave resisters. They were the useful idiots of the government in Pretoria. At a time when the truth of violent state repression could be easily read about in major newspapers, a neoliberal think tanker called for Ciskei to be added to the Freedom House rankings as a separate country, even though nobody but South African elites bought the idea of Bantustan independence. "I would urge that Ciskei be put in and highlighted and spotlighted," he said. "I think this is a beacon for all of us on South Africa, and I am very happy with what's going on there."[48] He asked of the United States: "Can we have a Ciskei here?" Like many other libertarians, he saw the height of economic freedom in a state unburdened by representative democracy, stripped of its capacity to tax and redistribute, and trained by the threat of capital flight to always put investors' needs first.

2.

Even as the Ciskei experiment showed what should have been rather troubling results for those who claimed to believe in freedom, Leon Louw sought to scale up the model of the business-friendly zone to a reform plan for the whole nation. He met with a Texas oil millionaire visiting South Africa and shared his own idea. The Texan had promised funding—money that eventually came from Charles Koch, whom Louw thanked in the opening pages of *South Africa: The Solution*, published in the Ciskei capital Bisho in 1986.[49] The book, which Louw cowrote with his wife, Frances Kendall, was one of South Africa's most successful political bestsellers at the time, selling close to forty thousand copies, and was released and widely reviewed internationally.[50]

In their book, the couple proposed a "Swiss solution" for South Africa, breaking up the existing system of states and Bantustans into a mosaic of "cantons," where residents could "vote with their feet" by leaving with their capital whenever they desired. Every South African would have multiple citizenships—national, cantonal, and local. The model of one person, one vote would be replaced with the Swiss model of one person, many votes.[51] The central government would control no major revenue sources, make no major transfers between cantons, and be constitutionally bound to respect private property rights. All education and land would be privatized, and high bars would be set for constitutional changes by referendum.

The outcome would be what Louw and Kendall called a "market-place in politics."[52] They believed that most cantons would be what they called "cosmopolitan"—that is, multiracial—but a key feature of their proposal was that "people of a particular race or ideology can cluster together in 'national' or 'ethnic' cantons to satisfy their particular preferences and escape the kind of governments they reject."[53] The freedom of movement would be constitutionally secured but, crucially, the right of *citizenship* in this or that canton would not be.[54] In other words, you might take a job in a segregated canton but might not be permitted to settle there permanently or receive the benefits of citizenship. This was precisely how the existing labor market worked in apartheid South Africa as Black workers moved in and out of white areas for employment but had limited rights of residence, let alone property ownership. What the authors called the "freedom of disassociation"—and the freedom to privately discriminate—was central.[55] Louw and Kendall hoped the re-parcelization of land into many cantons and the decentralization of control over natural resources would safeguard against policies of racialized revenge. Louw left no doubt about this implication when he told *Time* magazine, "We want to make it possible to let the tiger—the Black majority—out of the cage without whites being eaten."[56]

The libertarian solution to involuntary apartheid from above left the door open for voluntary racial segregation from below. Ensuring the right to move but not the right to settle—and including the right to expulsion—suggested a way to an enforced re-sorting of the population back to the status quo ante.[57] Louw and Kendall illustrated this in the epilogue to their book, which imagined a future thirteen years removed from their own, where their Swiss solution had been realized. They prophesied a variety of coexisting political forms, including a canton called Workers Paradise, where "everyone was issued with a copy of Mao's little red book" and racial segregation was reinstituted because Black and white leftist radicals "refused to mix with each other socially."[58] Another canton was called Cisbo, for Ciskei Border Region, where everything was deregulated and traditional land privatized, a "mini Monaco" in which pot, prostitution, and pornography were legal. An illustration showed a white man with golf clubs and fishing pole rushing toward Black and white chorus girls as a man in a Mao suit and another in a black bourgeois frock coat wagged their fingers in prudish disapproval.[59] A last speculative canton was dubbed Witwaterberg, "South Africa's radical white separatist canton," where automation and white labor replaced Black labor altogether and racial covenants ensured that residents remained white only.[60]

In the event, it was only the last one that came to be. In 1990, a group known as the Afrikaner Freedom Front bought a patch of land and buildings in central South Africa, evicted its informal mixed-race residents, and opened the white Boer enclave of Orania the following year.[61] Designs for the settlement dated back to the early 1980s, when Carel Boshoff, head of the Bureau of Racial Affairs, as well as son-in-law of assassinated apartheid president Hendrik Verwoerd, had pitched the so-called Plan Oranje for the establishment of a white homeland. As Boshoff described it at the time, because "white supremacy" was doomed in the long run in a majority Black environment, the best thing to do was withdraw to a white redoubt while continuing economic relations with the surrounding non-white communities.[62] In the 1990s, with Boshoff in residence, Orania took as its logo a small white boy rolling up his sleeves, a gesture signaling a willingness to work—but also, unmistakably, a willingness to fight.

The area where Orania was located had been settled in the 1830s by the Voortrekkers, Boers who left the British Cape Colony to move into the South African interior. Louw, whose combination of anti-apartheid libertarianism and cultural conservatism confounds the usual political classifications, had long idolized the Voortrekkers, calling the Great Trek "one of the most glorious histories of classical liberalism, of rugged individualism."[63] Kendall and Louw defended the viability of the modern-day white enclave. Before Orania was actually founded, they wrote that "people laugh at the proposal of Afrikaner separatists like Carel Boshoff to establish an independent homeland" in the near-desert. But the lack of natural resources should be no problem, they said. An "Afrikaner homeland" just needed a "low-tax or no-tax policy to attract high-tech, skills-intensive business to the region."[64] The miniature ethnostate need only become a zone.

Other South African market radicals have embraced the racial experiment of Orania. At the annual meeting of the South African Libertarian Society held there in 2015, Louw jokingly referred to it as an adaptation of the homeland model to create an "Afrikanerstan."[65] For libertarians, the foremost attraction is its structure as a private entity.[66] Orania's leader is the chief executive, and residents are shareholders in the mother company.[67] It also issues its own currency, the ora. Another South African libertarian described Orania as "a rare example of a libertarian enclave," where membership was governed by voluntary contract as a way of achieving freedom from "the tyranny of the majority."[68] The founder of the South African Libertarian Society used the example of Orania in some advice posted online. "Make your own country," he wrote, "South Africa is vast. Find an attractive piece of land far from the urban centres, ensure it has water, build a fence around it and invite like-minded people to live there with you. Go as far below the radar as you can. Have as little contact with the bureaucracy as possible. Build your own economy and polity. Arm yourselves well."[69]

Orania has gained traction worldwide. In 2019, Australian Far Right groups were using Orania as a template for creating "Anglo-European enclaves" as bases for a coming race war.[70] In the United States, the white nationalist group American Renaissance praised Orania as a place where Afrikaners "could keep white and where they could preserve their language and culture" and "set up a private corporation to run it, with the power to grant residency only to certain approved Afrikaners."[71]

A clear advantage of this cantonization scheme was that it could permit the persistence of patterns of racialized economic power without the stigma of formal apartheid.[72] A voluntary racial segregation from below would not be troubled by the same problems of legitimacy as the top-down separatist state. The post–Jim Crow United States offered a great precedent—a country where segregation happened through the market rather than overt state intervention.[73] According to the libertarian model, racial separation and racial inequality created by the push and pull of economic forces posed no threat to the principles of the free market. Citizen-customers would vote with their feet and sort out the population organically. If the outcome was a balance of economic power that looked much like it had at the outset, then so be it. In a polity reconceived as a constellation of zones, redistribution was no longer part of government's role.

3.

On February 11, 1990, footage of Nelson Mandela walking out of the front gates of Victor Verster Prison after twenty-seven years of incarceration appeared on television screens across the world. There were isolated looting and riots around the country, prompting the notoriously brutal South African police force to fire into crowds, killing many. When Mandela spoke from a balcony in Cape Town partially covered with a red Soviet flag, people pressing in and lifted up on shoulders and arms to see him, his message was clear and unambiguous: "Universal suffrage on a common voters roll in a united, democratic and non-racial South Africa is the only way to peace and racial harmony."[74] The next month, the Ciskei government of Lennox Sebe was overthrown in a coup, with a crowd chanting, "Viva ANC! Viva the South African Communist Party!" Sebe himself was not present. During a previous coup attempt, he had been courting investors in Israel, where he twinned Ciskei's capital city with the West Bank settlement of Ariel.[75] This time he was in the homeland of the zone: Hong Kong.[76]

The events of the early 1990s looked like a refutation of the canton schemes and their fantasy of fragmentation.[77] There would be no drastic redrawing of the maps. The inherited borders of the South

African state remained as they were, and the artificial homelands rejoined the unitary nation in 1994. When Mandela won in a free and fair election, he spoke of South Africa as a "rainbow nation at peace with itself and the world."[78] Historians mark the election as the twentieth century's last act of decolonization, proof that empire had passed from the world stage in a triumph of the nation-state.[79] But there were signs that the dream of the zone was not going quietly. In 1979, the *Far Eastern Economic Review* had reported that free trade zones, "artificially inseminated and easily transplantable into any developing nation . . . have spread across the Third World like a test tube baby boom."[80] What had happened in the hinterland of the Eastern Cape, with its clusters of sweatshops, was very modern and, in some ways, the future. In 1986, there were only 176 zones globally. By 2018, there were 5,400.[81]

The libertarian Bantustans were perhaps not so anomalous as they seemed. National containers were permeable after independence. Flows of labor and money into and out of countries changed the conditions of the possible and placed constraints on the hopes of unimpeded sovereignty that accompanied the vibrant colors of a new flag gliding up the pole.[82] The limits of national sovereignty can be illustrated by comparing the pseudo-independent Ciskei to its neighbor, the actual self-governing state of Lesotho, just a few hundred miles to its north.

I have a personal connection with Lesotho. My family came to the landlocked country in 1985, when I was six years old: my father was joining the Lesotho Flying Doctor Service, riding a Cessna into the mountains to service clinics unreachable by roads. We came via Bloemfontein, South Africa, lugging our ten big black suitcases, including forty-eight tins of smoked salmon we had been given by Kwakwaka'wakh fishermen friends on our departure from our last home, on a small island off Vancouver Island. Lesotho is a rugged country, in gray and tan and a little green, high above sea level, bisected north–south by mountain ranges with most of the population living along the western edge. Gaining independence from the British Empire in 1964 as an enclave in the middle of apartheid South Africa,

Lesotho hosted many expatriate arrivals besides my family—Peace Corps volunteers, engineers, teachers, and geologists. Alongside the children of the postcolonial elites, my childhood best friends were Indian, Israeli, and American.

Lesotho was an object of special attention in the era of international development. The country was an ideal space, of a manageable size and serving as a potential showcase of postcolonial Black rule right in the middle of a pariah state. It seemed like the opposite of the zone. It was an aspiring national economy, striving for growth and modernization. Experts and funders ought to have been able to make things happen here, even if nowhere else. But it turned out they could not make them happen here either.

There is a famous book about the effort to "develop" Lesotho, *The Anti-Politics Machine*, which I later found out was being researched and written when we were there. Its author, the American anthropologist James Ferguson, concludes that the error of the platoons of experts was in seeing Lesotho as the self-contained islet it appeared to be on the color-coded map. In fact, the border had little meaning when the work was beyond it.[83] Men went back and forth across the line to work in South African gold and diamond mines, coming back with wages in cash. Some would end up in fights; part of my father's job was stitching up injuries from knobkerries, the stout round-headed clubs that men often carried under the heavy wool blankets that protected them from the mountain country's cold nights.

Lesotho was a pool of surplus labor for the needs of the apartheid state. The borders also meant little to the South African Defense Forces, who slipped into Lesotho to assassinate opponents of the regime taking refuge there. On occasion, we could hear the helicopters and gunshots. I heard the sound of a coup—people marching along the main road to the border, the Kingsway—while I watched the luckdragons and rock biters of *The Never-Ending Story* on VHS at a friend's house. The lesson of Lesotho was that no nation is an island, and development made little sense if you pretended it was. Even if the borders were officially recognized, and independence was genuine, in contrast to the pseudo-nations of the Bantustans, there were ways that the state remained a zone in the era of globalization. Political autonomy meant nothing without the economic means of survival.[84]

4.

South Africa has had a second life in science fiction as a vision of politics beyond and after the democratic nation-state. In Masande Ntshanga's 2019 speculative novel *Triangulum*, set largely in Ciskei, the protagonist's parents have moved to the Bantustan to work in Sebe's government. A project that sounds like it could have been designed by Louw turns townships into "self-contained, privately owned zones with standardized populations of 200,000 and streamlined economic functions, including energy production, recycling, manufacturing, and urban farming."[85] A high-rise "Revolution Tower," the tallest on the continent, stands in Johannesburg, built by a foreign corporation to signal to investors that the climate is fine. Watching a debate on television, the narrator sees a sociologist denounce "the zones as a new form of apartheid," while a community organizer responds with resignation that "people needed to eat." "The usual," the narrator remarks, and she changes the channel.[86]

Ntshanga expressed the pessimism of a quarter century of actually existing postapartheid, in which the state had its agency constrained by the need to attract overseas capital and betrayed too many promises. Another novelist, closer in time to Mandela's balcony speech, took the canton model to a more radical conclusion. In two novels from the early 1990s, the American author Neal Stephenson conjured up a world very much like the libertarian fantasy. In his 1992 *Snow Crash*, the "New South Africa Franchulate" is an "apartheid burbclave," a fictional version of the real-life Orania: privately owned, privately governed.[87] He expanded on the vision in his next novel, *The Diamond Age*, which featured an Orania-like "clave" of Boers— "stocky blonds in suits or the most conservative sorts of dresses, usually with half a dozen kids in tow." Among the future cantons that

Kendall and Louw predicted was "Maoville"; Stephenson offered a more baroque "Sendero Clave," named after the Shining Path (Sendero Luminoso), Peru's Communist guerrilla movement. It stands "four stories high and two blocks long, one solid giant mediatron" showing Mao Zedong "waving to an unseen multitude" alongside the Peruvian revolutionary leader.[88]

Stephenson animated Louw and Kendall's cantons. Among his most evocative ideas was that of the phyle, taken from the ancient Greek word for "tribe" or "clan." *The Diamond Age* features phyles based on lineage but also "synthetic" ones, "tribes that people just made up out of thin air."[89] However artificial, these phyles became real through legal agreement and cohabitation, shared ritual and codes of conduct. This openness was made possible by the footloose investor capital of manufacturers scouring the world for low wages and government giveaways. Container ships and telecommunications made it as easy to set up in the rural Eastern Cape as in Youngstown or Sunderland—and much cheaper. The end of a world divided into two blocs or three worlds made more visible a shattered world, a fragmented political imagination.

In the 1990s, market radicals pursued a pixelated geography resembling Stephenson's dystopia, with ongoing processes of secession producing ever more polities as products, extending Milton and Rose Friedman's freedom to choose into new forms of elective filiation. After the Cold War's end, libertarians embraced the vision of a world where the right of secession was unlimited. As the journalist Tom Bethell put it: "There are about 160 countries in the world today. Since the Berlin Wall came down, I have frequently found myself thinking: Why not many more? Why not 500 countries?"[90]

UN member states and the decade they joined

The Wonderful Death of a State

It is not easy to start a new state. The earth's surface is already divided up. A new state implies territory taken from an existing one. For good reason, states prefer this not to happen. Not wanting their own borders challenged, states defend international law that sets them in stone. Even during decolonization in Africa and Asia, the often-arbitrary outlines of colonies usually retained their shape as new nations. Demands from minorities seeking self-determination were ignored or suppressed, and the international community agreed. Cartography was destiny.[1]

In the 1990s, these assumptions collapsed. The dissolution of the Soviet bloc yielded a raft of new and reestablished nations, scrambling the contours of Europe.[2] The red mass of the USSR on the map at my middle school sprouted a bloom of new republics at its edges; the oblong of Yugoslavia was in pieces by the time I left high school. Czechoslovakia underwent mitosis. The breakup of socialist Europe seemed to open Pandora's box. The spirit of nation making was afoot. New movements agitated for their own right to secede: Catalans in Spain, the Flemish in Belgium, Tamils in Sri Lanka. In my own country, the province of Quebec came within a percentage point of voting to leave Canada.

When I was fifteen, my family was living in Vanuatu, a tiny island nation between Fiji and Australia. The Chinese and the Americans jockeyed for influence there, donating Toyota trucks to local health projects and building infrastructure. This was not so much humanitarianism as a testament to what a seat in the United Nations meant. Vanuatu was a nation of under two hundred thousand people and only a few thousand square miles, and had only been independent since 1980—but it had the same vote in the General Assembly as a world superpower.[3] Japan lobbied tiny Pacific nations for their support to continue commercial whaling, China to build support for its material and strategic interests. In the 1990s, the UN granted seats to tiny nations long excluded: Andorra, San Marino, Monaco, and Liechtenstein.

Most people saw this wave of nations through the lens of politics—some worried about resurgent "neo-nationalism." Market radicals saw it through the lens of capitalism—and were happy with what they saw. Each state spawned by secession was a new jurisdiction, a start-up territory that might offer itself as a refuge for flight capital or a site of unregulated business or research. Micronations were zones, bound spaces of legal difference small enough to stage economic experiments. They were also phyles—voluntary gatherings of like-minded residents. Secession was a way to subdivide the earth and bring new territories into the bustling marketplace of global competition. Neo-nationalism could be the harbinger of a coming golden age of social sorting defined by ever-shrinking jurisdictions.

In the United States, two groups formed an alliance in response to this moment of geopolitical churn: market radicals seeking passage to a capitalist polity beyond democracy and neo-Confederates seeking to resurrect the Old South. As in Leon Louw and Frances Kendall's blueprints for South Africa, they wove together principles of decentralized capitalist competition and racial homogeneity. This right-wing alliance dreamed of Bantustans of choice—Grand Apartheid

from below. Though their immediate goal failed, their vision of
laissez-faire segregation lived on. For them, secession was the path
to a world that was socially divided but economically integrated—
separate but global.

1.

The most important figure in the secessionist alliance was Murray Rothbard. Born in the Bronx in 1926, he came up through the
world of neoliberal think tanks, becoming a member of the Mont
Pelerin Society in the 1950s.[4] Throughout his career, he developed
a particularly radical version of libertarianism known as *anarcho-
capitalism*. He had no tolerance for government of any kind, seeing
states as "organized banditry" and taxation as "theft on a gigantic,
and unchecked, scale."[5] In his ideal world, government would be
eliminated altogether. Security, utilities, infrastructure, health care:
all would be bought through the market with no safety net for those
unable to pay. Contracts would replace constitutions, and people
would cease to be citizens of any place, only clients of a range of service providers. These would be anti-republics, private ownership and
exchange displacing any trace of popular sovereignty.

How to arrive at such an extreme destination? Although the idea
of national self-determination was the basis of the modern state
system he wanted to escape, he thought a radicalization of national
self-determination might provide the means of exit. Accelerating the
principle of secession would spark a chain reaction of disintegration.
Most new polities would not be anarcho-capitalist, but the process of
breakup would strip the state of its most precious asset—its impression of permanence. Creating new flags and new countries eroded the
legitimacy of old ones and chipped away at their self-serving mythol-
ogies. If new territories avoided being crushed by the vengeful central
government, they would take on different shapes and forms. What if
some opted for his preferred mode of statelessness? "The more states
the world is fragmented into," Rothbard wrote, "the less power any

one state can build up." It was a first principle for him that secession movements should be celebrated and supported "wherever and however they may arise."[6] Crack-up was the flywheel of human progress.

Rothbard's life was marked by a search for signs of potential secession—fractures in the edifice of public faith in existing states. When he found them, he did his best to deepen them. In the 1960s, he saw promise in the New Left's opposition to the Vietnam War.[7] Rothbard hated the war too. He saw America's self-appointed role of global policeman as a pretext for centralizing state power and expanding the cronyism, waste, and inefficiency of the military-industrial complex.[8] A tax-funded standing army with a monopoly on modern weaponry was anathema to his principles, and conscription was "mass enslavement."[9] Although Rothbard's anarcho-capitalism was rejected by the socialist New Left, he wondered if their opposition to *some* actions of the state might be converted into hatred of the state *as such*. Taken seriously, wouldn't "dropping out" translate into exit? In a journal that Rothbard helped launch called *Left & Right*, he propagated secession as revolutionary praxis. Radicals should not seize the state but get out—and make new polities of their own.

As fuel for secession, Rothbard saw nationalism as a positive force. Separatist movements, from Scotland to Croatia to Biafra, were built on a common sense of group belonging in a nation or an ethnicity.[10] In the United States, he was especially interested in the potential of Black nationalism. He admired those in the Black freedom struggle who aimed for communal self-help and collective self-defense and endorsed Malcolm X's call for separatism over Martin Luther King Jr.'s call for restraint and nonviolence.[11] Rothbard and his collaborators believed that Black secession from the United States was achievable; indeed, communities should respect the principle of racial separation.[12] He became frustrated by the cross-racial collaboration of white and Black radicals. Blacks should work with Blacks, he thought, just as it was "the responsibility of whites to build the white movement."[13]

The deviation of the New Left from his preferred script of racial

exit turned Rothbard violently against it by the early 1970s. Their
dogged egalitarianism was an affront to his belief in the biologically
hardwired hierarchy of talent and ability in both individuals and
groups.[14] He condemned affirmative action and quotas for under-
represented groups, comparing them to a British dystopian novel
called *Facial Justice*, in which the state dictates medical operations to
ensure that "all girls' faces are equally pretty."[15] What was needed, he
thought, was a countermovement—a revolt against human equality.
After helping found the Cato Institute with Charles Koch in 1976, he
aided with the launch of a new think tank in the Deep South in 1982:
the Ludwig von Mises Institute for Austrian Economics in Auburn,
Alabama, named after Hayek's mentor, the Austrian economist whose
seminars Rothbard had attended in New York from 1949 to 1959.[16]

Although Mises was no anarcho-capitalist himself, the institute
which took his name became the flagship think tank for the most radical strain of libertarianism. Its distance from the Beltway signified its
rejection of the politics of lobbying used by more mainstream groups
like Cato and the Heritage Foundation. Instead, it pushed more politically marginal positions like the virtues of secession, the need for
a return to the gold standard, and opposition to racial integration.
Its director was Rothbard's kindred spirit and closest partner, Llewellyn "Lew" Rockwell Jr., both a radical libertarian and an advocate of
racial separatism ever since his first position at the conservative publisher Arlington House (named, with little subtlety, after the last residence of Confederate general Robert E. Lee). As an editor, Rockwell
commissioned books on the disastrous effects of desegregation and
the betrayal of white politics in southern Africa, published alongside
David Friedman's *Machinery of Freedom* and panic-mongering bestsellers like *How to Profit from the Coming Devaluation*.[17] One book
Rockwell pitched to an author was called *Integration: The Dream that
Failed*; his personal opinion was that the only option was a "de facto
segregation for the majority of both races."[18]

Like Rothbard, Rockwell combined extreme laissez-faire politics
with a fixation on race. In 1986, he began editing the investment

newsletter of the politician and coin dealer Ron Paul, which trafficked in similar themes.[19] The newsletters were lucrative—subscriptions brought in close to $1 million a year in revenue.[20] A kind of IKEA catalog for the coming race war, the newsletter—which changed its name to the *Ron Paul Survival Report* in 1992—riffed on current events and listed books and services on how to bury your belongings, convert your wealth into gold or stash it overseas, turn your home into a fortress, and defend your family.[21] "Be prepared," it read. "If you live anywhere near a big city with a substantial black population, both husband and wife need a gun and training in it."[22]

South Africa appeared as a cautionary tale, with articles lamenting its "dewhiteization" and advocating cantonization.[23] If Palestinians could have a "homeland," the newsletter asked, why couldn't white South Africans?[24] The *Survival Report* presented a vision of universal racial separatism. "Integration has not produced love and brother-hood *anyplace*," it proclaimed. "People prefer their own."[25] The "disap-pearing white majority" meant that the United States was becoming South Africa in slow motion. Whites were "not replacing themselves," and minority groups were capturing state resources.[26] The solution proposed was an old one. "The Old South had it exactly right: seces-sion means liberty," the *Survival Report* stated in 1994.[27]

Not coincidentally, the newsletters' themes echoed the *Rothbard-Rockwell Report*, which the duo began publishing in 1990.[28] (The publication was later renamed *Triple R*; when Paul returned to Wash-ington, his readers were given free subscriptions.) Rockwell called the ideology he and Rothbard were developing "paleo-libertarianism."[29] The prefix signaled their belief that libertarianism needed to be "deloused" of the libertine trends of the 1960s in favor of conservative values. The paleo-libertarians hoped to "hive off" the "hippies, drug-gies, and militantly anti-Christian atheists" of the broader libertarian movement to defend Judeo-Christian traditions and Western culture and restore the focus on the family, church, and community as both protection against the state and the building blocks of a coming state-less society.[30]

Paleo-libertarians wished for a capitalist anarchist future but they did not foresee an amorphous mass of atomized individuals. Rather, people would be nested in collectives scaling upward from the heterosexual nuclear family in what Edmund Burke called, in an often-repeated quote, the "little platoons we belong to in society." It was taken for granted that these little platoons would divide according to race. "Wishing to associate with members of one's own race, nationality, religion, class, sex, or even political party is a natural and normal human impulse," Rockwell wrote. "There is nothing wrong with blacks preferring the 'black thing.' But paleolibertarians would say the same about whites preferring the 'white thing' or Asians the 'Asian thing.'"[31]

The revival of secession at the end of the Cold War looked to paleo-libertarians like a prime opening for a new political geography. "This is what it must have been like living through the French Revolution," Rothbard wrote. "History usually proceeds at a glacial pace . . . And then, wham!"[32] Of the dissolution of the Soviet Union, Rothbard remarked that it was "a particularly wonderful thing to see unfolding before our very eyes, the death of a state."[33] By this he meant, of course, both a specific state but also, optimistically, the death of states altogether. Secession was the means; anarcho-capitalist society was the end. Paleo-libertarians hoped they could keep the dissolution rolling back across the Atlantic. Rothbard's rhetoric was severe. "We shall break the clock of social democracy," he wrote. "We shall break the clock of the Great Society. We shall break the clock of the welfare state. . . . We *shall* repeal the twentieth century."[34]

Paleo-libertarians saw their task as preparing for the day after the collapse. Looking at the fate of the USSR, they asked compelling questions: What would happen in their own country if the regime crumbled overnight? How could collective life continue to function? The thought was not unpleasant. It offered the tantalizing prospect of sweeping away decades of quixotic state intervention, leaving a blank slate. Rockwell fantasized about a self-administered shock therapy, privatizing air, land, and water; selling off highways and airports;

ending welfare; returning the dollar to gold; and letting the poor fend for themselves.[35] Yet paleo-libertarians also recognized they would need some way to construct a new order out of the wreckage at ground zero. They found common ground with the Far Right in the need for tradition and civilizational values to bind collectives together. Both groups embraced explicitly racial consciousness, a move that banished them to the margins of mainstream opinion but offering a space for collaboration.

Rothbard brokered an alliance with a Far Right group based out of the Rockford Institute in Illinois who called themselves "paleo-conservatives." Both sides of the "paleo alliance" felt it was time to stop denying the reality of cultural and racial difference, and redesign political entities to reflect basic facts of psychology and biology. They both scorned the programs of the "warfare-welfare state." Overseas military interventions, civil rights legislation, and federal antipoverty efforts were merely make-work programs for shiftless bureaucrats and platforms for parasitical politicians.

The paleo alliance held their first meeting in Dallas in 1990. The plains around Dallas and the veld of South Africa were not so different. Both places were crucibles of enduring myths. Both saw waves of white settlement and the nineteenth-century conversion of communally owned territory inhabited by indigenous people into individually owned properties. South Africa had Voortrekkers pushing into the interior; Texas had wagon trains that made their way from the West to the waters of the Gulf. A residue of stories remained in the wake of both migrations: about the malleability of political geography, white hands drawing value from supposed wasteland, and the need for racial solidarity against a darker-skinned existential enemy. Settler ideology united people half a world apart. Rothbard gave a special status to the pioneer and the settler, whom he saw as the ultimate libertarian actor—"the first user and transformer" of territory.[36] He placed the ownership of "virgin land" seized and made valuable by labor at the core of "the new libertarian creed."[37] To the objection that settlers never found land truly empty of humans, Rothbard had a rebuttal. North America's indigenous people, even if they did have a right to the land they cultivated under natural law, had lost this right through their failure to hold it as individuals. Indigenous people, he claimed, "lived under a collectivistic regime."[38] Because they were proto-communists, their claim to the land was moot.

The new group was called the John Randolph Club, named after a slaveholder whose catchphrase was "I love liberty, I hate equality."[39] It was a who's who of the Far Right.[40] A founding member was Jared Taylor, whose white nationalist journal *American Renaissance* protested the ongoing "dispossession" of whites by non-whites.[41] Another was Peter Brimelow, the most prominent opponent of non-white immigration, whose book *Alien Nation* brought an "explicitly white supremacist position" back into mainstream discussions.[42] Others included the columnist Samuel Francis, who called on Caucasians to reassert "identity" and "solidarity" through "a racial consciousness as whites,"[43] and the journalist and politician Pat Buchanan, whose nativist tirades against non-white immigration presaged the rhetoric of Donald Trump.[44]

Rather than indigenous self-determination, the John Randolph Club championed the demand of autonomy for white Southerners, better known as the neo-Confederate movement. And it was these enthusiasts for the Old South who most directly brought the global spirit of secession into US politics. The neo-Confederates attempted to make their case by constructing a wobbly body of research claiming that Southerners were ethnically distinct from Northerners, comprising migrants from Wales, Ireland, and Scotland rather than England.[45] The so-called Celtic South Thesis, based in large part on a 1988 book called *Cracker Culture*, was full of obvious holes—not to mention the small problem of the history of slavery and its demographic legacy—but it sufficed as a makeshift translation of parallel developments across the Atlantic. The neo-Confederates were explicitly inspired by European examples. Their main organization, the Southern League (later League of the South), took its name from the Lega Nord, a right-wing political party that sought to separate northern Italy from the rest of the country. The Southern League's "New Dixie Manifesto," published in the *Washington Post*, called for exit from the "multicultural, continental empire" of the United States and the creation of a Commonwealth of Southern States.[46] Their website included a page on "homelands," with web links to secessionists ranging from southern Sudan and Okinawa to Flanders and South Tirol. "Independence. If it sounds good in Lithuania, it'll play great in Dixie!" the site read.[47] The page also linked to a party that would eventually spark the successful departure of Great Britain from the European Union: the UK Independence Party (UKIP).

While the neo-Confederates were not anarcho-capitalists for the most part, Rothbard endorsed the need "to preserve and cherish the right of secession, the right of different regions, groups, or ethnic nationalities to get the blazes out of the larger entity; to set up their own independent nation."[48] He also held a revisionist interpretation of the Civil War. He compared the Union cause to the adventurist foreign policy of the United States in the 1990s: America roved the world looking for monsters to slay in the name of democracy and human rights, a perverse campaign whose outcome was death and destruction rather than any of the stated aims. "The tragedy of the southern defeat in the Civil War," he wrote, was that it "buried the very thought of secession in this country from that time forward. But might does not make right, and the cause of secession may rise again."[49]

At the inaugural meeting of the paleo alliance, Rothbard explained that their vision united around the twin ideas of social conservatism and exit from the larger state. In a world without central government, the shapes of new communities would be determined by "neighborhood-contracts" between property owners.[50] Elsewhere, he called these entities, which closely resembled Neal Stephenson's idea of the phyle, "nations by consent."[51] Disintegrate and segregate was the program, installing homogeneity as the basis of the polity.[52] Merely stopping new immigration would not suffice. The "Old American republic" of 1776 had been swamped and overwhelmed by "Europeans, and then Africans, non-Spanish Latin Americans and Asians." Because the United

States was "no longer one nation," he wrote, "we had better start giving serious thought to national separation."[53] They might start small, claiming only a portion of the national territory. "We must dare to think the unthinkable," he said, "before we can succeed at any of our noble and far-reaching goals."[54] If he had his way, the wonderful death of the state would come to America too.

2.

We often speak of secessionist and Far Right movements such as the neo-Confederates in purely political or cultural terms, as symptoms of a sometimes pathologized fixation on ethnicity that crowds out all economic concerns. But this is wrong. We should also think of the radical politics of the 1990s in terms of capitalism. Rothbard and Rockwell's own reasoning began with economics. As adherents of the gold standard, abandoned by the United States in the 1970s, they felt that the fiat money system was doomed to a coming period of hyperinflation. Breaking up large states was a way to get out ahead of the pending monetary meltdown and create smaller states more able to reorganize after the crash. Ron Paul spoke of his conviction that change would come "with a calamity and with a bang." "Eventually the state disintegrates under the conditions we have today," he said, comparing the United States to the Soviet Union. He described his daydream of a Republic of Texas with "no income tax and a sound currency and a thriving metropolis."[55]

Even for those without such dire prognoses of the near future, it was simply true that the globalization of the 1990s made small states more viable than ever before. Singapore showed that while focusing on exports and free trade might expose you to the vagaries of global demand, it was no longer necessary to grow your own crops to feed your population. As market radicals so often pointed out, microstates like Luxembourg and Monaco were among the richest in the world.

Paleo-libertarians hoped that the spread of secession as an option would help accelerate economic reform away from social democracy and toward a more stripped-down version of capitalism. The most eloquent proponent of this argument was Rothbard's protégé Hans-Hermann Hoppe, who carried the torch of his mentor's vision after Rothbard died of a heart attack in 1995. Trained as a sociologist in Frankfurt, Hoppe immigrated to the United States and joined Rothbard on the faculty at the University of Nevada, Las Vegas School of Business, in 1986.[56] An active member of the John Randolph Club, he felt that a reversal happened after the end of the Cold War, as the once somnolent socialist bloc of Eastern Europe became the vanguard of global capitalism. Estonia was governed by a man in his early thirties who claimed that the only economic book he'd ever read was Milton Friedman's *Free to Choose*.[57] Tiny Montenegro set up a libertarian private university.[58] Countries across the region introduced low flat taxes on the advice of neoliberal think tanks.[59] As Hoppe saw it, an Eastern Europe filled with small open economies would put pressure on the welfare programs of the West, as those economies sucked in investment and lured away manufacturing jobs. "The emergence of a handful of Eastern European 'Hong Kongs' or 'Singapores,'" he wrote, "would quickly attract substantial amounts of Western capital and entrepreneurial talent."[60]

Hoppe foresaw a supercharging of the dynamic of national self-determination promoted by Woodrow Wilson after World War I, when the once-sprawling Hapsburg and Ottoman Empires were broken up into constituent states and mandates. These future states would be internally homogeneous, he wrote, replacing "the forced integration of the past" with the "voluntary physical segregation of distinct cultures."[61] Hoppe believed that the new territories should be much smaller than the contemporary nation-state. "The smaller the country," he noted, "the greater pressure to opt for free trade rather than protectionism."[62] Citing micronations and city-states as templates, he called for "a world of tens of thousands of free countries, regions, and cantons, of hundreds of thousands of free cities." It was a vision of something like Europe's Middle Ages—the continent in the year 1000 had been a dense pattern of thousands of different

polities, reduced over time to a few dozen. Rothbard had said: repeal the twentieth century. Hoppe's message was more extreme: repeal the millennium.

In 2005, Hoppe held the first meeting of the Property and Freedom Society in the gilded ballroom of a hotel on the Turkish Riviera owned by his wife.[63] In its annual gatherings, the PFS unites former members of the John Randolph Club (which dissolved in 1996) with new advocates of stateless libertarianism and racial secession.[64] Prophets of racial and social breakdown share the stage with investment advisors and financial consultants. At one meeting, the psychologist and race theorist Richard Lynn presented his new book on racial intelligence, *The Global Bell Curve*, while other speakers gave talks on "Public Health as a Lever for Tyranny," "How to Enrich Yourself at Others' Expense Without Anyone Noticing It," and "The Mirage of Cheap Credit."[65] Leon Louw spoke the same year as Carel Boshoff's son, Carel Boshoff IV, who gave a talk on what he called the "experiment" of Orania.[66] One of the organizers praised Orania as a "rare example" of peaceful secession.[67] Peter Thiel, at home in this mélange of social conservatism and anti-democratic market radicalism, was scheduled to speak at one of the PFS meetings as well, but canceled at the last minute.[68]

At the 2010 annual meeting, a white man raised in Texas, younger than the other speakers, took the stage. In a tweed blazer, with a MacBook on the lectern in front of him, Richard Spencer looked like the history grad student he had recently been. He had just launched an online magazine titled *The Alternative Right*, a term that would make him notorious. In his talk, Spencer painted a picture of a coming world that looked a lot like the paleo alliance's vision. Racial separatism would be the new norm: "Latino nationalist communities" in California and the Southwest, Black communities in the "inner cities," a "Christian reconstructionist Protestant state" in the Midwest.[69] For Spencer, present-day politics were heading toward disintegration. The program was to accelerate the collapse while preparing for its arrival.

Spencer rose to prominence six years later when he translated the Nazi salute of "Sieg Heil" into English, shouting "Hail Trump! Hail our people! Hail victory!" at a rally in Washington, DC.[70] To some, the dream of fracture seemed to draw nearer after Trump's election. The president of the Mises Institute wrote that Trump had shown "the cracks in the globalist narrative" of one-world government and that libertarians should capitalize by supporting all forms of secession.[71]

Hoppe became an icon for the Far Right.[72] His reputation rested especially on his book *Democracy: The God That Failed*, which cast universal suffrage as modernity's original sin because it disempowered the caste of "natural elites" who had organized society under monarchy and feudalism.[73] The welfare state spawned by democracy had dysgenic effects, Hoppe argued, encouraging the reproduction of the less able and keeping the talented from excelling. He drew on racial scientists to support his idea that it was necessary to split up into smaller homogeneous communities to reverse the process of "decivilization."[74] The passage that most delighted the Far Right was the one that openly embraced the expulsion of political undesirables. "There can be no tolerance toward democrats and communists in a libertarian social order," Hoppe wrote. "They will have to be physically separated and expelled from society."[75] Hoppe's face appeared in a variety of online imagery on the theme of removal, often accompanied by a helicopter, in reference to Chilean dictator Augusto Pinochet's notorious disposal of the bodies of opponents from the air.

One of the last talks Rothbard gave before his death took place on a plantation outside Atlanta and envisioned the day when the statues of Union generals and presidents would be "toppled and melted down" like the statue of Lenin in East Berlin, and monuments to Confederate heroes would be erected in their place.[76] Of course, many such Confederate statues already existed. The defense of one of them, a statue of General Robert E. Lee in Charlottesville, Virginia, became a symbolic stand for white nationalists in August 2017. Dressed in matching white polo shirts and khaki pants, they carried tiki torches and marched through the city, channeling anxieties of white demographic decline in their chant: "You will not replace us."[77] One of the organizers of the rally, a white nationalist, was a Hoppe fan—he sold bumper stickers reading I ♥ PHYSICAL REMOVAL.[78]

Rather than disavow such support, Hoppe praised the insights. In 2018, he wrote the foreword for a book titled *White, Right, and Libertarian*; its cover featured a helicopter with four bodies dangling from it, their heads displaying the logos of communism, Islam, antifa, and feminism.[79] Hoppe felt that the Far Right's emphasis on common culture and even common race showed how to create social cohesion in a future stateless society. Its militant opposition to non-white immigration was also compatible with the closed-borders position that the paleo-libertarians had been promoting since the early 1990s.[80] In the end, he would seem to have no quarrel with an image that appeared on message boards. It showed Rothbard, Hoppe, and Mises (drawn in the style of the Far Right icon Pepe the Frog) standing in front of the gold-and-black anarcho-capitalist flag, with Hoppe carrying an assault rifle. In this extreme version of crack-up capitalism, the zone was defined by race and marked by militant intolerance.

3.

The dream of bringing back the Old South looked like an abject failure. No "Commonwealth of Southern States" emerged.[81] Yet there was something more to the paleo alliance than a fever dream of taffeta and chattel slavery. The idea of an independent free-trading South reflected shifting geographies of investment and manufacturing as factories gravitated to places where union laws were weaker and tax breaks were larger. Global logistic hubs were operating in Memphis (FedEx) and Louisville (UPS). Atlanta's airport was the busiest for passenger traffic in the world. The North Carolina Global TransPark brought sea, road, rail, and air links into a fifteen-thousand-acre zone.[82]

The rural stretches beyond Dallas, the city where the John Randolph Club first met, were grazing lands for most of the twentieth century, but in its last decade they became more profitable as fracking lands. As the shale revolution brought new wealth, the public ownership of land became ever more politicized. Less than 2 percent of Texas land was federally owned, but in Nevada—where Rothbard and Hoppe taught—84 percent of it was. For those with a vision of a totally privatized country like the paleo-libertarians, this was a continually waving red flag. In the 1990s and the first years of the twenty-first century, the desire for ownership fueled secessionist movements, ranging from the would-be Free State of Jefferson in Northern California to the militant ranchers who occupied the Malheur National Wildlife Refuge in Oregon. Such groups sought to seize territory from the collectivists of Washington, DC, stake out their own homesteads, and create parallel structures of power.[83] These were not nostalgic throwbacks to earlier eras of self-sufficiency but land grabs centered on the globally traded commodities of beef, oil, and timber.

Dallas itself could have showed the John Randolph Club that modern capitalism offered many ways to distance yourself from other populations without a flag or a seat in the United Nations while remaining interconnected economically. For over a century, the city had been a laboratory for the forms of contract, exclusion, and segregation that the paleo alliance dreamed of. In the 1920s, it passed a law prohibiting racial mixing on city blocks. Whites policed the divisions with vigilante violence. As the city grew, the whites seceded into incorporated enclaves; their tax dollars would pay for their own schools, not those of the city at large.[84]

The 1990s were not just a time of fracturing sovereignties in Europe. The same kind of thing was happening in American hinterlands. The decade saw an explosion of a new kind of housing complex: the gated community, the latest innovation in spatial segregation. Rothbard and Hoppe's home of Las Vegas was the fastest-growing city in the United States that decade, and the gated community was its favored form. An African American city councilor protesting the multiplication of the walled communities called them "private utopias."[85] The phrase was well chosen. To those who said that the paleo visions were far-fetched, one might respond that their future was already here, in the segregated realities of the American city and its sprawling surroundings. The gated enclaves and walled settlements, the object of much angst and editorializing from centrists and leftist liberals concerned about the decline of public culture, were one of the more stimulating bright spots for libertarians. They asked the question: What if these hated suburban forms were good, actually? Maybe here, in miniature, the project of alternative private government could take root, the creation of liberated zones within the occupied territory. This could be "soft secession" within the state, not outside it. The crack-up could begin at home.

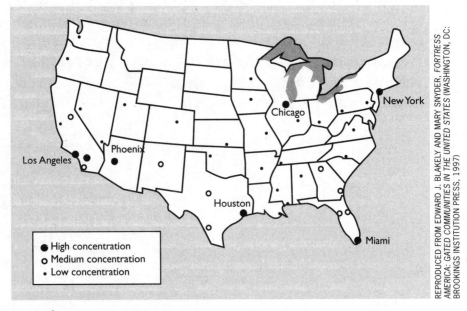

Concentration of gated communities in United States, 1996

Cosplaying the New Middle Ages

When neoliberal luminaries met in 1990 to crown Hong Kong the freest economy in the world, they chose a stunning location in which to do so.[1] The community of Sea Ranch has about ten thousand residents along ten miles of the Northern California coast. The bungalows are steep-roofed and striated in windbeaten gray and brown. They crouch behind lichen-covered bluffs and nestle in the soft swells of moors. The whole landscape is dipped in honey when the sun sets out on the flat line of the Pacific. The buildings have been lingered over in countless coffee table books, glossy features in *Dwell* and *Architectural Digest*, and latter-day Instagram feeds and Pinterest boards. The aesthetic lends itself to fetishization. The *New York Times* called Sea Ranch a modernist utopia.[2] But it was also, more mundanely, a gated community—a utopia of private property and rules. The population at the time of the 1990 meeting was 97 percent white.[3] Life was governed by a fifty-six-page document called *The Sea Ranch Restrictions*.[4] It limited the height of trees, enforced muted colors for drapes, and banned clothes hung from visible lines. The original planner called it a kibbutz without the socialism.[5] You were free to choose here but only insofar as you adhered to a greater edict: follow the fixed rules.

The coast had a long history of enclosure and exclusion. Russians arrived there in the 1840s, in pursuit of the "soft gold" of sea otter fur. They claimed a chunk of land and built walls out of tree trunks to make a settlement called Fort Ross (from *Rus*, the root of *Russia*). When a Muscovite of high culture arrived, she created a salon atmosphere, hosted dances, and built a glass conservatory.[6] But when the otters were gone, the Russians were, too, selling the buildings cheap to German farmers. The Mexican government took over the territory; for a month in 1846, the breakaway Bear Republic of California claimed sovereignty over the region, before giving way to the United States and leaving only the animal on the new state flag. A mill was built to turn felled trees into timber but burned down at the turn of the century. Decades later, the patch of land found new use as a real estate asset and a realm of sensory pleasure.

Founded in the 1960s, Sea Ranch was a pioneer in the revival of the walled settlement, the return of the fort to the coast after a century's absence. By the end of the century, gated communities were more than just a new kind of real estate—they became metaphors of the moment.[7] They seemed to capture the paradox of the post–Cold War decade, when two forces battled each other. One was a sense of ever-greater connection, of seamless mobility and communication. The other was a feeling of isolation, of social separation and new walls—*global apartheid*, to use a term that gained currency even as the system formally vanished in South Africa.[8] Gated communities were closed but interconnected, linked to the world by "ribbons of roadway, fiber-optic cables and digital electromagnetic signals."[9] Struggling to describe the emerging order, many reached to the deep past and diagnosed the return of a new Middle Ages. "We are building a kind of medieval landscape," an architecture critic lamented, "in which defensible, walled and gated towns dot the countryside."[10]

Market radicals were not depressed by these events—they were inspired. For them, the gated community was more than a metaphor.

Like the London Docklands and the Bantustan of Ciskei, it was a laboratory, a place to practice micro-ordering and keep the project of perforation rolling. They embraced the centrifugal force of settlement and the multiplication of different legal arrangements. Drafting new maps for decentralization, they drew up plans for the return of law and order, medieval style.

1.

Few took the fetish for the Middle Ages as literally as Milton Friedman's son, David Director Friedman, whose intellectual trajectory reflects the radicalization of libertarian thought in the late twentieth century. Born in New York City in 1945, David grew up in the academic enclave of Hyde Park, where his father taught at the University of Chicago. Though not a gated community, Hyde Park was a postage stamp of under two square miles surrounded by the poorer and blacker neighborhoods of the South Side, and a front line in the fight over race and property in midcentury America. Attempts to desegregate the enclave in the 1940s ran into a wall of opposition from its residents. In one pamphlet, homeowners described the neighborhood's racial covenants as "morally justified and not motivated by prejudice." They argued that the restrictive covenants were "private contracts" that offered security of investment and "safeguards against the deteriorating influence of undesirable neighbors."[11] In *Capitalism and Freedom*, Milton Friedman expressed his own opposition to laws against discrimination. He preferred that education be totally private, with people paying for it through state-provided vouchers. If they wanted to use their tax money to pay for a segregated school, then so be it.[12]

As an undergraduate at Harvard in the early 1960s, David was part of a conservative revival catalyzed by the presidential run of Barry Goldwater, whom his father was helping advise.[13] After returning to Hyde Park for a graduate degree in theoretical physics at the University of Chicago, he wrote a regular column for the conservative youth publication the *New Guard*. The tone was pugnacious. "Student rebels are our enemies," began one column. "The rebels, if they resort to force, should be hung from the nearest lamppost."[14] The *New York Times Magazine* singled him out as among the "most brilliant and articulate spokesmen" of the libertarian movement. "Ask not what government can do for you . . . ask rather what government is doing to you," he proclaimed.[15] With horn-rimmed glasses and his longish hair in a frizzy halo, he delivered provocative banter with the relish of a dorm-room debate champion. For public occasions, he sometimes added a gold medallion with a torch of liberty wrapped in the DONT TREAD ON ME snake of the Gadsden flag and the letters TANSTAAFL, for his father's well-known coinage: "There Ain't No Such Thing as a Free Lunch."[16]

David Friedman's politics leaned much further toward actual statelessness than those of his father. Milton was a skeptic of public education but he believed that government was necessary for a range of other functions, from law and order to property rights, printing and controlling money, and even, at times, fighting monopoly and punishing polluters.[17] As he often insisted, he was no anarchist. His son, by contrast, was. Two years out from his physics doctorate, David published a manifesto titled *The Machinery of Freedom: Guide to a Radical Capitalism*.[18] The book staked out an extreme position, joining Murray Rothbard's call for anarcho-capitalism, defined as a system in which all state services—from roads to courts and the police—would be privatized. Public law would cease to exist altogether, along with any semblance of democracy.

From the outset, anarcho-capitalism had the quality of a thought experiment. Debates about it often revolved around the difficulty of actually realizing a fully privatized world in the context of existing state structures. A common objection was the problem of defense. How could any private community protect itself against a nuclear-armed enemy? Because of such difficulties of practical realization in the present, anarcho-capitalists enjoyed taking refuge in the past. In 1970, a letter to the editor of the *New Guard* warned that the idea of privatizing protection would lead not to economic freedom but to "a new Feudalism."[19] The correspondent was closer to the truth than he might have known.

In fact, David Friedman's work was hard to separate from his extracurricular persona as an early-twelfth-century upper-class Berber named Duke Cariadoc of the Bow. He was an active member of the Society for Creative Anachronism (SCA), a group that had started in Berkeley in the 1960s.[20] In persona as Cariadoc, Friedman forwent glasses, used only his right hand to eat, always followed the name of God with an honorific, and sometimes followed the name of a dead non-Muslim with "curses on him for an unbeliever." He wrote advice to people on how to be a medieval Muslim and signed his name in Arabic.[21] In 1972, he launched an annual SCA gathering called the Pennsic Wars, a portmanteau of Pennyslvania and Punic. The first one drew 150 people; by the late 1990s, the two-week medieval camping event regularly attracted 10,000.[22]

The topos of the Middle Ages fed into Friedman's research. In an article in the prestigious *Journal of Political Economy*, he offered a "theory of the size and shape of nations," crunching measurements of the length of medieval trade routes into formulae.[23] But it was in 1978 that he made his most enduring contribution to the literature of the New Middle Ages. While his father was talking to the camera about the miracle of Hong Kong, David was praising another rock in the sea: Iceland, where he felt he could find traces of an anarcho-capitalist civilization.

From the tenth to the thirteenth centuries, he wrote, the Nordic island "might almost have been invented by a mad economist to test the lengths to which market systems could supplant government in its most fundamental functions."[24] In medieval Iceland, he wrote, law was privately enforced; even murder was a civil offense for which one paid a fine to the victim's family.[25] The attractive feature of this model was that retribution was transferrable. Someone who suffered a crime could sell the contract for retribution to a third party—they had a property right in their own victimhood. Friedman admired the durability of the Icelandic system, which lasted over three hundred years, and suggested it could offer inspiration for the present day. Medieval Iceland showed that "the American legal system is a mere thousand years behind the cutting edge of legal technology."[26]

Others picked up the thread from Friedman. Most important was his fellow anarcho-capitalist economist Bruce Benson.[27] In his 1990 book *The Enterprise of the Law: Justice Without the State*, Benson also proposed a rebooted medievalism as a model of criminal justice reform for the late twentieth century. In Benson's narrative, German tribes brought the model of *wergeld*, or "man-price," to the British Isles in the fifth century.[28] Economic payback rather than imprisonment was the ideal mode of punishment. In the Middle Ages, it was dispensed by self-organized bodies called "hundreds," which he praised as "cooperative protection and law enforcement associations."[29] Already by the eleventh century, though, law and order started to become more top-down. The king appointed sheriffs and took a portion of fines.[30] It became illegal to settle thefts without appealing to royal law.[31] As Norman centralism replaced Saxon localism, what had been interpersonal offenses became "crimes." By the twelfth century, tax collectors and justices were part of the court, granted license to extract revenue from the population by royal imprimatur.[32] Permission to operate jails—also obtained through the king—became lucrative, with prisoners charged for their own imprisonment.[33] Benson saw incarceration itself as an unnecessary state function. The nadir for him came in the nineteenth century, when a public prison system financed by taxes emerged in Britain.[34]

Benson's gallop through legal history traced an arc from private to authoritarian law.[35] As an anarcho-capitalist, he believed that all government-imposed forms of taxation, fines, and penalties were theft. The further we moved from the self-organization of Germanic war chiefs, the closer we came to tyranny. But he held out some hope. He observed that the public monopoly on policing was quite recent. Into the nineteenth century, there were private "thief-takers" as well as private police forces. In the late twentieth century, privatization might be turning the enterprise of law into a business again. He pointed to companies like Mesa Merchant Police and Guardsmark, which offered private security alongside long-standing agencies like Pinkerton and Wackenhut. He highlighted Behavioral Systems Southwest, which housed detained undocumented immigrants on behalf of the former Immigration and Naturalization Service.[36] His biggest argument for privatizing law and order was that it would slash payroll.[37] Police forces and prisons were highly unionized; privatization would solve that problem immediately.

Versions of neo-medieval private justice were common in the cyberpunk of the 1990s. In William Gibson's *Virtual Light*, "skip-tracers" track people down on contract.[38] In *Battle Angel*, an anime miniseries set in 2036, a class of enterprising freelancers pursues criminals for profit. "Once there was something called the police whose purpose was to prevent crime," one explains. "These days The Factory just puts a bounty on the head of wanted criminals and lets hunter warriors like me do the dirty work."[39] In the contemporary United States, Benson proposed other ways of reviving lost traditions. Turning ownership of streets over to residents meant people could keep out suspicious outsiders by self-policing and deepening a sense of community. He practiced what he preached, living in a gated community in Tallahassee, Florida, that had private streets, a single entrance, and a neighborhood Crime Watch.[40] Privatization was bringing back the spirit of the Anglo-Saxon hundreds.[41]

Benson was not just whistling into the wind. He was well funded and fêted by think tanks. In 1998, his arguments went straight into a report for the William I. Koch Commission on Crime Reduction and Prevention for the State of Kansas. Privatizing law and order, he said, was "actually a return to historical practices rather than something new."[42] For those perplexed by the turn of libertarian funders like the Charles Koch Foundation toward prison abolition in the twenty-first century, Benson's argument sheds some light. Market radicals of his ilk believe that prison itself is a perversion of punishment, which would be better served by private restitution rather than statist attempts at rehabilitation.[43] Mercenary thief-takers, justice by private posse, and

tradable contracts in payback; these were the components of a reform
inspired by the deep past.

2.

In the last decades of the twentieth century, the neoliberal movement's
center of gravity moved westward. An unlikely vortex formed in a
place better known for its protest and dropout culture: San Francisco's
Bay Area. Milton and Rose Friedman blazed the trail, moving out in
1979. They bought a second home in Sea Ranch and a primary residence in Royal Towers, the tallest building on San Francisco's Russian
Hill, rising twenty-nine stories above a thicket of bay-windowed ter-
race houses. At the base of the hill was the Cato Institute, founded by
Charles Koch, Ed Crane, and Murray Rothbard. Steps away were the
offices of *Inquiry* and *Libertarian Review*.[44] The Friedmans were often
joined for dinner by their neighbor Antony Fisher—former chicken
magnate, failed sea turtle rancher, and think tank impresario. Fisher
set up the Pacific Research Institute in 1979 and the Atlas Foundation
in 1981, filling out the roster of what would become highly influential
pushers of privatization policies in the Reagan years.[45] It was PRI that
funded Bruce Benson's work on the Middle Ages.

By the 1990s, the most exciting parts of the West were those places
that were parceled off and governed like Sea Ranch. Praising the
phenomenon of gated communities, the vice president of the Cato
Institute wrote that people were responding rationally "by walling
[themselves] off from barbarian threats."[46] Another libertarian wondered whether using covenants to create "voluntary cities" like Sea
Ranch would help solve the problem of "crack houses" in American
cities—presumably by simply expelling users.[47] But gated communities were more than just refuges. They were zones to experiment in.
A pair of economists described them as "contractual governments . . .
formed by entrepreneurs who produce and sell constitutional rules."[48]
Votes were allotted by housing unit, or even by the size of the housing
unit, instead of the old model of "one person, one vote," which to their

mind was producing suboptimal outcomes.[49] Looked at this way, the new walled towns became exhibits in the case for capitalism without democracy.

The most detailed investigation came courtesy of Gordon Tullock, who made the case for the gated community as a template for redesigning the future. Trained as a lawyer, he served the US State Department in Hong Kong, Seoul, and Tianjin before settling down for a career in the academy. He was an intellectual magpie, collecting and combining insights from far-flung disciplines and locations. His syncretic approach was on display when he touched down in 1979 in a favorite site for libertarian thought experiments: apartheid South Africa. Anticipating Louw and Kendall, he suggested the country should fragment into smaller units rather than uniting under universal suffrage.[50] By way of illustration, Tullock pulled an unexpected rabbit from his hat: the People's Republic of China. The communist revolution there had left much intact, he argued. Local government still resembled the system of Imperial China, broken up into "a federation of villages" of one thousand to two thousand residents overseen by "street governments," leaving a high degree of local control.[51]

A few years later, Tullock mined another surprising source for insights: the Ottoman Empire. Living at the time in a Virginia condominium with armed private police, he wondered whether "little private governments" might be generalized on the model of Ottoman *millets*. Under the system that lasted until the dissolution of the Ottoman Empire after the First World War, one was both an imperial subject and a member of a self-governing religious community. Why, Tullock asked, couldn't ethnic communities similarly govern themselves in the United States? School funds could be distributed, for instance, to "a Polish community in Chicago or the Cubans of Miami," rather than allotted geographically by school district. He indulged in an even further flight of racialized fancy when he suggested that, in contemporary US cities, Black Muslims used "police force" on "their citizens . . . engaging in violence up to and including executions." Perhaps to reassure his audience this was not meant negatively, Tullock noted that he approved of the order and prosperity brought by these Black Muslims. Under similar circumstances, he "would voluntarily join."[52]

In the fall of 1990, Tullock embarked on a lecture tour to Yugoslavia, speaking on the topic of decentralization and federalism. He was surprised to find that the Balkan socialist republics were not sorted out cleanly by ethnic differences but included significant minority populations. This struck him as a fatal flaw, an intuition confirmed soon after when ethnic conflict tore the country apart. He decided to write a handbook for federalizing the state, with the hope it could be used in countries across the world to preempt further violence.[53] Ever attentive to his surroundings, Tullock found an early draft of his ideal polity in his own neighborhood when he moved into a gated community of about 250 homes in the sun-bleached, saguaro-blanketed hillocks north of Tucson. What he called in his writing the Sunshine Mountain Ridge Homeowners Association became the template for his ambitious effort to write a global blueprint for federalism based on elective self-sorting.[54]

The virtue of the master-planned community was that it was voluntary. It had a tailored set of rules, visible from the outset, which you could either opt into and buy a home, or choose not to, and shop elsewhere. As opposed to the larger jurisdiction of a city, county, or state, the homeowner association (HOA) was a compact unit, an opportunity for micro-ordering. "What does this little 'government' do?" Tullock asked. They owned and maintained the streets and installed fire hydrants. Private companies provided fire protection, gas, electricity, cable, and garbage collection. The community was defended by the local sheriff but added its own guards for night shifts. It also had precise aesthetic prescriptions, including how one's garden could look from the street and the color of one's house. "If we get some eccentric who would like to paint his house purple," Tullock noted, "he can be stopped."[55] Zany taste was not covered by this version of freedom—it would be too likely to clash with too many of one's fellow property owners.

Not satisfied to see his HOA as an idiosyncratic example of a functioning private government, Tullock used the community as evidence for a theory he called "sociological federalism," which stated frankly that the most pertinent sociological categories are ethnicity and race. The population of Sunshine Mountain Ridge was "rather homogenous," he noted—that is, almost entirely white and non-Hispanic, whereas almost a third of the people in the surrounding Pima County were of Mexican background. For Tullock, this was not a problem but a confirmation of his assumption: "It seems that people, on the whole, like living with other people who are similar to them."[56]

Why would people want to "secede" to gated communities? "Are they seeking to avoid people of other races?" Cato's David Boaz asked skeptically in 1996.[57] Tullock's analysis pointed toward yes. He defended segregation for both its voluntary quality and its utilitarian outcomes. No state forced division; people would do it themselves. And once they had done so, their binding contracts would define the limits of their exercise of individual expression, and private security forces would ensure the exclusion of undesirables. This was the vision of an orderly checkerboard of racial homogeneity, enabled by the abandonment of any prospect of redressing inequality through collective action. Writing from the scrublands of southern Arizona, Tullock saw the fortified Caucasian citadel as both a speculative dream and an existing reality.

3.

David Friedman saw one path to a stateless future in building alternative institutions, or what he called "the skeleton of anarcho-capitalism" within society.[58] Gated communities modeled polycentric law. According to this theory, there need not be a single code of law applicable to all. In fact, things work more smoothly when there are many codes. It was a shortcoming of the modern world that only one set of laws applied within the whole of a given territory. By contrast, libertarians celebrated the idea of different groups carrying their law around with them. This was what Hans-Hermann Hoppe called the "hierarchic-anarchic" order of the medieval era.[59] Market radicals should take their "cues from the European Middle Ages," he wrote, "striving to create a U.S. punctuated by a large and increasing number of territorially disconnected free cities."[60] Authority was not the problem. Rules were not the problem. The problem was not having enough authorities and rules to choose from.

That this understanding of the Middle Ages was based more on imagination than rigorous scholarly study goes without saying. The medieval world was regularly reduced to a few convenient bullet points. But to nitpick historical accuracy would be to miss the point. Just before Friedman wrote his article on Iceland, he published another in which he described medieval reenactment as a "joint fantasy."[61] At the re-creationist gatherings, he introduced something called the Enchanted Ground, an area sectioned off by a golden rope and a sign reading WITHIN THESE BOUNDS THE TWENTIETH CENTURY DOES NOT EXIST. This kind of re-creation is also known as LARPing (live action role playing) or cosplay (from the "costume play" of devoted fans of fictional characters). In political discussions, *cosplay* is sometimes used as a term of derision for a kind of politics that is escapist, not engaged with the real world. But as Friedman himself points out, his own response to the Middle Ages is unique in that it is real. You wear the period clothing, get blisters on your hands from the sword, prepare and eat the medieval food. In the same way, the historical LARPing of anarcho-capitalists had real-world outcomes. They invite us to speculate but to do so concretely—to play for real.

An example of this was David's son, Patri Friedman—named after his father's fellow creative anachronist, a Harvard history of science PhD who went by the name Patri du Chat Gris. Patri attended the Pennsic Wars in his youth, and later became a fan of the celebrated Burning Man cultural festival in the Nevada desert. He reveled in the ingenuity and creativity of the participants who made "two-mile-long laser images . . . visible from space in a dusty environment" and not one but two "forty-foot-long fire-breathing dragon cars."[62] But he had one complaint: there was no commerce permitted at the event. In his vision of utopia, as in those of anarcho-capitalists before him, commodification was not checked at the door but rather dominated everything in sight.

Patri's goal was to re-create the enchanted ground of Burning Man but put utopia up for sale. The emblem of Burning Man was a stick figure with its arms in the air. The Seasteading Institute's logo placed a cargo ship in its hands. "Atlas swam," quipped one critical article.[63] This was a gated community at sea, an aquatic take on the voluntary city, and a floating jurisdiction. When David Friedman spoke at the second conference of the institute, he explained its significance by returning to the familiar trope of the Ottoman Empire. "The world as a whole is a polylegal system," he said. Usually this meant that different patches of land were attached to different legal regimes. But what if the territory could be mobile, plugging into one set of laws one year and another the next? Or it could use flags of convenience as ships do, carrying the labor law or intellectual property law of Liberia or Panama with it to a more highly regulated part of the world. Seasteads could be legal mobile homes.

Anarcho-capitalists believed that through serial acts of opting out, the lineaments of a future society without a state could come into definition. Playacting a private society could take on its own momentum. Reality seemed to track the fantasy. When David Friedman was a kid, the University of Chicago created its first police force. In *The Machinery of Freedom*, he proposed the idea of privatizing security altogether.[64] By 2000, the University of Chicago had one of the country's largest private forces. True to Friedman's desires, it had been granted jurisdiction over the neighborhood, policing sixty-five thousand people. That same year, about half of all new developments in the US West and South were gated and master-planned, and seven million American households lived behind walls or fences.[65] Homeschooling looked like another bright spot. In the 1970s, there were an estimated twenty thousand children being homeschooled. By 2016, there were 1.8 million.[66] A John Randolph Club member, Gary North, was critical to getting homeschool laws passed in all fifty states.[67]

"The modern state with its unitary legal system is less tolerant of diversity than the states of the Middle Ages," David Friedman has claimed.[68] Yet if gated communities were neo-medieval islands, they testified to the opposite. Tullock praised the way that one could "vote with one's feet" between communities, but one could not really shop meaningfully between mini-governments. The covenants signed by HOA residents were written in boilerplate hashed out by lawyers and insurance companies.[69] They varied even less from community to community than the enclaves' architectural styles and fanciful names, and they tended to narrow the parameters of acceptable behavior rather than expand residents' freedom. Political signs and the distribution of newspapers were prohibited. A California couple received a daily fine for having a wooden rather than a metal swing set. A Florida woman was taken to court for a dog that weighed over thirty pounds.[70] The private governments of the gated community constrained free choice in the belief that homogeneity best secured their long-term investment. Economic freedom meant less room for individual expression.

It is to David Friedman's credit that he conceded that the anarcho-capitalist society would not necessarily be "a society in which each person is free to do as he likes with himself and his property as long as he does not use either to initiate force against others."[71] It is just as likely, he admitted, that privatizing law and order could lead to more restrictions on personal freedom. Residents of the American West needed only look to the recent past for a sense of what this would mean in practice. Well into the twentieth century, the United States was dotted with hundreds of company towns. Built and owned by private individuals, these were enclaves of paternalistic rule. Houses were built by the company, with their appearance and color fixed by the boss. Stores were owned by the company, too, with workers sometimes paid in "scrip" that could only be used there. Sociological federalism was the order of the day, with races and ethnicities living in segregation. Behavior was controlled, with frequent prohibitions on liquor and almost universal prohibitions on joining a union or taking labor actions. Strikes were met with termination and expulsion from the community. Some coal towns made workers sign agreements that they would not even host union members as visitors in their homes.[72] In copper mining towns like Bisbee and Jerome, armed freelance vigilantes were used to round up and eject members of undesirable labor unions. A coal boss from Washington State who owned and ran his own town had a well-known saying that doubles as a slogan for the anarcho-capitalist dream: "A good kingdom is better than a poor democracy."[73] He said nothing about the bad kingdoms. Only in anarcho-capitalist fantasies do people live under laws of their own choosing.

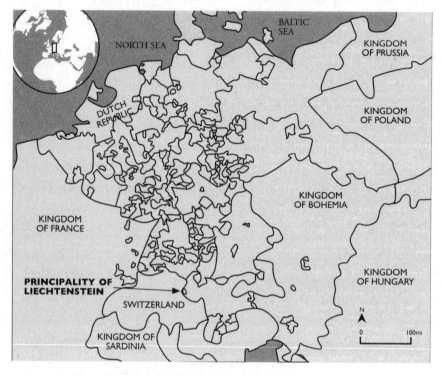

Mosaic of polities in Europe around 1789

Your Own Private Liechtenstein

It's been said that if you light a cigarette when you enter Liechtenstein on the highway from Switzerland, you'll still be smoking it when you cross into Austria.[1] The principality is about the length of Manhattan, a craggy green valley along the river Rhine. It seems an unlikely place to offer a template for political organization for the twenty-first century. Yet despite—and because of—its miniature size, the aura of the principality shines bright in the libertarian mind. In 1985, the *Wall Street Journal* called Liechtenstein "the supply-siders' Lilliputian lab."[2] The year after, Leon Louw and Frances Kendall used it to argue for cantonization in apartheid South Africa.[3] Radical libertarians celebrate it as the "first draft" of a state designed as a service provider with citizens as customers, and dream about "a world of a thousand Liechtensteins."[4]

Among its virtues is the presence of a resident libertarian theorist. Prince Hans-Adam II von und zu Liechtenstein, the world's fourth-wealthiest monarch, with a net worth of over $2 billion, has offered himself as a tribune for the cause, sketching blueprints for what he calls "the state in the third millennium"—an alternative globalism based on secrecy, autocracy, and the right of secession. To some market radicals, this last bit of confetti from the Holy Roman Empire is the preview of a potential coming future.[5]

1.

The charm of Liechtenstein begins with its origins: it was bought for cash.[6] At the beginning of the 1700s, a member of the Viennese court purchased two stretches of land from the bankrupt Hohenems dynasty and melded them into a single principality. The territory was rechristened with the surname of its new owners.[7] Becoming a fully sovereign state in 1806, Liechtenstein was part of the German Confederation until that confederation dissolved in the middle of the century, after which it came under the umbrella of the Hapsburg Empire. Neither the principality's original buyer nor any of his heirs lived there; until 1842, none even visited it.[8] They enjoyed diplomatic immunity in Vienna, four hundred miles away. Liechtenstein was just one of their many properties, strewn across what was still the aristocratic patchwork of central Europe.[9]

When the Hapsburg Empire broke up after its defeat in the First World War, Liechtenstein affiliated itself with Switzerland. Austrian currency, made worthless by hyperinflation, was ditched for the Swiss franc, which became legal tender in the microstate in 1924.[10] The war dealt a blow to the House of Liechtenstein: most of its scattered properties lay in what became the new state of Czechoslovakia, which followed a policy of economic nationalism and expropriated foreign-owned holdings. The princely family lost more than half its land, with compensation at what they reckoned was a fraction of the true value.[11] Liechtenstein's application to join the League of Nations was rejected in 1920, but the microstate still had its sovereignty and sought ways to make use of it. Ideas for a lottery and a horse-betting operation surfaced and vanished, as did a proposal to launch an extranational currency unit known as the *globo*.[12] Plans to mimic Monaco and become an alpine Monte Carlo also came to naught. In the end, Liechtenstein chose instead to become something that did not yet properly have a name: a tax haven.

The central institution of the tax haven is the trust. Invented in England, the trust dates back to the time of the Crusades, when people departing to fight in the Holy Wars sought to leave their property in the hands of a confidant. In the medieval and early modern period, putting land in trust with friends or living relatives was a way to avoid it being confiscated upon their death by authorities or tax collectors. They were a means of asserting the power of elites against the rise of tax-collecting rulers. Into the twentieth century, they have filled a similar purpose. The sociologist Brooke Harrington has shown how trust and estate professionals adopted some of the code of earlier knights, bound by personal ties that float above and beyond the confines of terrestrial nation-states.[13] For centuries the heart of the profession was the City of London, but the introduction of income tax in many countries around the time of the First World War created more incentive for secreting away personal wealth, and companies whose businesses were fragmented among the newly created states looked for a single seat of incorporation.[14] Liechtenstein and Switzerland stepped in to fill the gap.

Liechtenstein's status as a remnant of the premodern feudal system made the posture of chivalrous keeper of secrets all the more convincing. In 1920, a multinational consortium created a new bank there.[15] The same year, the first holding company was created.[16] In 1926, the microstate passed a law that allowed foreign companies to act as if they were domiciled in the mountain valley. All that was required was having a local lawyer act as your agent. In the eyes of the tax collector, their residence became your residence. The number of registered companies quadrupled within a few years, rising to around twelve hundred in 1932; by the early twenty-first century, there would be seventy-five thousand of them. Accounts were anonymous, registration could be in any language, the shares could be denominated in any currency, and all the subsidiaries of the mother company would be covered anywhere in the world.[17] One of the enduring features of the Liechtenstein system is that a corporation could be made up of just a single person, their identity vanishing inside a legal black box.[18] Liechtenstein's trademark offering was the Anstalt, originally developed in Austria as a type of foundation for charitable purposes. Liechtenstein adapted it as a way to shield family fortunes from inheritance taxes.[19]

"Considered as a country," a journalist wrote in 1938, "Liechtenstein is much too small to be independent. But considered as a safe it is a very large one, practically the largest one ever built."[20] The quaint streets of Liechtenstein's capital, Vaduz, with a population of a few thousand, were lined with the corporate offices of the world's largest companies, including IG Farben, Thyssen, and Standard Oil. Liechtenstein also debuted another practice beloved of the superrich: letting them buy citizenship. In 1938, the price was $5,500. (Adjusted for inflation, this is about $110,000 in today's money—similar to the current entry level for naturalization "by investment" in countries like Vanuatu and Grenada.)[21] Most of the newly minted Liechtensteiners did not stay. They drove in, took the oath of citizenship, and drove away. Liechtenstein became known as "the capital of capital in flight."[22]

In 1938, Liechtenstein's monarch took up residence in the principality itself for the first time, as Prince Franz-Josef II fled the annexation of Austria by Nazi Germany. By an agreement whose terms remain opaque, the country was left untouched by German forces. There was a small domestic Nazi movement, and Hitler sympathizers were allowed in the fifteen-person parliament, but a slightly comical attempt at a putsch was put down with the aid of Boy Scouts.[23] An international commission of historians later found that although forced laborers were used on lands owned by the royal family in Austria, Liechtenstein—unlike its neighboring Switzerland—did not traffic in gold or art stolen from Jews.[24]

After the war, Liechtenstein continued to develop its status as an "Eden for nervous capitalists."[25] The 1950s saw the expansion and extension of the offshore world, as more corporations sought to escape taxation by creating holding companies outside the country they operated in. By 1954, Liechtenstein had between six thousand and seven thousand holding companies, including a subsidiary of Ford, alongside other companies disguised behind made-up names like Up and Down Trading Corporation.[26] As one trustee explained, someone showing up with a briefcase full of cash would be given a range of options for placing it in an account either personally or through a nominee.[27] A charter was needed, but it only had to include the company's name, the date of incorporation, and the name of the nominee; an annual meeting was required, but it could be held by your nominee—and could be a meeting of one.[28] As with the famous numbered bank accounts of Switzerland, secrecy was what was being paid for—a bolt-hole beyond the sight of the expanding postwar state. "Swiss bankers keep their lips sealed," a saying went, "but the Liechtenstein bankers don't even have tongues."[29]

The era from the early 1970s to the late 1990s were the "golden years" for tax havens.[30] Liechtenstein was joined by others, including Bermuda, the Bahamas, and, above all, the Cayman Islands. By the late 1970s, Liechtenstein hosted more companies than citizens and boasted a GDP per capita second only to Kuwait.[31] Alongside its regular corporate clients were some shadier ones. In the 1960s, the CIA used Liechtenstein to register front organizations for its covert involvement in the civil war in the Congo. (The generic name of its holding company was Western International Ground Maintenance Organization.)[32] A few decades later, the International Confederation of Free Trade Unions accused Liechtenstein of facilitating investments into apartheid South Africa.[33] An Austrian company built a plant in South Africa through an anonymous Liechtenstein subsidiary, while a British business selling asbestos sourced from South African mines to the United States used a Liechtenstein shell company to avoid sanctions.[34]

As for individuals with Liechtenstein connections, they included the Nigerian military ruler Sani Abacha as well as the newspaper tycoon Robert Maxwell, who siphoned his employees' pensions into a secret account in Liechtenstein.[35] Intelligence reports also linked the Colombian drug lord Pablo Escobar and the Zairean dictator Mobuto Sese Seko to banks of the microstate.[36] Even more prominent were Ferdinand and Imelda Marcos, who used Liechtenstein trusts to stash away some of their embezzled fortune, estimated at $1–$5 billion. (When they wanted money, they would send the phrase *Happy Birthday* to their Swiss banker, who would retrieve cash from Liechtenstein and then contact their agent in Hong Kong for delivery to Manila.)[37] Another notable client was the Ukrainian president Viktor Yanukovych, whose lavish holiday residence was technically owned by a company in the tony London neighborhood of Fitzrovia, which was, in turn, owned by P&A Corporate Services Trust of Vaduz. Liechtenstein was a portal to "Moneyland," as one journalist put it, a domain beyond tax-collecting states.[38]

Liechtenstein did not put all its energies into what was tactfully called *wealth management*. As an early commentator put it, even though Liechtenstein's taxes and fees were very low, there was more than enough gold dust to float up and coat the small country. Wealth gained through its novel status as a tax shelter let it move into industrialization. By the 1980s, Liechtenstein was one of the most industrialized nations in the world, with factories manufacturing products ranging from fake teeth to central heating plants. It went from exporting laborers as farmhands to importing them as factory workers. Over half its workforce commuted from neighboring countries—with no chance of naturalization.[39]

Citizenship was governed by a radical spirit of communitarianism. After they ended their early practice of selling passports, the only way to become a citizen was by approval from community members voting via secret ballot, followed by approval from the parliament and the prince. So few ever made it through that most did not even try. As the number of corporations registered in the country soared into five digits, the number of immigrants per year averaged only a couple of dozen. Liechtenstein was applying its version of the Singapore Solution: a microstate with maximal openness to capital and closed borders for new citizens. It was a land both of the future and of the past: women did not have the right to vote until 1984.

2.

Liechtenstein is usually treated as a curiosity—a fairy-tale kingdom in the heart of Old Europe. What made it part of the libertarian war of ideas was the adventurous ideological entrepreneurship of Prince Hans-Adam II. Born in 1945 and baptized as Johannes Adam Pius Ferdinand Alois Josef Maria Marko d'Aviano von und zu Liechtenstein, Hans-Adam was the first monarch to be raised in the territory. After working briefly in a London bank and interning at the US Congress, he attended business school in St. Gallen, an hour's drive north of Vaduz.[40] The country was still poor enough in the 1960s that Hans-Adam's father sold a Leonardo da Vinci painting from their collection to the National Gallery in DC, in part to pay for his son's lavish wedding.[41] Hans-Adam recalled being educated in an era that taught that "the bigger, the better." Smaller nations seemed destined to be swallowed by one of the two feuding Cold War camps. Liechtenstein's lack of even its own seat in the United Nations made Hans-Adam wonder if he was being set up for failure.

Given supervision of the country's finances in 1970 and taking over duties from his father as regent in 1984, Hans-Adam was described as "the technological age's manager-prince," bringing his business school mentality to the task of government.[42] Worried that Liechtenstein was being lapped by other tax havens like Panama and the Channel Islands, he set up branch offices in Zurich, Frankfurt, and New York City, and increased the number of the country's banks from three to fifteen.[43] Assets under management tripled in the mid-1980s.[44] He also went on a charm offensive. The Metropolitan Museum of Art hosted a blockbuster show of pieces from the princely collection.[45] The principality's fairy-tale air was only enhanced by the 3,100-pound golden stagecoach on display in the exhibition.

Another one of the prince's goals was reversing the embarrassment of rejection from the League of Nations and earning a seat in the UN, which succeeded in September 1990. In his first address from the floor of the General Assembly, Hans-Adam did not follow tradition by delivering bromides about international cooperation. Instead, he made an astonishing argument: that all nations were ephemeral and should remain open to the possibility of their imminent dissolution. States cannot live forever, he argued. They have "life cycles similar to the human beings who created them." Extending their life spans could sometimes end up causing more violence than letting them peacefully die. To cling too tightly to the existing configuration was "to freeze human evolution." Borders themselves were arbitrary— "the product of colonial expansion, international treaties or war and very seldom have people been asked where they want to belong."[46]

Such proclamations verged on the scandalous as breakaway movements threatened national crack-ups from Quebec to Belgium to Belgrade. The UN had a formal policy against secession and discouraged minorities inside existing nation-states from seeking independence.[47] But the mood was changing as Hans-Adam spoke. The Soviet Union's stepwise dissolution seemed to be showing that peaceful disintegration was possible. In his address, the prince welcomed the Baltic states Latvia and Estonia, which entered the UN at the same time as the microstate. He also welcomed both North and South Korea as new members. The Cold War's end was allowing for the recognition of multiple claims on a single people along with a surge of new nations.

The prince proposed that the way to help rather than hinder human evolution was to create a means for continuous churning of the world map. This would happen through referendums. Such a rearrangement could move by stages, devolving first responsibilities for local affairs and taxation; but if that did not satisfy a population, it could go all the way to the splitting of a state into two or more new entities. The idea originated in a parlor game that Hans-Adam's family used to play: speculating about how their erstwhile patron and protector, the Hapsburg Empire, might have survived. Hans-Adam believed that it could have happened if the empire had allowed for the proliferation of smaller self-determining units—a decentralization within a loose union to save the interdependent whole.[48] He thought the model was just as valid a century later. The high-pressure system of globalization could only preserve the all-important economic unity if polities were given the option of splitting into fragments.

Hans-Adam cross-fertilized the Holy Roman Empire's model of aristocratic state ownership, which had given rise to Liechtenstein itself, with the fluid idea of sovereignty represented by the global clients of Liechtenstein's banks. Those corporations' tangle of overseas subsidiaries and shell companies suggested that sovereignty could be unbundled, relocated, and recombined. Hans-Adam's own family had ruled Liechtenstein from afar for centuries. Why shouldn't the modern state also be a "service provider," where all capacities except for national defense were contracted out to private actors?[49] This was an opt-in, opt-out vision of citizenship, explicitly designed as an analogue to the marketplace. The people, he wrote, should be "the shareholders of the state."[50]

The conclusion of the First World War had enshrined the idea of Wilsonian self-determination, usually understood as based on a common language, common territory, and common history. This was the justification by which Czechoslovakia had expropriated his family's properties. Hans-Adam countered that a nation should not be premised on a transcendent idea of the state as a bearer of an ineffable essence, or even of a community of shared fate. He preached instead a premodern idea of statehood. It was nebulous, open to adaptation, even—as his own state showed—open to purchase and sale. Liechtenstein set itself up as the international champion of the contractual communities that people like Murray Rothbard dreamed of. Given a pulpit at the UN, Hans-Adam espoused a libertarian blueprint for what he called "the state in the third millennium," or what Rothbard called "nations by consent."[51] It was anarcho-capitalism by way of the Alps.

The prince practiced what he preached, bringing his version of self-determination into his own country. In the year 2000, a red booklet arrived in the mailboxes of every citizen in Liechtenstein with Hans-Adam's proposed revision to the constitution.[52] The proposal greatly increased the prince's power, giving him the right to put forward and veto bills, dissolve parliament, and enact emergency laws. It also included something remarkable: a nuclear option that permitted the population to hold a referendum to abolish the monarchy itself.[53] And true to Hans-Adam's UN speech, the proposal permitted any of Liechtenstein's eleven communes to secede after a majority vote (while reserving the right for the prince to order a second vote). The clause was watered down from the prince's original version, which included the possibility of *individuals* to secede without the need for approval from the parliament or the prince.[54] When members of the parliament balked at what was called a "princely power grab," Hans-Adam showed he was serious about his transactional relationship to the territory. He suggested he would be happy to sell the country to Bill Gates and rename it Microsoft if the constitutional reform did not go his way.[55] "My ancestors bailed out Liechtenstein when it was bankrupt and thus acquired sovereign rights," he told the *New York Times*. "If ever the people decided time is up for this ruling family, they would have to find someone else rich enough to take our place."[56]

The prince had no intention of letting go of his investment cheap—but finding someone as rich as he would have been a tall order. The House of Liechtenstein was wealthier than the House of Windsor.[57] The proposed constitutional revision passed in 2003, making Hans-Adam Europe's "only absolute monarch" but also the only one building in a constitutional exit from the monarchy and the country itself.[58] The combination was odd, out of step with the times. There was talk of Liechtenstein being ejected from the Council of Europe.[59] But the confrontation with parliament meant that Hans-Adam's model had passed its stress test. The next year, the "tycoon-monarch" passed the governing duties on to his son.[60]

3.

Hans-Adam's Liechtenstein was a combination of hereditary male autocracy and direct democracy chained to a dependency on capital hypermobility and secrecy. The *Economist* called it "democratic feudalism."[61] The prince's hybrid version of medieval and modern politics sparked the imagination of libertarians in the 1990s and the first years of the twenty-first century, becoming an important touchstone for their criticism of European integration. Liechtenstein was the avatar of a different Europe and an alternative way of relating to the world economy. "Europe's enclaves could be more than amusing anomalies," wrote John Blundell (seen earlier as a champion of the homeland of Ciskei). "They could contain the seeds to subvert the European Union."[62] Specifically, critics argued that the European Union should follow Liechtenstein's example by including a clause allowing for popular referendums to leave the union.[63]

Underpinning the libertarian critique of the EU was a romanticizing of the continent's earlier fragmentation. Historian Paul Johnson argued that "the so-called feudal system, often used as a synonym for backwardness, was in fact a series of ingenious devices to fill the power vacuum left by the fall of Rome."[64] "When the Roman Empire in the West disintegrated," he wrote, "the ensuing Dark Ages saw state functions assumed by powerful private individuals or defensible cities."[65] A German economist proposed that "the European culture is the most successful in world history not despite but because it is fragmented into so many small countries that compete with one another."[66] Far from being impractical, the messy jumble of polities on the European peninsula dead-ending in the Atlantic was a source of strength. The ideal Europe was a "free market of states" with a common repository of rule of law and entrepreneurial spirit, a fractured assembly of sovereignties in a pool of shared culture.[67]

This counternarrative turned the official history of European integration on its head. The sign of progress was not fusing sovereignties and decision-making and overlaying the continent with ever more shared laws and regulations. The arc of progress did not bend toward "ever closer union." Rather, Europe had been on the path to greater liberty when it was politically fissured. Advocates of Brexit praised the success of Liechtenstein, Monaco, Luxembourg, Singapore, Hong Kong, and other small territories in the "age of the statelet."[68] Among the celebrants of medieval Europe was the founder of the Far Right party that would help win the Brexit vote.[69] The fact that Liechtenstein was in the European Free Trade Area (EFTA) and European Economic Area (EEA) without joining the EU meant that it had free trade without free movement of people—another model of partial integration attractive to advocates of Brexit.[70]

Hans-Adam II stood alongside other Euroskeptics. In 2013, he appeared at a gathering of neoliberals and nationalists with the economist Bernd Lucke, who had just founded the Alternative for Germany (Alternative für Deutschland, or AfD), soon to become the first Far Right party to enter the Bundestag.[71] The prince also became a member of the Hayek Society, which included key members of the AfD in its ranks.[72] Another member of the House of Liechtenstein, Prince Michael, a wealth manager by profession, was the founder of the European Center of Austrian Economics Foundation, which translated Alvin Rabushka's book on the flat tax into four languages.[73]

Hans-Adam presented his argument about the state as service provider at the conference of the Ludwig von Mises Institute alongside people advocating the breakup of Switzerland and the European Union. The prince's proposals bore a striking resemblance to those of the institute's namesake, another child of central Europe and an icon for the libertarian Right. In a famous book from 1927, Mises had argued for secession by plebiscite and speculated on the possibility of the secession of the individual.[74] In his regal style, Hans-Adam included references to no other thinkers in his writing, but the shared spirit of Mises connected his proposals to the ideas of Rothbard and the other paleo-libertarians across the Atlantic.

Part of the reason for libertarians to defend the Liechtenstein model was that the Liechtenstein model was under attack. Tax avoidance and money laundering, long allowed to proliferate unchecked, became politicized after the Cold War amid renewed concerns over drug trafficking, corruption, and, after 2001, terrorism. A first sign was a report on "harmful tax competition" published by the intergovernmental organization of the richer nations, the Organisation for Economic Co-operation and Development (OECD), in 1998.[75] A task force set up by another club of the world's most powerful nations, the G8, put Liechtenstein on a blacklist of fifteen "non-cooperative states" related to money laundering in 2000; it was the only one from Europe.[76] The blacklisting dealt a blow to Liechtenstein's reputation. A major leak in 2008—the first of a string that would include the Panama, Paradise, and Pandora Papers—showed that among those holding accounts in Liechtenstein through a trustee was a German dog named Günter.[77] Financial institutions were forced to change regulations to cut back on the possibility of anonymous account holders.[78] Liechtenstein's primary bank lost nearly 10 percent of its assets as customers pulled out when they could no longer remain unknown.[79]

The targeting of Liechtenstein did not dim its glamour for market radicals. On the contrary, it became possible to narrate the tax haven as a capitalist David fighting against a globalist regulatory Goliath. Paradoxically, a place that was among the wealthiest per capita in the world, tailor-made to protect the finances of the even wealthier, was cast as the underdog—a victim of "financial imperialism." Hans-Adam led the defense, arguing that the OECD was threatening to develop into a global tax cartel and even a world government.[80] Borrowing a line invented by Swiss bankers in the 1960s, he defended the origins of Liechtenstein's bank secrecy as part of an effort to save persecuted Jews—an interpretation made doubtful by the fact that some of Hitler's closest corporate allies, IG Farben and Thyssen, housed their corporations there years after the Nazi seizure of power.[81] In an even more eyebrow-raising claim, the prince cast his country as the end station of an Underground Railroad for the superrich. "So long as you have tax pirates," he said, "I don't feel any moral guilt about being a tax haven just as people once took up slaves to help them escape their poor fate."[82] When the German government sought more insight into the internal workings of Liechtenstein's banks, which were found to hold tens of millions of German accounts, he described it as the "Fourth Reich."[83]

4.

To libertarians, Liechtenstein looked like a wormhole back to an earlier form of global political economy, free of the treaties and international regulations that seemed to be tightening the noose around secrecy jurisdictions by the first decade of the twenty-first century, and the integration that libertarians feared would lead to redistribution and infringements on private property. Like Hong Kong and Singapore, it was a living example of the way things could be, premised on a globally interconnected world with no barriers to the movement of goods and money—a strip of rural land inserted almost invisibly into the circuitry of international finance, one of the "fragile islands of freedom" threatened by the expansion of the regulatory state.[84] Recall that the end of the Cold War saw two apparently contradictory trends. On the one hand, there was greater economic interdependence, with globalization the buzzword on everyone's lips. On the other hand, the political landscape was more fragmented than ever, as the UN tacitly opened up the possibility for something it had never accepted before: secession and nationalist movements by minority populations were now considered legitimate politics. The originality of Liechtenstein was its particular spin on this new form of politics. If new groups could make claims, then what if they began to make them as clients of services rather than as members of a national community?

There was something genuinely ideological about this vision of a world of tax havens that the mythology around Liechtenstein helps us to understand. It was not merely escape or exit in the negative sense but a fully formed philosophy of radical decentralization with secession as an ever-present option. The billionaire prince promoted his vision through the Liechtenstein Institute on Self-Determination, founded in Princeton with a $12 million gift, as well as the Liechtenstein Foundation for Self-Governance, which seeks to disseminate the country's model abroad. The libertarian world pays attention. In 2018, the Ludwig von Mises Institute's Jeff Deist praised "breakaway movements of the kind that Prince Hans of Liechtenstein is writing about, that government be rethought of as more of a service provider and subjects being thought of, or citizens being thought of, as customers."[85] A libertarian think tanker who helped blunt the OECD campaign against tax havens never fails to mention that the right to secede is enshrined in the Liechtenstein constitution. "Shouldn't people in other nations have the same freedom?" he asks.[86]

One person who took the rhetoric literally was Daniel Model, a corrugated packaging mogul and former curling champion. After moving from his native Switzerland to Liechtenstein, he went one step further, releasing a "declaration of sovereignty" that rejected membership in any human collective he had not expressly consented to and condemned democracy as a system of organized theft.[87] Model declared his independent state Avalon, headquartered in a dove-gray mansion the size of a city block in a rural Swiss village. He drew its name from *The Mists of Avalon*, a fantasy novel written by Marion Zimmer Bradley that revisits the legends of King Arthur from the point of view of women. Avalon became Model's own private Liechtenstein. In 2021, he hosted a conference called Liberty in Our Lifetime, devoted to finding places all around the world where one could escape the state. One of the speakers, who praised the Liechtenstein model of secession by referendum and designed his own scheme of "free private cities" with citizenship by contract, said that the attendees were driven by one question: "Are there possibilities to opt out?"[88]

The search for such fantasy escapes took libertarians from Central London to East and Southeast Asia to European microstates. But sometimes they also went farther afield, seeking economic freedom in what they misidentified as the earth's remaining empty lands.

PART III

FRANCHISE NATIONS

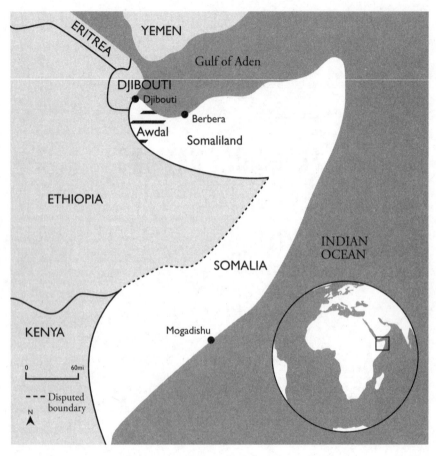

Somalia

A White Man's Business Clan in Somalia

In Bruce Sterling's 1988 novel *Islands in the Net*, the global government is known by the metonym "Vienna." Public enemy number one is a white US Special Forces colonel named Jonathan Gresham, who has defected. At the end of the book, Gresham speaks from a "liberated zone" in a "heavily guarded, supersecret mountain fortress" in the Aïr Mountains of Algeria, wearing the "male chador" of the Tuareg people. On video, he sits "turbanned, veiled, and cloaked, his massive head and shoulders framed in a spreading wicker peacock chair" flanked by armed lieutenants.[1] He is a caricature of radicalism past: a Caucasian libertarian Huey Newton. But the absurdity of his pose suggests the scrambling of politics at the end of the Cold War. "I'm a postindustrial tribal anarchist," he says, giving a name to a peculiar new school of thought.[2] Laura, the novel's protagonist, is a public relations consultant. She seems to inhabit a different world than Gresham does, one of power suits and boardrooms instead of desert hideaways and automatic weapons. But she, too, revels in the fissures of the new world, ruminating on "little Pacific island states whose 'national sovereignty' could be had for a price." These islands, she observes, "were on the Net, and where there were phones, there was credit. And where there was credit, there were airline tickets. And where there were jets, there was home."[3] The libertarian guerrilla and the consultant were kindred spirits—champions of the age of crack-up capitalism.

The previous chapter showed how anarcho-capitalists were electrified by the disintegration of states and the commodification of sovereignty in the 1990s. Among their more startling inspirations was the northeast African nation of Somalia, where a bloody civil war left the international community in shock and the country with no functioning government after 1991. This apparent catastrophe was a stirring vision of hope for the most radical capitalists. Rather than a humanitarian nightmare, Somalia offered a preview of the world to come and a chance to combine "postindustrial tribal anarchy" with sovereignty for sale. The war-torn Horn of Africa offered the prospect, as the Mises Institute put it, of being "stateless . . . and loving it."[4]

1.

Our guide to this alternative future is the globe-trotting Dutch libertarian Michael van Notten. Perhaps more than anyone, he embodied the furious political experimentation of the market radicals. Born in the thousand-year-old Dutch town of Zeist in 1933, Michael (also spelled Michiel) van Notten trained as a lawyer and eventually took a position with the European Economic Community in Brussels. He worked in the Directorate-General for Competition, often described as a special site of neoliberal thought in action for its ability to overrule national government rules about state spending and public ownership.[5] After nearly a decade in Brussels, van Notten abandoned the citadel of European integration to form the Libertarian Center in Holland, then set up the Institutum Europaeum libertarian think tank. A major Dutch newspaper described him as being "at home in the conservative strongholds of the Hoover Institution at Stanford University, the Heritage Foundation in Washington, DC and the Institute of Economic Affairs in London."[6] He also became a member of the Mont Pelerin Society in 1977, co-translated the abridged *Reader's Digest* version of Hayek's *Road to Serfdom* into Dutch, and did a Dutch translation of Milton and Rose Friedman's *Free to Choose*.[7]

Van Notten was a generic foot soldier in the neoliberal "war of ideas" until 1978, when he hatched the idea that would become his trademark: the tax-free T-zone, which would also be defined by deregulation.[8] He introduced the notion at a Mont Pelerin Society meeting in Paris that was opened by then-mayor Jacques Chirac, who praised Hayek for diagnosing the ills performed under the banner of "social justice." One economist in attendance praised van Notten's idea for the way it could begin to punch holes in the existing system. By lifting taxation in discrete areas, van Notten's T-zones would "give rise to a stimulating jealousy," as towns and regions would compete to emulate the low-tax enclaves. They would offer a demonstration effect, "discrediting the surrounding system."[9]

Like other champions of zones before him, van Notten saw the anomalous jurisdictions less as straightforward economic entities than as experiments in new ways of living and battlefronts in an ongoing war. In a 1982 pamphlet, he referred to the zone as a "political crowbar."[10] Zones were to be "paradises on earth for entrepreneurs." Arrayed against them were governments, trade unions, employers' associations, and environmentalists, all of whom feared change and sought to protect their own special interests and block innovation.[11] As he saw it, the ultimate goal of zones was to "make governments compete for people."[12] Because citizens of modern democracies were seduced by ideas of social justice, the quickest way to teach them "the virtues of a deregulated society" was "to create among them some mini-societies."[13] Once T-zones existed, he predicted, all European states would be forced to replicate them for fear of losing investors. The bottom-up compulsion of competing for scarce resources would be more effective than any design from above.[14] The zone would act as pedagogue and disciplinarian.

Like many others, van Notten's prototype was Hong Kong. But he gave the model a twist. While everybody was talking about the need for new Hong Kong–style arrangements worldwide, he suggested that the T-zones be populated by Hong Kongers themselves.[15] He wondered if Europe might help accelerate an "exodus," suggesting that "one million Chinese could be divided over twenty European nations." Hong Kong emigrants would act as agents of capitalist spread: "a hundred little enclaves" would push three hundred million Europeans to change their social democratic ways. The dream was stillborn, however: Brussels played the role of spoiler, shortening tax holidays, blocking T-zones in cities, and limiting them to distressed areas.[16] The "Euro–Hong Kongs" that van Notten hoped would exert the discipline that democracies refused to, and undermine the political cartel at the heart of Europe, morphed into workaday technology parks.

Having failed at home, van Notten searched farther afield. Just below Hong Kong on his list of ideal free zones was the less familiar territory of Aruba, a Caribbean island off the northern coast of Venezuela.[17] In the early 1980s, he worked with political leaders to draft a libertarian constitution for the nation as it pondered a still-unrealized independence from the Netherlands.[18] He envisioned privatizing police and judges, and replacing taxes with voluntary contributions.[19] When this effort also failed, van Notten turned his attention to another remnant of the Dutch Empire: the nation of Suriname on the South American mainland, which had gained full independence in 1975. Van Notten connected with exiled opposition leaders and freelance guerrillas to plan a coup.[20] His daughter describes him advising would-be insurrectionaries by shortwave radio from their home in Holland. He kept his constitution for a libertarian Suriname under lock and key in the attic of his sister's home. After his death, the document, marked TOP SECRET, was opened to find a proposal to build a dream zone with all state functions privatized and taxes eliminated altogether.[21]

By the early 1980s, van Notten had gone from a gadfly in Brussels to a border-crossing would-be libertarian guerrilla. As the Berlin Wall fell, his attention again shifted continents, from South America to Africa. There, he would devise a novel form of legal thinking by retrofitting what he saw as an archaic social form perfectly suited for anarcho-capitalism: the Somali clan.

2.

Van Notten had spent time in Africa before.[22] Between his job at the European Economic Community and his trek through the world of free-market think tanks, he made various forays into southern Africa. According to his daughter, one of van Notten's first ventures was building fiberglass coffins; he secured a contract with Zambia's vice president, who reportedly wanted bodies from deaths in guerrilla training camps interred before the president's return. Van Notten's daughter recounts a mad scramble to produce fifty coffins, with the paint drying on the way to the Brussels airport for shipment. Ultimately, the enterprise went no further than another business scheme, a hovercraft service across the Kalahari Desert.[23]

After his plans for a libertarian revolution in Suriname ran aground, van Notten turned from insurrection to the more conventional field of consulting, taking an assignment for the UN International Development Organization to investigate the possibility of setting up free trade zones in the Horn of Africa.[24] Shaped like the number 7, the Horn of Africa had been divided in the nineteenth century among colonial powers. France had established French Somaliland at the top left of the 7, at the bottleneck between the Gulf of Aden and the Red Sea; after decolonization in 1977, it became the country of Djibouti. The rest of the top bar had been the protectorate of British Somaliland, and the diagonal slash had been Italian Somaliland. Because the whole stretch of coast spoke the same language and identified as the same ethnicity, it followed the standard principle of self-determination that the former British and Italian territories should be one nation. This was what happened in 1960, as the two colonies merged to become the single state of Somalia.

After less than a decade of relative democracy, Somalia descended into dictatorship under Siad Barre. But in the 1980s, forces built against him, starting in the north. By 1991, the country had fallen entirely into civil war, becoming the most notorious "failed state" of the decade. The UN launched a humanitarian and military peacekeeping mission that lasted until 1995, bringing in some thirty thousand troops and civilian support staff.

Van Notten was in the middle of events. No longer an innocuous NGO consultant, he had found a patron in an insurgent military leader who was willing to take his advice on the design of a constitution for a future Somali state. Ensconced in a hotel in Mogadishu, the country's capital, he ruminated underneath a mango tree as the rumblings of conflict began in the streets.[25] He believed he had the chance here to create a utopia. He called his ideal form of alternative ordering *kritarchy*, "the rule of judges." This would be an anarchist society— without a central state—but not a lawless one. Although there would be no legislature or parliament (and thus no way of creating new laws), there would be a codified set of prohibitions, sanctions, and punishments, which would be overseen and administered by judges. Somalia was an ideal locale for a test run of this form of government because he believed it already hosted a rare, existing form of kritarchy: traditional Somali law, also known as *xeer*.[26]

The Horn of Africa had long been of special interest for anarchists and libertarians. In the 1940s and 1950s, British colonial anthropologists had documented what they saw as a remarkable form of social order in the region, organized along the hereditary unit of the "clan."[27] They described a nomadic people without a centralized government but with strong patrilineal ties, tracing each person back to a male ancestor from which the clan's name derived. Each clan had its own unwritten set of sanctions, punishments, and rules governing marriage, murder, theft, and other matters. Clan law allowed for what one scholar called "ordered anarchy," a term that libertarians later honored by adopting it to describe their own ideal social arrangement.[28]

Relying on ethnographies of the Horn of Africa, van Notten wrote something extraordinary: a constitution for a polity without a state.[29]

In his view, it was only by abandoning both democracy and the idea of the central state itself that Somalia could overcome its colonial legacy. "Somalia will become the first country in the world not to be ruled by the democratic dictatorship of 51 percent of the vote," he wrote in a letter to his daughter.[30] It was not alien rule that constituted the essence of colonialism but government itself.[31] True decolonization required the deconstruction of the state. This principle, he believed, had been missed by the international community and by Somalia's initial leaders, who had reached for multiparty elections but created chaos.[32] "The United Nations invaded Somalia with a multinational army of 30,000 to re-establish a democracy," he wrote, but it only deepened the civil war.[33]

The traditional Somali system of law and order in van Notten's writings resembled the anarcho-capitalist constructions of the medieval system described in an earlier chapter: crimes were dealt with through restitution and compensation, rather than imprisonment.[34] Families functioned as insurance pools: relatives shared their incomes, and the perpetrator's whole family would pay the victim in the event of a transgression. He included lists of the number of camels due for the loss of an eye, a nose, or a toe and a sliding scale of compensation for rape, with the highest amount paid when the victim was a virgin and the lowest when she was a widow.[35]

Somali customary law seemed to offer a coherent form of social order without a state. Van Notten wondered if foreign businesspeople could adopt it and use it for themselves. The obvious obstacle was that Somali law was based on kinship rooted in clan—but was there a way around this? Discussing the idea with a group of Somali elders, he heard a radical suggestion. "Gather with your business friends and form a new clan," they told him. "If the new clan prospers, the existing clans will not lose a moment in adopting its superior business environment as their own custom." The elders even suggested a name—*Soomaali 'Ad*, or the "White Somalis."[36]

The wild innovation of a White Somali business clan was grafted by van Notten onto the more conventional proposal of a free port on the Somali coast, a delimited area where tariffs are suspended and incentives are given to businesses to invest and operate.[37] The "manager" of the free port, presumably van Notten himself, would act as "the head of an extended Somali family," settling disputes but not being a ruler per se, more like the manager of a shopping mall or the captain of a cruise ship.[38] Members of the "freeport-clan" would be related not by kinship but by a network of contracts.

Van Notten saw stateless Somalia as a "huge network of hundreds if not thousands of mini-governments, each wholly independent of the others."[39] He found this compelling, in part, because he saw it as a dry run for the near future. He believed the monetary system in the industrialized world was doomed to collapse, with multiparty elections and central governments soon to follow. People would turn to mercenaries, private companies, and freelancers for infrastructure and services in the new state of anarchy. "It is at that moment," he wrote, "that the Somali experience can offer us some guidance."[40] If libertarians had once praised a Portable Hong Kong for its flat rate income tax, a Portable Somalia would be even more portable. As van Notten put it, "With their nomadic lifestyle, the Somalis can't afford to have a big government. Theirs must be small, so small that it can be transported on the back of a camel."[41] Here was a path back to Hans-Hermann Hoppe's vision of Europe in the year 1000, comprising many hundreds or thousands of independent territories.[42] Somalia had led the way as "the first nation to have rid themselves of their foreign political system" of democracy.[43] The Horn of Africa was the germ of a global anarcho-capitalist future.

3.

In the late 1990s, van Notten found an ally in a man with a biography almost as unusual as his own. Writing for the libertarian Foundation for Economic Education, the anthropologist Spencer Heath MacCallum described having met "a Somali tribeswoman traveling in the United States with her European husband." This was van Notten and his new wife, Flory Barnabas Warsame, who hailed from the Awdal region in the northwest corner of Somalia.[44] She explained to Mac-Callum that her people had come to realize that "Somalia's statelessness might prove to be a uniquely valuable asset in the modern world." The idea was for clans to capitalize on their "statelessness by opening areas within their tribal lands for development, inviting businessmen and professionals the world over to come to take advantage of the absence of a central government or other coercive authority." Clans would lease territory, and van Notten would have a chance to realize his plans. MacCallum declared himself inspired by the "social experiment with far-reaching implications for human freedom" underway in Somalia.[45]

MacCallum had been working on designs for his own "mini-societies" for decades. His investigations began with the idiosyncratic insights of his namesake and grandfather Spencer Heath, an amateur theorist and professional inventor made wealthy by his design of airplane propellers.[46] In Heath's telling, after the fall of Rome central European "barbarians" had established small-scale forms of ownership and self-government, which they brought with them to the British Isles. It was there, far from the authoritarian undertow of the Roman tradition, that ideal-typical forms of "free feudal" communities developed, reaching their peak in the ninth century before the unpleasant intrusion of the Continental mindset via Norman conquest in the eleventh.[47] Incubated in island isolation, the patrimony of "the Teutonic tribes" remained the key payload of cultural evolution, a treasure brought by the colonists to what became the United States.[48]

Heath found some of the last islands of Saxon self-ownership in an unlikely place in mid-twentieth-century America: its hotels and resorts. With their shared utilities, security, and amenities, hotels modeled what he called *proprietary communities*—voluntary agglomerations of humans in a space overseen and owned by a private agent.[49] MacCallum took up the investigation from his grandfather. He moved from hotels to shopping malls, office buildings, mobile home parks, and marinas, all examples of the "multi-tenant income property."[50]

Heath had overwhelmingly focused on the Germanic antecedents for a future of capitalist anarchy, only briefly touching on the "voluntary feudalism" of ancient Mexico and Japan.[51] MacCallum was more earnest in his explorations beyond the Western world. While he pored over the management model of the shopping center, he also completed a doctorate in anthropology to better study what he called the "traditionally stateless society" of Indigenous communities.[52] In an inversion common among Western romantics, he argued that "the concepts of property, freedom of contract, and justice were discovered and first developed not by the technologically advanced societies but by tribal societies."[53]

In 1971, MacCallum began his first effort at writing a lease outlining rules of conduct, rights, and responsibilities for a future minisociety. He was employed for the purpose by Werner Stiefel, a refugee from Nazi Germany and the head of a family-owned dermatological company whose most well-known product was the skin cream Lubriderm. Stiefel wanted to create his own country—"a community on the high seas outside the political jurisdiction of any nation," modeled on Galt's Gulch in Ayn Rand's *Atlas Shrugged*.[54] He owned a motel in upstate New York. MacCallum suggested, consistent with his father's theories, that it could act as a laboratory.[55]

The motel became what they called *Atlantis I*, a prototype for an alternative society. New residents were called "immigrants" and they created their own "Atlantean" currency. The second "immigrant" recounts helping sell the silver coins of the currency along with bars of soap and bumper stickers. Satisfied by the prototype, Stiefel sought out locations in the Caribbean and set to work building a geodesic dome and a concrete ship, christened *Atlantis II*. Launched into the Hudson River, the ship tipped onto its side and got stuck in the mud. Eventually it managed to reach the Bahamas, where it remained until sinking in a hurricane.[56]

MacCallum tinkered with the lease he drafted to govern Atlantis, including innovations taken from Ciskei in South Africa.[57] His hope was to replace constitutional arrangements with something more like a business contract. A polity should be like a shopping mall, he thought. Nobody who rented retail space in a mall would expect to exercise popular sovereignty over the building. That would be absurd. Likewise, MacCallum hoped for a political environment that set politics aside. Collective life would be reduced to a problem of administration. You entered if the terms of the contract were to your liking and left if they were not. Vague ideas of the demos and "the people" would have no place. He and van Notten saw stateless Somalia as a chance to roll out their anarcho-capitalist system in miniature. They leased a patch of territory from the local clan, dubbed it Newland, and planned for the business clan to govern inside of it.[58]

Free-port clans would pave the path to the future by looking backward. "If the 'new Somalia' comes about," MacCallum wrote, "it will simply be an evolved version of traditional, pre-colonial Somalia. It will provide a navigational light in a world ravaged by political democracy, a beacon for a humanity that has lost its bearings."[59] MacCallum's grandfather and mentor Spencer Heath had emphasized the foundational importance of kinship for unifying the "blood-bonded group."[60] The notion of free-port clans made the audacious proposition that voluntary agreements between commercial partners would prove as robust as familial ties. Murray Rothbard had spoken of "nations by consent." This went one further, imagining contracts transmuted into kinship in "clans by consent."

Van Notten and MacCallum were first-class anarcho-capitalist fantasists, but they also needed financial backing. In 1995, van Notten partnered with American businessman Jim Davidson to focus on the first step to a post-democratic free-port clan future: building private toll roads.[61] A couple of years later, the duo registered the Awdal Roads Company in the tax haven of Mauritius. The company's website included a link to something called Freedonia, which it noted was "looking for land near Awdal." A click took you to a page reading "Good Evening, Welcome to the Principality of Freedonia Embassy." Freedonia, one would discover, was not just a riff on the mythical country in the Marx Brothers' Duck Soup (1933) but had enjoyed eight years of existence, with consulates worldwide and passports available to its citizens. Like Atlantis before it, Freedonia had also created its own currency: it had coins stamped with the Freedonian crest and the word SUPERIBIMUS, a misspelling of the Latin phrase "we shall overcome."

Freedonia was ostensibly a principality under the reign of a certain Prince John II. More prosaically, it was the pet project of a group of young Texan men. Photographs of its treasury secretary, prime minister, and minister of defense featured them posing graduation-style in a wood-paneled basement in front of a green satin Freedonian flag with a yellow saltire and six white stars, wearing the boxy hat and brass buttons of US Marines.[62] The would-be state of Freedonia was a nation without a territory: a "non-territorial nation, like Palestine," they explained. The youths had a few ideas for addressing that shortcoming. One was "to build a large island in international waters." Another was to "buy a small amount of land from a country (possibly Caribbean, latin american, or pacific [sic]) and buy the governing rights to the land as well." Most ambitious was the plan beloved by libertarians from Robert A. Heinlein to Elon Musk: "claiming land on the Moon and Mars."[63]

In 1999, Prince John, now a college student, connected with Davidson, who in turn connected him to van Notten, who promised him land in Awdal.[64] The jurisdiction of Freedonia seemed to have finally found a territory. Its founders aspired to make it "a part time residence for the world's wealthy" as well as a site for incorporation, ship registration, and resource extraction through cheap labor.[65] Freedonia captured in miniature much of the secessionist imagination of the late twentieth century. It also mimicked much of the offshore reality that had come into existence: the use of enclaves for concealment of assets in low-tax or no-tax jurisdictions, the registration of ocean vessels under flags of convenience, and the possibility of multiple passports.

In January 2001, though, the secessionists felt the sting of the scorpion tail of sovereignty. According to a long and sheepish message posted by Prince John, a member of the Somali diaspora living in

Toronto had faxed a printout of the Freedonian website back home.[66] When local authorities discovered the young Americans were claiming they had been granted a swath of coastline for their imaginary nation, the deal was canceled and van Notten and Davidson were deported for their complicity in the scheme.[67] The Texan teenage monarch's offshore tax haven was not meant to be.

4.

The white man's business clan in Somalia could also seem like a lark, the pipe dream of a pair of neocolonial eccentrics. But there was more to their flight of fancy than one might expect. The Somalia of the 1990s and 2000s did, in fact, challenge some of the basic expectations about how a state should act and how an economy should be. Beyond concern over the humanitarian calamity of the civil war, the question of how life persists without a state posed a basic sociological riddle. Somalia became a place to understand how people adapted to develop what some called "governance without government."[68] Scholars observed that the end of the state had not led to a Hobbesian war of all against all. Somalia seemed to offer a category error. Could there really be "economy without a state"? After all, as one scholar put it, "if a state were a required component, then the Somali economy could not exist."[69] And yet not only did the Somali economy exist, but something even more remarkable was happening: it was doing better than ever.

Somalia first showed signs of "commerce without a state" in the 1990s.[70] After the government collapsed, GDP grew, exports increased, and investment rose.[71] Even life expectancy improved.[72] For libertarian scholars, Somalia became "a unique test" of statelessness as a sustainable condition.[73] "While Somalia lacks a central government," one wrote, "the private sector has developed governance mechanisms to fill the void."[74] A dissertation titled "Money Without a State" described the extraordinary fact that the Somali shilling functioned as a token of exchange and a store of value long after the central bank and treasury had disappeared.[75] The shilling's value actually stabilized in relation to the dollar, and it was used for exchange into neighboring countries.[76] One German anarcho-capitalist perhaps went the furthest when he gathered funds for translating the works of Ludwig von Mises, Friedrich Hayek, and Hans-Hermann Hoppe into Somali. Their writings would further aid the residents of Mogadishu from taking the "road to serfdom"—by which he meant the reestablishment of a central state.[77]

In a widely cited article, a young economist named Peter Leeson made the case that Somalia was "better off stateless" in comparison to the dictatorial state that preceded it.[78] He went as far as to suggest that it might actually become a template for other intractable situations. "Allowing government to crumble and anarchy to emerge" in the West African state of Sierra Leone, he suggested, "may actually improve its state of development."[79] He saw a historical parallel with nineteenth-century Angola, where the export trade—including in enslaved humans—was, he wrote, "extensive and durable, though there was no government enforcement of property rights."[80]

There was no denying that Somalia was especially well equipped for survival under conditions of statelessness. For one thing, neither the colonial nor the postcolonial states had ever attempted to capture most of the population, in the sense of incorporating them into the standard bureaucracy of education, taxation, and registration.[81] While the Italians had made some effort at developing the infrastructure of a modern state, the British presence had been especially thin. With no natural resources to lure them deeper inland, the colonists had stuck to the coast. They did not seek to develop the interior, nor did they make many efforts to educate or convert the local population, which was not prone to stay in the same place for very long.

The nomadic groups kept their wealth in their herds of livestock, traveling to find grazing land and water sources. Somalia's postcolonial state also had little to do with the nomads, concentrating its efforts in the urban centers. So when the government vanished, the transition was not as abrupt as it would have been in other countries, leading to the emergence of a marketplace for political services and a "commodification of warlordism."[82] The territory became not stateless so much as composed of many miniature states: a "mosaic of fluid, highly localized polities—some based on traditional authority, others reflecting hybrid arrangements."[83]

Kinship was part of the glue that kept the country together. Family ties also help explain the paradox of stateless prosperity in another way: those who fled to wealthier countries often remitted money back to their relatives. Money earned elsewhere, especially by the large numbers of Somalis working in the Gulf nations, became a disproportionate source of local wealth.[84] For those refugees in Western countries, some of the remittances could come from social security and other transfers. Ironically, the welfare state itself helped to subsidize the supposed anarchist miracle.[85]

But there were omissions in the story that the libertarians told. They either ignored or glossed over the fact that the most successful part of Somalia after the state's collapse was the place where a new state had been rapidly reestablished. Just months after Somalia's central government dissolved, the Islamic Republic of Somaliland declared its independence in the north of the country, within the borders of the old British protectorate. It was here that security returned most quickly, and the basic fundamentals of the state emerged quite early. The very scholar whose work on "economy without state" spawned libertarian dissertations also pointed out that "in stark contrast to southern Somalia," the de facto state of Somaliland had government ministries, carried out development planning exercises, and collected minimal taxes and fees.[86] While van Notten's wife advertised the statelessness of her clan's territory to lure in overseas investors, this was hardly the case. In fact, his wife's clan had been part of the conference that created Somaliland in 1991.[87] Members of the clan were vice presidents in the Somaliland government.[88]

The territory of Somaliland is a peculiar place. Although it functions like a state, it lacks UN recognition so has been called "a country that does not exist."[89] Still, reestablishing the institutions of government gave investors confidence. Lack of UN recognition did not prevent France's Total from spending $3.5 million refurbishing its oil storage facility there, in exchange for a monopoly on oil supply and distribution.[90] Lack of recognition did not keep five airlines and five private telecommunications companies from setting up shop within the first decade in Hargeisa, Somaliland's capital.[91] Somaliland has also experimented with its own kind of old-fashioned politics. In December 2002, six months after van Notten died, what he had dubbed the "monster of democracy" returned when half a million people voted in the first multiparty elections held in the region since the 1960s.[92] Subsequent competitive elections have seen smooth transfers of power between opposing parties.[93] To many outside observers, Somaliland was an "overlooked success story" not of ordered anarchy but of decentralized post-conflict democracy.[94]

The port of Berbera, on the Somaliland coast, embodied well the model of development that worked best. It was the greatest economic success story in the region. For more than a thousand years, goods from the African interior had arrived there to be shipped to the Middle East, onward to South and East Asia, and up the Red Sea to Cairo, Alexandria, and Europe. During the time of the British protectorate, it served as the colonial capital. After independence, Berbera was a classic site of Cold War competition. The Soviets built one wharf; the Americans built another.[95] In the 1980s, three-quarters of the still-intact nation of Somalia's foreign currency came from exports from the port.[96] After state collapse in the 1990s, it exported more than it had the decade before.[97] In June 2021, a new terminal big enough for the world's largest ships opened in Berbera with a half-billion-dollar investment from Dubai.[98] The company has an agreement with Somaliland to manage its port for thirty years in return for a 65 percent stake in the venture, complete with plans to build an adjoining free zone for foreign manufacturers to set up factories.[99]

The wealthy emirate was a lifeline for the Somali economy in the years of statelessness. Mobile phone networks and mobile payment systems were established by companies headquartered in Dubai. Electric generators purchased in Dubai were attached to local homes by local entrepreneurs (or rentiers) who charged by the lightbulb.[100] Planes leased by Somali carriers were parked in Dubai in the evenings. Somalis had already traveled in large numbers to work as laborers in the Gulf. Now the Gulf came to them.

The recipe for success in the age of high globalization, it seemed, lay not in the Somali clan but in becoming an outpost of Dubai.

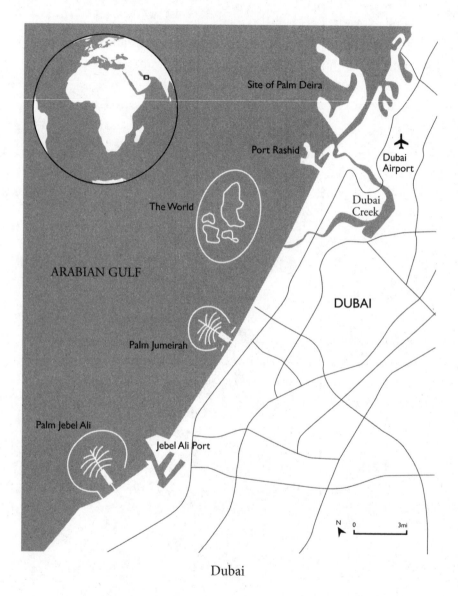

Dubai

The Legal Bubble-Domes of Dubai

If there is any place in the world that has contributed to global zone fever as much as the Asian juggernauts of Hong Kong and Singapore, it is Dubai. In a few short decades, the emirate on the Persian Gulf staged a dizzying ascent from a gold-smuggling outpost with houses built of coral and sand to the gilded home of the world's tallest hotel, the world's only ski slope in a desert, and the world's highest tennis court, among many other records. In 2003, plans were announced for an amusement park three times the size of Manhattan.[1] The same year, ground broke—or emerged—on an archipelago of three hundred artificial islands loosely shaped like a map of the world. The developer soon announced a sequel: the Universe, an archipelago of planets and the moon.[2] In the first decade of the 2000s, Dubai's economy grew by 13 percent a year on average, outpacing even China.[3] Skyscrapers were built at the rate of a floor every three days.[4] In six years, the city's population doubled and its footprint quadrupled.[5]

"When you first arrive in Dubai and see the glitzy high-rise buildings, you think you could be driving through Canary Wharf," wrote a

British employee of a construction company. Then you realized how much larger it was. "The scale of things is scary." A major property development in the UK would be 150 acres; the main free zone in Dubai was a hundred times larger. Things got done. "In two years they have built and opened a metro system," he said. "In the UK it would take that long to refurbish one station."[6] Dubai made use of the most advanced forms of engineering and architecture to achieve visually stunning, gravity-defying feats in the built environment. It was unapologetic in its ostentatious celebration of wealth unburdened by hang-ups about inequality.

How did they do it? Authoritarianism was part of the answer. Dubai was a case study in capitalism without democracy. Through the early 2000s, it ranked as one of the least politically free places in the world, owing to the absence of popular elections, protection of free expression, and rights for noncitizens, as well as the arbitrary use of police force and practice of forced labor.[7] As early as 1985, the CIA reported that in Dubai "ideology is dismissed as irrelevant to business."[8] Of course, dismissing ideology in favor of business amounted to an ideology of its own. But what kind of ideology? Most striking was the resemblance to corporate governance. Both power and ownership were concentrated entirely in the figure of the sheikh, who was frequently referred to as the CEO of Dubai, Inc. The city-state's executive council was made up of the heads of state-owned enterprises rather than elected officials.[9] The result was a short-circuiting of public deliberation—indeed, the elimination of any idea of the public at all. "The delays, the disputes, the litigation, the whole messy business of 'Not in My Back Yard' simply doesn't exist in the country," one architectural critic wrote. The city was an advertisement: "Look at what enlightened, corporate, efficient and non-democratic government *can do*."[10]

"Milton Friedman's beach club" is what Mike Davis called Dubai in 2006, "a society that might have been designed by the Economics Department of the University of Chicago."[11] It had "achieved what American reactionaries only dream of—an oasis of free enterprise without income taxes, trade unions or opposition parties."[12] But the charm of Dubai was lost on Friedman himself, who never mentioned it. The emirates were not discussed at the meetings on designing an Economic Freedom of the World index, where Hong Kong, Singapore, and even Ciskei were the stars. Dubai's fans sat further right on the spectrum. In the early 2000s, the emirate began to catch the attention of market radicals less of the Chicago school variety than the anarcho-capitalist strain.

What the *Financial Times* called Dubai's "paradoxical blend of laissez-faire and rigid authoritarianism" was no paradox to right-wing libertarians.[13] One German anarcho-capitalist wrote that Dubai was the best evidence that Hans-Hermann Hoppe was right: monarchy was superior to democracy, since monarchs tended to the long-term wealth of their territories while elected officials plundered theirs during their time in office.[14] Two Dutch anarcho-capitalist authors wrote that the absence of democracy was not a problem but rather the key to the city-state's success. Elections would only decrease economic freedom.[15] The meteoric rise of Dubai offered the best evidence yet that democracy and capitalism need not go together.

Perhaps the most impassioned take on the emirate came from the self-described neo-reactionary and tech worker Curtis Yarvin, who blogged under the pseudonym Mencius Moldbug and moved in the same circles as Patri Friedman and Peter Thiel.[16] Along with Singapore and Hong Kong, Dubai proved to Yarvin that "*politics is not necessary to a free, stable and productive modern society.*"[17] Dubai was run like a business, and this was as it should be, he said. Instead of citizens, it had customers, who expected nothing more from the state than that which was outlined in their contract.[18] He felt that bonds of citizenship were mere instruments for extorting the state for benefits, which, in turn, had to be extorted from others through taxation. Abstract ideas of civic belonging or obligation had no place in Dubai. By the early 2000s, Dubai's population was, by some estimates, 95 percent foreigners.[19]

If Dubai's rejection of democracy was one attraction for Yarvin, another was its scale. Like Hoppe and Rothbard before him, he thought the smaller the jurisdiction, the better.[20] Dubai had a massive free trade zone but the entire polity was smaller than the smallest US state, Rhode Island. Yarvin's term for his normative ideal was a "patchwork"—"a global spiderweb of tens, even hundreds, of thousands of sovereign and independent mini-countries."[21] *Patchwork* was also a term used by scholars to describe what Dubai became in the 2000s, holding the real secret of the emirate's charm for the anarcho-capitalist.[22]

From the outside, Dubai was marked by its dazzling gigantism, its quality of having sprung straight from the high-definition screen of an architectural rendering. But this wasn't what made it attractive to the right-wing libertarians. What they liked was harder to see: it was Dubai's embrace of radical legal pluralism and its willingness to design bespoke jurisdictions to satisfy investors. Dubai was not just a "city-corporation."[23] It was one state with many systems, and a test run of Yarvin's patchwork in practice.

1.

In February 1979, as pigeons foraged in half-frozen mountains of garbage left by striking sanitation workers in London, Queen Elizabeth went off to a place where the workers never struck. Accompanied by her husband and the foreign secretary, she took the brand-new British Airways Concorde to Kuwait, then switched to the royal yacht *Britannia* for her three-week tour, the first British monarch to visit the Arabian Peninsula. In the boom that followed the quadrupling of oil prices, British connections to the Gulf were a bright spot amid the doldrums of the 1970s. At the time of the royal visit, Britain exported more to the Gulf than to the Commonwealth countries Canada, Australia, and New Zealand combined.[24] One British company alone was engaged in works valued at £1.8 billion, and British firms were taking the "lion's share" of new construction in the Gulf.[25]

The tastes of the Gulf elite had made them familiar fixtures of the

British tabloid press. Just as a common royal culture had bound European sovereigns together in the nineteenth century, so a jet-setting circuit of horse races, luxury ski resorts, and prestigious real estate enclaves bound the British monarchy to their Middle Eastern counterparts. The Gulf sovereigns did not scrimp on hospitality. Every journalist got their own limousine and the monarch received extravagant gifts at every stop. Dubai's Sheikh Rashid presented her with a three-hundred-diamond necklace, plus a sculpture of solid gold camels standing under solid gold palm trees with rubies for dates.[26] Crowds lined the roads along her route, including many of the ten thousand British citizens resident in the Gulf and thousands of Pakistanis and Indians.

Some of the older members of the latter group were former British subjects, but were the Emiratis themselves? Not quite. Although the Persian Gulf had been treated like a "British lake" since the early nineteenth century, England never claimed suzerainty over the coast of the Arabian Peninsula where the emirates lay. In 1820, the British had deployed a thirty-thousand-strong force to defeat the "Qawassim pirates" of the territory, but the upshot was a truce that transformed the pirates into rightful rulers. Among them were the Al Makhtoum family, who remain the hereditary leaders of Dubai.

A new word was coined to describe the legal relationship of the British to the littoral region on the south of the Persian Gulf, which fell short of direct administration. Because of the truce, the sheikhdoms were dubbed the Trucial States or the Trucial Coast.[27] This form of semi-sovereignty meant Dubai was both inside and outside the British Empire. For the most part, it reflected the fact that the area was little noticed by the Great Powers, beyond the products of its waters labeled on maps as Great Pearl Bank.

Britain began to take more notice of Dubai in the 1960s, when London banks found a new source of profit by selling wafer-sized gold bars in bulk quantities to buyers in the sheikhdom. The buyers would then strap these to their bodies, or stash them under fish, and smuggle them in souped-up skiffs over a thousand miles to Mumbai to dodge Indian trade restrictions.[28] The sheikh turned a blind eye to the tariff wall jumping, claiming the gold was legal when it entered his territory. "So far as we are concerned," one customs official said, "trade out of Dubai is not smuggling but free enterprise."[29] Smuggling networks were complex, linking sites across the Indian Ocean and into the South China Sea. One, called the "Ring," worked out of import–export businesses in the free port of Hong Kong, which served as a convenient base, with no tariffs or duties. The merchandise was sourced specifically for smuggling purposes: the gold biscuits forged in Switzerland or London weighed ten tolas, a measurement used only in India; Japanese textiles were manufactured in six-yard lengths specifically for saris. The smugglers' management of long supply chains impressed journalists. The Ring's "efficiency would put to shame the operations of some of the best-managed multinational corporations," one wrote.[30] Until Indira Gandhi cracked down, the "smuggler kings" of Mumbai who controlled contraband trade from Dubai were described as running a "state within a state."[31]

Britain's relationship with Dubai was hands-off but steady until 1968, when Prime Minister Harold Wilson declared the accelerated withdrawal of the British military from outposts "east of Suez." The leaders of the Trucial States watched the British go with regret. Sheikh Rashid said that "the whole coast, people and rulers, would all support retaining British forces in the Gulf."[32] For over a century, as one historian put it, the sheikhs were able to "outsource their military and external affairs to Britain."[33] Now they were required to not only oversee those affairs themselves but also fashion a terrain marked by familial ties, overlapping jurisdictions, and long-simmering border disputes into something that conformed to the Westphalian model of firm borders and exclusive sovereignty. With the concept of the nation-state as much of an ill fit with local reality as the idea of government by popular consent, the sheikhs opted for something other than the standard model of Wilsonian national self-determination.[34] In 1971, they formed the federation of the United Arab Emirates, with Abu Dhabi as the capital.

Economically, the UAE was born under a lucky star. The quadrupling of oil prices after the 1973–74 oil embargo made it rich. The Gulf's oil money was recycled through financial centers like the City of London, leaving a huge pool of cash available to be loaned out. While most of the oil was in Abu Dhabi, Dubai confirmed the presence of a commercially viable amount of oil in 1967, and sent off its first tankerful to a refinery in Britain two years later.[35] By the end of 1975, Dubai's oil revenue was $600 million a year.[36] During her 1979 visit, Queen Elizabeth unveiled some of the emirate's signature new projects financed by oil wealth. She pushed a button to bring water rushing into a dry dock built for oil tankers of up to one million tons and longer than the height of the Empire State Building. She cut the ribbon on the Dubai World Trade Centre, the Middle East's first skyscraper. Most important, she opened the port at Jebel Ali, which would become a vast free trade zone and, at sixty-six berths, the world's largest man-made port.[37]

Advertisements for Jebel Ali in British newspapers included aerial photographs with the port in the foreground and an empty expanse of desert stretching behind it to the horizon, a blank slate about which investors in the cramped space of East London could only fantasize. Even more important than its vast scale was its legal status. To dodge complications with the UAE authorities in Abu Dhabi, Dubai had unilaterally carved out the Jebel Ali Free Zone as a formally extraterritorial space, five thousand acres of land paved, wired, and ready for construction.[38] Perks included the possibility of 100 percent foreign ownership, no corporate taxes for fifteen years, no personal income taxes, full repatriation of profits and capital, and, of course, the guarantee of no labor unrest, thanks to the policy of importing labor constantly threatened by deportation.[39] Dubai worked by accessing a steady stream of labor from South Asia drawn by wages higher than in their own country even though they had no right of residence, guaranteeing hire-and-fire-and-deport in perpetuity. An added risk braved by workers was that thin legal protection left them vulnerable to often not being paid at all.[40] While foreign residents from richer countries (known as *expats* rather than *migrants*) enjoyed all-you-can-drink brunches and the creature comforts of the West, manual workers were kept in barbed-wire encampments in the desert to minimize flight risk and costs of upkeep.[41]

Jebel Ali ended up being Dubai's most important innovation. It followed the model of special economic zones the world over but became more than just another industrial park. In time, it became the template for Dubai's signature model of patchwork urbanization as the emirate built zone after zone within its borders, each with its own distinct sets of laws united by a common goal—to draw in foreign investors.

2.

We are used to thinking of a nation as a unified legal space: one territory inhabited by citizens under one set of rules. But this is never really the case. States and provinces have their own laws, municipalities have their own laws, and we often live in smaller units (such as public housing projects, condo associations, or university campuses) that have their own regulations and sometimes private security forces. What was special about Dubai is that it took this reality of legal diversity and turned it into an organizing principle for the whole emirate. As observers have noted, walking between neighborhoods in Dubai is effectively like walking from one country to another. The journalist Daniel Brook compares the situation to the nineteenth-century treaty ports in China. There, the rule of extraterritoriality meant that different laws applied to different citizens; in Dubai, different laws applied to different patches of land.[42] In Mike Davis's memorable metaphor, zones were placed under "regulatory and legal bubble-domes," each with its own set of rules.[43]

New jurisdictions proliferated. They were clustered by function— the Silicon Oasis for tech manufacturing, Dubai Healthcare City for medical companies, and Dubai Knowledge Village (now called Knowledge Park) for branches of universities.[44] There were gated zones called Media City and Internet City, where web access was unfiltered.[45] In 2006, $100 billion in projects were underway, including

"an Aviation City and a Cargo Village, an Aid City and a Humanitarian Free Zone, an Exhibition City and a Festival City, a Healthcare City and a Flower City."[46] Perhaps the most striking experiment in zone making was the Dubai International Financial Centre (DIFC), opened in 2004. It was overseen by the Australian finance regulator Errol Hoopmann, who said his goal was to cordon off 110 acres of land, empty it of existing laws, and then "write our own laws to fill up that vacuum." He compared the DIFC to the Vatican. It was "a state within a state," he said.[47]

Until 2002, land ownership by foreigners was permitted only in Jebel Ali. After that year, it became legal for foreigners to own property anywhere in the emirate. The result was a land rush. The housing that sprang up to accommodate newcomers and absentee investors followed the familiar format of gated communities, such as the master-planned communities of the southwestern United States. These had a regional forerunner in the faux-suburban towns like the American Camp built near the Aramco oil refinery in Saudi Arabia in the 1930s—a fenced compound of ranch-style houses for white families, complete with swimming pool and movie theater and surrounded by far more numerous migrant workers and Saudis, who lived in low-quality segregated quarters.[48] The Dubai suburbs of the 2000s offered a range of styles from Spanish villa to traditional Arabic, from Santa Fe to Bauhaus cubes.[49] Their car-centric model of air-conditioned suburbanization echoed the Sunbelt model of Houston and Los Angeles, but amplified it. In even more extreme weather conditions, Gulf populations consumed more water, electricity, and gasoline per capita than anyone else on earth.[50]

"Buy land," goes the apocryphal quote from Mark Twain, "they're not making it anymore." But this was not even true when he was supposed to have said it. Boston built half its downtown from reclaimed sand flats in the nineteenth century. Lower Manhattan, Singapore, and Hong Kong followed suit. Running out of waterfront property in the early 2000s, Dubai similarly created more, piling sand into the shape of a giant palm tree extending out into the sea, its slender fronds designed to maximize beach access. The Palm Jumeirah, built with 385 million tons of sand, was followed by the Palm Jebel Ali and, finally, the artificial islands of the World, whose pseudo-countries of sand sold for up to $30 million each.[51] Dubai real estate became a bolt-hole for globally mobile cash, especially for "the magnates and kleptocrats of the Middle East, North Africa, South Asia and the former Soviet Union." In a particularly eyebrow-raising case, the Azerbaijani head of state bought nine Dubai mansions in two weeks "in the name of his eleven-year-old son."[52]

Dubai captured the three qualities of the millennium's global city: verticality, novelty, and exclusivity.[53] Its developers, especially the state-owned colossus Nakheel Properties, internalized the injunction of global urbanism to be a recognizable brand: distinctive but not strange, exotic but not upsetting, diverting but not too unfamiliar, able to catch the eye of investors but not representing too much of a risk. Like money, a contemporary city needed to be both a store of value and a unit of exchange. As with superluxury apartments in London and New York, many of the flats in Dubai high-rises were bought but never occupied, part of what critics have called the zombie architecture of the twenty-first century.[54]

To someone arriving by air across the vast tan plain of the desert interrupted by islands of desalination plants, grand estates, and industrial bunkers, Dubai's zones appear like "computer motherboards."[55] This is how the emirate presented itself to investors, too, a flat space where "multinationals can plug in their regional operations."[56] Yet at ground level, Dubai loses the appearance of a unified design. Decentralized laws translate into visual chaos, a streetscape of "squarish ovals, rounded squares, curvaceous pyramids . . . globes atop boxes, teardrops mounted on pillars, bent slabs fastened to concrete goal posts."[57] The effect is less the clean lines of high modernism and more like a supersized version of the jumble of American highway neon. This is what the logic of capital looks like.

When the Emiratis broke ground on Jebel Ali in 1968, the plan was for it to be the future capital of the UAE.[58] Four decades later,

it had become, instead of a part of the tool kit for assembling legal
modules inside nations, a piece of patchwork that could be lifted up
and set down anywhere. No longer bound to being merely a political
capital for a federation or a nation-state, it was a flexible container for
new arrangements of labor, capital, and technology.

Just add territory.

3.

If one injunction for the twenty-first century was to be inoffen-
sively iconic, another was to be connected, smoothly linked to all
other nodes in the global economy. In the language of logistics, you
needed to be both a gateway and a corridor. At the turn of the millennium, Dubai set about replicating itself overseas, building franchise zones, portable Jebel Alis. This happened through a tangle of
new state-owned subsidiaries.

One of these so-called parastatal organizations was DP World
(Dubai Ports World), which united transportation, real estate, logistics, and light industry under one roof—an agency governing a city
within a city, charged with the task of cloning itself overseas and
bringing the "legal-regulatory bubble-dome" with it.[59] DP World got
its start in 1999, when it took over from Dubai the comanagement
of the Jeddah Islamic Port on the Red Sea. The following year, Jafza
International (Jebel Ali Free Zone Authority International) was created to advise foreign governments on setting up their own special
economic zones—globalizing the patchwork model.[60] Jafza International described its job as providing "Dubai expertise."[61] In 2004, it
began managing Port Klang in Malaysia.[62] By the end of 2005, it had
signed contracts with five African countries to oversee the development of their ports.[63] That same year, Dubai bought the US company
CSX World Terminals, becoming the world's sixth-largest container
terminal operator.[64]

Dubai was expanding at a furious pace. It signed a joint venture
partnership with the Indian conglomerate Tata Group to create seven

logistics parks in India.[65] It advertised its entry into Russia, where it would advise on the construction of special economic zones, and signed a memorandum of understanding with Libya.[66] It announced the construction of an $800 million tax-free port in Senegal.[67] Romanian officials visited Dubai to look into creating "a Jafza-like platform," presumably on their short stretch of coast on the Black Sea.[68] In 2006, DP World won a bidding war with Singapore for the UK company P&O, the shipping line that had serviced the British Empire. Coaling stations, naval bases, and free ports had once strung together the empire from Colombo to Gibraltar—shipping lanes were what the political scientist Laleh Khalili calls the "sinews of war and trade."[69] Now the biggest port operators were the empire's former possessions and protectorates: Singapore, Hong Kong, and Dubai.

Dubai did not hesitate before the metropole itself. It bought 20 percent of the London Stock Exchange, as well as a stake in the London Eye. The name of the Dubai flag carrier, Emirates, appeared on the shirts of a London football team, Arsenal, and their new pitch opened as Emirates Stadium. In 2013, DP World also opened London Gateway port. Thirty miles downstream from the Isle of Dogs, London Gateway was everything that the Docklands was not: a logistics park, a business park, and a deepwater harbor for the world's largest container ships.[70] Much of the construction was done by robots and automated cranes and trucks.[71] A semicolony just a few decades earlier, Dubai now managed the entryway to the metropole's most important waterway.

Another point of focus was the coast along the Bab el-Mandeb Strait between Yemen and Djibouti, where twenty thousand ships a year passed through on their way to the Suez Canal, carrying 30 percent of Europe's oil.[72] DP World took over management of the Port of Djibouti in 2000. Two years later, it assumed management of Djibouti–Ambouli International Airport.[73] Dubai also built the country's first five-star hotel and took over the management of Djibouti customs.[74] A Dubai World subsidiary bought Djibouti's airline.[75] As mentioned in the previous chapter, a few years later, DP World expanded the port in Berbera, the de facto state of Somaliland.

It was difficult not to compare the hyperactive, dynamic, and successful Dubai with Iraq, its distorted double farther up the Gulf. There was Iraq, democracy being enforced by a foreign occupier at the barrel of a Tomahawk missile. Here was Dubai, without democracy, hosting pool parties and brunches, ribbon cuttings and new acquisitions every month. Curtis Yarvin, the blogger yearning for a patchwork of mini-states, was among those who posed them as opposites. In Iraq you had democracy without law, and in Dubai you had law without democracy. Which was preferable?

But the choice was false, as was the opposition. Dubai's rise was hard to separate from US military interventions in its neighboring countries. The UAE had allowed the United States to base equipment in the federation since 1991, and by the early 2000s, Jebel Ali was the US Navy's busiest port of call.[76] The economic boom was fed entirely by the surge in oil prices that followed the US invasion of Iraq and Afghanistan. In a telling move, the oil and construction company Halliburton relocated from its home state of Texas to the Jebel Ali Free Zone in 2007.[77] When Djibouti's Doraleh oil terminal opened, the ceremony happened on the guided missile cruiser USS *Vicksburg*. The US military had invested in the terminal to the tune of $30 million.[78]

The close partnership between Dubai and the US military made it ironic that the loudest outcry over the emirate's overseas expansion should come from the United States itself. Among the terminals operated by the P&O shipping company were twenty-two in the United States. When DP World bought P&O in 2006, American policymakers opposed the deal as a supposed security risk, eventually leading the Dubai company to sell off the management contracts of those terminals. The protest was particularly incongruous given that DP World's ports were cutting-edge in their security. In fact, as the geographer Deborah Cowen observed, the United States was collaborating with Dubai to screen containers while following them in subjecting port workers to abnormally high levels of surveillance.[79]

A few years later, Dubai returned to the United States by a southern back door. In March 2008, four officials from Orangeburg County,

South Carolina, a district of about eighty thousand, boarded a fourteen-hour flight to Dubai to carry out negotiations on a $600 million investment by the emirate. Emphasizing what they saw as uniting flora between the two geographies, the South Carolinians brought palmetto palm tree pins and palm tree neckties. One member of the delegation expressed hope that the palm tree and crescent moon on their state flag would be welcomed by a Muslim country.[80] Jafza International bought 1,300 acres of land in Orangeburg and announced plans for a business park with light manufacturing, warehousing, and distribution.[81]

The union of the moons was not in the stars. Just as the Dubai model peaked, it hit the wall of the global financial crisis. In November 2008, DP World requested a suspension of repayments on its loans, and Dubai itself needed to be bailed out by Abu Dhabi.[82] Jafza pulled out of Orangeburg. The Trump Tower Dubai planned for the trunk of the Palm Jumeirah was not built.

4.

Dubai was a new kind of state, tailor-made for globalization. Deregulation of shipping and trucking allowed for intermodal transport that supercharged maritime trade. Technical innovations in gantry cranes made it faster than ever to get ships loaded and unloaded. Wide-body long-haul aircraft allowed for a place distant from most business centers to become a key node in the global network—an "aerotropolis," as a journalist dubbed it.[83] (One textbook observed that nearly any two places in the world could be linked by a stopover in Dubai.)[84] The end of capital controls and the fluidity of money turned the emirate's gleaming towers and villas into three-dimensional tax-free savings accounts. Dubai was a perfect symbol of the global economy taking shape in the early twenty-first century.

It is significant that the rise of Dubai in the early 2000s happened parallel to the practice of nation branding. Previously a topic for corporations, branding began to be applied to nations. Consultants and

PR agencies packaged the qualities and virtues of countries into easily digestible sound bites. Nation-branding indexes quantified what average people thought of various countries in new league tables. Such indexes helped direct the flows of ever-larger numbers of tourist dollars, investments in real estate, and relocations of companies, framed in terms of livability for employees, the ease of doing business, the degree of economic freedom, and the intangible additions to the value of your product to be described as "Made in Country X." A famous early example of nation branding was Britain, where the idea of Cool Britannia became closely linked to Tony Blair and New Labour after 1997. Another was Hong Kong, which crafted a campaign billing itself as Asia's World City, launched in 2001.[85] Uniquely Singapore was launched in 2004, Incredible India in 2005.[86] Dubai's skyline and the city's many world records made it the flagship brand of the UAE and a leading world tourist city. In 2014, it was the fifth most visited city in the world.[87]

After all the talk in the 1990s about democracy and capitalism going together, one thing that nation-branding consultants discovered early on was how little value democracy added when it came to a country's reputation. In fact, it was undemocratic countries like Dubai and Singapore that ranked especially high with tourists and investors. There was an important lesson to be learned here. Winning the capitalist game globally seemed to have little to do with abstract questions of democratic liberty. People in the industry saw this as no coincidence: centralizing power in a CEO-like head of state allowed for a unity of message.[88] Democracy was messy. It folded in different visions of a country, left loose ends and dangling, ragged narratives. Capitalism without democracy could hit the target every time. Indeed, if one judged countries the way one judged companies—as everything about the global market was saying we should—then Dubai won in all metrics. What was a dismal Freedom House ranking compared to the world's tallest skyscraper? Next to land valuations that rose 10 percent a year, what was a place at the bottom of the World Press Freedom list? Concerns over political and civil liberties could seem like sentimental anachronisms of an earlier time, indulgences one could no longer afford in the constant combat of global competition.

An urban planner notes how Dubai creates monumental infrastructure while hiding it from sight.[89] The Port of Jebel Ali is behind barbed wire. The epic land reclamation projects of the World and Palm Jumeirah are gated communities inaccessible to the public. Dubai is both hyperreal—reproduced endlessly in glossy pictures of the skyline and dramatic aerial footage—and impossible to grasp, a place seen only from above and not at street level, where the buses with bars in place of windows shuttle workers to their encampments. It is perhaps the way Dubai offers itself deliberately as a projection screen that makes it available for constant reappropriation.

Mainstream reportage about Dubai is careful not to follow the script of the Brand Dubai media office (opened in 2009) too closely. Journalists tend to note the absence of democracy as part of Dubai's dark side, along with sex trafficking, child jockeys, and the exploited and often unpaid workforce. Reactionary thinkers like Yarvin found this unnecessary. Instead, he pushed the success of Dubai to more radical conclusions. He proposed his own solution for Iraq that would borrow the virtues of fragmented governance from Dubai. Begin by breaking it up, he wrote, back into its Ottoman-era provinces. Then put each territory under the control of a for-profit "sovereign security corporation." These companies would be privately owned, privately run, and publicly traded on the Dubai financial exchange. The "new emirates of Mesopotamia" would have a dual share structure. People born in the former Iraq would get a share in the corporation but no vote. Shares with voting rights would be sold at auction in Dubai. Internal dissent would not be tolerated, nor would there be protection for political or civil freedoms. Under the sovereign security companies, Yarvin wrote, "the business of Iraq will be business, just as in Dubai."[90]

This was not so far from the de facto administration of Iraq by private contractors. Yarvin wrote his piece in the spring of 2007. In the first quarter of 2008, there were as many contractors in Iraq as military personnel.[91] The involvement of private interests in the war was unprecedented and highly lucrative. The *Financial Times* found the top earner was KBR, part of Halliburton until 2007, which gained at least $39.5 billion in federal contracts in Iraq.[92] Halliburton got in on a no-bid contract.

Yet even if "Dubai Inc." was the template, the emirate was not literally a corporation. Dubai did still have citizens, albeit a minuscule minority of the people living in the emirate, and it did still have a traditional head of state, albeit one unaccountable to the people and ruling through the privilege of bloodline. In other words, Yarvin's dream was only half-realized. He wondered if it was possible for sovereign corporations, or sovcorps, to do Dubai one better by eliminating the hereditary monarch and moving to the more traditional corporate model of anonymous public ownership.[93] Imagine if Dubai could do an IPO, he wrote.[94]

In one of his provocative asides, Yarvin mused on whether it would be a good idea to let Dubai's Sheikh Al Makhtoum run Baltimore.[95] In the coming years, others in his circle would ask another version of the same question: What if Silicon Valley ran Honduras? Something like the sovcorp was about to come closer to reality.

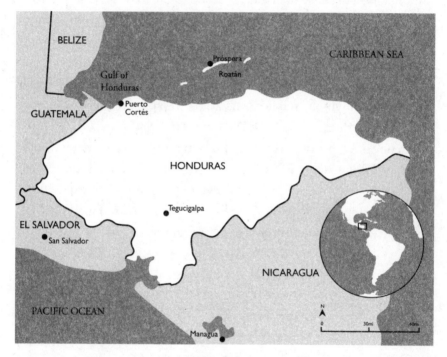

Honduras

Silicon Valley Colonialism

In 2009, a Stanford economics professor named Paul Romer gave a talk on reviving colonialism. He asked the following: Why had some countries grown rich while some remained poor? It was not just about having the right location or the right natural resources, he said. It was about something more intangible: the right set of rules. Rules meant the laws that set tax rates, regulated labor, and protected property. They also meant the overall style of government. At a deeper level, rules were cultural norms, values, and beliefs. They were the way we were made to behave, but also the way we behaved without thinking. The history of capitalism was a history of struggle among rules. The nations with the best rules won.

Hong Kong—a scrap of coastline organized under different rules than the adjacent mainland since the nineteenth century—was Romer's prime example. When China imported the Hong Kong model to the Pearl River Delta in the late 1970s, he said, a "process of copying" helped China begin catching up to the West. Romer waved away objections that Hong Kong was undemocratic. Until the handover, the colony's governor was appointed by the UK parliament, which was elected by British voters. Hong Kong *was* a democracy—"it just happened to be not a democracy that involved the local residents." As for the Opium Wars—the violence that had made the whole thing possible—Romer insisted they were incidental. In his telling, Hong Kong got to where it was because of the "historical accident" of being colonized by the British.[1]

How could such historical accidents be made to happen again? The shortcut to Hong Kong that Romer offered was called the charter city. The formula: persuade poor nations to surrender patches of uninhabited territory to be managed by richer ones. Pollinate the empty land with rules known to make capitalism work and watch it grow. This would be colonialism by consent, occupation by invitation. Using the jargon of Silicon Valley, he called them "start-up political jurisdictions."[2] Charter cities could happen anywhere. Displaying a nighttime map of Africa unlit by artificial light, he pointed out the "enormous amount of land on earth that's very underutilized."[3] Leaders only had to face the fact that sovereignty under conditions of globalization was already moot. Why not go all the way and give over your country to external management? You had nothing to lose and Hong Kong to gain.

1.

The tech sector at the turn of the millennium was defined by the relentless search for the next world-changing "killer application," or *killer app.* The way Silicon Valley saw it, the world was full of problems in need of technological fixes.[4] Airbnb set out to solve the hotel. Uber set out to solve the taxi. Theranos set out to solve the blood test. The idea of the charter city borrowed its sheen from the idea of charter schools, the privately backed start-up educational institutions that tripled in number from 2000 to 2012.[5] The *Wall Street Journal* made the connection, comparing Romer's charter city model to a charter school "free of union contracts and public bureaucracy."[6] For mainstream America in the 2000s, charter schools were targeting the outmoded institutions of public schools. Charter cities targeted the outmoded institution of nation-states.

The first place where Romer's plan touched down was on the island of Madagascar, off the southeastern coast of Africa. His ally was Marc Ravalomanana, a dairy tycoon who became president of Madagascar in 2002. Ravalomanana made headlines six years later with revelations of a scheme to lease 1.2 million hectares of agricultural land free of charge for ninety-nine years to a South Korean conglomerate.[7] The deal was one of the most prominent attempted land grabs in Africa as richer nations sought to secure overseas agricultural sites after a spike in world food prices.[8] Host countries were offering land for nothing, or next to nothing, in hopes of securing some jobs for locals and spillover effects from foreign investment. Romer saw Ravalomanana as a man willing to rethink sovereignty even in the face of controversy. He flew to Madagascar to pitch the charter city model and was delighted when the president agreed to create two of them.[9] Other elites were less persuaded by the subdivision of the nation. They backed a coup, which overthrew Ravalomanana in 2009.[10]

As one coup closed a door, another opened one. This time, the site was Honduras. Honduras had been an enclave economy in the nineteenth century, with plantations run by foreign companies. From the 1960s onward, it fell under successive US-supported military dictatorships.[11] In 1976, the country joined the first wave of export processing zones, giving tax breaks to companies in Puerto Cortés, a port city on the Caribbean coast named after the conquistador who landed there in 1526. From there, zones spread to ever more locations, until finally a 1998 law decreed that EPZs could be created anywhere in the country.[12] The zones sucked in workers, with manufacturing mostly in the low-wage textile sector. The labor force in EPZs grew from nine thousand in 1990 to a hundred thousand a decade later,[13] though by the 2000s the very success that Romer highlighted in the manufacturing zones of China was beginning to undercut Honduras's wage advantage.[14]

The coup in 2009 was carried out by the National Party of Porfirio

"Pepe" Lobo. Among his advisors were graduates of elite US universities. Like Romer, they were seeking solutions and gimmicks, ways
to extend what they saw as the success of the EPZs. One of their ideas
was upgrading them into something closer to the nineteenth-century
concession. They floated the label "superembassy," described by one
advisor as "an area governed by another country's laws."[15] Lobo's team
was primed for Romer's arguments, and when his charter city talk
was posted online, they contacted him. By late 2010, the Honduran
leadership had met with Romer and agreed to make their country
"the site of an economic experiment."[16]

The legal form for the charter city in Honduras was the Región
Especial de Desarrollo (special development region), or RED, an extraterritorial entity to be managed by a foreign partner country.[17] Created by the National Congress of Honduras through a constitutional
amendment, REDs would be veritable colonies within the nation. A
foreign nation would establish and staff courts; train police; set up
schools, health-care systems, and prisons.[18] Policy would come from a
nine-member Transparency Commission and governor appointed by
the Honduran president in the first instance and internally thereafter.[19]
REDs resembled nineteenth-century concessions but, in some ways,
went beyond them. Most remarkable was the fact that they would
have their own juridical standing: REDs could enter treaties with
other nation-states, determine their own immigration policies, and
conduct diplomacy alongside the Honduran government.[20] In terms
of international law, the REDs would have at least as much autonomy
as the Special Administrative Region of Hong Kong. True to Romer's
rhetoric, the model was "one country, two systems." Freeing patches of
territory from national oversight and granting all state functions to a
foreign country, the REDs put sovereignty on the auction block.

"Who wants to buy Honduras?" asked the *New York Times*,
reporting the expectation that Romer would be the "chairman" of a
charter city of ten million people (in a country where the entire population currently numbered eight million).[21] The *Wall Street Journal*
praised Romer's supervision of "the development of an instant city."[22]

The *Economist* marveled at the prospect of "Hong Kong in Honduras," reproducing Romer's publicity to imagine "scores of skyscrapers and millions of people" around a natural harbor.[23] The *Atlantic* asked, "Should Struggling Countries Let Investors Run Their Cities?" and answered yes: "It may very well be easier to solve the country's systemic governance challenges by starting afresh, even within small parts of its territory."[24] Voices from the libertarian corner were even more effusive. The *Freeman* called the REDs "a revolution in governance."[25] Populated by "citizen-customers," they could be a site of "field testing" for other experiments in governance.[26] One British libertarian blogger effused: "*These zones are a frontier. They are a new thing, an adventure, and a new addition to humanity.*"[27]

Romer had managed to secure the necessary domestic conditions in the host country, but he was having trouble finding a patron state, a richer country willing to manage the charter city. One of his dream candidates was Canada. In early presentations of the charter city, he fantasized about Canadians taking over the Cuban enclave of Guantánamo Bay from the United States and turning the notorious prison of the Global War on Terrorism into a bustling commercial hub for the region.[28] He pitched Canada on a similar role for Honduras.[29] This was no humanitarian mission, he insisted; it was a business proposition.

Canada was already one of the primary investors in Honduras, accounting for an average of 28.7 percent of foreign direct investment in the early 2000s, more than the United States. The Canadian company Gildan, producer of socks, T-shirts, and other clothing, was the single biggest employer in the Honduran EPZs.[30] A charter city in the country would be a captive market and a client for Canadian services. Canada could offer education, health care, environmental management, and tax administration on a fee-for-service basis.[31] Romer even imagined a Caribbean contingent of the Royal Canadian Mounted Police patrolling the zones with wages drawn from land revenues.[32] He repeated a popular slogan: "The world wants more Canada."[33] But Canada demurred.

The charter city connected to the dreams of Silicon Valley, but also to the context of larger geopolitics. Romer talked about the need to "rethink sovereignty" as if this were a new idea. But the United States had been rethinking sovereignty in earnest since its invasion and occupation of Afghanistan in 2001 and Iraq in 2003. When Romer gave his first charter cities lecture, the United States still had 130,000 troops in Iraq. His presentation at Stanford was attended by Condoleezza Rice, who had just walked away from the calamities she helped conduct as secretary of state in the Bush administration, taking on a prestigious new position as director of the Hoover Institution—the West Coast outpost of Mont Pelerinians.[34] Romer referred to her by her nickname, mentioning Condi in the audience.[35] The actual existing rethinkers of sovereignty were Romer's colleagues.

The wars in the Middle East had untethered the world-making imagination of many US and UK elites. Assorted historians and public intellectuals mused that empire had been maligned and needed rehabilitation.[36] One such cheerleader, Niall Ferguson, adjunct fellow at Hoover, called himself a "fully paid-up member of the neoimperialist gang."[37] With the failures of American "nation building" a constant thrum in the daily news, the press was happy to showcase Romer's dreams for a less militarized version of imperialism with economic freedom as its goal.

The few critical voices pointed out that the coverage of Romer's ideas glossed over the nature of the government in Honduras he was dealing with. Just as with coverage of the Chicago school's influence on Pinochet's Chile, the innovative quality of Romer's economic proposals were reported without attention to the thousands of illegal detentions and the murders and disappearances of protesters and activists.[38] One of the lawyers who filed a complaint against the constitutionality of the scheme for REDs was shot dead in what appeared to be an assassination, just hours after a television interview in which he denounced the ceding of land to investors for self-governing "model cities."[39] But what were such isolated episodes of police violence and human rights violations compared to the death toll of attempting to

bring (back) popular elections to the Middle East? US foreign policy and Romer's charter city proposals worked in tandem to shift the
Overton window on the idea of alien rule. If the world's most prestigious publications could get behind a project of colonialism by invitation, what else might be possible? Curtis Yarvin was, as usual, willing
to say the quiet part out loud. He wondered why Romer insisted his
charter cities were not colonialism. They were "*exactly* colonialism,"
he wrote, and this was no reason for apology. Non-European populations did better when they were ruled by Europeans, he proclaimed.
Romer was blazing the trail toward what Yarvin called a "colonialism
for the 21st century," and he was thrilled.[40]

2.

Those who became most excited about Romer's plan for Honduras
were not existing states like Canada but entrepreneurial libertarians
who thought it might be nice to have a mini-state of their own. The
conference where Peter Thiel speculated about a world of a thousand nations? Romer was scheduled to speak there too. The positive reception of the charter cities idea (not to mention the boom
for military contractors and construction companies in the Middle
East) suggested that the taboo against subdividing and recolonizing
territory was weakening. Why shouldn't private citizens get in on the
act of government, the most lucrative line of business yet created?
Patri Friedman pointed out that government services accounted for
30 percent of global GDP. "People talk about disrupting medicine or
energy or education," Friedman said. "Those are small potatoes. This
is the big one." Government was the biggest cartel in the world. "Let's
think of countries as firms and citizens as customers," he proposed.
If there was such a thing as state failure, then "can we cash in on it
as entrepreneurs?"[41] As a pure enterprise, start-up cities looked like a
field waiting for an investor with enough guts to enter.

"If laws were software," Friedman asked, then why was "America's
operating system . . . written in 1787?"[42] Reforming domestic laws

was too slow. Better to find a place where one could write new code from scratch. Friedman hoped that Honduras would be the country to make this happen. He gathered people from Thiel's circle to back an investment group called Future Cities Development, which announced plans to bring the "Silicon Valley spirit of innovation to Honduras." In 2011, they signed a memorandum of understanding with Honduras to build a RED.[43]

A series of other investors were attracted to the Honduras project by the prospect of a free market in statecraft. Some were more politically motivated than others. One member of the Seasteading Institute board who also signed a memorandum of understanding with the government claimed he wanted to make the zones into an "anarcho-capitalist paradise."[44] He imagined zones perforating existing polities and drawing away people and capital until the surrounding territories were left as husks. "Ultimately in 20, 30, 40 years," he said, "we'll get to the point where the nation-state system atrophies." He compared the nation-state to the US postal service, eroded more every day by email and private couriers. The proliferation of zones meant that the "nation state government exists like the post office for a while but at some point" it will wither away.[45]

Another saw the Honduran zone as the answer to the only relevant question: "Which state would you buy?"[46] He saw it as a place where "contract citizens" could come together in a true social contract, with no chance of infringement on private property in the name of "the common good." There would be no collective politics beyond atomized individuals, who would be "the sovereign of themselves."[47] As "the old order is visibly coming to an end, but a new one has not yet been established," he wrote, libertarians had no option but to retreat to liberated territories.[48] The Honduran zone could serve as a redoubt and a bastion in a troubled time—a version of Galt's Gulch, the millionaires' Colorado hideaway from *Atlas Shrugged*, but with better beaches.

Yet another investor, Erick Brimen, referred to his métier as "countrypreneurship," and started a venture capital fund offering seed capital for creating new societies "from scratch."[49] Working with Patri Friedman, Brimen broke ground in May 2021 on a fifty-eight-acre zone on the island of Roatán, off the north coast of Honduras, with $17.5 million in capital.[50] Called Próspera, the zone was not a RED but its legal successor, a ZEDE (*zona de empleo y desarrollo económico*, "zone of employment and economic development"), one of two in the country.[51] ZEDEs remained under Honduran international and criminal law; they could no longer enter treaties independently, but otherwise offered a blank slate for building new internal institutions from scratch. ZEDEs were freed of import and export taxes and could have their own courts, security forces, education systems, and legal system.[52] "We are a private venture in which all relationships are determined by contracts between the organizer and the individual business or residents," said one advisor. "We are the epitome of free market principles."[53]

Luxury accommodations, offices, and laboratories were planned for the ZEDE, but one of the selling points of living in Próspera was also that you didn't have to live there—no more than Próspera's investors lived in the Cayman Islands, where their fund was registered. Proponents of the start-up society insisted that the twenty-first-century city was not made of concrete and glass so much as out of laws.[54] True to Romer's vision, the most important thing about a place was its rules. While earlier settlers once sought wealth in gold, crops, or railroads, the treasure of zones like Próspera in the twenty-first century was their status as a jurisdiction—their potential as a new place to pick and choose among regulations and licensing requirements. Such zones offered vivid examples of what had become standard practice in the conduct of global capitalism. When people form a business contract anywhere in the world, they already have the choice of which law they elect to use; most commercial contracts are written in either New York State or English law.[55] For what one scholar calls "roving capital," laws are selected and combined à la carte.[56] The VC firm funding Próspera, for example, was registered in Wyoming.[57] The business itself was registered in Delaware.[58] These jurisdictions were portals to what Oliver

Bullough calls Moneyland, where people can select whichever laws "are most suited to those wealthy enough to afford them at any moment in time."[59]

Próspera hoped to build a new portal to Moneyland but also to accelerate the dynamic of the choice of laws. Their vision was premised on a faith in the frictionless possibilities of governance by internet. One of their templates was the small Baltic state Estonia, birthplace of Skype, which strove to become what one journalist called a "digital republic" in the 2000s, allowing you to vote, dispute parking tickets, and even give testimony in a criminal case online.[60] After 2014, Estonia launched an e-residency program, which allowed people to become "virtual residents" for a small fee, registering their business in the country and gaining access to its range of online services as well as entry to the European Union's Digital Single Market.[61] The architect of that program was an advisor.[62]

Anarcho-capitalists long dreamed of making the metaphor of the "social contract" discussed by political theorists into a literal contract, printed on paper or displayed on a screen, which a customer would sign to agree to be bound by certain rules. This was brought to life in the classic speculative novel of anarcho-capitalism, *Alongside Night* from 1979, in which the United States has collapsed into a currency crisis and true believers in the free market have gathered in enclaves and strongholds run by an underground organization known as the Cadre. Members hail one another with their greeting—"Laissez-faire!"—and enjoy libraries stocked with Mises, Rand, and Rothbard and services provided by the First Anarchist Bank and Trust Company, NoState Insurance, and the TANSTAAFL Café (short for There Ain't No Such Thing as a Free Lunch).[63]

To enter one of the redoubts, you first had to sign a General Submission to Arbitration, which bound you to settle all future disputes of any kind through third-party private courts. Parts of such a system already exist in the commercial world. A business contract usually includes a note about where a dispute would be settled should a disagreement arise. Cross-border cases are often handled by international centers, with London, Hong Kong, and Singapore being leading seats of arbitration. In *Alongside Night*, this extends to all aspects of civil law and conduct. Nobody who refused the contract was allowed to enter, and those who rejected a judgment were submitted to boycott and ostracism, "a 'casting out' that is virtually equivalent to being turned naked over to one's enemies."[64]

As in the strongholds of the Cadre, arbitration in Próspera would cover everyday affairs unrelated to business.[65] The "agreement of coexistence" signed on joining the ZEDE meant that infractions would be treated not as crimes but as breaches of contract. The senior arbiters of the Próspera Arbitration Center that governed disputes were three elderly white men from Arizona.[66]

This was a different vision of government than one based on rights and obligations, let alone popular sovereignty. It was a self-conscious choice to make corporate governance the foundation of human community, a fulfillment of the anarcho-capitalist blueprint drafted by David Friedman and many others.

A Próspera advisor praised the decision of Honduras to surrender control over the territory. "Honduras is letting go," he said, "and that's an absolutely unique phenomenon in the world. You have to be very desperate as a territory and as a political class to understand that the problem might be that you have to . . . let others take over."[67] The symbolism of the ZEDE as an act of desperation was not lost on the Honduran population. Debate over the zones reopened a larger conversation in the country about fragmentation of national territory. Critics saw a through line in the historical perforation of national sovereignty, from the banana enclave to the *maquila* sweatshops to the start-up zones.[68] One journalist noted the fact that zones were legalized on the hundred-year anniversary of General Manuel Bonilla's granting similar privileges to US banana companies.[69] Another pointed out that one ZEDE was planned for the place where William Walker, the nineteenth-century American mercenary who declared himself the president of Nicaragua, was eventually tried and executed by the Honduras government.[70] Locals complained of an "invasion of model cities created for the benefit of the rich."[71]

The charter city dream in Honduras was made possible only by a violently repressive government, by thousands of illegal detentions and the murders and disappearances of protesters and activists.[72] The project was rolled out even as the government launched a campaign of terror against its opponents, with women and LGBTQI activists as specific targets.[73] The ZEDEs became a focal point of anger at the regime and the complicity of the United States and other foreign powers in upholding it. In June 2021, a National Movement Against ZEDEs and for National Sovereignty, formed by human rights lawyers and church representatives, complained that Próspera had broken the provisions of the International Labour Organization by failing to consult Indigenous residents before going ahead with the development.[74] The ZEDEs drew criticisms from not just locals but also UN representatives in Honduras, who worried about oversight against discrimination in the zones, and the nongovernmental National Anti-Corruption Council.[75]

In September 2020, Brimen had a shouting confrontation with Roatán locals as his security guards stood off against local police.[76] He appeared on a local news station in an attempt to smooth over the conflict. "When you think about Roatán Próspera," he said, "you need to think about a platform." Yes, he said, the goal was a low-tax environment, but "the whole point of Próspera is to create an environment where human rights and property rights are both protected and defended." As he put up slides of statistics from the accounting firm Ernst & Young and headshots of advisors from Tallinn, Dubai, and London, Brimen seemed unable to understand why people with centuries of history of subordination to more powerful countries were so sensitive about his campaign to "disrupt" their government.[77] It was grimly humorous for Brimen to disparage foreign aid as "colonialism with a human face" while he himself operated a territorial concession governed by foreign laws and overseen by foreign advisors.[78]

3.

In one of his many glosses on the charter city idea, Paul Romer said elliptically that they were an attempt "to propose a different metarule for changing the rules in developing countries, one that could, in some sense, circumvent many of the roadblocks that stop changes in rules."[79] Of course, the "metarule" was the cession of territorial control to a foreign power, and the "roadblocks" it detoured around were the domestic democratic control over decisions made in or about that territory. But as we have seen, economic freedom without political freedom was no paradox for libertarians. In fact, when a libertarian think tank published a historical retrospective analysis of economic freedom, it ranked Honduras under the 1975 military dictatorship as the second most economically free territory in the world—second only to Hong Kong.[80]

The start-up city was the same fantasy that had drawn libertarians and neoliberals to Hong Kong in the 1970s, Singapore in the 1990s, and Dubai in the 2000s: the dream of capitalism without democracy. They sometimes described this as "shrinking the state," but a Honduran fisherman offered a better metaphor: the ZEDEs, he said, allowed investors to "kidnap the state."[81]

Late in 2021, the old-fashioned mechanism of popular elections creaked its levers and democracy took its revenge. A new government came to power in Honduras: the election was won by Xiamaro Castro, the wife of the president deposed in Pepe Lobo's 2009 coup. She put the ZEDEs at the top of her list of targets, seeking to revise the constitutional amendment that allowed for the creation of zones, or to put their continued existence to a popular vote.[82] Meanwhile, the champions of start-up cities hoped that their foothold would be defended by treaties such as the Dominican Republic–Central America–United States Free Trade Agreement, which permitted investors to sue host governments if their investments were negatively affected by legal changes.[83] As one former investor put it without irony, "Libertarians don't like international trade law but it turns out international trade law is tremendously helpful."[84]

The mounting opposition put the long-standing model of the enclave under inspection. In April 2022, Xiomara Castro's predecessor, who had overseen the creation of ZEDEs, was extradited to the United States on charges of trafficking tons of cocaine and using the proceeds to fund his political operations.[85] The same month, the Honduran congress voted unanimously to overturn the ZEDE law as unconstitutional. Existing ZEDEs, such as Próspera, were slated to be abolished within a year.[86]

Might the future move away from anarcho-capitalist paradises after all? Another member of Próspera's board of advisors was Oliver Porter, the godfather of charter cities, who had overseen the secession of Sandy Springs, Georgia, from Atlanta in 2005—a move that cut off tax revenue to the inner city and outsourced all government services to private providers, in what Naomi Klein called "the glimpse of a disaster-apartheid future."[87] Porter spoke often and glowingly about Próspera. Yet he never mentioned the fact that Sandy Springs had struck its own reverse course in 2019, bringing government services back in-house. As with many other instances where privatization of publicly owned utilities led to higher prices and less choice, private contractors in Sandy Springs had become too expensive. The city's leaders concluded the public option was cheaper and turned their back on the open market.[88]

The road of secession, pointing toward the illusory promised land of unencumbered economic freedom, was not a one-way street. In the 2020s, convening a constituent assembly to revise a country's constitution has gained popularity as a tool for rewriting the contract between state and people. Castro proposed one for her new government, carrying through her husband's plans that got derailed by the coup. Farther south, Chile is seeking to revise the constitution put in place under the military dictatorship of Augusto Pinochet. The government in Peru is also hoping to create a new constitution. The vision of the earth's surface as a circuit board with swappable components still has a formidable opponent in the elusive dream of people speaking in a democratic voice.

And yet zone fever burns on. With Honduras looking ever less hospitable, enthusiasts of start-up cities have begun eyeing its neighbors. In 2019, Nayib Bukele became the prime minister of El Salvador and immediately rolled out an aggressive campaign to brand his nation as a global center for another kind of exit: cryptocurrency. In November 2021, he unveiled plans for a Bitcoin City, with power generated by a volcano, and a giant central square in the shape of the Bitcoin logo.[89] Proponents of the start-up city spoke at the gathering about how Bitcoin could contribute to the dream of "opting out on every layer."[90] They were in talks with Bukele about turning it into a "free private city" even as they pursued opportunities farther south in Jair Bolsonaro's Brazil, through the University of Chicago–educated minister of the economy Paulo Guedes.[91] History shows there is always another fantasy island on the horizon.

CENTRALIZED
(A)

DECENTRALIZED
(B)

DISTRIBUTED
(C)

← Link

← Station

Network types

A Cloud Country in the Metaverse

While much of the action in Neal Stephenson's 1992 novel *Snow Crash* takes place in a fractured geography of gated communities, private prisons, racist enclaves, and jerry-rigged refugee ships, the heart of the plot is in a place that is a non-place: the Metaverse. Characters put on goggles and earbuds to escape their gig jobs delivering pizza or packages and traverse a virtual reality in their avatars as gorillas, samurai, or dragons. They buy, sell, and develop property in the Metaverse, though the underlying land, as in Singapore and Hong Kong, is owned by a single body that reinvests the revenue into expanding infrastructure. Certain areas are exclusive, but anyone with access to a computer can drop out of everyday reality and pop up in the online world. As one character says, "When you live in a shithole, there's always the Metaverse."[1]

In 2021, Facebook, one of the few companies in history to achieve a market capitalization exceeding $1 trillion, announced it was changing its name to Meta Platforms behind a push toward something it also called the metaverse. This metaverse sought to meld the worlds of gaming, social media, and workplace internet use by allowing you to have identities, appearances (or "skins"), and payment systems that you could carry across platforms—from chatting with family on Facebook to sitting in an office meeting on Zoom to staging a raid in a massive multiplayer online role-playing game like *Final Fantasy* or *World of Warcraft*. In the promotional video, users played a game of cards as cartoonish avatars, and Mark Zuckerberg engaged an employee in a staged conversation as a copy of *Snow Crash* lay on the coffee table between them.[2] Other tech companies followed suit. Microsoft bought the company that produced *World of Warcraft*, and the pages of the business press began to fill with a term that only science fiction readers had heard of a year before.

While the term was new to many, the phenomenon was not. The idea of an immersive online experience had featured in tech futurism for longer than many millennials had been alive. William Gibson coined the term *cyberspace* in his 1984 novel *Neuromancer*, and as early as 1992, the film *Lawnmower Man* featured a protagonist strapped into a headset descending into a megalomaniac rage in a three-dimensional computer space. Long used to train soldiers and pilots, virtual reality headsets entered arcades in the 1990s and were a fixture of tech-booster magazines like *Wired*. The 1999 hit *The Matrix* brought the cyberpunk idea of jacking into an alternative reality into popular consciousness at a time when one-third of Americans began to use the internet. *Habbo*, launched in 2000, and *Second Life*, launched in 2003, offered rudimentary versions of the metaverse, where avatars walked jerkily around three-dimensional rooms and cityscapes and occasionally socialized with strangers.

As some people showed themselves willing to pay for accessories and buildings in these games, there were many articles about the novel idea of "making real money in virtual worlds" and "investing in the online property boom."[3] One person watching the numbers was the financier Stephen K. Bannon, who would later go on to become a top Trump advisor. Bannon raised $60 million in 2007, mostly from his former employer Goldman Sachs, to invest in a Hong Kong–based company that recruited low-wage Chinese workers to play *World of*

Warcraft. By completing simple tasks, these "gold farmers" earned virtual currency and other items that could be sold to Western gamers for real money at a profit. Beyond the clever arbitrage play, Bannon credits the experience with alerting him to the extent of online energies. Bannon described seeing the "monster power" of disaffected young white men online, which he later channeled into his media platform *Breitbart*, one of the forums for the eruption of the alt-right after 2016.[4]

It is impossible to talk about political ideology in the last twenty years without talking about the influence of gaming and the internet. While so far we have mostly looked at *places* in the conventional sense, recent radical capitalist visions of exit have had one eye on the everyday world and the other on the virtual. With a tsunami of money crashing into the tech sector, and later into cryptocurrencies like Bitcoin, the libertarian mind has oscillated for the last two decades between the two domains of online and off. From the late 1990s, anarcho-capitalists saw the internet as a place to strip social rules down to the steel girders of private property and contract. As we have seen time and again, their goal has been not to take a wrecking ball to the state but to hijack, disassemble, and rebuild it under their own private ownership. They built toy models of the state with real-world effects.

1.

The urtext of twenty-first-century tech libertarianism was published in 1997. It carried a mercenary title—*The Sovereign Individual: How to Survive and Thrive During the Collapse of the Welfare State.*[5] The authors were the American venture capitalist James Dale Davidson and the British journalist and businessman William Rees-Mogg, whose oeuvre included a previous book called *Blood in the Streets: Investment Profits in a World Gone Mad.*[6] (Its title references Baron de Rothschild's axiom that "the time to buy is when there's blood in the streets.") Rees-Mogg described himself and Davidson as "instability forecasters" and "discontinuists."[7] Their genre was the recognized one of futurism combined with business advice—how to profit from the coming collapse.

By 1991, they were already touting the "subversive invention" of the microchip and its capacity to "destroy the nation-state."[8] The argument crystallized around the internet, which they argued was eroding received ideas of territorial government. "Cybercash," they said, would let people take their money wherever they wanted through anonymous transactions; as the wealthy fled high-tax jurisdictions, this portability would starve the welfare state. They combined this observation about capital flight with a speculative argument, drawn from epigenetics, that humans had entered a more rapid phase of evolution. The result, they said, would be the emergence of a hypermobile superclass of high-IQ individuals, who could remotely coordinate placid low-IQ workforces while stashing their wealth far from the grasping hands of governments.

Davidson and Rees-Mogg called this tiny, rarefied fraction of the world's population "sovereign individuals," and estimated their coming number at a hundred million worldwide.[9] The nation-state form was dysgenic. It worked against the dictates of evolutionary advance and survival. In an era of hypermobility, it served evolutionary interests to escape national constraints. Scales would fall from the eyes of the new global elites, they predicted. The elites would cease to see national identity as anything meaningful, and the conceit that they owed anything to their so-called fellow citizens would be laughable. They would understand that one's countrymen were actually "the main parasite and predator," their brains contaminated by the idea that they were owed a share of someone else's hard-earned income.[10] Sovereign individuals knew they had no obligations to anyone but themselves.

The authors spoke of a return to the diverse political geography of the Middle Ages. "Before the nation-state," they wrote, "it was difficult to enumerate precisely the number of sovereignties that existed in the world because they overlapped in complex ways and many varied forms of organization exercised power. They will do so again. In the new millennium, sovereignty will be fragmented once more."[11] Disintegration would favor the few. "Every time a nation-state cracks up, it will facilitate further devolution and encourage the autonomy of Sovereign Individuals. We expect to see a multiplication of sovereign entities, as scores of enclaves and jurisdictions more akin to city-states emerge from the rubble of nations."[12]

This was a model of capitalism without democracy. Since majoritarian decision-making could not deliver the choices needed for economic survival, democracies would slowly be outcompeted. They would simply wither away, no coups necessary.

The Sovereign Individual has enjoyed an extraordinary afterlife among Silicon Valley libertarians. Marc Andreessen, prominent venture capitalist and co-creator of the first web browser, called it "the most thought-provoking book on the unfolding nature of the 21st Century that I've yet read."[13] Another reader influenced by the book on its release was Peter Thiel, who created the online payment system PayPal partly as an attempt to realize the book's visions of "encrypted cybercash."[14] He said the book made him realize that success came from thinking in the time frame of ten or twenty years in the future.[15]

One of the attractions of *The Sovereign Individual* is how it worked against what could be called the "commune story" of the internet. The commune story finds the origins of Silicon Valley in the failure of the hippie settlements of the 1970s—a failure that led people like Stewart Brand, publisher of the *Whole Earth Catalog*, to try building their utopias in the clean space of computer code rather than the stubborn muck of the outdoors.[16] The "Declaration of Independence of Cyberspace," written by former Grateful Dead songwriter John Perry Barlow and released at the World Economic Forum in Davos in 1996, praised cyberspace as the "new home of the Mind." Casting the web as a kind of psychedelic dreamland, Barlow wrote that "legal concepts of property, expression, identity, movement, and context do not apply to us. They are all based on matter, and there is no matter here."[17]

Anarcho-capitalists, by contrast, argued that matter *did* still apply in the creation of a digitally mediated world, and that property would too. If played right, property could be even more inviolable online than off. No doubt what appealed to a conservative like Thiel about *The Sovereign Individual* was its recognition of this fact and its indifference to the sentimentality of the commune story. Davidson and Rees-Mogg were frank that the rewards of the new paradigm would be distributed unevenly. As they saw it, the internet would not erase distinctions, in a realization of the failed dream of the 1970s, but rather lead to a rightful hardening of hierarchy based on merit. Their vision would be borne out by events. By the year 2000, the most successful companies, including Amazon and eBay, had turned the internet into online shopping malls—privately owned public spaces, where the parameters of your actions were set by the owners, and rents were collected both from your purchases and eventually from the data produced by every motion of your cursor.[18] The actual existing web was not a utopia beyond property; it was a utopia *of* property. It became clear that the new frontier of the web would work like the old frontier: new land to be grabbed by first movers. New territory meant new possibilities of ownership.

2.

Among the most articulate radical capitalist exponents of the new political geography of the virtual world was another fan of *The Sovereign Individual*, Balaji Srinivasan. Born on Long Island in 1980 to Indian immigrant parents, Srinivasan earned a PhD in electrical engineering from Stanford before launching a biotech start-up that offered an at-home genetic screening kit for hereditary diseases. Tipped by *MIT Technology Review* in 2013 as one of the leading "innovators under 35," Srinivasan promptly entered the venture capital world, becoming a principal at Marc Andreessen's firm.[19]

In the heady early 2010s, when the American public was looking to Silicon Valley for solutions for everything from health care to education, Srinivasan became one of the most high-profile advocates for what he called, in a notorious talk, "Silicon Valley's ultimate exit."[20]

By his account, the American Northeast, previously dominant, had entered a permanent and irreversible decline. In an analogy to the Steel Belt of the Midwest, which had become the Rust Belt by the late 1970s, the "Paper Belt" of the Northeast was doomed. The paper he referred to included the laws made in Washington, DC; the newspapers, magazines, and advertising of New York City; and the diplomas of Harvard and Yale.

Srinivasan cited Andreessen on the coming proliferation of countries, as well as Google's Larry Page, who said in 2013 that "maybe we could set apart a piece of the world . . . where people can try new things."[21] Along with Thiel, Srinivasan invested in Curtis Yarvin's company Tlon, devoted to building a new internet that would come closer to his vision of society run as a business.[22]

Srinivasan did not advocate literal exit in the sense of secession. "They have aircraft carriers, we don't," he quipped. But he did introduce a novel variation on the start-up city that he would develop over the next decade. He called it the cloud country.[23] It began from the observation that people were finding new kindred spirits online. The internet had made it possible to form affinity groups and create meaningful bonds without physical connection, often across lines of gender, geography, class, and nationality. "Hundreds of millions of people have now migrated to the cloud," he wrote, "spending hours per day working, playing, chatting, and laughing in real-time HD resolution with people thousands of miles away . . . without knowing their next-door neighbors." The result was a new geography that people had not even begun to map. He described a "cloud cartography" etched out in social networks, "mapping not nation states but states of mind."[24] Where you lived in three dimensions was less important than who you were linked to online.

Secession and exit were emotionally loaded terms, but it was true that people were entering new forms of sociability through voluntary attachments to online games, brands, services, platforms, and companies. Srinivasan pointed to social media. Most people in a city like New York used a service like Facebook every day, but if we weren't one of the company's engineers or marketing executives, we had no way of knowing how many did, where, and for how long. What if the company's flag unfurled from the window of everyone who logged on?[25] Facebook blue would stream in the wind, sometimes covering whole faces of buildings, sometimes ebbing, moving like the shadow of a cloud across the sun. Watching the spreading pattern of flags from week to week and year to year might be startling and begin to look something like a takeover. Facebook went from 1 million monthly active users in 2004 to 2.4 billion by 2019, nearly a third of the world's population. What if we thought of these as defections to a new state in utero?

Connections to these private actors and firms could be a lot stronger than bonds to one's nation. When did people consciously interface with their national government or think about their nationality? If you were a school-age child in the United States, you started every morning by pledging allegiance to the flag, but what about adults? Mouthing the national anthem at the occasional baseball game, showing a passport at the border if you happen to travel, filing your taxes every April, voting every couple of years. By contrast, most Americans clicked the icon of their favored social media platform once, twice, dozens, or even hundreds of times every day. For half a century, intellectuals had criticized the displacement of civic identity by consumerism.[26] Srinivasan flipped the script. Why shouldn't consumerism swallow patriotism? Aren't companies ultimately more benign than the murderous twentieth-century state? What was the body count of Facebook or Google compared to those of Mao Zedong or Adolf Hitler? If the social media companies were dictatorships of a new kind, with power centralized in a CEO, nobody seemed to mind.

The idea of "netizens" and online communities was hardly a new insight; what was novel was the leap that Srinivasan made from elective online communities to the possibility that the cloud might come back down to earth.[27] "Rather than starting with the physical territory, we start with the digital community," he wrote. "We recruit online for a group of people interested in founding a new virtual social network, a new city, and eventually a new country. We build the embryonic state as an open source project, we organize our internal economy around remote work, we cultivate in-person levels of civility, we simulate architecture in VR, and we create art and literature that reflects our values."[28] The numbers of members and perhaps their investments or fees would register on a publicly viewable dashboard, until a tipping point was reached where a spattering of droplets became a cloud—first a cloud town, then a cloud city, and eventually a cloud country.

Srinivasan envisioned two steps toward the destination. To start with, exit would be virtual. People would remain where they lived, but they would be encouraged to imagine their home as an embassy for a future cloud country. Physically, the cloud country would be noncontiguous, but that was no problem. Srinivasan cited the example of Indonesia, an archipelago of more than seventeen thousand islands that nonetheless retained a strong sense of national identity since its independence from Holland in 1945. Why couldn't digital users create their own archipelago? "It can connect a thousand apartments, a hundred houses, and a dozen cul-de-sacs in different cities into a new kind of fractal polity with its capital in the cloud," he wrote.[29]

Much of this already existed. It was possible to use third-party payment systems, open online bank accounts, and register businesses remotely. It was also possible to spend your entire waking day in immersive gaming worlds like *Fortnite*, *Minecraft*, or *Roblox*. Many did. The difference was what Srinivasan saw as the end goal: putting out the flag of the private company to declare membership in a different polity.

Instead of simply being online, you would eventually start "crowdfunding" territory to establish a settlement somewhere on earth.[30] Where this cloud country would be was never mentioned and there was little reason to think Srinivasan would avoid the pitfalls that had sunk so many other would-be founders of micronations in the past. But he was tweaking the usual plotline in his idea of going "cloud first, land last," building up an online customer base as a prelude to settling a new zone.[31] Social media platforms had shown the possibility of scaling up rapidly. Srinivasan put the project in comparative terms. Facebook had 2.89 billion monthly active users, Instagram had 1 billion. By contrast, 20 percent of actual countries in the world had less than a million citizens apiece. These were, as he put it in tech terms, feeble user counts.[32] "Imagine 1000 startup cities around the world competing for residents," he said.[33] The move would be made from the sovereign individual to the "sovereign collective."[34]

Srinivasan's "cloud country" idea of exit was very different from the goldbug scenario of a well-stocked and well-armed hinterland retreat. Such retreats do exist in literature and in reality. Lionel Shriver's novel *The Mandibles*, for example, features the Free State of Nevada, founded after a devastating financial crisis. In the real world, New Hampshire has seen similar efforts from libertarians trying to create a "Free State,"[35] while white supremacists have been moving to the Idaho woods to build a would-be homeland since the 1990s.[36] There are people selling decommissioned missile silos in North Dakota, while Thiel's crowd builds luxury postapocalyptic retreats in New Zealand.[37] Essential to all these scenarios is the isolation of the place, a move back to something more self-sufficient and less dependent on global economic ties. Srinivasan, by contrast, had no interest in either self-sufficiency or roughing it. His model was not Theodore Kaczynski's cabin but Lee Kuan Yew's Singapore. One of his favorite books was Lee's *From Third World to First*.[38] He described his model as "collective exit." "The founder doesn't just move to the cabin," he said. "They whistle for backup and they bring their friends there and turn the cabin into a little settlement and then a town and then a city and then a bigger thing until they outshine the city they left."[39]

Like many tech libertarians, Srinivasan was often at pains to portray his state-building projects as business plans, complete with corporate-style pitch decks and charts. It seemed important for libertarians to insist that they were rejecting the tradition of republican democracy in favor of something more rigorous and empirically driven—"a society funded by subscription and seignorage," as Srinivasan called his cloud country.[40] But the republican political imagination still had a grip even on those who saw themselves seeking an exit from politics. Srinivasan's description of his project as moving from sovereign individuals to the "sovereign collective" sounded very much like the classical notion of groups of people coalescing as a single demos. He referred to those who would create cloud countries as "founders," with deliberate echoes of Silicon Valley but only slightly less obvious echoes of the American Revolution; the Declaration of Independence occasionally appeared in his slide decks.

Unlike Thiel and Friedman, Srinivasan was also notable for his use of the language of democracy. He said that the existing system in a place like the United States was a "51% democracy" while he was advocating "100% democracy," through models where one had to actively opt in.[41] It is only when you look twice that you see that the difference lies in the question of ownership. The basic principle of republican democracy is one person, one vote. Srinivasan's cloud city blueprints were curiously silent on the question of decision-making, but one can assume that they would take their cue from corporate governance: one share, one vote. When asked about property ownership in a future cloud city, Srinivasan surprised the interviewer by replying that an individual would not actually own land—the corporation that developed it would. The individual would instead own a share in the city as a whole.[42] This model made perfect sense in the world of social media platforms. You don't own your Facebook profile; you are granted Facebook's service in exchange for your user data. There was even a real-world example that Srinivasan cited as a model: New Songdo City in South Korea, built by a private corporation in which citizen-customers held shares.[43] The cloud country was a world of terms and conditions rather than rights and obligations. It was a realization of Yarvin's vision of sovcorp, the sovereign corporate republic.

One reason why Srinivasan seemed confident about something as far-fetched as founding a new country may have been that he had done something like it before. He was an active and early player in the world of cryptocurrency, which began with the launch of Bitcoin in 2009. The idea of competing private currencies had been widely discussed in libertarian circles since Friedrich Hayek wrote about the "denationalization of money" in 1976.[44] They had never caught on, partly because of the difficulty of finding the right technical means.

Bitcoin, designed by a mysterious figure named Satoshi Nakamoto, was an ingenious system in which digital "coins" could be securely transferred between participants, with all transactions and holdings recorded on a public ledger called the blockchain. The coins could be "mined"—that is, acquired—by running computer programs solving difficult equations, and the system limited the total number of bitcoins that could ever be mined to twenty-one million. If you distrusted the management of money by the organs of the democratic state, and especially if you were concerned about state-led inflation, this cap on the total bitcoin supply was very appealing. At the same time, the publicly visible blockchain seemed to promise both radical transparency and ironclad protection against meddling. Bitcoin offered the prospect of money beyond central banks. Bringing *The Sovereign Individual*'s "cybercash" into reality would remove the human factor from money. It also offered the tantalizing possibility of substituting technology for trust, enabling algorithmically governed "smart contracts" without judges or courts. In that sense, putting money and laws "on the blockchain" was the ultimate form of exit.

In 2015, Srinivasan left Andreessen Horowitz to work full-time at a new company devoted to mainstreaming Bitcoin.[45] The cryptocurrency was trading at about $258 per bitcoin when he started. Six years later, it peaked at about $58,000, translating into a return on investment of over 24,000 percent. In economic terms, he had borne witness to something as close to magic as you were ever likely to see. To describe the creation of cryptocurrency, Srinivasan reached for a term we have seen earlier in relation to the "joint fantasy" of David Friedman's medieval re-creationism: live action role-playing, or LARPing.

Bitcoin proponents had "LARPed" a currency into existence, he said. They had treated a line of code as if it were money, and enough people were convinced by the quality of their model that it *became* money.[46] It had grown from a figment of an individual's imagination in 2008 to a trillion-dollar part of the world financial system by 2021, with central banks worldwide contemplating their own moves into digital currencies. And if you could LARP money, one of the central filaments of social fabric, then why couldn't you LARP a nation?[47] "Where we are: start your own currency," Srinivasan said in 2017. "Where we will be going to now: start your own country."[48]

Again, this was not quite so wild as it sounded. Political historians have written for decades on the "invented traditions" of modern nationalism: the way that modern nations were, effectively, brought into existence through the creation of mass rituals and pageantry, the codification of language in dictionaries and folk stories in anthologies, the writing and performance of national poems and plays, the erection of monuments, and the formalization of traditional forms of dress.[49]

A classic of cultural history explains how print capitalism created the "imagined communities" of modern nations, as people who read the same newspapers, novels, biographies, and poems began to see themselves as part of a common collective. Sociologists have adapted the point to suggest that online media are having a similar effect, connecting people from all over the globe into new collectives, often based on the anticipation of a future outcome. Retail investors and cryptocurrency enthusiasts alike can become part of such "speculative communities."[50]

Srinivasan praised the internet as a "non-rivalrous frontier," where anybody could re-create themselves and remix their identities.[51] His parents had come to the United States to find opportunity, but the next generation would go to the cloud. A phrase he liked to use to describe this was "reverse diaspora." He saw the real reorganization of global society after the end of the Cold War happening online, as speculative communities rearranged loyalties across national borders (at least insofar as firewalls permitted them). The territorial United States was to the internet what Great Britain had been to the United States in 1776: an incumbent polity destined to be abandoned and superseded.

Srinivasan's tweak to the start-up city model was to suggest that the online and offline worlds might be not alternatives to each other but complementary: you build online first, then you come down to earth. His replacement of the sovereign individual with "the sovereign collective" seemed like a break from Davidson and Rees-Mogg, but the difference was really only semantic. All three saw the same things: the possibility of exit created by new technology, the creation of a new global caste of meritocratic adepts, and the abandonment of the taxing, regulatory state in favor of new affiliations and even new territories organized along the lines of private corporations.

3.

The dream of the cloud country was based on a series of fairly obvious omissions. First of all, lost in Srinivasan's scorn for the Paper Belt was the debt that Silicon Valley owed to it. The internet itself was a paper product, created by government and universities. Srinivasan's former boss Andreessen invented the first web browser at a land-grant university in Illinois. Sergey Brin and Larry Page invented Google on a National Science Foundation grant. The NSF itself built the backbone of the internet before allowing it to be privatized in the 1990s.[52]

Second was the silence on the question of resources. Nothing is created out of thin air. The cloud is anchored in sprawling data centers, which run hot and get cooled by rivers and coal-burning power plants. Cryptocurrency is a particularly notable resource hog. By the early 2020s, its rise in value was putting strains on electrical grids worldwide, as people wired together vast warehouses of computers running day and night to solve the equations that mined new coins. The more people tried to solve the equations, the harder they became. The harder they became, the more the computers needed to run. The more the computers needed to run, the more the strain on power grids. Iran banned bitcoin mining in 2021 after it led to blackouts and possibly the shutdown of a nuclear reactor. China, one of the world's biggest bitcoin producers, banned it, too, leading miners to relocate their rigs to places like Canada, South Dakota, and Texas, sites of more traditional commodity extraction.[53] The annual electricity consumption of bitcoin mining is estimated to be higher than that of the entire country of Sweden.[54] Srinivasan's discussion of cloud country made no mention of energy usage or climate change. The burdens of adjustment to rising tides, floods, fires, and ever more frequent extreme weather events would presumably be borne by others.

Most glaring was the idea of "bare land." Srinivasan swallowed the frontier myth whole.[55] He described himself as part of the "*Oregon Trail* generation," referring to the popular 1980s computer game that let you role-play as a settler in a covered wagon heading westward. In his understanding, US history until the 1890s had been marked by openness, where "anybody could go out West and take a plot of land and turn it into something."[56] He saw the nineteenth century as a time of "equality of opportunity." But opportunity has always depended on who one was. I remember *Oregon Trail*'s glowing green graphics from the school computer lab, too—but I also know that my great-grandfather, a Métis man of mixed Indigenous and European ancestry born in Montana, was ejected with his family from the lands of the American West as an illegal squatter. The bison herds his own father had hunted for trade and survival were dead, and families like his were left to gather bones for sale as fertilizer. The frontier was not a land of freedom for them.[57]

Srinivasan made frequent reference to his own background and the need to draw in those not fortunate enough to be born with the right passport. But his version of the earth operates utterly innocent of the trail of suffering wreaked in the name of the settler-colonial fantasy. Where, after all, is the bare land? Is it in the sparsely populated Canadian North, where Indigenous communities have fought unsuccessfully for centuries for the right to shape the territory that their people have inhabited for millennia? Is it in the Australian West, where the

Rio Tinto mining company dynamited sacred Aboriginal sites for iron ore in 2020? Is it in the South Pacific of French Polynesia, which the French used for nuclear testing into the 1990s? Or is it in the Indonesia that Srinivasan himself cited approvingly, where the Dayak people have been opposing gold-mining companies since the 1960s? These were all dark spaces on the map of the world at night that start-up city champions like Romer used to make their case. But this was a crude cartography of the earth's inhabitants, a PowerPoint slide in place of understanding.

Srinivasan preferred blue-sky (or, better, blank-whiteboard) speculation to real-world examples. Yet one of the successful examples he offered was telling: the state of Israel. This was indeed a reverse diaspora, organized through newspapers and texts that produced a kind of cloud country of a Jewish homeland through the media of the time. Kicked off by the publication of Theodor Herzl's *Jewish State* in 1896, the Zionist plan translated only slowly into facts on the ground through small-scale acts of colonization, which were eventually accepted and given legitimacy by the dominant imperial powers of the day. But consider the consequences of this example. The land in Palestine was no more bare than anywhere else in the world, and it remains rent by competing historical claims over territory. Israel's solution to the problem of demographic and political geography has been to create a two-tier system separating primarily Jewish citizens of the country from Muslim inhabitants of the region. Its fenced boundary—policed by cameras, drones, armed soldiers, and heat-sensing technology at the limit of the technological frontier—puts the Berlin Wall's death strip to shame.[58]

Perhaps there was an honesty in this example. Srinivasan and his fellow tech investors expressed frustration with the problems of San Francisco—a place rife with visible inequality and untreated mental illness, the legacy of centuries of racialized poverty, violence, and discriminatory immigration policy stretching back to the original expropriation of the land on which the city was built. It is clear that Srinivasan, with his resources, could find somewhere better. But as he seemed to admit himself, it would probably look like the state of Israel: militarized, paranoid, defiant—and also very invested in technology. It was not for nothing that a bestselling book on Israel praised by Srinivasan called it the "start-up nation."[59] Here was a template: a cloud country with a twenty-six-foot-tall border wall.

4.

In 2021, Srinivasan wrote that "an evacuation point is an interesting way of thinking about collective exit, about the sovereign collective, about what comes after the sovereign individual. When the state fails, pull the fire alarm and gather your community in a new hub."[60]

Srinivasan thought the trigger for the move to the cloud country had finally come when the COVID-19 pandemic swept the globe in early 2020. He rang the alarm early on the repercussions of the pandemic, foretelling a division of the world map into "green zones" that had contained the virus and "red zones" that had not. First used in West Africa during the Ebola epidemic, such zones, designated by public health officials, seemed poised to become the basis for a new political economy. Color-coded zones were rolled out to control the coronavirus in Malaysia, Indonesia, northern Italy, and France; the strategy was also considered by the White House. India divided its 1.3 billion people into a patchwork of green, yellow, and red zones, with different freedoms and restrictions in each. Global investors took note. The global citizenship broker Henley & Partners forecast that "as the curtain lifts, people will seek to move from poorly governed and ill-prepared 'red zones' to 'green zones' or places with better medical care."[61]

Across the United States, regional "compacts" sprang up as competition intensified for lifesaving ventilators and protective equipment. The atmosphere was one of competitive federalism, with states reconfigured as economic units bidding in a marketplace. Governor Gavin Newsom termed California a "nation-state"; Maryland's governor confessed to keeping COVID-19 tests in an undisclosed location under armed guard, in part to prevent their seizure by federal author-ities.[62]

"We are entering this fractal environment in which the virus breaks centralized states," Srinivasan told a virtual summit organized by Startup Societies Foundation in the spring of 2020. Since the virus does not stop at borders, neither would the process of fragmenta-tion. As regions seal themselves off to prevent contagion, "you can drill down to the state, or even the town or county level," Srinivasan observed. Any state without the virus under control would "face defection" in an intensified contest for talent and capital. After the pandemic has passed, he predicted, "nations are going to turn into effectively vendors and entrepreneurs and relatively mobile people will be applicants."[63] The move to remote work, the reliance on deliv-ery services, and the evaporation of face-to-face interaction, along with increasing fears of urban unrest and uprising—all of this made fertile ground for new settlements in the cloud.

Talk of a "techxodus" picked up during the pandemic. As people increasingly departed the Bay Area to work remotely, the pandemic pushed many of Silicon Valley's elites to the boiling point regarding California and what they saw as its ungrateful political ruling class. "San Francisco's fall will catalyze the rise of startup cities," Srinivasan tweeted in 2020.[64] "Some folks will go remote in the exurbs or rural locales . . . Others may recoalesce around new, themed cities."[65] He hyped Próspera, in which he had invested, and Starbase, a patch of land in Texas bought by Elon Musk to launch SpaceX rockets, which Musk also pictured as a community that would sustain future shuttles commuting to off-world settlements.[66]

In the event, the most important destinations for Srinivasan's col-leagues were less Mars than Mar-a-Lago. Miami opened its arms to the tech sector in 2020, making it what the *Financial Times* hyped as "the most important city in America."[67] Thiel bought two houses on Dubai-like artificial islands near Miami Beach for $18 million.[68] Keith Rabois, a partner at Thiel's venture capital firm, bought a home on the same islands for $29 million.[69] Miami seemed to be simply following the well-worn playbook of Sunbelt cities luring investors through low taxes and light-touch regulation, but Srinivasan hyped it as "the first of a new set of international cloud capitals and start-up cities."[70] He touted Miami as the "Singapore of Latin America," although it would probably be better described as its Dubai: an enclave of conspicuous consumption and a laundromat for dirty money from the region. While Singapore was known for its intolerance of corruption, Florida was among the most corrupt places in the nation.[71]

For all the talk of building from scratch, cloud country boosters were mostly on the lookout for someone willing to give them the infrastructure they needed—from military protection to cheap energy to a docile workforce to an infinity pool and a room with an ocean view. Their metaphors were meteorological, but the reality looked more like something from the animal kingdom: the remora attached to the side of the whale shark of the state. A particularly revealing moment came in 2017, when Thiel was advising Trump on his new cabinet appointments. Srinivasan's Twitter feed suddenly went blank and his name surfaced in the news—as a candidate for the next commissioner of the FDA.[72] It seems the only thing better than exiting the state would be taking it over.

"What's the next step for the global freedom class?" Srinivasan asked in 2021. He himself opted for Singapore, an authoritarian city-state far from the disorder that he complained of in San Francisco. There he launched a more earnest campaign for a cloud country, including an online lecture series and a website that paid people in bitcoins for solving potential future problems for a city built on the blockchain.[73] Srinivasan's writings continued his update of *The Sovereign Individual*, arguing that states do not matter, cryptography had solved the problems of government, and the internet was enabling "a digital Atlantis—a new continent floating in the cloud where old powers compete and new powers arise."[74]

Yet the course of the pandemic had not been kind to his predictions. People did not defect en masse, the center of government held, and state capacity became more important to ordinary people, not less. Cryptocurrency had not changed the nature of the money game—it just added one more horse to bet on. As a speculative asset, bitcoins and other digital tokens rose and fell with the broader stock market, artifacts of a financial moment where liquidity had nowhere to go except to unproductive ends that promised short-term pay-outs. If the goal of blockchain technology was to eliminate the factor of trust, this seemed unwise. A study in the *Lancet* showed that it was precisely "trust in government and interpersonal trust" that correlated with how well a country minimized casualties from the pandemic.[75]

Those seeking an exit in the metaverse would also find nothing of the sort. The platforms that we log on to are owned by private actors. Our every keystroke (and when we are strapped into a VR rig, our every twitch, bend, and nod) is minutely tracked, traced, sorted, cal-ibrated, and sold onward to advertisers and other developers. It says a lot that one of Silicon Valley's most successful companies—Uber—did not offer an empty prairie on which to roam and build. Rather, if you were a driver, it pulled you along like a dog on a leash, punishing you for any deviation while preserving the fiction that you were a free contractor. The metaverse, as one critic has astutely observed, is probably best thought of as a cubicle.[76] The private government of corporations has little space for the alternative visions of collectives, other than those that reproduce its own dominance.

As one of the foundational texts of tech criticism notes, Silicon Valley often forgets its Hegel at its own risk.[77] The German philoso-pher taught that the master is always dependent on the slave. Neither island nor cloud can exist without its underclass. Beyond the masses of app-mediated gig workers, even the vaunted artificial intelligence programs work only because of the often repetitive routines and ef-forts of labor both skilled and unskilled.[78] From Honduras to Dubai, the waged service class is the easiest for the visionaries to forget and the hardest for them to live without. When the COVID-19 pandemic broke out, Singapore initially thought it had flattened the curve, until it was hit by a wave of infections from the migrant workers living in cramped quarters away from the public eye. The city's leaders had seemingly forgotten they existed. The cloud floats because the underclass holds it up. Time will tell if they drop their arms one day and make something new.

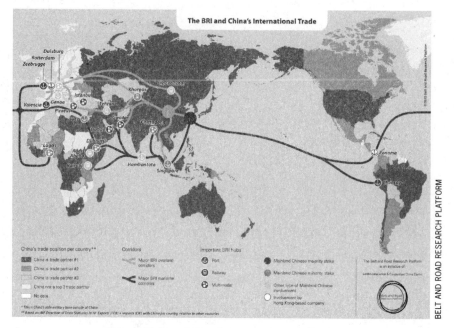

China's Belt and Road Initiative, circa 2021

BE WATER

In early 2022, Patrik Schumacher, the principal of Zaha Hadid Architects, one of the most famous architecture firms in the world, unveiled plans for an extraordinary ensemble of buildings. There were images of galleries and auditoriums, meeting halls and restaurants. They showcased the trademark sweeping, sinewy lines of his architecture, something between art nouveau and the airbrushed art of H. R. Giger.

Schumacher's firm had made its name in megaprojects around the world, from a stadium and an airport in Beijing to the BMW plant in Leipzig to a hotel in Dubai that looked like an ice cube melting from the inside out. Buildings in the works included the Shenzhen Science and Technology Museum, the spaceship-like Shenzhen OPPO headquarters, and the Shenzhen Bay Super Headquarters Base.[1] In Chengdu, a complex was underway called Unicorn Island, named after the term for companies that it hoped to attract: start-ups with valuations over $1 billion apiece.[2] Ad copy for the project spoke of the incentives offered to investors and proclaimed that it "may become the next Silicon Valley."[3]

Most of the work done by Zaha Hadid Architects was in Asia,

specifically in capitalist countries without democracy. Things went faster there, Schumacher explained. He called the Emirates a "research and development lab" for the firm: "We are trying things out for the first time which we wanted to try out, but couldn't."[4] Hong Kong continued to be another such "social experiment."[5] The firm had recently released the concept for a gently twisting high-rise in the Hong Kong city center, touted as the most expensive real estate site in the world.[6]

Although these projects had made headlines worldwide, it was this new one that Schumacher felt came closest to his political principles. A socialist in his younger years, he had been shaken by the global financial crisis in 2008, and turned to the works of Murray Rothbard and Ludwig von Mises, which declared that economic systems built on fiat money were inevitably doomed to failure.[7] The problem, Schumacher felt, was trying to stave off the collapses through bailouts and easy money. The crisis should be allowed to come. He scandalized the architecture world when he laid out this anarcho-capitalist vision at the World Architectural Congress, arguing that governments should abolish all social and affordable housing, eliminate all housing standards, and privatize all streets, squares, public spaces, and parks.[8] The status quo was doomed—"the hope lies in what we dare to build afterwards."[9] The new city he proposed would offer the chance to "irradiate the collective imaginary within the advanced societies, and become a torch leading the way forward for a long overdue political revolution."[10] Utopian architecture had too often tried to work against the trends of the free market and capitalism; he wanted to lean into them.[11]

There was only one problem with Schumacher's new city: it did not exist. It was made of bits and pixels, accessible only through computer interfaces through which you could perambulate as a white-shelled android. The people were simulated and the sky was blank. At the same time, it was more than a video game. As in Balaji Srinivasan's vision, it was a cloud city with coordinates that matched a real patch of territory: a muddy slip of land of just over two square miles, at an elbow of the Danube between Serbia and Croatia. Left unclaimed when Yugoslavia disintegrated in the 1990s, it was symbolically "claimed" in 2015 by an enterprising Czech, who named it Liberland. In addition to its flag and regalia, Liberland had all the traits of a start-up country. All land would belong to the state, as in Singapore; one person, one vote would be replaced by a system weighted to the amount of property owned, as in a gated community. Some parts of the country would be set aside for business, others for pleasure, and a "wild zone" would remain unregulated altogether.[12]

Croatian border guards in speedboats kept the would-be Liber-landers from even setting foot on the land, much less erecting a high-tech enclave there.[13] The project had a near-zero chance of success. So why would the principal of one of the world's highest-paid architecture firms commit so much time and effort to the project of reclaiming a mudflat? Schumacher explained his motivation, disarmingly, by invoking Karl Marx. Marx, he said, had taught that politics reflects changes in the nature of capitalism. In a world based on agriculture, feudalism made sense. When a hereditary elite owned most of the land and the peasants merely tilled it, there was no reason to let them help make decisions. In the age of industrialization, the new class of the bourgeoisie started creatively recombining the world's resources and innovating new technologies, making it rational for a new political form—democracy—to give them a role in managing the state. This was followed by votes for the working class, binding them to the nation.

In the twenty-first century, however, the situation changed again, Schumacher said. As manufacturing grew more automated, and advances in artificial intelligence promised a "man–machine symbiosis" on the horizon, democracy no longer made sense. It was an antique ideology, an artifact of an earlier, superseded moment in the history of capitalism—a dumbly literal reading of the world map, as if everything were penned inside its colored containers. What made sense in the twenty-first century were dots on the map like Liberland: blank-slate enclaves that could be anchor points for virtual enterprises, getaways for the global elite, or new citadels of financial services, marketing, design, software engineering, and other lines of work that needed little more than an electrical outlet and a robust internet connection. "The revolution comes when the political system becomes a barrier to the forces of production," Schumacher said. "And that's what we've reached."[14]

The zone was the political form appropriate to twenty-first-century capitalism. Margaret Thatcher and Ronald Reagan had made progress by privatizing public assets, breaking unions, and reducing top marginal tax rates, but their reforms were too tentative. They clung to the nation form. The pace needed to accelerate. The European Union had to be broken up. Spain, Germany, and Italy had to be broken up too. Schumacher saw crack-up as an ongoing project. "In the next round of crises which are bound to come," he said, maybe a country like Scotland would secede and fail as a socialist project, at which point right-libertarians would come in—the people "who have been predicting this."[15] All that was needed was the courage to imagine what should come after the crash. "Crisis is a galvanizer," he said.[16]

1.

Anarcho-capitalists like Schumacher turned the conventional post–Cold War narrative on its head. Instead of democratic capitalism flowing outward from a Western source, they saw a more efficient, nondemocratic form of capitalism, perfected in Asia, rolling westward to revive the "sclerotic European race."[17] Instead of regarding places like China as monoliths, they saw them as patchworks of law, status, and access—a model of "fragmented authoritarianism."[18]

As China oriented its economy to global trade since the 1970s, it used zones to subdivide the nation. By the 2010s, it was also creating zones far from its own territory. Under the Belt and Road Initiative, launched in 2013, China funded infrastructure stretching from its own borders through chains of zones, reaching out to Turkey, Kenya, and beyond. A high-speed rail line was built running through Laos and Cambodia and down the Malay Peninsula to Singapore.[19] The Belt and Road Initiative bought the Greek port of Piraeus, in Athens, and funded outposts in the London Docklands. Chinese companies took over the Djibouti harbor from Dubai's DP World, and spent $4 billion on a railway connecting Djibouti to the much larger Ethiopia, a country of a hundred million next door.[20] China also built a military base in Djibouti, its first one overseas, alongside the bases of France, Japan, and the United States.[21] In Sri Lanka, a Chinese company signed a ninety-nine-year lease for a deepwater port and invested in an adjacent "Port City" the size of Central London.[22] In El Salvador, a Chinese conglomerate proposed a series of zones that would involve a hundred-year lease on one-sixth of the country's territory.[23] Although proceeding in an often haphazard and unplanned way, the Chinese government and Chinese corporations were establishing enclaves that resembled the concessions imposed on them a century and a half earlier.[24]

"You could say that these Chinese companies are like the British East India Company of our days," said one diplomat after China signed a long-term lease for a port in the Solomon Islands. "They are the vanguard of their nation's push into new markets and new spheres of influence." A local resident asked: "Are they looking at turning Solomon Islands into a colony?" It makes more sense to say they are turning the country into a zone. Special economic zones on islands of the Philippines; fishery zones off leased islands near Papua New Guinea; an economic development zone along the railway in Cambodia; a proposal to build a rival to the Panama Canal through Nicaragua—despite all the talk of "deglobalization," China seems to be continuing with many of the familiar techniques of the last half century.[25] Its vision is of corridors—seaways, highways, and railways—linking nodes of capitalism across borders.[26]

China follows well-worn tracks, retracing the network of coaling stations and free ports that upheld the British Empire in the nineteenth century. Other countries also draw on earlier precedents of extraterritoriality. Since the sixteenth century, the Ottoman sultan had granted citizens of some Western nations immunity from local law and the right to be tried in their own courts through so-called capitulations—a practice perceived by Western nations as a symptom of its supposed civilizational inferiority.[27] In 2017, Saudi Arabia, under Ottoman rule until the 1920s, announced a spectacular extraterritorial zone near the Jordanian and Egyptian border: a $500 billion megaproject called NEOM with backing from some of the world's biggest investors.[28] Planned from scratch, NEOM is intended to cover over ten thousand square miles of desert and Red Sea coastline. The plans include a "linear city" with a pair of twin skyscrapers to stretch horizontally for dozens of miles, billed as "the largest buildings ever constructed."[29] The scheme is not only a feat of architecture and engineering (and, arguably, magical thinking when it comes to water procurement) but also a laboratory of private government. It is to be run by shareholders rather than the Saudi state—"an autonomous government whose laws will be chartered by investors."[30] Shares are to be sold on the Saudi stock exchange. The only obligation of the NEOM board of directors would be protecting the shareholders' investment. The Saudi crown prince Mohammed bin Salman has called it "the first zone floated in the public markets" and "the first capitalist city in the world."[31]

"There is nothing in the desert," reads a line from *Lawrence of Arabia*, yet even here the land was not empty. Twenty thousand Bedouins had to be cleared from the region. One who resisted removal was shot dead.[32] As of 2022, ten thousand workers were beginning construction, including on a floating automated port and logistics hub called Oxagon.[33] Part of NEOM's sales pitch is the promise that the labor problem bedeviling the Gulf will eventually be solved by robots. In a country where about a third of the residents are expats, there was a public relations blitz around the granting of Saudi citizenship to a humanoid robot—the first time in the world a machine received legal personhood.[34] Her name was Sophia, she wore a power suit, and she was bald, presumably as a way around the Saudi norm of women not showing their hair in public.

Meanwhile, keen to join the club of dynamic Asian juggernauts after leaving the European Union, Britain has sought out partners on the Arabian Peninsula. Dubai—whose DP World bought the storied P&O Shipping Line and built the London Gateway port—has figured particularly prominently. The CEO of DP World UK sat on the post-Brexit trade advisory board.[35] Through its new state investment arm, Britain became a junior partner in DP World's development of three African ports, including the one in Somaliland. A major player in London's post-Brexit scheme for a "Singapore-style" free port, DP World was slated to harvest £50 million in direct subsidies and ongoing tax breaks for its investments in the program.[36] An economic advisor insisted that it is necessary to compete with the enticements offered by similar zones in the Middle East. "Our freeports are only going to work if we think of them as being little offshore islands," he said.[37]

The risks of bargaining away slivers of sovereignty became clear in 2022 when DP World–owned P&O Ferries, seeking to lower the wages it was paying, fired its entire workforce of eight hundred employees without warning on a single day. Asked why the company did not try to negotiate with the union first, the CEO said that it would have been a waste of time because no union would ever have accepted their terms.[38] The workers were welcome to come back—at an hourly wage of £5.15, barely half the British minimum wage.[39] How could P&O do this? Through a trick of the zone. The ships sailed from UK ports, but they flew flags of Bermuda, the Bahamas, and Cyprus, and operated under *their* labor laws. They were in British waters but not of Britain. Such fiascos did not deter others from dealing with Dubai. Just weeks after the mass firing, Quebec's public pension fund announced a $2.5 billion investment in DP World, the first major foreign direct stake in the state-owned company.[40] The retirement savings of Canada's second-largest province now rested on the emirate's global pursuit of profit.

2.

Hong Kong and Singapore, London and Liechtenstein, Somalia and Dubai: what we are seeing is not the union of capitalism and democracy but their increasing divergence. The relative performance of the different nations in the early twenty-first century has only made the story line clearer. Undemocratic capitalism is the winning brand. Libertarians' expressions of admiration for authoritarian Asian governments are more common all the time. In a conversation with a young Bitcoin guru who had just moved from Australia to Dubai to escape COVID lockdown, the president of the Mises Institute applauded the efficiency of places like the Emirates and Singapore. He took the lesson of the pandemic to be that freedoms were provisional everywhere and could be removed at a moment's notice. "In Singapore, things work. In Dubai, things work." he said. "If we're increasingly becoming authoritarian in the West, you can be authoritarian and nothing works or you can be authoritarian and things work."[41]

Looking around the world, one sees zones everywhere. During the pandemic, China moved forward with plans to turn the island of Hainan into a special economic zone with tax holidays for investors, duty-free shopping, and relaxed regulations on pharmaceuticals and medical procedures.[42] As a development strategy in Africa, zones are "on a steep upward trend and projected to proliferate in a large majority of countries."[43] Postapartheid South Africa is a galaxy of privately owned and managed enclaves.[44] Indian prime minister Narendra Modi's government, often described purely in terms of its Hindu chauvinism, has been ramping up special economic zones. "Lots of business will be shifted from Singapore and Dubai because of these incentives," says the government representative in charge.[45] Hungary has turned to a more nationalist form of economic development, yet at the same time it opened new special economic zones for Korean investment.[46] The City of London is returning to its twentieth-century roots by trying to invent itself as an offshore market for cryptocurrency banking, doubling down on the one thing it has been able to do well: take fees to move money around for the benefit of a tiny stratum of the wealthy.[47] The tallest pencil tower yet opened in Manhattan in 2022, twenty-four times higher than it is wide. Prices for an apartment ranged from around $8 million to $66 million. "This isn't housing," one sociologist noted. "It isn't serving any social purpose. It's a luxury good, more like a land-bound yacht."[48] Dubai real estate got a boost from the pandemic, with a record-breaking number of properties sold. New homeowners included "Afghan warlords and the political elite from countries like Nigeria, Syria and Lebanon, all searching for a safe place to park their savings."[49]

Zones are everywhere, but contrary to the rhetoric of boosters, they do not seem to be creating islands of liberation from the state. Rather, states are using them as tools to advance their own purposes. NEOM is a telling example. Saudi Arabia, an economy owned and operated by a royal family, is contracting with the Chinese company Huawei to wire its agglomeration in the desert as a "smart city."[50] As one consultant conceded, zones have proceeded through government-enabled confiscation, running roughshod over basic libertarian principles of property rights.[51] Creating a land market in rural China, for example, was projected to leave 110 million villagers without land by 2030.[52] Zones are not turning the world into a patchwork of a thousand private polities in dynamic competition. They are strengthening the position of a handful of state capitalist superpowers.

In a new preface to *The Sovereign Individual*, written in 2020, Peter Thiel said that the rise of China was the one megatrend that the book had missed. But, he asked, was China so different after all? Despite the fact that the ruling party still had the word *communist* in its name, it showed little interest in redistributive equality. Instead, it was happily playing the game of winner-take-all capitalism and "jurisdictional competition," allowing investors to shop between territories for laws that suited them best.[53] Thiel himself has rethought his antipathy toward government.[54] After he supported and helped advise President Trump, his company Palantir began securing major contracts with Immigration and Customs Enforcement and the US military.[55] In

2022, Palantir was in discussions to begin managing the crown jewel of the British welfare state, the National Health Service.[56] The science fiction author and international lawyer China Miéville once argued that exit is for losers. Good capitalists know the real game is capturing the existing state, not going through the hassle of creating a new one.[57] Thiel seemed to agree that a world of one thousand new state contracts was preferable to one of a thousand nations.[58]

Besides, the United States itself looks more like a zone all the time. In 2022, it edged out Switzerland, Singapore, and the Cayman Islands to take the top spot in an index of financial secrecy, crowned as the best place in the world to illegally hide or launder assets.[59] Its own status as a democracy has been called into question. It was briefly downgraded by a well-respected index to a so-called anocracy, a system mixing features of democratic and autocratic rule.[60] Soon, Americans may no longer need to go elsewhere to realize the perfect zone. What one scholar calls the "boomerang effect" may bring those zone policies back home.[61]

3.

Where the secessionist dream lives on, it is often overlaid with a hint of panic. Partly this is a matter of political polarization. In the United States, deep animosity toward and even fear of political opponents have driven support for the breakup of the country higher than ever before.[62] Talk of a "national divorce" has become commonplace; in late 2021, 50 percent of Trump voters and 40 percent of Biden voters were sympathetic to the idea of splitting the country.[63] In the UK, the prospect of Scotland, which voted for increased self-rule in the 1990s, leaving the union altogether seems ever stronger in the wake of Brexit. In Spain, Catalonia remains in low-level conflict with the central government in Madrid over the suppression of its separatist ambitions.[64]

Secessionism is also driven by a desire for a flight to safety. From the pandemic to climate change, the zone has come to figure ever more as a refuge. In the decade since "seasteading" efforts first launched, it has become routine to frame enclave-building projects in terms of climate. Overnight, projects that continue to look like varieties of gated communities have begun to be pitched as models of sustainability, responsible solutions to sea-level rise, and paragons of a low-carbon lifestyle. NEOM, for example, is sold as a net-zero city, with promises to include all amenities within walking distance and convert the sand of the desert into silicon for solar panels. Eko Atlantic, a luxury community for 250,000 being built by a billionaire on an artificial island in Lagos, Nigeria, comes with its own flood defense.[65] (The anchor tenant is to be a half-billion-dollar US consulate.)[66] Dubai's artificial archipelago, built through destruction of local reefs and the importing of sand from as far away as Australia, is also now perversely pitched as a climate-friendly environment. Its most grotesque feature is the Heart of Europe, being built on and around Germany Island in the man-made archipelago. The brainchild of Josef Kleindienst, a former Austrian police officer and high-ranking member of the Far Right Freedom Party, the Heart of Europe will include, among other things, Oktoberfest, German Christmas markets, Swiss timber chalets, olive trees imported from Andalusia, villas modeled on Viking longboats, and a mechanism for creating a rainy and even snow-covered street—all packaged as "the world's most sustainable tourism project."[67]

A different kind of zone that recurs in climate discussions is the idea of the *sacrifice zone*, an area where human settlements are abandoned to sea-level rise. Globally, new forms of inequality are already coming into focus, as poorer communities are designated as sacrifice zones and enter "managed retreat" while richer areas begin to plan for seawalls, berms, dikes, and other forms of containment.[68] When the Seasteading Institute had a short-lived partnership with the South Pacific nation of Tahiti, its executives spoke in rather vague ways about how its floating structures could provide an alternative space of habitation for Tahitian residents as sea levels continue to rise.[69] Beyond the obvious question of looming extreme weather patterns that would likely destroy such structures, the vision of how, in fact, the locals would be folded into the new Waterworld was little discussed. Would they be full members or a permanent underclass?

This was the zone as lifeboat—or, more likely, as cruise ship. It is telling that cruise ships are such a common point of reference for advocates of start-up societies: the floating resorts are microcosms of racialized hierarchy, picking and choosing from the world's laws to keep the workforce as disempowered as possible.[70] One promoter of start-up societies wrote of the superluxury cruise ship *The World* as a model for a future seastead or private city.[71] Instead of cabins rented to vacationers, the ship had residences with permanent owners, who could check in and out as it circled the globe. But at the outbreak of the pandemic, these vessels of escapism became petri dishes of contagion. In March 2020, after being at sea continually for eighteen years, *The World* evacuated its passengers and entered hibernation in the Canary Islands.[72] The dream of extra-national escape revealed itself to be uncomfortably tethered to the existing world of nations.

4.

No matter the rhetoric, zones are tools of the state, not liberation from it. No matter the exit fantasies, zones cannot escape the earth. The third truth about them is perhaps the most banal but most consequential: zones have inhabitants. There is no such thing as a blank slate.

We can see this clearly back in the ur-zone of Hong Kong. I began this book with Milton Friedman gazing out affectionately at the city's skyline, which he imagined as a perfect container for the conduct of capitalism, with decision-making insulated from disruptions by the absence of democratic elections. In 2017, when I presented an early version of that chapter at the University of Hong Kong, a professor from the law school laughed. Milton's description of a quiescent city-state was borderline ridiculous in the middle of one of the most convulsive periods in Hong Kong history, with the population taking to the streets time and again to demand political self-determination. A few months before I gave my talk, two newly elected lawmakers had been barred from taking their positions because they had expressed Hong Kong nationalism and cursed China while taking their oaths of office.[73] A few years earlier, the Occupy Central movement had stopped traffic on the city's main artery for seventy-nine days.

I realized later that I was giving my talk in a landmark year. It had been twenty years since the handover, with thirty years left until the planned end of "one country, two systems" with Hong Kong's full reabsorption into China. Riding through the city on a bus, I passed by Hong Kong Polytechnic University. The kids in their Flyknit sneakers, with plastic figurines bouncing off their backpacks, gave no hint of the fact that many of them would be combatants on a battlefield on this very campus just two years later. In September 2019, Polytechnic University became the scene of an almost medieval siege, with protesters using slingshots and catapults to launch bricks at the police from inside while tear gas and hoses of blue ink assaulted them from outside.[74] The promise of democracy buried in the Basic Law, which Hong Kong activists had tried to pry out and make real, was being denied and snuffed out again.

In 2020, as Beijing grew concerned about a rising wave of pro-democracy candidates within Hong Kong's rubber-stamp government, a national security law was imposed from the mainland that made it illegal to call for secession. Critical newspapers closed down, and once-open critiques of Beijing went silent. Politicians, professors, lawyers, and journalists associated with the pro-democracy movement were arrested, their previous social media posts and utterances now retroactively made grounds for persecution. Speedboats were intercepted as pro-democracy activists attempted to flee to Taiwan. What neoliberals once praised as "Adam Smith's other island" had become a new kind of East Berlin—but an odd one, where international capital still enjoyed the full freedom of movement.[75]

Hong Kong has always been marked by what one book famously calls the politics of disappearance.[76] Its smallness has brought with it both extraordinary success and the vertiginous feeling of proximity to extinction. In the 1994 anime series *Genocyber*, the city is destroyed at the end of the first episode. The intertitle reads: "On that day, Hong Kong mysteriously exploded and vanished from the face of the earth." It now looks like this might be coming to pass, politically by diktat, infrastructurally by degrees. Plans are advancing for the absorption of Hong Kong into the Greater Bay Area, a single vast mega-cluster that includes Shenzhen, Guangzhou, and Macao.[77] Hong Kong's leading position in finance and shipping had already been chipped away. The Shanghai Stock Exchange is on the rise as an alternative site for IPOs. In 2012, Hong Kong was the third-biggest container port in the world, after Shanghai and Singapore; by 2020 it had slipped to number eight, passed by four Chinese ports along with Busan, South Korea.[78] The same year, the United States revoked its status as a separate customs territory. "Made in Hong Kong" became simply "Made in China." The neoliberals themselves have lost faith. In 2021, the new edition of the Heritage Foundation index of economic freedom was released with an absence at the top.[79] For them, too, Hong Kong had vanished into the mainland.

But Hong Kong, as one native son writes, is "a city that refuses to die."[80] How will it live on? One popular proposal imagines it as a city-state in the style of the early modern empire, with devolved power and a high degree of autonomy within a Chinese federation. Some are demanding outright independence for Hong Kong; others hold out for rejoining a China that had been itself democratized.[81] Some imagine a reconstituted Hong Kong in exile. Tycoon Ivan Ko, advised by some of the same people behind Próspera, has been exploring the possibility for an escape pod of Hong Kong émigrés, a charter city implanted on the Irish coastline.[82]

When the Hong Kong activists demanding democracy and self-determination in 2019 faced ever-harsher repression from the police, they found a way to engage with both the authorities and the city through rapidly shifting protests. They borrowed a term from one of their city's icons, Bruce Lee. "Be water," they said, and faced down sixteen thousand rounds of tear gas. What this means might only be discovered in the process of becoming.

NOTES

INTRODUCTION

1. Peter Thiel, "Back to the Future" (keynote speech), Seasteading Institute Conference, September 29, 2009, San Francisco, CA, video, 30:55, https://vimeo.com/7577391.
2. Peter Thiel, "The Education of a Libertarian," *Cato Unbound*, April 13, 2009, https://www.cato-unbound.org/2009/04/13/peter-thiel/education-libertarian.
3. Thiel, "Back to the Future."
4. After writing this passage, I came across a similar thought experiment in a book supported financially by the Charles Koch Foundation. See Tom Bell, *Your Next Government?: From the Nation State to Stateless Nations* (Cambridge: Cambridge University Press, 2017), 1; for pioneering work on zones, see Aihwa Ong, *Neoliberalism as Exception: Mutations in Citizenship and Sovereignty* (Durham, NC: Duke University Press, 2006); Keller Easterling, *Extrastatecraft: The Power of Infrastructure Space* (New York: Verso, 2014); Ronen Palan, *The Offshore World: Sovereign Markets, Virtual Places, and Nomad Millionaires* (Ithaca, NY: Cornell University Press, 2003); Nicholas Shaxson, *Treasure Islands: Tax Havens and the Men Who Stole the World* (New York: St. Martin's Griffin, 2011); and Patrick Neveling, "Free Trade Zones, Export Processing Zones, Special Economic Zones and Global Imperial Formations 200 BCE to 2015 CE," in *The Palgrave Encyclopedia of Imperialism and Anti-Imperialism*, ed. Immanuel Ness and Zak Cope (Basingstoke, UK: Palgrave Macmillan, 2015).
5. François Bost, "Special Economic Zones: Methodological Issues and Definition," *Transnational Corporations* 26, no. 2 (2019): 142. One scholar solves the problem by simply referring to the capitalized Zone. Jonathan

Bach, "Modernity and the Urban Imagination in Economic Zones," *Theory, Culture & Society* 28, no. 5 (2011): 99–100.

6. Aihwa Ong, "Graduated Sovereignty in South-East Asia," *Theory, Culture & Society* 17, no. 4 (2000): 68.

7. Gabriel Zucman, *The Hidden Wealth of Nations* (Chicago: University of Chicago Press, 2015).

8. Gabriel Zucman, "How Corporations and the Wealthy Avoid Taxes (and How to Stop Them)," *New York Times*, November 10, 2017, https://www .nytimes.com/interactive/2017/11/10/opinion/gabriel-zucman-paradise -papers-tax-evasion.html.

9. Oliver Bullough, *Moneyland: Why Thieves and Crooks Now Rule the World and How to Take It Back* (London: Profile Books, 2018), 53, 79.

10. "Obama Targets Cayman 'Tax Scam,'" *PolitFact*, January 9, 2008, https:// www.politifact.com/article/2008/jan/09/obama-targets-cayman-islands -tax-scam/.

11. As is often pointed out, the United States itself is one of the world's biggest tax havens. Ana Swanson, "How the U.S. Became One of the World's Biggest Tax Havens," *Washington Post*, April 5, 2016, https://www.washingtonpost .com/news/wonk/wp/2016/04/05/how-the-u-s-became-one-of-the-worlds -biggest-tax-havens/.

12. In 2019, the United Nations Conference on Trade and Development (UNCTAD) proposed referring to all zones as *special economic zones*. This does not include the zone-like tax havens. UNCTAD, *World Investment Report: Special Economic Zones* (Geneva: United Nations, 2019), xii.

13. The United States has almost three hundred such foreign-trade zones.

14. Tim Looser, "21st Century City Form in Asia: The Private City," in *The Routledge Handbook of Anthropology and the City*, ed. Setha Low (New York: Routledge, 2018).

15. Kimberly Adams and Benjamin Payne, "Nevada Considers Bringing Back the 'Company Town' for the Tech Industry," *Marketplace*, June 30, 2021, https://www.marketplace.org/shows/marketplace-tech/nevada-considers -bringing-back-the-company-town-for-the-tech-industry/.

16. Quinn Slobodian, "Rishi Sunak's Free Ports Plan Reinvents Thatcherism for the Johnson Era," *Guardian* (UK edition), March 1, 2020, Global Newsstream.

17. Grégoire Chamayou, *The Ungovernable Society* (Cambridge: Polity, 2021), 231.

18. Bost, "Special Economic Zones," 151.

19. Stuart M. Butler, "The Enterprise Zone as a Political Animal," *Cato Journal* 2, no. 2 (Fall 1982): 374.

20. Lionel Shriver, *The Mandibles: A Family, 2029–2047* (New York: Harper Perennial, 2016), 48.

21. Jeff Deist, "The Prospects for Soft Secession in America," *Mises Wire*, September 21, 2021, https://mises.org/wire/prospects-soft-secession-america.

22. Jeff Deist, "Secession Begins at Home," LewRockwell.com, January 31, 2015, https://www.lewrockwell.com/2015/01/jeff-deist/secession-begins-at-home/.

23. Stephen Graham and Simon Marvin, *Splintering Urbanism: Networked Infrastructures, Technological Mobilities and the Urban Condition* (London: Routledge, 2001), 272.

24. Ola Uduku, "Lagos: 'Urban Gating' as the Default Condition," in *Gated Communities: Social Sustainability in Contemporary and Historical Gated Developments*, ed. Samer Bagaeen and Ola Uduku (London: Earthscan, 2010).

25. Sanjay Srivastava, *Entangled Urbanism: Slum, Gated Community, and Shopping Mall in Delhi and Gurgaon* (New York: Oxford University Press, 2014).

26. Michael P. Gibson, "The Nakamoto Consensus—How We End Bad Governance," *Medium*, April 3, 2015, https://medium.com/@William_Blake/the-nakamoto-consensus-how-we-end-bad-governance-2d75b2fa1f65.

27. Albert O. Hirschman, *Exit, Voice and Loyalty: Responses to Decline in Firms, Organizations, and States* (Cambridge, MA: Harvard University Press, 1970).

28. Bruce Sterling, *Islands in the Net* (New York: Arbor House, 1988), 17.

29. Stéphane Rosière and Reece Jones, "Teichopolitics: Re-considering Globalisation Through the Role of Walls and Fences," *Geopolitics* 17, no. 1 (2012): 218.

30. For these two points and a powerful interpretation see Wendy Brown, *Walled States, Waning Sovereignty* (New York: Zone Books, 2010), 35.

31. For documentation see the International Organization on Migration's Missing Migrants Project, https://missingmigrants.iom.int/region/mediterranean.

32. Francis Fukuyama, "The End of History?," *National Interest*, no. 16 (Summer 1989): 3–18.

33. Angus Cameron and Ronen Palan, *The Imagined Economies of Globalization* (London: Sage, 2003), 157; and Vanessa Ogle, "Archipelago Capitalism: Tax Havens, Offshore Money, and the State, 1950s–1970s," *American Historical Review* 122, no. 5 (December 2017).

34. Thomas Piketty, *Capital in the Twenty-First Century* (Cambridge, MA: Belknap Press of Harvard University Press, 2014); Zucman, *Hidden Wealth of Nations*.

35. Chuck Collins, *The Wealth Hoarders: How Billionaires Pay Millions to Hide Trillions* (London: Polity, 2021).

36. Raymond Plant, "Restraint and Responsibility," *Times* (London), October 16, 1990, The Times Digital Archive, Gale.

37. Andrew Kaczynski and Paul LeBlanc, "Trump's Fed Pick Stephen Moore Is a Self-Described 'Radical' Who Said He's Not a 'Big Believer in Democracy,'" CNN.com, April 13, 2019, https://www.cnn.com/2019/04/12/politics/stephen-moore-kfile/index.html.
38. Deist, "Soft Secession in America."
39. Hari Kunzru, *Red Pill* (New York: Knopf, 2020), 226.

CHAPTER 1: TWO, THREE, MANY HONG KONGS

1. Patri Friedman, "TSI Strategy & Status: The Future" (speech), Seasteading Institute Conference, September 29, 2009, San Francisco, CA, video, 26:42, https://vimeo.com/8354001.
2. Patri Friedman, "Beyond Folk Activism," *Cato Unbound*, April 6, 2009, https://www.cato-unbound.org/2009/04/06/patri-friedman/beyond-folk-activism.
3. Patri Friedman and Brad Taylor, "Seasteading: Competitive Governments on the Ocean," *Kyklos* 65 (May 2012): 225.
4. Friedman and Taylor, "Seasteading," 230.
5. Friedman, "Beyond Folk Activism."
6. Chris Ip, "Hong Kong Is Model for Ocean Utopias," *South China Morning Post*, December 4, 2011, Global Newsstream.
7. Milton Friedman, *Capitalism and Freedom* (Chicago: University of Chicago Press, 2002), ix.
8. Friedman, "TSI Strategy & Status."
9. Let a Thousand Nations Bloom home page, (capture March 2, 2013), https://athousandnations.com.
10. Michel J. Crozier, Samuel P. Huntington, and Joji Watanuki, *The Crisis of Democracy* (New York: New York University Press, 1975), 2.
11. Peter Brimelow, "Why Liberalism Is Now Obsolete: An Interview with Nobel Laureate Milton Friedman," *Forbes*, December 12, 1988, 176.
12. "Hong-Kong," *Penny Magazine of the Society for the Diffusion of Useful Knowledge*, December 24, 1842, 500.
13. Barry Naughton, *The Chinese Economy: Transitions and Growth* (Cambridge, MA: MIT Press, 2007), 42; and John M. Carroll, *A Concise History of Hong Kong* (Lanham, MD: Rowman & Littlefield, 2007), 68.
14. Maria Adele Carrai, *Sovereignty in China: A Genealogy of a Concept Since 1840* (Cambridge: Cambridge University Press, 2019), 51.
15. Wellington Koo quoted in Maria Adele Carrai, "China's Malleable Sovereignty Along the Belt and Road Initiative: The Case of the 99-Year Chinese Lease of Hambantota Port," *Journal of International Law & Politics* (2019): 1078.
16. Eunice Seng, *Resistant City: Histories, Maps and the Architecture of Development* (Singapore: World Scientific, 2020), 94.

17. Lawrence Mills, *Protecting Free Trade: The Hong Kong Paradox 1947–97* (Hong Kong: Hong Kong University Press, 2012), 33.

18. Naughton, *The Chinese Economy*, 35.

19. Yin-Ping Ho, *Trade, Industrial Restructuring and Development in Hong Kong* (London: Palgrave Macmillan, 1992), 173.

20. Mills, *Protecting Free Trade*, 8.

21. Y. C. Jao, "The Rise of Hong Kong as a Financial Center," *Asian Survey* 19, no. 7 (July 1979): 686.

22. Alvin Y. So, "The Economic Success of Hong Kong: Insights from a World-System Perspective," *Sociological Perspectives* 29, no. 2 (April 1986): 249.

23. Jao, "Rise of Hong Kong," 677.

24. Jamie Peck, "Milton's Paradise: Situating Hong Kong in Neoliberal Lore," *Journal of Law and Political Economy* 1, no. 1 (2021): 192.

25. "Uncle Miltie," *Time*, March 10, 1980, https://content.time.com/time/subscriber/article/0,33009,950360,00.html.

26. James C. Roberts, "Milton Friedman, Superstar," *Human Events*, November 22, 1980, 40.

27. Mark Tier, "Hong Kong," *Reason*, June 1977, 60.

28. Simon Hoggart, "Where Even the Poor Are Rich," *Observer*, February 28, 1982.

29. "The Power of the Market," *Free to Choose*, https://www.youtube.com/watch?v=dngqR9gcDDw.

30. See Melinda Cooper, *Family Values: Between Neoliberalism and the New Social Conservatism* (New York: Zone, 2017).

31. Catherine Schenk, "Negotiating Positive Non-interventionism: Regulating Hong Kong's Finance Companies, 1976–1986," *China Quarterly*, no. 230 (June 2017): 350.

32. Jon Woronoff, *Hong Kong: Capitalist Paradise* (Hong Kong: Heinemann, 1980), 232.

33. Alvin Rabushka, *The Changing Face of Hong Kong: New Departures in Public Policy* (Washington, DC: American Enterprise Institute for Public Policy Research, 1973), 2.

34. Alvin Rabushka, *Hong Kong: A Study in Economic Freedom* (Chicago: Graduate School of Business, University of Chicago, 1979), 67.

35. Rabushka, *Hong Kong*, 33, 39.

36. Rabushka, 64.

37. The Liberty Fund, "Hong Kong: A Story of Human Freedom and Progress," 1981, https://www.youtube.com/watch?v=RchkEruI1FA.

38. Rabushka, *Changing Face*, 1.

39. Carroll, *Concise History*, 171.

40. Steve Lohr, "Unabashedly, the Business of Hong Kong Is Money," *New York Times*, September 27, 1982, ProQuest Historical Newspapers.

41. See, for example, F. A. Hayek, "A Rebirth of Liberalism," *Freeman*, July 28, 1952, 731.

42. For a thorough insider history of the libertarian movement, see Brian Doherty, *Radicals for Capitalism: A Freewheeling History of the Modern American Libertarian Movement* (New York: PublicAffairs, 2007).

43. Stanford University, Hoover Institution Archives, F. A. Hayek Papers, Box 34, Folder 10, MPS Hong Kong, List of Guests.

44. Rosemary McClure, "Hong Kong: Mandarin Celebrates Its First 50 Years and Its Next 50," *Los Angeles Times*, February 15, 2013, ProQuest Historical Newspapers.

45. "Film Designer Who Built the Replica of the Bridge on the River Kwai and Later Created Interiors for Luxury Hotels," *Daily Telegraph* (UK), September 1, 2004, Westlaw; and William Rees-Mogg, "When Is a Bribe Just a Friendly Gesture?," *Times* (London), November 7, 1994, The Times Digital Archive, Gale.

46. Henry Wai-chung Yeung, *Transnational Corporations and Business Networks: Hong Kong Firms in the ASEAN Region* (London: Routledge, 1998), 74.

47. Nancy Yanes Hoffman, "Clavell Can Tell Hong Kong Fortunes," *Los Angeles Times*, May 3, 1981, ProQuest Historical Newspapers.

48. Terry Teachout, "James Clavell, Storyteller," *National Review*, November 12, 1982, 1422.

49. Jennifer Burns, *Goddess of the Market: Ayn Rand and the American Right* (Oxford: Oxford University Press, 2009); and Marsha Familaro Enright, "James Clavell's Asian Adventures," Atlas Society, https://www.atlassociety.org/post/james-clavells-asian-adventures.

50. Linda Ashland, "Hong Kong's New Taipans," *Town & Country*, May 1980, 133.

51. Carroll, *Concise History*, 160–62; and Ho-Fung Hung, *City on the Edge: Hong Kong Under Chinese Rule* (Cambridge: Cambridge University Press, 2022), 154.

52. Seng, *Resistant City*, 91.

53. John Chamberlain, "There'll Always Be a Hong Kong," *Human Events*, October 14, 1978, 13.

54. Michael Ng-Quinn, "Living on Borrowed Time in a Borrowed Place," *San Francisco Examiner*, September 14, 1981, Newspapers.com.

55. Tim Summers, *China's Hong Kong*, 2nd ed. (London: Agenda, 2021), 17.

56. Lorenz Langer, "Out of Joint?—Hong Kong's International Status from the Sino-British Joint Declaration to the Present," *Archiv des Völkerrechts* 46, no. 3 (September 2008).

57. Chamberlain, "There'll Always Be," 13.

58. Robert Poole Jr., "The China Decision," *Reason*, March 1979, 6.

59. "Hong-Kong," 501.

60. Geoffrey Howe, *Conflict of Loyalty* (New York: St. Martin's, 1994), 318.

61. Margaret Thatcher, "Interview for Wall Street Journal," January 24, 1990, https://www.margaretthatcher.org/document/107876.

62. Margaret Thatcher, *The Downing Street Years* (New York: HarperCollins, 1993), 259.

63. Confidential Annex to Minutes of Full Cabinet, September 30, 1982, https://www.margaretthatcher.org/document/123921.

64. Thatcher, "Wall Street Journal."

65. This had also been proposed for the Falklands. Michael Frenchman, "Britain Puts Forward Four Options on Falklands," *Times* (London), November 28, 1980, The Times Digital Archive, Gale. See also Peter J. Beck, "The Future of the Falkland Islands: A Solution Made in Hong Kong?," *International Affairs* 61, no. 4 (Autumn 1985): 643–60; and Louisa Lim, *Indelible City: Dispossession and Defiance in Hong Kong* (New York: Riverhead, 2022), 103.

66. Ezra F. Vogel, *Deng Xiaoping and the Transformation of China* (Cambridge, MA: Belknap Press of Harvard University Press, 2011), 477.

67. Barry Naughton, *Growing Out of the Plan: Chinese Economic Reform, 1978–1993* (Cambridge: Cambridge University Press, 1995), 54.

68. Don Graff, "Hong Kong Principle," *Indiana Gazette*, October 5, 1982, Newspapers.com.

69. Vogel, *Transformation of China*, 494.

70. Quoted in Steve Tsang, *A Modern History of Hong Kong* (London: I.B. Tauris, 2004), 214.

71. Brian Eads, "Murdoch, Made for Hong Kong," *Spectator*, November 15, 1986, Periodicals Archive Online.

72. Edward W. Cheng, "United Front Work and Mechanisms of Countermobilization in Hong Kong," *China Journal*, no. 83 (2019): 5–7; and Leo F. Goodstadt, *Uneasy Partners: The Conflict Between Public Interest and Private Profit in Hong Kong* (Hong Kong: Hong Kong University Press, 2005), 132.

73. Vogel, *Transformation of China*, 506.

74. Quoted in Chi Kuen Lau, *Hong Kong's Colonial Legacy* (Hong Kong: Chinese University Press, 1997), 84.

75. Francis Yuan-hao Tien quoted in Leo F. Goodstadt, "Business Friendly and Politically Convenient—the Historical Role of Functional Constituencies," in *Functional Constituencies: A Unique Feature of the Hong Kong Legislative Council*, ed. Christine Loh and Civic Exchange (Hong Kong: Hong Kong University Press, 2006), 53.

76. Lim, *Indelible City*, 138.

77. Bart Wissink, Sin Yee Koh, and Ray Forrest, "Tycoon City: Political Economy, Real Estate and the Super-Rich in Hong Kong," in *Cities and the Super-Rich: Real Estate, Elite Practices, and Urban Political Economies*, ed. Ray Forrest, Sin Yee Koh, and Bart Wissink (New York: Palgrave Macmillan, 2017), 230.

78. Denis Chang, "The Basic Law of the Hong Kong Special Administrative Region: Economics and Norms of Credibility," *Journal of Chinese Law* 2, no. 1 (Spring 1988): 31.

79. Shu-hung Tang, "Fiscal Constitution, Income Distribution and the Basic Law of Hong Kong," *Economy and Society* 20, no. 3 (1991): 284–85; see also Tang Shu-hung, "The Hong Kong Fiscal Policy: Continuity or Redirection?," in *Political Order and Power Transition in Hong Kong*, ed. Li Pang-kwong (Hong Kong: Chinese University Press, 1997), 224; on the clauses, see also Gonzalo Villalta Puig, "Fiscal Constitutionalism and Fiscal Culture: A Comparative Study of the Balanced-Budget Rule in the Spanish Constitution and the Hong Kong Basic Law," *Hong Kong Law Journal* (2013); Miron Mushkat and Roda Mushkat, "The Economic Dimension of Hong Kong's Basic Law: An Analytical Overview," *New Zealand Journal of Public and International Law* 7, no. 2 (December 2008); and Hong Kong Legislative Council, Official Report of Proceedings, Wednesday, July 13, 1988, p. 1848.

80. Alvin Rabushka, "A Free-Market Constitution for Hong Kong: A Blueprint for China," *Cato Journal* 8, no. 3 (Winter 1989): 647.

81. "Record of a discussion between the Prime Minister and Premier Hua Guofeng, 1 November 1979," https://www.margaretthatcher.org/document/138424.

82. Langer, "Out of Joint?," 328.

83. Summers, *China's Hong Kong*, 105–6.

84. Chien-Min Chao, "'One Country, Two Systems': A Theoretical Analysis," *Asian Affairs* 14, no. 2 (Summer 1987): 107.

85. Those more aware of Chinese history would recognize it as part of the ongoing process of turning the multiethnic Qing Empire into a single nation-state. The method used to absorb Hong Kong closely resembled that used to incorporate Tibet in the 1950s. Hung, *City on the Edge*, 106.

86. Jun Zhang, "From Hong Kong's Capitalist Fundamentals to Singapore's Authoritarian Governance: The Policy Mobility of Neo-liberalising Shenzhen, China," *Urban Studies Journal* 49, no. 13 (October 2012): 2866; for the origins of the phrase, see Isabella M. Weber, *How China Escaped Shock Therapy: The Market Reform Debate* (New York: Routledge, 2021), 118–19.

87. Weber, *How China Escaped*, 146.

88. Min Ye, "Policy Learning or Diffusion: How China Opened to Foreign Direct Investment," *Journal of East Asian Studies* 9, no. 3 (September–December 2009): 410.

89. Dennis Bloodworth, "Awakening China Courts Hong Kong," *Observer*, April 1, 1979, ProQuest.

90. Juan Du, *The Shenzhen Experiment: The Story of China's Instant City* (Cambridge, MA: Harvard University Press, 2020), 6, 37; for the latter phrase, see Emma Xin Ma and Adrian Blackwell, "The Political Architecture of the First

and Second Lines," in *Learning from Shenzhen: China's Post-Mao Experiment from Special Zone to Model City*, ed. Mary Ann O'Donnell, Winnie Wong, and Jonathan Bach (Chicago: University of Chicago Press, 2016), 135.

91. Mary Ann O'Donnell, "Heroes of the Special Zone: Modeling Reform and Its Limits," in *Learning from Shenzhen*, 44.

92. O'Donnell, "Heroes of the Special Zone," 45.

93. Zhang, "Hong Kong's Capitalist Fundamentals," 2858.

94. Daniel You-Ren Yang and Hung-Kai Wang, "Dilemmas of Local Governance Under the Development Zone Fever in China: A Case Study of the Suzhou Region," *Urban Studies* 45, no. 5–6 (May 2008): 1042.

95. Zhang, "Hong Kong's Capitalist Fundamentals," 2860.

96. Yehua Dennis Wei, "Zone Fever, Project Fever: Development Policy, Economic Transition, and Urban Expansion in China," *Geographical Review* 105, no. 2 (April 2015): 159.

97. Carolyn Cartier, *Globalizing South China* (Malden, MA: Wiley-Blackwell 2002), x.

98. Du, *The Shenzhen Experiment*, 56.

99. Mihai Cracuin, "Ideology: Shenzhen," in *Great Leap Forward*, ed. Chuihua Judy Chung et al. (Cologne: Taschen, 2001), 83; for the latter phrase, see Jonathan Bach, "Shenzhen: From Exception to Rule," in *Learning from Shenzhen*, 30; for details on the development of land policy, see Meg Rithmire, *Land Bargains and Chinese Capitalism: The Politics of Property Rights Under Reform* (Cambridge: Cambridge University Press, 2015).

100. Vogel, *Transformation of China*, 403.

101. Zhang, "Hong Kong's Capitalist Fundamentals," 2860.

102. Vogel, *Transformation of China*, 403.

103. Jin Wang, "The Economic Impact of Special Economic Zones: Evidence from Chinese Municipalities," *Journal of Development Economics* 101 (2013): 137.

104. See Naughton, *Growing Out of the Plan*, chap. 4.

105. Shaohua Zhan, "The Land Question in 21st Century China," *New Left Review*, no. 122 (March/April 2020): 118.

106. Milton Friedman, "A Welfare State Syllogism" (speech), Commonwealth Club of California, June 1, 1990, San Francisco, CA, transcript in *Commonwealth*, July 2, 1990, 386.

107. This is not to imply that Friedman's model was adopted by the Chinese reformers. For details, see Isabella M. Weber, "Origins of China's Contested Relation with Neoliberalism: Economics, the World Bank, and Milton Friedman at the Dawn of Reform," *Global Perspectives* 1, no. 1 (2020): 1–14; and Julian Gewirtz, *Unlikely Partners: Chinese Reformers, Western Economists, and the Making of Global China* (Cambridge, MA: Harvard University Press, 2017).

108. Milton Friedman, "The Real Lesson of Hong Kong" (lecture), Mandel Hall, University of Chicago, May 14, 1997, transcript, https://miltonfriedman .hoover.org/objects/57006/the-real-lesson-of-hong-kong.

109. Simon Xiaobin Zhao, Yingming Chan, and Carola B. Ramón-Berjano, "Industrial Structural Changes in Hong Kong, China Under One Country, Two Systems Framework," *Chinese Geographical Science* 22, no. 3 (2012): 308.

110. Vogel, *Transformation of China*, 397; see also Ye, "Policy Learning or Diffusion," 409.

111. Taomo Zhou, "Leveraging Liminality: The Border Town of Bao'an (Shenzhen) and the Origins of China's Reform and Opening," *Journal of Asian Studies* 80, no. 2 (2021): 337–61.

112. Milton Friedman, "Questions and Answers with Milton Friedman," *HKCER Letters* 23, November 1993, https://hkcer.hku.hk/Letters/v23/rq&a.htm.

113. See Maurice Adams et al., eds., *The Constitutionalization of European Budgetary Constraints* (Portland, OR: Hart, 2014); and Hilary Appel and Mitchell A. Orenstein, *From Triumph to Crisis: Neoliberal Economic Reform in Postcommunist Countries* (New York: Cambridge University Press, 2018), 100.

114. Germany in 2009, Austria in 2011, and Italy in 2012.

115. Milton Friedman, *Capitalism and Freedom*, rev. ed. (Chicago: Chicago University Press, 1982), 9.

116. Walter Block in Milton Friedman, "A Statistical Note on the Gastil-Wright Survey of Freedom," in *Freedom, Democracy and Economic Welfare*, ed. Michael Walker (Vancouver, BC: Fraser Institute, 1988), 134.

117. James Gwartney, Walter Block, and Robert Lawson, "Measuring Economic Freedom," in *Rating Global Economic Freedom*, ed. Stephen T. Easton and Michael A. Walker (Vancouver, BC: Fraser Institute, 1992), 156.

118. Gwartney, Block, and Lawson, "Measuring Economic Freedom," 160.

119. James Gwartney and Robert Lawson, *Economic Freedom of the World: 1997 Annual Report* (Vancouver, BC: Fraser Institute, 1997), 27.

120. James Gwartney, Robert Lawson, and Walter Block, *Economic Freedom of the World: 1975–1995* (Vancouver, BC: Fraser Institute, 1995), 64.

121. Richard B. McKenzie and Dwight R. Lee, *Quicksilver Capital: How the Rapid Movement of Wealth Has Changed the World* (New York: Free Press, 1991).

122. Ian Vásquez and Tanja Porcnik, *The Human Freedom Index 2016* (Washington, DC: Cato Institute, 2016), 5–7.

123. Goodstadt, "Business Friendly and Politically Convenient—the Historical Role of Functional Constituencies," 53, https://www.basiclaw.gov.hk.

124. Ngok Ma, "Reinventing the Hong Kong State or Rediscovering It? From Low Interventionism to Eclectic Corporatism," *Economy and Society* 38, no. 3 (2009): 510, 516; and Jeffrey Wasserstrom, *Vigil: Hong Kong on the Brink* (New York: Columbia Global Reports, 2020), 45.

125. Keith Bradsher and Chris Buckley, "Hong Kong Leader Reaffirms Unbending Stance on Elections," *New York Times*, October 20, 2014, https://www.nytimes.com/2014/10/21/world/asia/leung-chun-ying-hong-kong-china-protests.html.

126. Samuel P. Huntington, "Democracy's Third Wave," *Journal of Democracy* 2, no. 2 (Spring 1991): 12–35.

127. Brian Fong, "In-between Liberal Authoritarianism and Electoral Authoritarianism: Hong Kong's Democratization Under Chinese Sovereignty, 1997–2016," *Democratization* 24, no. 4 (2017): 724–25.

128. See Jane Burbank and Frederick Cooper, *Empires in World History: Power and the Politics of Difference* (Princeton, NJ: Princeton University Press, 2010), 2.

129. Lauren A. Benton, *A Search for Sovereignty: Law and Geography in European Empires, 1400–1900* (New York: Cambridge University Press, 2010), 290.

130. Ogle, "Archipelago Capitalism," 1432.

131. James Ferguson, *Global Shadows: Africa in the Neoliberal World Order* (Durham, NC: Duke University Press, 2006), 48.

132. Vogel, *Transformation of China*, 415.

133. Bach, "Shenzhen," 24.

134. Carolyn Cartier, "Zone Analog: The State–Market Problematic and Territorial Economies in China," *Critical Sociology* 44, no. 3 (2018): 465.

135. Andrew Mertha, "'Fragmented Authoritarianism 2.0': Political Pluralization in the Chinese Policy Process," *China Quarterly*, no. 200 (December 2009): 995.

136. Wasserstrom, *Vigil*, 42.

137. Carroll, *History of Hong Kong*, 229.

138. Thomas K. Cheng, "Sherman vs. Goliath?: Tackling the Conglomerate Dominance Problem in Emerging and Small Economies—Hong Kong as a Case Study," *Northwestern Journal of International Law & Business* 37, no. 1 (2017): 89.

139. Cheng, "Sherman vs. Goliath," 90.

140. Thomas Piketty and Li Yang, "Income and Wealth Inequality in Hong Kong, 1981–2020: The Rise of Pluto-Communism?," *World Inequality Lab Working Paper*, no. 18 (June 2021): 2.

CHAPTER 2: CITY IN SHARDS

1. Yair Mintzker, "What Is Defortification? Military Functions, Police Roles, and Symbolism in the Demolition of German City Walls in the Eighteenth and Nineteenth Centuries," *German Historical Institute Bulletin*, no. 48 (Spring 2011): 46.

2. Fernand Braudel, *Civilization and Capitalism, 15th–18th Century*, vol. 1, *The Structures of Everyday Life: The Limits of the Possible* (London: William Collins Sons, 1979), 510.

3. Maria Kaika, "Architecture and Crisis: Re-Inventing the Icon, Re-Imag(in)ing London and Re-Branding the City," *Transactions of the Institute of British Geographers* 35, no. 4 (October 2010): 459. In 2006, the Corporation of London's name was changed to the City of London Corporation.

4. Shaxson, *Treasure Islands*, 71.

5. Shaxson, 71.

6. Matthew Eagleton-Pierce, "Uncovering the City of London Corporation: Territory and Temporalities in the New State Capitalism," *Environment & Planning A: Economy and Space* (2022): 5, https://doi.org/10.1177/0308518 X221083986.

7. Kaika, "Architecture and Crisis," 459.

8. Nicholas Shaxson, *The Finance Curse: How Global Finance Is Making Us All Poorer* (New York: Grove, 2019), 59. The colonial background is important, as they often inherited British Common Law. Manuel B. Aalbers, "Financial Geography I: Geographies of Tax," *Progress in Human Geography* 42, no. 6 (2018): 920.

9. Lewis Mumford, *The Culture of Cities* (New York: Harcourt Brace Jovanovich, 1938), 22.

10. The story of the redevelopment of the Docklands is a set piece in the popular textbook Peter Hall, *Cities of Tomorrow: An Intellectual History of Urban Planning and Design Since 1880*, 4th ed. (Malden, MA: Wiley Blackwell, 2014), 423–35. Enterprise zones have been objects of close critical academic examination since their creation. For two excellent recent accounts see Timothy P. R. Weaver, *Blazing the Neoliberal Trail: Urban Political Development in the United States and the United Kingdom* (Philadelphia: University of Pennsylvania Press, 2016), chap. 6; and Sam Wetherell, "Freedom Planned: Enterprise Zones and Urban Non-Planning in Post-War Britain," *Twentieth Century British History* 27, no. 2 (2016): 266–89. For "Hong Kong on Thames," see Martin Pawley, "Electric City of Our Dreams," *New Society*, June 13, 1986, 12.

11. Hall, *Cities of Tomorrow*, 390.

12. Geoffrey Howe, "A Zone of Enterprise to Make All Systems 'Go,'" Conservative Central Office News Service, June 26, 1978, https://www.margaretthatcher.org/document/111842.

13. Ezra Vogel, *Japan Is Number One: Lessons for America* (Cambridge, MA: Harvard University Press, 1979).

14. James Anderson, "The 'New Right,' Enterprise Zones and Urban Development Corporations," *International Journal of Urban and Regional Research* 14, no. 3 (September 1990): 474.

15. John Hoskyns and Norman Strauss, *"Stepping Stones" Report* (final text), Centre for Policy Studies, November 14, 1977, https://www.margaretthatcher .org/document/111771.

16. Schenk, "Negotiating Positive Non-interventionism," 352.

17. GDP data available through the World Bank, https://data.worldbank.org.

18. Howe, *Conflict of Loyalty*, 361.

19. Peter Hall, "Enterprise Zones and Freeports Revisited," *New Society*, March 24, 1983, 460. On the non-plan, see Anthony Fontenot, *Non-Design: Architecture, Liberalism, and the Market* (Chicago: University of Chicago Press, 2021), 243–51; and Wetherell, "Freedom Planned: Enterprise Zones and Urban Non-Planning in Post-War Britain," 275.

20. Madsen Pirie, "A Short History of Enterprise Zones," *National Review*, January 23, 1981, 26.

21. Harvey D. Shapiro, "Now, Hong Kong on the Hudson?," *New York*, April 26, 1982, 35–37.

22. Stuart M. Butler, "The Enterprise Zone as a Political Animal," *Cato Journal* 2, no. 2 (Fall 1982): 373.

23. Butler, "Political Animal," 376.

24. Butler, 377.

25. Paul Johnson in Butler, "Political Animal," 374.

26. Jonathan Potter and Barry Moore, "UK Enterprise Zones and the Attraction of Inward Investment," *Urban Studies* 37, no. 8 (2000): 1280.

27. Sue Brownill and Glen O'Hara, "From Planning to Opportunism? Re-Examining the Creation of the London Docklands Development Corporation," *Planning Perspectives* 30, no. 4 (2015): 549.

28. Wetherell, "Freedom Planned," 287.

29. Barry M. Rubin and Craig M. Richards, "A Transatlantic Comparison of Enterprise Zone Impacts: The British and American Experience," *Economic Development Quarterly* 6, no. 4 (1992): 435; and "Enterprise Zones: Do They Go Too Far or Not Far Enough?," *Sunday Times* (London), August 12, 1984, The Sunday Times Historical Archive, Gale.

30. Chris Tighe, "Slow Go in Go-Go Areas," *Sunday Times* (London), August 1, 1982, The Sunday Times Historical Archive, Gale.

31. John Harrison, "Buy a Building for Free," *Sunday Times* (London), February 8, 1987, The Sunday Times Historical Archive, Gale.

32. Peter Shearlock, "How to Build a Tax Haven," *Sunday Times* (London), February 3, 1985, The Sunday Times Historical Archive, Gale.

33. Alan Walters to Margaret Thatcher, July 5, 1982, https://www.margaretthatcher .org/document/218360.

34. Quoted in Anderson, "The 'New Right,' Enterprise Zones and Urban Development Corporations," 479.

35. Anderson, "The 'New Right,'" 468.
36. Doreen Massey, "Enterprise Zones: A Political Issue," *International Journal of Urban and Regional Research* 6, no. 3 (1982): 429.
37. David Harvey, "The Invisible Political Economy of Architectural Production," in *The Invisible in Architecture*, ed. Ole Bouman and Roemer van Toorn (New York: Academy Editions, 1994), 426.
38. Perry Anderson, letter to author, September 11, 2018.
39. Anderson, "The 'New Right,'" 483.
40. Göran Therborn, *Cities of Power: The Urban, the National, the Popular, the Global* (New York: Verso, 2017), 50.
41. Pawley, "Electric City," 12.
42. Jo Thomas, "London Financial District Going to the Isle of Dogs," *New York Times*, January 7, 1986, ProQuest Historical Newspapers.
43. Sara Stevens, "'Visually Stunning' While Financially Safe: Neoliberalism and Financialization at Canary Wharf," *Ardeth* (2020): 87–89, http://journals .openedition.org/ardeth/1153.
44. Pawley, "Electric City."
45. Sue Brownill, *Developing London's Docklands: Another Great Planning Disaster?* (London: Paul Chapman, 1990), 50; Thomas, "Going to the Isle of Dogs"; and Roy Porter, *London: A Social History* (London: Penguin Books, 1994), 381.
46. Nigel Broackes quoted in Weaver, *Blazing the Neoliberal Trail*, 262.
47. Anderson, "The 'New Right,'" 483.
48. E. J. Hobsbawm, *The Age of Empire, 1875–1914* (New York: Pantheon Books, 1987), 38.
49. David Edgerton, *The Rise and Fall of the British Nation: A Twentieth Century History* (London: Penguin, 2018), 290.
50. Edgerton, *Rise and Fall*, 310–11.
51. Rob Harris, *London's Global Office Economy: From Clerical Factory to Digital Hub* (London: Routledge, 2021), 6.
52. Edgerton, *Rise and Fall*, 472.
53. Maureen Mackintosh and Hillary Wainwright, eds., *A Taste of Power: The Politics of Local Economics* (London: Verso, 1987), 354.
54. Jo Littler and Hillary Wainwright, "Municipalism and Feminism Then and Now: Hilary Wainwright Talks to Jo Littler," *Soundings*, no. 74 (Spring 2020): 12.
55. Hillary Wainwright, "Bye Bye GLC," *New Statesman*, March 21, 1986, 10, ProQuest Periodical Archives Online; Cutler to Thatcher, March 26, 1981, https://www.margaretthatcher.org/document/126349.
56. Mackintosh and Wainwright, *A Taste of Power*, 303, 310.
57. Jade Spencer, "A Plan for a People's London," *Tribune*, May 16, 2022, https://tribunemag.co.uk/2022/05/peoples-plan-royal-docks-london

-thatcherism-glc-neoliberalism. See also Owen Hatherley, "Going Back to NAM," *Tribune*, September 16, 2021, https://tribunemag.co.uk/2021/09 /going-back-to-nam.

58. Charles Moore, *Margaret Thatcher: The Authorized Biography*, vol. 3, *Herself Alone* (New York: Knopf, 2019), 55.

59. Quoted in Muhammet Kösecik and Naim Kapucu, "Conservative Reform of Metropolitan Counties: Abolition of the GLC and MCCs in Retrospect," *Contemporary British History* 17, no. 3 (2003): 89.

60. Marion Roe quoted in Kösecik and Kapucu, "Conservative Reform," 89.

61. Sylvia Bashevkin, *Tales of Two Cities: Women and Municipal Restructuring in London and Toronto* (Vancouver: University of British Columbia Press, 2006), 57–58.

62. Leo Panitch, Colin Leys, and David Coates, *The End of Parliamentary Socialism: From New Left to New Labour* (London: Verso, 2001), 171–72.

63. Chris Toulouse, "Thatcherism, Class Politics, and Urban Development in London," *Critical Sociology* 18, no. 1 (1991): 70.

64. A. Merrifield, "The Canary Wharf Debacle: From 'TINA'—There Is No Alternative—to 'THEMBA'—There Must Be an Alternative," *Environment & Planning A* 25 (1993): 1256.

65. Warren Hoge, "Blair's 'Rebranded' Britain Is No Museum," *New York Times*, November 12, 1997, https://www.nytimes.com/1997/11/12/world/london -journal-blair-s-rebranded-britain-is-no-museum.html.

66. Desiree Fields, "Constructing a New Asset Class: Property-Led Financial Accumulation After the Crisis," *Economic Geography* 94, no. 2 (2016); and Manuel B. Aalbers, "Financial Geography III: The Financialization of the City," *Progress in Human Geography* 44, no. 3 (2020): 599.

67. Joshua K. Leon, "Global Cities at Any Cost: Resisting Municipal Mercantilism," *City* 21, no. 1 (2017): 7–8.

68. Leon, "Global Cities," 16.

69. Michael Freedman, "Welcome to Londongrad," *Forbes*, May 23, 2005, https:// www.forbes.com/forbes/2005/0523/158.html. See Oliver Bullough, *Butler to the World: How Britain Helps the World's Worst People Launder Money, Commit Crimes, and Get Away with Anything* (London: Profile, 2022).

70. Jae-Yong Chung and Kevin Carpenter, "Safe Havens: Overseas Housing Speculation and Opportunity Zones," *Housing Studies* (2020): 1, https://doi .org/doi.org/10.1080/02673037.2020.1844156.

71. Joe Beswick et al., "Speculating on London's Housing Future," *City* 20, no. 2 (2016): 321.

72. Chung and Carpenter, "Safe Havens," 7.

73. Rodrigo Fernandez, Annelore Hofman, and Manuel B. Aalbers, "London and New York as a Safe Deposit Box for the Transnational Wealth Elite," *Environment & Planning A* 48, no. 12 (2016): 2444.

74. Judith Evans, "The Gilded Glut," *FT.com*, June 8, 2017, ProQuest.

75. Quoted in Brett Christophers, *The New Enclosure: The Appropriation of Public Land in Neoliberal Britain* (London: Verso, 2018), 172.

76. Alexandra Stevenson and Julie Creswell, "Bill Ackman and His Hedge Fund, Betting Big," *New York Times*, October 25. 2014, https://www.nytimes.com/2014/10/26/business/bill-ackman-and-his-hedge-fund-betting-big.html.

77. Matthew Soules, *Icebergs, Zombies, and the Ultra-Thin: Architecture and Capitalism in the 21st Century* (New York: Princeton Architectural Press, 2021), 99.

78. Nikita Stewart and David Gelles, "The $238 Million Penthouse, and the Hedge Fund Billionaire Who May Rarely Live There," *New York Times*, January 24, 2019, https://www.nytimes.com/2019/01/24/nyregion/238-million-penthouse-sale.html.

79. Saskia Sassen, *The Global City* (Princeton, NJ: Princeton University Press, 1991).

80. Leon, "Global Cities."

81. Owen Hatherley, "Renzo Piano's Shard," *Artforum*, Summer 2011, https://www.artforum.com/print/201106/renzo-piano-s-shard-28344.

82. Paul C. Cheshire and Gerard H. Dericks, "'Trophy Architects' and Design as Rent-Seeking: Quantifying Deadweight Losses in a Tightly Regulated Office Market," *Economica*, no. 87 (2020): 1081.

83. Luna Glucksberg, "A View from the Top: Unpacking Capital Flows and Foreign Investment in Prime London," *City* 20, no. 2 (2016): 251.

84. Glucksberg, "A View from the Top," 246.

85. Fernandez, Hofman, and Aalbers, "Safe Deposit," 2450.

86. Anna White, "The 200 Home Tower Block That Sold Out in Under Five Hours," *Daily Telegraph* (UK), July 12, 2015, Westlaw.

87. Rowland Atkinson, Simon Parker, and Roger Burrows, "Elite Formation, Power and Space in Contemporary London," *Theory, Culture & Society* 34, no. 5–6 (2017): 184.

88. Margaret Thatcher, Speech to the First International Conservative Congress, September 28, 1997, https://www.margaretthatcher.org/document/108374.

89. Julia Kollewe, "Canary Wharf Owner Rescued by China and Qatar," *Guardian*, August 28, 2009, https://www.theguardian.com/business/2009/aug/28/songbird-canary-wharf-china-qatar; and Guy Faulconbridge and Andrew Osborn, "Thatcher's Legacy: A Citadel of Finance atop Once-Derelict Docks," Reuters, April 16, 2013, https://www.reuters.com/article/uk-britain-thatcher-wharf/thatchers-legacy-a-citadel-of-finance-atop-once-derelict-docks-idUKBRE93F0S920130416.

90. Brenda Goh, "Chinese Developer to Revamp London Docks for Asian Firms," Reuters, May 29, 2013, https://www.reuters.com/article/cbusiness -us-abp-londondocks-idCABRE94S0W720130529.

91. Matt Kennard, "Selling the Silverware: How London's Historic Dock Was Sold to the Chinese," *International Business Times*, June 7, 2016, https://legacy .pulitzercenter.org/reporting/selling-silverware-how-londons-historic -dock-was-sold-chinese.

92. Art Patnaude, "Chinese Investors Bet on U.K. Land," *Wall Street Journal*, September 19, 2014, ProQuest.

93. Wissink, Koh, and Forrest, "Tycoon City," 235.

94. Cheng, "Sherman vs. Goliath?," 91.

95. Alice Poon, *Land and the Ruling Class in Hong Kong* (Hong Kong: Enrich, 2011), 51.

96. Christophers, *The New Enclosure*, 310.

97. Atkinson, Parker, and Burrows, "Elite Formation," 193.

98. Atkinson, Parker, and Burrows, 194.

99. Boris Johnson, "We Should Be Humbly Thanking the Super-Rich, Not Bashing Them," *Daily Telegraph* (UK), November 18, 2013, Westlaw.

100. Samuel Stein, *Capital City: Gentrification and the Real Estate State* (New York: Verso, 2019), 150.

101. Thomas J. Sugrue, "America's Real Estate Developer in Chief," *Public Books*, November 27, 2017, https://www.publicbooks.org/the-big-picture -americas-real-estate-developer-in-chief/.

102. See Stein, *Capital City: Gentrification and the Real Estate State*, 137.

103. Charles V. Bagli, "A Trump Empire Built on Inside Connections and $885 Million in Tax Breaks," *New York Times*, September 17, 2016, https:// www.nytimes.com/2016/09/18/nyregion/donald-trump-tax-breaks-real -estate.html.

104. Garth Alexander, "Donald Trump Dreams Up a New City in Manhattan," *Times* (London), July 24, 1994, The Times Digital Archive, Gale.

105. Nick Davies, "The Towering Ego," *Sunday Times Magazine*, April 17, 1988, The Sunday Times Digital Archive, Gale.

106. Donald Trump, "Remarks at an Opportunity Zones Conference with State, Local, Tribal, and Community Leaders," April 17, 2019, https://www.govinfo .gov/app/details/DCPD-201900229.

107. Jesse Drucker and Eric Lipton, "How a Trump Tax Break to Help Poor Communities Became a Windfall for the Rich," *New York Times*, August 31, 2019, https://www.nytimes.com/2019/08/31/business/tax-opportunity -zones.html.

108. Brett Theodos, "The Opportunity Zone Program and Who It Left Behind," *Statement Before the Oversight Committee, Ways and Means Committee,*

U.S. House of Representatives, November 16, 2021, https://waysandmeans .house.gov/sites/democrats.waysandmeans.house.gov/files/documents/B .%20Theodos%20Testimony.pdf.

109. Quoted in Ray Forrest, Sin Yee Koh, and Bart Wissink, "Hyper-Divided Cities and the 'Immoral' Super-Rich: Five Parting Questions," in *Cities and the Super-Rich: Real Estate, Elite Practices, and Urban Political Economies*, ed. Ray Forrest, Sin Yee Koh, and Bart Wissink (New York: Palgrave Macmillan, 2017), 274.

110. Matthew Haag, "Amazon's Tax Breaks and Incentives Were Big. Hudson Yards' Are Bigger," *New York Times*, March 9, 2019, https://www.nytimes .com/2019/03/09/nyregion/hudson-yards-new-york-tax-breaks.html.

111. Michael Kimmelman, "Hudson Yards Is Manhattan's Biggest, Newest, Slickest Gated Community. Is This the Neighborhood New York Deserves?," *New York Times*, March 14, 2019, https://www.nytimes.com/interactive /2019/03/14/arts/design/hudson-yards-nyc.html.

112. Kriston Capps, "The Hidden Horror of Hudson Yards Is How It Was Financed," *Bloomberg CityLab*, April 12, 2019, https://www.bloomberg .com/news/articles/2019-04-12/the-visa-program-that-helped-pay-for -hudson-yards.

113. Kimmelman, "Slickest Gated Community."

114. Rowland Atkinson, "London, Whose City?," *Le Monde Diplomatique*, July 2017, https://mondediplo.com/2017/07/06london; and Gordon MacLeod, "The Grenfell Tower Atrocity: Exposing Urban Worlds of Inequality, Injustice, and an Impaired Democracy," *City* 22, no. 4 (2018): 464.

115. George Monbiot, "With Grenfell Tower, We've Seen What 'Ripping Up Red Tape' Really Looks Like," *Guardian* (UK Edition), June 15, 2017, https:// www.theguardian.com/commentisfree/2017/jun/15/grenfell-tower-red -tape-safety-deregulation.

116. David Madden, "A Catastrophic Event" (editorial), *City* 21, no. 1 (2017): 3.

117. Graham and Marvin, *Splintering Urbanism*, 325.

118. James Vernon, *Modern Britain, 1750 to the Present* (Cambridge: Cambridge University Press, 2017), 501.

119. Jacob Rowbottom, "Protest: No Banners on My Land!," *New Statesman*, November 1, 2004, Gale OneFile.

120. Paul Mason, "New Dawn for the Workers," *New Statesman*, April 16, 2007, Gale OneFile.

121. Anna Minton, "The Paradox of Safety and Fear: Security in Public Space," *Architectural Design* 88, no. 3 (May 2018): 89.

122. Anna Minton, *Ground Control: Fear and Happiness in the Twenty-First Century City* (London: Penguin, 2009), 61.

123. Stephen Graham, "Luxified Skies: How Vertical Urban Housing Became an Elite Preserve," *City* 19, no. 5 (2015): 620, 638.

124. Soules, *Icebergs, Zombies, and the Ultra-Thin: Architecture and Capitalism in the 21st Century*, 93.

125. Hatherley, "Renzo Piano's Shard."

126. Alan Wiig, "Incentivized Urbanization in Philadelphia: The Local Politics of Globalized Zones," *Journal of Urban Technology* 26, no. 3 (2019); and Stein, *Capital City: Gentrification and the Real Estate State*, 57.

127. Paul Watt, "'It's Not for Us': Regeneration, the 2012 Olympics and the Gentrification of East London," *City* 17, no. 1 (2013): 101. For a pioneering analysis, see Neil Smith, *The New Urban Frontier: Gentrification and the Revanchist City* (New York: Routledge, 1996).

128. Wiig, "Incentivized Urbanization in Philadelphia," 112.

129. Jack Brown, "If You Build It, They Will Come: The Role of Individuals in the Emergence of Canary Wharf, 1985–1987," *London Journal* 42, no. 1 (2017): 71.

130. Richard Disney and Guannan Luo, "The Right to Buy Public Housing in Britain: A Welfare Analysis," *Journal of Housing Economics*, no. 35 (2017): 51–53.

131. Stuart Hodkinson, "The New Urban Enclosures," *City* 16, no. 5 (2012): 510–14; and Christian Hilber and Olivier Schöni, "In the United Kingdom, Homeownership Has Fallen While Renting Is on the Rise," *Brookings Institution*, April 20, 2021, https://www.brookings.edu/essay/uk-rental-housing-markets/.

132. Ella Jessel, "Behind the Story: How Did Boris's Business Park Become a Ghost Town?," *Architects Journal*, February 11, 2022, https://www.architectsjournal.co.uk/news/behind-the-story-how-did-boriss-business-park-become-a-ghost-town.

133. Alastair Lockhart, "Big Changes Announced for London Skyscraper That's as Tall as the Shard," *MyLondon*, January 26, 2022, https://www.mylondon.news/news/east-london-news/big-changes-announced-london-skyscraper-22883066.

134. Patrick Radden Keefe, "How Putin's Oligarchs Bought London," *New Yorker*, March 28, 2022, https://www.newyorker.com/magazine/2022/03/28/how-putins-oligarchs-bought-london.

135. Mackintosh and Wainwright, *A Taste of Power*; and Adrian Smith, "Technology Networks for Socially Useful Production," *Journal of Peer Production* (2014). See Ben Tarnoff, *Internet for the People: The Fight for Our Digital Future* (New York: Verso, 2022), 167–70. See also Spencer, "A Plan for a People's London."

136. Alan Lockey and Ben Glover, *The "Preston Model" and the New Municipalism* (London: Demos, May 2019), https://demos.co.uk/wp-content/uploads/2019/06/June-Final-Web.pdf; Matthew Brown, "Preston Is Putting Socialist Policies into Practice," *Tribune*, January 20, 2022, https://tribunemag.co.uk/2022/01/community-wealth-building-preston-trade-unions-labour

-party; Bertie Russell, "Beyond the Local Trap: New Municipalism and the Rise of the Fearless Cities," *Antipode* 51, no. 3 (2019); and Susannah Bunce, "Pursuing Urban Commons: Politics and Alliances in Community Land Trust Activism in East London," *Antipode* 48, no. 1 (2016).

137. Harvey, "The Invisible Political Economy," 421.

138. Loraine Leeson, "Our Land: Creative Approaches to the Redevelopment of London's Docklands," *International Journal of Heritage Studies* 25, no. 4 (2019): 371–72.

CHAPTER 3: THE SINGAPORE SOLUTION

1. Moore, *Margaret Thatcher: The Authorized Biography*, vol. 3, *Herself Alone*, 802.

2. Owen Paterson, "Don't Listen to the Terrified Europeans. The Singapore Model Is Our Brexit Opportunity," *Telegraph.co.uk*, November 21, 2017, Westlaw.

3. Mark R. Thompson, "East Asian Authoritarian Modernism: From Meiji Japan's 'Prussian Path' to China's 'Singapore Model,'" *Asian International Studies Review* 17, no. 2 (December 2016): 131.

4. Benjamin Tze Ern Ho, "Power and Populism: What the Singapore Model Means for the Chinese Dream," *China Quarterly* 236 (2018): 968.

5. Milton Friedman and Rose D. Friedman, *Two Lucky People: Memoirs* (Chicago: University of Chicago Press, 1998), 327.

6. Milton Friedman, "The Invisible Hand in Economics and Politics," *Inaugural Singapore Lecture, Sponsored by the Monetary Authority of Singapore and Organized by the Institute of Southeast Asian Studies*, October 14, 1980, https://miltonfriedman.hoover.org/internal/media/dispatcher/271090/full.

7. Linda Y. C. Lim, "Singapore's Success: The Myth of the Free Market Economy," *Asian Survey* 23, no. 6 (June 1983): 761.

8. The biggest sovereign wealth funds are Government of Singapore Industrial Corporation (GIC), founded in 1981, and Temasek Holdings, founded in 1974. As of 2021, they are, respectively, the first and fifth most active state-owned investors in the world. Rae Wee, "GIC Retains Position as Most Active State-Owned Investor: Report," *Business Times* (Singapore), January 13, 2021, https://www.businesstimes.com.sg/companies-markets /gic-retains-position-as-most-active-state-owned-investor-report. State-owned enterprises are called Government-Linked Corporations (GLCs). In 1998, two-thirds of the one hundred largest Singaporean companies by sales were GLCs. Linda Low, "Rethinking Singapore Inc. and GLCs," *Southeast Asian Affairs* (2002): 288. On state-led capitalism see Adam D. Dixon, "The Strategic Logics of State Investment Funds in Asia: Beyond Financialisation," *Journal of Contemporary Asia* 52, no. 1 (2022): 127–51.

9. S. Rajaratnam, "Singapore: Global City (1972)," in *S. Rajaratnam on Singapore: From Ideas to Reality*, ed. Kwa Chong Guan (Singapore: World Scientific Publishing, 2006), 233.

10. Rajaratnam, "Singapore," 231.

11. Michael D. Barr, *Singapore: A Modern History* (London: I.B. Tauris, 2019), 161.

12. W. G. Huff, "What Is the Singapore Model of Economic Development?," *Cambridge Journal of Economics* 19, no. 6 (December 1995): 753.

13. Alexis Mitchell and Deborah Cowen, "The Labour of Global City Building," in *Digital Lives in the Global City: Contesting Infrastructures*, ed. Deborah Cowen et al. (Vancouver: University of British Columbia Press, 2020), 213.

14. Gordon P. Means, "Soft Authoritarianism in Malaysia and Singapore," *Journal of Democracy* 7, no. 4 (October 1996): 106–9. Since 2000, a small "Speaker's Corner" has been established as a designated zone for gathering and demonstration in a central city park.

15. Beng Huat Chua, *Liberalism Disavowed: Communitarianism and State Capitalism in Singapore* (Ithaca, NY: Cornell University Press, 2017), 40.

16. For a recent overview see Chong Ja Ian, "Democracy, Singapore-Style? Biden's Summit Spotlights Questions of How to Categorize Regimes," *Academia SG*, December 20, 2021, https://www.academia.sg/explainer/democracy-singapore-style/.

17. On pragmatism see Kenneth Paul Tan, "The Ideology of Pragmatism: Neoliberal Globalisation and Political Authoritarianism in Singapore," *Journal of Contemporary Asia* 42, no. 1 (February 2012); Chua, *Liberalism Disavowed: Communitarianism and State Capitalism in Singapore*, 6–7; and Denny Roy, "Singapore, China, and the 'Soft Authoritarian' Challenge," *Asian Survey* 34, no. 3 (1994): 234.

18. Francis Fukuyama, "Asia's Soft-Authoritarian Alternative," *New Perspectives Quarterly* (Spring 1992): 60.

19. Janet Lippman Abu-Lughod, "The World System in the Thirteenth Century: Dead-End or Precursor?," in *Islamic and European Expansion: The Forging of a Global Order*, ed. Michael Adas (Philadelphia: Temple University Press, 1993), 83.

20. Not mentioned are the South Asian convict workers who built the roads and bridges throughout the island, as well as the Government House, a military battery, and a church. Anand A. Yang, "Indian Convict Workers in Southeast Asia in the Late Eighteenth and Early Nineteenth Centuries," *Journal of World History* 14, no. 2 (2003): 201.

21. Carl A. Trocki, *Singapore: Wealth, Power and the Culture of Control* (London: Routledge, 2006), 13.

22. Quoted in Paul H. Kratoska, "Singapore, Hong Kong and the End of Empire," *International Journal of Asian Studies* 3, no. 1 (2006): 2.

23. Jeevan Vasagar, *Lion City: Singapore and the Invention of Modern Asia* (New York: Pegasus, 2022), 32.

24. Barr, *Singapore*, 147.

25. Vasagar, *Lion City*, 36.

26. Daniel Immerwahr, *How to Hide an Empire: A History of the Greater United States* (New York: Farrar, Straus and Giroux 2019), 197.

27. Immerwahr, *How to Hide an Empire*, 4.

28. Vasagar, *Lion City*, 225.

29. Lee Kuan Yew, *From Third World to First: The Singapore Story, 1965–2000* (New York: Harper Collins, 2000), 14–15.

30. Ang Cheng Guan, *Lee Kuan Yew's Strategic Thought* (New York: Routledge, 2013), 96.

31. Jim Glassman quoted in Chris Meulbroek and Majed Akhter, "The Prose of Passive Revolution: Mobile Experts, Economic Planning and the Developmental State in Singapore," *Environment & Planning A* 51, no. 6 (2019): 6.

32. The quote is from a 1982 oral history quoted in UNDP, *UNDP and the Making of Singapore's Public Service: Lessons from Albert Winsemius* (Singapore: UNDP Global Centre for Public Service Excellence, 2015), 11.

33. The officer was Jan Pieterszoon Coen. Debates over removing his statue in his hometown emerged again during confrontations with the national colonial past. Olivia Tasevski, "The Dutch Are Uncomfortable with Being History's Villains, Not Victims," *Foreign Policy*, August 10, 2020, https://foreignpolicy .com/2020/08/10/dutch-colonial-history-indonesia-villains-victims/.

34. Barr, *Singapore*, 162; and UNDP, *UNDP and the Making of Singapore's Public Service: Lessons from Albert Winsemius*, 11.

35. "Singapore's Successful Drive to Become Brain Centre of Southeast Asia," *Financial Post*, October 7, 1972, Newspapers.com.

36. UNDP, *UNDP and the Making of Singapore's Public Service: Lessons from Albert Winsemius*, 8. On Puerto Rico see César J. Ayala and Rafael Bernabe, *Puerto Rico in the American Century: A History Since 1898* (Chapel Hill: University of North Carolina Press, 2009), chap. 9.

37. Kees Tamboer, "Albert Winsemius: 'Founding Father' of Singapore," *IIAS Newsletter*, no. 9 (Summer 1996): 29.

38. Vasagar, *Lion City*, 71.

39. Catherine Schenk, "The Origins of the Asia Dollar Market 1968–1986: Regulatory Competition and Complementarity in Singapore and Hong Kong," *Financial History Review* 27, no. 1 (2020): 22.

40. Vasagar, *Lion City*, 76.

41. J. K. Galbraith, "Age of Uncertainty" (1977), ep. 10, https://www.youtube .com/watch?v=Rv8b_ou-NQM.

42. Daniel P. S. Goh, "Super-Diversity and the Bio-Politics of Migrant Worker Exclusion in Singapore," *Identities* 26, no. 3 (2019): 359.

43. Arif Dirlik, "Confucius in the Borderlands: Global Capitalism and the Reinvention of Confucianism," *boundary 2* 22, no. 3 (Autumn 1995): 239.

44. Dirlik, "Confucius in the Borderlands: Global Capitalism and the Reinvention of Confucianism," 232–36; and Roy, "'Soft Authoritarian' Challenge," 232.

45. Dirlik, "Confucius in the Borderlands: Global Capitalism and the Reinvention of Confucianism," 239. For the US reception see Jennifer M. Miller, "Neoconservatives and Neo-Confucians: East Asian Growth and the Celebration of Tradition," *Modern Intellectual History* (2020), 1–27.

46. Fareed Zakaria, "Culture Is Destiny: A Conversation with Lee Kuan Yew," *Foreign Affairs* 73, no. 2 (1994): 115.

47. Wen-Qing Ngoei, *Arc of Containment: Britain, the United States, and Anticommunism in Southeast Asia* (Ithaca, NY: Cornell University Press, 2019), 126.

48. Mario Rossi, "Singapore Run Like Corporation," *Santa Cruz Sentinel*, October 5, 1980, Newspapers.com.

49. Quoted in Chua, *Liberalism Disavowed: Communitarianism and State Capitalism in Singapore*, 50.

50. Yew, *From Third World to First: The Singapore Story, 1965–2000*, 304.

51. See Maurice Meisner, *Mao's China and After*, 3rd ed. (New York: Free Press, 1999), 291–412.

52. Pang Eng Fong, "Growth, Inequality and Race in Singapore," *International Labour Review* 111, no. 1 (1975): 16.

53. Deng Xiaoping, "Excerpts from Talks Given in Wuchang, Shenzhen, Zhuhai and Shanghai (January 18–February 21, 1992)," http://www.china.org.cn/english/features/dengxiaoping/103331.htm.

54. They borrowed the term from the World Bank. He Li, "The Chinese Discourse on Good Governance: Content and Implications," *Journal of Contemporary China* 29, no. 126 (2020): 831.

55. Elsa van Dongen, *Realistic Revolution: Contesting Chinese History, Culture, and Politics After 1989* (New York: Cambridge University Press, 2019), 6; and Carolyn Cartier, "'Zone Fever,' the Arable Land Debate, and Real Estate Speculation: China's Evolving Land Use Regime and Its Geographical Contradictions," *Journal of Contemporary China* 10, no. 28 (2001).

56. Wang Hui, *The End of the Revolution: China and the Limits of Modernity* (New York: Verso, 2011), 51.

57. Hui, *End of the Revolution*, 57. A Chinese intellectual, Wang Huning, traveled to the United States and published a book called *America Against America* in 1991. By 2022, he ranked fourth in the hierarchy of the CCP. Chang Che, "How a Book About America's History Foretold China's Future," *New Yorker*, March 21, 2022, https://www.newyorker.com/books/second-read/how-a-book-about-americas-history-foretold-chinas-future.

58. Lye Liang Fook, "Suzhou Industrial Park: Going Beyond a Commercial Project," in *Advancing Singapore-China Economic Relations*, ed. Swee-Hock Saw

and John Wong (Singapore: Institute of Southeast Asian Studies, 2014), 68; and Yang Kai and Stephan Ortmann, "The Origins of the 'Singapore Fever' in China 1978–92," in *China's "Singapore Model" and Authoritarian Learning*, ed. Stephan Ortmann and Mark R. Thompson (London: Routledge, 2020).

59. Kean Fan Lim and Niv Horesh, "The 'Singapore Fever' in China: Policy Mobility and Mutation," *China Quarterly* 228 (2016): 995, 1006.

60. Connie Carter, "The Clonability of the Singapore Model of Law and Development: The Case of Suzhou, China," in *Law and Development in East and South-East Asia*, ed. Christoph Antons (London: RoutledgeCurzon, 2003), 212.

61. See Mary G. Padua, *Hybrid Modernity: The Public Park in Late 20th Century China* (London: Taylor & Francis, 2020), chap. 5.

62. Tu Weiming, "Multiple Modernities: A Preliminary Inquiry into the Implications of the East Asian Modernity," *Globalistics and Globalization Studies* (2014).

63. Hedley Bull, *The Anarchical Society: A Study of Order in World Politics* (New York: Columbia University Press, 1977), 258.

64. Margaret Tan, "Plugging into the Wired World: Perspectives from Singapore," *Information Communication & Society* 1, no. 3 (1998). A shrewd observer wondered if they were not trying to get ahead of the technology to digitally ring-fence the island for reasons of censorship to protect "Asian values"—which turned out to be true. Warwick Neville, "Managing the Smart City-State: Singapore Approaches the 21st Century," *New Zealand Geographer* 55, no. 1 (1999): 39.

65. This followed conversations in the field of Law and Development at the time. Carter, "The Clonability of the Singapore Model of Law and Development: The Case of Suzhou, China," 208–20.

66. See Chris Gifford, *The Making of Eurosceptic Britain* (Aldershot: Ashgate, 2008); Quinn Slobodian and Dieter Plehwe, "Neoliberals Against Europe," in *Mutant Neoliberalism: Market Rule and Political Ruptures*, ed. William Callison and Zachary Manfredi (New York: Fordham University Press, 2019), 89–111; Quinn Slobodian, "Demos Veto and Demos Exit: The Neoliberals Who Embraced Direct Democracy and Secession," *Journal of Australian Political Economy*, no. 86 (2020): 19–36; and Roberto Ventresca, "Neoliberal Thinkers and European Integration in the 1980s and the Early 1990s," *Contemporary European History* 31, no. 1 (2022): 31–46.

67. Margaret Thatcher, "Speech in Korea," September 3, 1992, https://www.margaretthatcher.org/document/108302.

68. See, e.g., Margaret Thatcher, "Speech to the International Free Enterprise Dinner," April 20, 1999, https://www.margaretthatcher.org/document/108381.

69. Margaret Thatcher, "Speech Receiving Aims of Industry National Free Enterprise Award," October 17, 1984, https://www.margaretthatcher.org/document/105766.

70. Youyenn Teo, "Interrogating the Limits of Welfare Reforms in Singapore," *Development and Change* 46, no. 1 (January 2015): 99. See Cooper, *Family Values: Between Neoliberalism and the New Social Conservatism*. Another legacy of the earlier period was race science and eugenics, openly embraced by Lee in attempts to increase births from highly educated women and decrease births from those less so. See Michael D. Barr, "Lee Kuan Yew: Race, Culture and Genes," *Journal of Contemporary Asia* 29, no. 2 (1999).

71. Kwasi Kwarteng et al., *Britannia Unchained: Global Lessons for Growth and Prosperity* (Houndmills, UK: Palgrave Macmillan, 2012), 57.

72. "Making the Break," *Economist*, December 8, 2012, Gale.

73. Tony Rennell, "Brexit Bloodletting," *Daily Mail*, October 31, 2016, Gale OneFile; and Ben Chapman, "'Singapore on Steroids,'" *Independent*, November 13, 2019, Gale In Context: Global Issues.

74. Daniel Hannan, "Free Trade: Have We Lost the Argument?," *Initiative for Free Trade*, https://ifreetrade.org/?/article/free-trade-have-we-lost-the-argument.

75. Jeremy Hunt, "Why I'm Looking East for My Vision of Post-Brexit Prosperity," *Daily Mail*, December 29, 2018, https://www.dailymail.co.uk/debate/article-6539165/Why-Im-looking-east-vision-post-Brexit-prosperity-writes-JEREMY-HUNT.html.

76. Paterson, "Don't Listen to the Terrified Europeans. The Singapore Model Is Our Brexit Opportunity."

77. Glen Owen, "Let's Make Britain the Singapore of Europe!," *Mail on Sunday*, January 17, 2021, https://www.pressreader.com/uk/the-mail-on-sunday/20210117/281719797231656.

78. On this point see William Davies, "Leave, and Leave Again," *London Review of Books*, February 7, 2019, https://www.lrb.co.uk/the-paper/v41/n03/william-davies/leave-and-leave-again.

79. This is Sajid Javid. Fraser Nelson, "Javid's Home Truths," *Spectator*, February 11, 2017, https://www.spectator.co.uk/article/javid-s-home-truths; and Jamie Grierson, "Going Up: Sajid Javid, the Tory from 'Britain's Worst Street', Is Back," *Guardian* (UK Edition), June 27, 2021, https://www.theguardian.com/politics/2021/jun/27/going-up-sajid-javid-the-tory-from-britains-worst-street-is-back.

80. This is Jacob Rees-Mogg. Alan Livsey, "Brexiter Jacob Rees-Mogg's Lacklustre Record as a Fund Manager," *Financial Times*, October 15, 2017, ProQuest; and James Meek, "The Two Jacobs," *London Review of Books*, August 1, 2019, https://www.lrb.co.uk/the-paper/v41/n15/james-meek/the-two-jacobs.

81. Boris Johnson, "Boris Johnson's First Speech as Prime Minister," Gov.uk, July 24, 2019, https://www.gov.uk/government/speeches/boris-johnsons-first-speech-as-prime-minister-24-july-2019; and Arj Singh, "Liz Truss Plan for Singapore-Style Freeports 'Will Create Tax Havens' in Britain,"

Huffpost (UK Edition), August 1, 2019, https://www.huffingtonpost.co .uk/entry/freeports-brexit-liz-truss-tax-havens-money-laundering_uk _5d431469e4b0ca604e2eb8f4.

82. Case in point was Eamonn Butler of the Adam Smith Institute who offered advice to both Thatcher and Johnson administrations on free ports. Eamonn Butler and Madsen Pirie, eds., *Freeports* (London: Adam Smith Institute, 1983); and Eamonn Butler, "Now's the Time to Finally Get Freeports Right and Reinvigorate the British Economy," *Telegraph.co.uk*, August 2, 2019, Westlaw.

83. "Post-Brexit Plans Unveiled for 10 Free Ports," *BBC News*, August 2, 2019, https://www.bbc.com/news/49198825.

84. Martina Bet, "EU Could Tear Up Rishi Sunak's Freeport Plan with Measure Agreed in Brexit Trade Deal," *Express Online*, March 4, 2021, https://www .express.co.uk/news/uk/1405449/eu-news-rishi-sunak-freeports-brexit -trade-deal-exports-spt. The first round of trade agreements with twenty-three countries post-Brexit actually made it *less* advantageous to produce in free ports than outside of them. Jim Pickard, "UK Freeports Blow as Exporters Face Tariffs to 23 Countries," *Financial Times*, May 9, 2021, https://www .ft.com/content/625d1913-9242-4d97-9d0b-9cd6925c4e0e.

85. Margaret Thatcher, "Speech to Australian Institute of Directors," October 2, 1981, https://www.margaretthatcher.org/document/104711.

86. Gavin Shatkin, "Reinterpreting the Meaning of the 'Singapore Model': State Capitalism and Urban Planning," *International Journal of Urban and Regional Research* 38, no. 1 (January 2014): 124.

87. Tan, "The Ideology of Pragmatism: Neo-liberal Globalisation and Political Authoritarianism in Singapore," 76.

88. Shatkin, "Reinterpreting the Meaning of the 'Singapore Model': State Capitalism and Urban Planning," 135.

89. Seth S. King, "Modern Building Changes Face of Romantic Singapore," *New York Times*, August 12, 1963, https://www.nytimes.com/1963/08/12/archives /modern-building-changes-face-of-romantic-singapore-tide-of.html.

90. "Apartments Rising Fast in Singapore," *Los Angeles Times*, July 12, 1963, Newspapers.com.

91. Michael A. H. B. Walter, "The Territorial and the Social: Perspectives on the Lack of Community in High-Rise/High-Density Living in Singapore," *Ekistics* 45, no. 270 (June 1978): 237.

92. Susan S. Fainstein, "State Domination in Singapore's Public–Private Partnerships," *Journal of Urban Affairs* 43, no. 2 (2021): 283.

93. See series of seven posts beginning with Dominic Cummings, "High Performance Startup Government & Systems Politics: Some Notes on Lee Kuan Yew's Book," *Dominic Cummings Substack*, August 2, 2021,

https://dominiccummings.substack.com/p/high-performance-startup
-government?s=r.

94. One academic called this a program "more akin to Taiwan-on-Trent; an
activist, entrepreneurial state that supports technology-intensive industries
and relies on exporting services to compete in the global economy." Adrian
Pabst, "Power Without Purpose," *New Statesman*, February 14–20, 2020,
https://www.newstatesman.com/magazine/power-without-purpose. In this
interpretation, Brexit might be most relevant for escaping the EU's doctri-
naire prohibitions on state subsidies. "Opening the Taps," *Economist* (September 19, 2020): 26.

95. Charmaine Chua, "Sunny Island Set in the Sea," in *Digital Lives in the
Global City: Contesting Infrastructures*, ed. Deborah Cowen et al. (Vancouver: University of British Columbia Press, 2020), 238–47.

96. Paul R. Krugman, "The Myth of Asia's Miracle," *Foreign Affairs* (November–
December 1994): 71.

97. Goh, "Migrant Worker Exclusion," 360.

98. Goh, 358.

99. Ahead of the vote, 93 percent of those who planned to vote Leave were worried about high immigration rates. Harold D. Clarke, Matthew Goodwin,
and Paul Whitely, *Brexit: Why Britain Voted to Leave the European Union*
(New York: Cambridge University Press, 2017), 12.

100. Dominic Cummings, "How the Brexit Referendum Was Won," *Spectator*,
January 8, 2017, https://www.spectator.co.uk/article/dominic-cummings
-how-the-brexit-referendum-was-won.

101. Youyenn Teo, *This Is What Inequality Looks Like* (Singapore: Ethos, 2018).

CHAPTER 4: LIBERTARIAN BANTUSTAN

1. Martín Arboleda, *Planetary Mine: Territories of Extraction Under Late Capitalism* (Brooklyn: Verso, 2020), 61.

2. Patrick Cox, "Spotlight: South African Individualist," *Reason*, December 1,
1980, 61.

3. Milton Friedman, "The Fragility of Freedom," in *Friedman in South Africa*,
ed. Meyer Feldberg, Kate Jowell, and Stephen Mulholland (Cape Town:
Graduate School of Business, 1976), 8.

4. Kogila Moodley, "The Legitimation Crisis of the South African State," *Journal of Modern African Studies* 24, no. 2 (1986): 187–201.

5. Laura Phillips, "History of South Africa's Bantustans," in *Oxford Research
Encyclopedia of African History* (2017), n.p.

6. Henry Kamm, "Transkei, a South African Black Area, Is Independent,"
New York Times, October 26, 1976, https://www.nytimes.com/1976/10/26

/archives/transkei-a-south-african-black-area-is-independent-transkei
-becomes.html.

7. For details see Jamie Miller, *An African Volk: The Apartheid Regime and Its Search for Survival* (New York: Oxford University Press, 2016).

8. Laura Evans, "Contextualising Apartheid at the End of Empire: Repression, 'Development' and the Bantustans," *Journal of Imperial and Commonwealth History* 47, no. 2 (2019): 373.

9. Miller, *An African Volk*, 22.

10. "Say No to Ciskei Independence," *South African History Online*, https://www.sahistory.org.za/archive/say-no-ciskei-independence.

11. Quoted in Ferguson, *Global Shadows: Africa in the Neoliberal World Order*, 59.

12. Les Switzer, *Power and Resistance in an African Society: The Ciskei Xhosa and the Making of South Africa* (Madison: University of Wisconsin Press, 1993), 334.

13. Herbert Grubel, "Discussion," in *Freedom, Democracy and Economic Welfare*, ed. Michael Walker (Vancouver, BC: Fraser Institute, 1988), 240.

14. Anthony Robinson, "The Supply-Siders of Ciskei," *Financial Times*, November 19, 1986, Financial Times Historical Archive, Gale; and n.a., "The Sunday Times Reports That Ciskei, the Small Self-Governing Territory Within South Africa, Is Enjoying an Economic Boom," *Sunday Times* (London), June 2, 1985, Sunday Times Historical Archive, Gale.

15. Andre Jordaan, "Ciskei's Tax Reform Benefits Explained," *Daily Dispatch* (East London, South Africa), March 23, 1985, https://archive.org/stream/DTIC_ADA337700/DTIC_ADA337700_djvu.txt.

16. n.a., "The Sunday Times Reports That Ciskei." For details see John Blundell, "Ciskei's Independent Way," *Reason*, April 1, 1985, https://reason.com/1985/04/01/ciskeis-independent-way/.

17. George Stigler to Max Thurn, April 7, 1978. Hoover Institution Archives, Mont Pelerin Society Papers, Box 20, Folder 5.

18. Claire Badenhorst, "Meet Leon Louw of the FMF; Marxist Turned Free Marketeer: The Alec Hogg Show," *Biz News*, September 23, 2020, https://www.biznews.com/thought-leaders/2020/09/23/leon-louw-free-market.

19. "Introducing the South African Free Market Foundation," *Die Individualist— The Individualist*, no. 1 (December 1975): 1.

20. Walter E. Williams, "After Apartheid: An Interview with Leon Louw and Frances Kendall," *Reason*, July 1, 1988, https://reason.com/1988/07/01/after-apartheid1; and Deborah Posel, "The Apartheid Project, 1948–1970," in *The Cambridge History of South Africa*, ed. Robert Ross, Anne Kelk Mager, and Bill Nasson (Cambridge: Cambridge University Press, 2011), 330–31.

21. Cox, "Spotlight: South African Individualist," 61; and Dan O'Meara, *Volkskapitalisme: Class, Capital and Ideology in the Development of Afrikaner*

Nationalism, 1934–1948 (Cambridge: Cambridge University Press, 1983). On the broader debate over economic policy between economic liberals and conservatives in which other Mont Pelerin Society neoliberals were involved see Antina von Schnitzler, "Disciplining Freedom: Apartheid, Counterinsurgency, and the Political Histories of Neoliberalism," in *Market Civilizations: Neoliberals East and South*, ed. Quinn Slobodian and Dieter Plehwe (New York: Zone Books, 2022), 163–88.

22. Republic of Ciskei, *Report of the Commission of Inquiry into the Economic Development of the Republic of Ciskei* (Bisho: Government of the Republic of Ciskei, 1983), 14. The recuperation of an indigenous African property tradition was part of a revised—and sometimes even reversed—civilizational discourse in the 1980s and 1990s in some libertarian circles whereby tribal mentalities were redefined as truly free-market—comparable to those of the "Germanic tribes" of the Visigoths who are claimed to have preserved a property-rights-respecting tradition destroyed by the Roman law tradition, which they saw as originating in Persia. In this narrative, the Enlightenment rationalization model becomes itself an invasion from the East against the decentralized medieval model that was coded as the "true" Western tradition. In this new narrative, the Black population did not need to be educated into the market—they simply needed to have their inherent market natures liberated. As leading neoliberal voice and Mont Pelerin Society member Michael O'Dowd put it in a Free Market Foundation publication in 1992, "The rights-protecting Germanic tribes that survived into the Middle Ages and the African tribes that have survived into the present time have a great deal in common." Introduction to Leonard Liggio, *The Importance of Political Traditions* (Johannesburg: Free Market Foundation, 1992), 4.

23. Republic of Ciskei, *Report of the Commission of Inquiry*, 13.

24. On the history of Foreign Trade Zones see Dara Orenstein, *Out of Stock: The Warehouse in the History of Capitalism* (Chicago: University of Chicago Press, 2019).

25. Cameron and Palan, *The Imagined Economies of Globalization*.

26. Statement of Noel Beasley, chairperson, Indiana Save-Our-Jobs Campaign, Business agent, Indiana/Kentucky Joint Board, Amalgamated Clothing & Textile Workers Union, AFL-CIO, CLC. 97th Congress, second session, March 22, 1982, 51–52. For work by the authoritative scholar on EPZs see Patrick Neveling, "Export Processing Zones, Special Economic Zones and the Long March of Capitalist Development Policies During the Cold War," in *Decolonization and the Cold War: Negotiating Independence*, ed. Leslie James and Elisabeth Leake (London: Bloomsbury, 2015), 63–84.

27. Allister Sparks, "Foreign Companies Profit from Apartheid in S. Africa," *Washington Post*, April 10, 1987, Gale OneFile: Business.

28. Colin Nickerson, "Asian Companies Find Bonanza in S. African Market-place," *Boston Globe* (May 22, 1988), ProQuest Historical Newspapers; Askold Krushelnycky, "Intelligence File," *Sunday Times* (London), August 2, 1987, The Sunday Times Historical Archive, Gale.

29. Roger Thurow, "Ciskei Makes Offer Firms 'Can't Refuse,'" *Wall Street Journal*, March 5, 1987, ProQuest Historical Newspapers.

30. Nickerson, "Asian Companies Find Bonanza in S. African Marketplace."

31. Alan Hirsch, "Industrialising the Ciskey: A Costly Experiment," *Indicator South Africa* 3, no. 4 (1986): 16.

32. Melanie Yap and Dianne Leong Man, *Colour, Confusion and Concessions: The History of the Chinese in South Africa* (Hong Kong: Hong Kong University Press, 1996), 422.

33. n.a., "The Sunday Times Reports"; and Brian Stuart, "Financial Aid for Black States Detailed," *Citizen* (Johannesburg), April 11, 1985, https://archive.org/stream/DTIC_ADA337700/DTIC_ADA337700_djvu.txt. Companies would only receive the tax-free status if they forsook incentives from the government—but they would still receive "concessions relating to transport, rebates, housing and electricity supplies" and would be allowed to write off all previous benefits received. The generous incentives of the South African developmentalist state continued for the first few years after the tax cuts. Jordaan, "Ciskei's tax reform."

34. Gillian Hart, *Disabling Globalization: Places of Power in Post-apartheid South Africa* (Berkeley: University of California Press, 2002), 144.

35. Thurow, "Ciskei Makes Offer."

36. Hirsch, "Industrialising the Ciskey," 17.

37. n.a., "The Sunday Times Reports"; and Thurow, "Ciskei Makes Offer."

38. Truth and Reconciliation Commission, June 13, 1997, Name: Priscilla Maxongo, Case: Mdantsane, https://www.justice.gov.za/trc/hrvtrans/hrvel2/maxongo.htm.

39. "Commuters Shot Dead in Ciskei," *Times* (London), August 5, 1983, Times Digital Archive, Gale.

40. Michael Hornsby, "Black Union Chief Challenges Ciskei Self-Rule," *Times* (London), December 17, 1981, The Times Digital Archive, Gale.

41. Michael Hornsby, "South Africa Releases Black Union Leader," *Times* (London), March 5, 1982, The Times Digital Archive, Gale; and "Unionist 'Was Tortured,'" *Times* (London), March 24, 1983, The Times Digital Archive, Gale.

42. Paul Vallely, "Amnesty Reports Priest Whipped in Church Raid," *Times* (London), June 30, 1986, The Times Digital Archive, Gale; and Robert W. Poole Jr. et al., "Havens of Prosperity and Peace in South Africa's Back Yard," *Reason*, January 1, 1986, https://reason.com/1986/01/01/trends-203/.

43. Hermann Giliomee, "True Confessions, End Papers and the Dakar Conference: A Review of the Political Arguments," *Tydskrif vir Letterkunde* 46, no. 2 (2009): 37.

44. Ray Kennedy, "Lawyers Seek Retrial for 'Death-Squad Hitman,'" *Times* (London), November 20, 1989, The Times Digital Archive, Gale.

45. John Blundell was a Mont Pelerin Society member, head of the Institute for Humane Studies, and later head of the Atlas Economic Research Foundation and the Charles Koch Foundation. John Blundell, "Africa: Ciskei: A Trojan Horse to Topple Apartheid?," *Wall Street Journal*, March 18, 1985, ProQuest; Blundell, "Ciskei's Independent Way."

46. Brian Kantor, comment in P. T. Bauer, "Black Africa: Free or Oppressed?," in *Freedom, Democracy and Economic Welfare*, ed. Michael Walker (Vancouver, BC: Fraser Institute, 1988), 239.

47. Gordon Tullock, comment in Bauer, "Black Africa: Free or Oppressed?," 239.

48. Walter Block, comment in Bauer, "Black Africa: Free or Oppressed?," 239.

49. Leon Louw and Frances Kendall, *South Africa: The Solution* (Bisho: Amagi, 1986), xii.

50. Michael Johns, "Swiss Family Buthelezi," *Policy Review* (Spring 1988): 84.

51. Louw and Kendall, *South Africa*, 126.

52. Williams, "After Apartheid: An Interview with Leon Louw and Frances Kendall."

53. Leon Louw, "A Non-Left Anti-Apartheid Program," December 5, 1986, Stanford University, Hoover Institution Archives, Heartland Institute Papers, Box 87.

54. Louw and Kendall, *South Africa*, 136.

55. Louw and Kendall, 103.

56. Bruce W. Nelan, "306 Solutions to a Baffling Problem," *Time*, March 23, 1987, Academic Search Premier.

57. On the right of expulsion see Louw and Kendall, *South Africa*, 138.

58. Louw and Kendall, 215.

59. Louw and Kendall, 221. The model here was likely Sol Kerzner's casinos and resorts, some of which were built in Bantustans. Alan Cowell, "Sol Kerzner, South African Casino Tycoon, Is Dead at 84," *New York Times*, March 27, 2020, https://www.nytimes.com/2020/03/27/business/sol-kerzner-dead.html.

60. Louw and Kendall, *South Africa*, 217.

61. James Kirchik, "In Whitest Africa: The Afrikaner Homeland of Orania," *Virginia Quarterly Review* 84, no. 3 (2008): 78.

62. Stanley Uys, "Is Partition the Answer?," *Africa Report* (September–October 1981): 45.

63. Louw particularly praised their Klein Vrystaat (Little Free State) at the northeast corner of the Transvaal, which existed with a population of under

three hundred for five years in the 1880s as what Louw called a "constitutional anarchy," in which the vote was restricted to property owners and the government had only one rule: they were forbidden to make any additional laws. Leon Louw, "The Solution 1 of 6," [1985?], https://www.youtube.com/watch?v=46E-rdMDxY4.

64. Frances Kendall and Leon Louw, *Let the People Govern* (Bisho: Amagi Publications, 1989), 210.

65. Leon Louw, "Why People Do Not Want Orania to Secede," Libertarian Seminar, Orania, 2015, https://www.youtube.com/watch?v=iBVgyeON53o.

66. Andrew Kenny, "Welkom in Orania," *politicsweb*, October 29, 2015, https://www.politicsweb.co.za/news-and-analysis/welkom-in-orania.

67. Erwin Schweitzer, *The Making of Griqua, Inc.: Indigenous Struggles for Land and Autonomy in South Africa* (Münster: Lit Verlag, 2015), 37.

68. Ivo Vegter, "The Elusive Libertarian Enclave," *Daily Maverick*, December 11 2012, https://www.dailymaverick.co.za/opinionista/2012-12-11-the-elusive-libertarian-enclave/.

69. Trevor Watkins, "The Future in South Africa," *LibertarianSA Google Group* (March 17, 2016), https://groups.google.com/forum/print/msg/libsa/edXGhAbGG-w/OSqaFaUAEgAJ?ctz=4404831_72_76_104100_72_446760.

70. Michael McGowan, "Australian White Nationalists Reveal Plans to Recruit 'Disgruntled, White Male Population,'" *Guardian* (UK Edition), November 11, 2019, https://www.theguardian.com/australia-news/2019/nov/12/australian-white-nationalists-reveal-plans-to-recruit-disgruntled-white-male-population.

71. "The New South Africa," *American Renaissance* (January 2003); and "Keep Hope Alive?," *American Renaissance* (February 2001).

72. To offer one piece of evidence of many: Fred Macaskill, the founder and director of the Free Market Foundation who was invited to join the MPS by Hayek and attended their meeting in Hong Kong, wrote in 1979, "In a free society entirely racialistic communities could develop . . . the individual has the right to practice any form of discrimination he chooses with regard to his own property." Frederick Macaskill, *In Search of Liberty: Incorporating a Solution to the South African Problem* (New York: Books in Focus, 1979), 91. Jan Lombard, another attendee at the MPS meeting in Hong Kong in 1978, wrote in the same year that the key mechanism of his schema was that "People can even vote 'with their feet,' in the sense that under systems of multiple jurisdictions they will have the choice of a large variety of mini-political systems throughout the country," adding that "the principle of voluntary exclusiveness is also a vital element of this approach . . . If a purely white homeland is organized by a particular group of people somewhere in South Africa, this should not be regarded as contrary to the spirit of the laws of liberty." J. A. Lombard, *On Economic Liberalism in South*

Africa, BEPA Economic Papers, (Pretoria: Bureau for Economic Policy and Analysis, 1979), 23.

73. On this, see Lombard: "In this new order, people will for the foreseeable future continue to live in separate urban areas determined by the homogeneity of their life styles and their collective demand preferences. In so far as the colour of a man's skin and his language together represent a reasonable indicator of his life style, the question arises whether the physical appearance of the urban scene in South Africa will differ very much from that which has been developing under restrictions of the Group Areas Act." Lombard, *On Economic Liberalism in South Africa*, 24.

74. "Transcript of Mandela's Speech at Cape Town City Hall," *New York Times*, February 12, 1990, https://www.nytimes.com/1990/02/12/world/south-africa-s-new-era-transcript-mandela-s-speech-cape-town-city-hall-africa-it.html.

75. Eric Marsden, "Inside Johannesburg," *Sunday Times* (London), December 7, 1986, The Sunday Times Historical Archive, Gale; and Robinson, "Supply-siders of Ciskei."

76. "'Homeland' Leader Deposed in Ciskei," *New York Times*, March 5, 1990, https://www.nytimes.com/1990/03/05/world/homeland-leader-deposed-in-ciskei.html.

77. This was a vision also shared by some chiefs and Bantustan leaders who had profited from the more federal system. On the negotiations to dissolve the homeland system see Hilary Lynd, "The Peace Deal: The Formation of the Ingonyama Trust and the IFP Decision to Join South Africa's 1994 Elections," *South African Historical Journal* 73, no. 2 (2021): 318–60.

78. Quoted in Saul Dubow, *Apartheid, 1948–1994* (New York: Oxford University Press, 2014), 268.

79. See, e.g., Frederick Cooper, *Africa Since 1940: The Past of the Present* (New York: Cambridge University Press, 2002), 1. Some political scientists cavil that South Africa was already formally independent so decolonization is an inapt description. Timothy William Waters, *Boxing Pandora: Rethinking Borders, States, and Secession in a Democratic World* (New Haven, CT: Yale University Press, 2020), 59.

80. Orenstein, *Out of Stock: The Warehouse in the History of Capitalism*, 216.

81. UNCTAD, *World Investment Report: Special Economic Zones*, xii.

82. For this process of disenchantment see Patrick Bond, *Elite Transition: From Apartheid to Neoliberalism in South Africa* (London: Pluto Press, 2000).

83. James Ferguson, *The Anti-Politics Machine: "Development," Depoliticization, and Bureaucratic Power in Lesotho* (New York: Cambridge University Press, 1990).

84. Ferguson makes this point by comparing Lesotho to Transkei in Ferguson, *Global Shadows: Africa in the Neoliberal World Order*, 55–65. See also Laura Evans, "South Africa's Bantustans and the Dynamics of 'Decolonisation':

Reflections on Writing Histories of the Homelands," *South African Historical Journal* 64, no. 1 (March 2012): 122–23.

85. Masande Ntshanga, *Triangulum* (Columbus, OH: Two Dollar Radio, 2019), 210.

86. Ntshanga, *Triangulum*, 211.

87. Neal Stephenson, *Snow Crash* (New York: Del Rey, 1992), 40. Apartheid burbclaves are one of what he calls Franchise-Organized Quasi-National Entities (FOQNEs).

88. Neal Stephenson, *The Diamond Age: or, A Young Lady's Illustrated Primer* (New York: Bantam Spectra, 1995), 31.

89. Stephenson, *The Diamond Age*, 30.

90. Tom Bethell, "Let 500 Countries Bloom," *Washington Times*, May 8, 1990, Newsbank.

CHAPTER 5: THE WONDERFUL DEATH OF A STATE

1. The legal principle is *uti possidetis*—from the Latin *uti possidetis ita possideatis* ("may you have what you have had"). This opening section draws on Waters, *Boxing Pandora: Rethinking Borders, States, and Secession in a Democratic World*. The opposition to secession is based in the Saving Clause in the Declaration on Principles of International Law Concerning Friendly Relations and Co-operation Among States adopted by the UN General Assembly on October 24, 1970. See also Umut Özsu, *Completing Humanity: The International Law of Decolonization, 1960–82* (Cambridge: Cambridge University Press, forthcoming).

2. The Baltic states Latvia, Lithuania, and Estonia were not technically new nations as they remained de jure independent even as they were de facto incorporated into the Soviet Union as socialist republics after 1940.

3. For an extraordinary episode of libertarian state making at the moment of Vanuatu's independence see Raymond B. Craib, *Adventure Capitalism: A History of Libertarian Exit from Decolonization to the Digital Age* (Oakland, CA: PM Press, 2022), chap. 4.

4. Justin Raimondo, *An Enemy of the State: The Life of Murray N. Rothbard* (Amherst, NY: Prometheus Books, 2000), 46–54.

5. Murray N. Rothbard, "Free Market Police, Courts, and Law," *Reason* (March 1973), https://reason.com/1973/03/01/free-market-police-courts-and/.

6. Murray N. Rothbard, *Never a Dull Moment: A Libertarian Look at the Sixties* (Auburn, AL: Ludwig von Mises Institute, 2016), 48.

7. Daniel Bessner, "Murray Rothbard, Political Strategy, and the Making of Modern Libertarianism," *Intellectual History Review* 24, no. 4 (2014): 445.

8. Murray Newton Rothbard, *For a New Liberty: The Libertarian Manifesto (1973)* (Auburn, AL: Ludwig von Mises Institute, 2006), 350.

9. Rothbard, *Never a Dull Moment*, 48; and Rothbard, *For a New Liberty*, 102.

10. Murray N. Rothbard, "For Bengal," *Libertarian Forum* 3, no. 5 (May 1971); Murray N. Rothbard, "For Croatia," *Libertarian Forum* 4, no. 2 (February 1972). Complete run of issues available at https://mises.org/library/complete -libertarian-forum-1969-1984.

11. Rothbard, *Never a Dull Moment*, 102.

12. Murray N. Rothbard, Leonard Liggio, and H. George Resch, "Editorial: The Black Revolution," *Left and Right* 3, no. 3 (Autumn 1967): 13; and Murray N. Rothbard, Leonard Liggio, and H. George Resch, "Editorial: The Cry for Power: Black, White, and 'Polish,'" *Left and Right* 2, no. 3 (Autumn 1966): 12–13. On this larger history see Edward Onaci, *Free the Land: The Republic of New Afrika and the Pursuit of a Black Nation-State* (Chapel Hill: University of North Carolina Press, 2020).

13. Murray N. Rothbard, "Editor's Comment: The Panthers and Black Liberation," *Libertarian* 1, no. 4 (May 15, 1969), https://www.rothbard.it/articles /libertarian-forum/lf-1-4.pdf.

14. Murray N. Rothbard, *Egalitarianism as a Revolt Against Nature and Other Essays*, 2nd ed. (Auburn, AL: Ludwig von Mises Institute, 2000), 16.

15. Rothbard, *Egalitarianism as a Revolt Against Nature*, 7.

16. Janek Wasserman, *Marginal Revolutionaries: How Austrian Economics Fought the War of Ideas* (New Haven, CT: Yale University Press, 2019), 257. On the friction between the Cato and Mises Institutes see Doherty, *Radicals for Capitalism: A Freewheeling History of the Modern American Libertarian Movement*, 607–13.

17. Nathaniel Weyl, *Traitors' End: The Rise and Fall of the Communist Movement in Southern Africa* (New Rochelle, NY: Arlington House, 1970); Harry Browne, *How to Profit from the Coming Devaluation* (New Rochelle, NY: Arlington House, 1970); and David Friedman, *The Machinery of Freedom: Guide to a Radical Capitalism* (New Rochelle, NY: Arlington House, 1978).

18. Rockwell to Weyl, February 11, 1970, Stanford University, Hoover Institution Archives, Nathaniel Weyl Papers Box 34, Folder 8 (hereafter Weyl 34.8).

19. Paul had three stretches in the House of Representatives: from 1976 to 1977, 1979–1985, and 1997–2013.

20. Julian Sanchez and David Weigel, "Who Wrote Ron Paul's Newsletters?," *Reason*, January 16, 2008, https://reason.com/2008/01/16/who-wrote-ron -pauls-newsletter/.

21. "We Will Survive, and Prosper!," *Ron Paul Investment Letter* 8, no. 12 (December 15, 1992): 2; and "How to Store Your Gold at Home," *Ron Paul Investment Letter* 4, no. 2 (March 15, 1988): 8.

22. "Annie Get Your Gun . . . and Susie, Millie, and Marcia Too," *Ron Paul Investment Letter* 8, no. 6 (June 15, 1992): 2.

23. "Gold and South Africa," *Ron Paul Survival Report* 9, no. 1 (January 15, 1993): 2.

24. "There Goes South Africa," *Ron Paul Survival Report* 10, no. 6 (June 15, 1994): 5.

25. "Ethnic Hatreds May Raise the Gold Price," *Ron Paul Investment Letter* 6, no. 6 (June 15, 1990): 3; and "People Prefer Their Own," *Ron Paul Survival Report* 9, no. 1 (January 15, 1993): 3.

26. "The Disappearing White Majority," *Ron Paul Survival Report* 9, no. 1 (January 15, 1993): 7.

27. "Ron Paul's Bookstore," *Ron Paul Survival Report* 10, no. 2 (February 15, 1994): 8.

28. Murray N. Rothbard and Llewellyn H. Rockwell, "Why the Report?," *Rothbard-Rockwell Report* 1, no. 1 (April 1990): 1.

29. See Melinda Cooper, "The Alt-Right: Neoliberalism, Libertarianism and the Fascist Temptation," *Theory, Culture & Society* 38, no. 6 (2021): 29–50; and Quinn Slobodian, "Anti-68ers and the Racist-Libertarian Alliance: How a Schism Among Austrian School Neoliberals Helped Spawn the Alt Right," *Cultural Politics* 15, no. 3 (2019): 372–86.

30. Llewellyn H. Rockwell, "A New Right," *Rothbard-Rockwell Report* 1, no. 1 (April 1990): 11; and Llewellyn H. Rockwell, "The Case for Paleo-Libertarianism," *Liberty* 3, no. 3 (January 1990): 35.

31. Rockwell, "The Case for Paleo-Libertarianism," 37.

32. Murray N. Rothbard, "The Freedom Revolution," *Free Market* 7, no. 8 (August 1989): 1.

33. Murray N. Rothbard, "A Strategy for the Right," *Rothbard-Rockwell Report* (March 1992): 6.

34. Rothbard, "A Strategy for the Right," 16. See also John Ganz, "The Year the Clock Broke," *Baffler* (November 2018), https://thebaffler.com/salvos/the-year-the-clock-broke-ganz.

35. Lew Rockwell, "Rockwell's Thirty-Day Plan," *Free Market* 9, no. 3 (March 1991): 1–5.

36. Rothbard, *Egalitarianism as a Revolt Against Nature*, 11, 103.

37. Murray N. Rothbard, "The New Libertarian Creed," *New York Times*, February 9, 1971.

38. Murray N. Rothbard, *Conceived in Liberty* (Auburn, AL: Ludwig von Mises Institute, 2011), 177.

39. Thomas Fleming, Opening Remarks, JRC Meeting, December 1, 1990, The Howard Center for Family Religion and Society, Rockford Illinois Records in the Regional History Center, Northern Illinois University, RC 238, Allan Carlson Papers, Box 173, Folder 12 (hereafter Carlson 173.12).

40. For membership lists and lists of attendees at meeting see Carlson 173.12. Also available from the author on request; on the paleoconservatives see

George Hawley, *Right-Wing Critics of American Conservatism* (Lawrence: University Press of Kansas, 2016); and Nicole Hemmer, *Partisans: The Conservative Revolutionaries Who Remade American Politics in the 1990s* (New York: Basic Books, 2022).

41. n.a., "Who Speaks for Us?," *American Renaissance* 1, no. 1 (November 1990), https://www.amren.com/archives/back-issues/november-1990/#cover.

42. Aristide R. Zolberg, *A Nation by Design: Immigration Policy in the Fashioning of America* (Cambridge, MA: Harvard University Press, 2008), 396.

43. Samuel Francis, "Why Race Matters," *American Renaissance* (September 1994), https://www.amren.com/archives/back-issues/september-1994/#cover.

44. John Ganz, "The Forgotten Man," *Baffler* (December 15, 2017), https://thebaffler.com/latest/the-forgotten-man-ganz; Daniel Denvir, *All-American Nativism* (New York: Verso, 2020), 64; and Joseph E. Lowndes, "From Pat Buchanan to Donald Trump: The Nativist Turn in Right-Wing Populism," in *A Field Guide to White Supremacy*, ed. Kathleen Belew and Ramón A. Gutiérrez (Berkeley: University of California Press, 2021).

45. Euan Hague, Heidi Beirich, and Edward H. Sebesta, *Neo-Confederacy: A Critical Introduction* (Austin: University of Texas Press, 2008), 104–18.

46. Hague, Beirich, and Sebesta, *Neo-Confederacy: A Critical Introduction*, 1; Michael Hill and Thomas Fleming, "New Dixie Manifesto," *Washington Post*, October 29, 1995, ProQuest; and Carlson to Antony Sullivan, "Report on 'The New Politics' Conference," funded by a grant from the Earhart Foundation, n.d.

47. Dixienet: The Southern League Website, https://web.archive.org/web/19961102130200/http://www.dixienet.org/slhomepg/foreign.html.

48. Murray N. Rothbard, "The Nationalities Question (August 1990)," in *The Irrepressible Rothbard*, ed. Llewellyn H. Rockwell (Burlingame, CA: The Center for Libertarian Studies, 2000), 231.

49. Rothbard, *Never a Dull Moment*, 48.

50. Murray N. Rothbard, "The 'New Fusionism': A Movement for Our Time," *Rothbard-Rockwell Report* 2, no. 1 (January 1991): 8.

51. As noted in the article, it was first presented as a talk at the regional meeting of the Mont Pelerin Society in Rio de Janeiro in September 1993. Murray N. Rothbard, "Nations by Consent: Decomposing the Nation-State," *Journal of Libertarian Studies* 11, no. 1 (Fall 1994): 1.

52. "Beyond a small quantity, national heterogeneity simply does not work," he wrote, "the 'nation' disintegrates into more than one nation, and the need for separation becomes acute." For South Africa, he advocated not less apartheid but more: a "partitioning" into separate ethnic groups. Murray N. Rothbard, "The Vital Importance of Separation," *Rothbard-Rockwell Report* 5, no. 4 (April 1994): 5, 7.

53. Rothbard, "Importance of Separation," 10.

54. Rothbard, 10.

55. Ron Paul, "The Moral Promise of Political Independence," *Secession, State and Economy Conference*, April 7–9, 1995, https://mises.org/library/moral -promise-political-independence.

56. For biographical details see the materials in Hoover Institution Archives, Center for Libertarian Studies Papers, Box 4, folder 4.

57. Richard Rahn, "Why Estonia Is a Country for the Future," *Cato Institute*, September 22, 2015, https://www.cato.org/commentary/why-estonia-country -future.

58. Mila Jonjić and Nenad Pantelić, "The Mediterranean Tiger: How Montenegro Became a Neoliberal Role Model," in *Market Civilizations: Neoliberals East and South*, ed. Slobodian and Plehwe. See also Torben Niehr, "Viva Montenegro! Lasst tausend Monacos blühen!," *Eigentümlich Frei* 9, no. 63 (June 2006): 13.

59. Appel and Orenstein, *From Triumph to Crisis: Neoliberal Economic Reform in Postcommunist Countries*, 91.

60. Hans-Hermann Hoppe, "The Economic and Political Rationale for European Secessionism," in *Secession, State & Liberty*, ed. David Gordon (New Brunswick, NJ: Transaction, 1998), 222.

61. Hoppe, "The Economic and Political Rationale for European Secessionism," 218.

62. Hans-Hermann Hoppe, "The Political Economy of Centralization and Secession," *Secession, State and Economy Conference*, April 7–9, 1995, https: //mises.org/library/political-economy-centralization-and-secession.

63. Hans-Hermann Hoppe, "The Property and Freedom Society—Reflections After Five Years," *Libertarian Standard* (2010), accessed September 1, 2017, http://libertarianstandard.com/articles/hans-hermann-hoppe/the -property-and-freedom-society-reflections-after-5-years/.

64. Hawley, *Right-wing Critics of American Conservatism*, 200. Other former JRC members hosted in Bodrum include Joseph Salerno and Thomas DiLorenzo. Salerno expressed a very Rothbardian affinity between Malcolm X and Mises in Joseph T. Salerno, "Mises on Nationalism, the Right of Self-Determination, and the Problem of Immigration," *Mises Institute*, March 28, 2017, https://mises.org/wire/mises-nationalism-right-self-determination -and-problem-immigration.

65. "PFS 2010 Annual Meeting—Speakers and Presentations," https://property andfreedom.org/2018/02/pfs-2010-annual-meeting-speakers-and -presentations/.

66. "PFS 2014 Annual Meeting—Speakers and Schedule," https://propertyand freedom.org/2013/11/pfs-2014-annual-meeting-speakers-and-schedule/.

67. Robert Grözinger, "Freie Stadt in Südafrika," *Eigentümlich Frei* (May 2013), 18.

68. Agenda, Wayback Machine capture, June 4, 2016, https://propertyand
freedom.org/; and Brandon Thorp and Penn Bullock, "Peter Thiel Cancels
Appearance at Fascist Conference," *Towleroad*, July 29, 2016.

69. Richard Spencer, "The 'Alternative Right' in America," *Property and Freedom Society*, June 3–7, 2010, https://vimeo.com/12598049.

70. Joseph Goldstein, "Alt-Right Gathering Exults in Trump Election with
Nazi-Era Salute," *New York Times*, November 20, 2016, https://www
.nytimes.com/2016/11/21/us/alt-right-salutes-donald-trump.html.

71. Jeff Deist, "Self-Determination, Not Universalism, Is the Goal," *Mises Institute*,
May 29, 2017, https://mises.org/blog/self-determination-not-universalism
-goal.

72. John Ganz, "Libertarians Have More in Common with the Alt-Right Than
They Want You to Think," *Washington Post*, September 19, 2017), Gale
Academic OneFile; Quinn Slobodian, "A Brief History of Neoliberal Prob-
lems: How Race Theory Spawned the Alt Right," *Harvard University New
Directions in European History Colloquium* (September 21, 2017); and Slobo-
dian, "Anti-68ers and the Racist-Libertarian Alliance," 378–82.

73. Hans-Hermann Hoppe, *Democracy: The God That Failed* (New Brunswick,
NJ: Transaction, 2001), 73.

74. See, e.g., citation of race scientist Philippe Rushton in Hoppe, *Democracy*, 141.

75. Hoppe, *Democracy*, 218.

76. Murray N. Rothbard, "America's Two Just Wars: 1775 and 1861," in *The
Costs of War: America's Pyrrhic Victories*, ed. John V. Denson (New Brunswick, NJ: Transaction, 1999), 133.

77. See Nicole Hemmer, "The Alt-Right in Charlottesville: How an Online
Movement Became a Real-World Presence," in *A Field Guide to White
Supremacy*, 287–303.

78. "Christopher Cantwell Radical Agenda," accessed September 16, 2017,
https://christophercantwell.com/product/i/.

79. Chase Rachels, *White, Right, and Libertarian* (Createspace Independent
Publishing, 2018).

80. Hans-Hermann Hoppe, "Libertarianism and the Alt-Right: In Search of a Libertarian Strategy for Social Change," The Ludwig von Mises Centre (UK),
October 20, 2017, https://misesuk.org/2017/10/20/libertarianism-and-the
-alt-right-hoppe-speech-2017/. See, e.g., Hans-Hermann Hoppe, "The Case
for Free Trade and Restricted Immigration," *Journal of Libertarian Studies*
13, no. 2 (1998): 221–33; and Rothbard, "Nations by Consent: Decomposing
the Nation-State," 7.

81. To date, the most successful efforts at creating self-contained white nationalist communities have been in the other corner of the country, in the
Pacific Northwest. See Kathleen Belew, *Bring the War Home: The White*

Power Movement and Paramilitary America (Cambridge, MA: Harvard University Press, 2018).

82. Graham and Marvin, *Splintering Urbanism: Networked Infrastructures, Technological Mobilities and the Urban Condition*, 360.

83. Jim Surowiecki, "Bundynomics," *New Yorker*, January 25, 2016, https://www.newyorker.com/magazine/2016/01/25/bundynomics. For excellent studies of this topic see Phil A. Neel, *Hinterland: America's New Landscape of Class and Conflict* (London: Reaktion, 2018); Daniel Martinez HoSang and Joseph E. Lowndes, *Producers, Parasites, Patriots: Race and the New Right-Wing Politics of Precarity* (Minneapolis: University of Minnesota Press, 2019), chap. 5; and James R. Skillen, *This Land Is My Land: Rebellion in the West* (New York: Oxford University Press, 2020). On the related Posse Comitatus, "sovereign citizen," and "redemptionist" movements see Anna Merlan, *Republic of Lies: Conspiracy Theorists and Their Surprising Rise to Power* (New York: Metropolitan, 2019), chap. 7.

84. Michael Phillips, *White Metropolis: Race, Ethnicity, and Religion in Dallas, 1841–2001* (Austin: University of Texas Press, 2006), 64. For a reflection on Spencer and Dallas see Michael Phillips, "The Elite Roots of Richard Spencer's Racism," *Jacobin*, December 29, 2016, https://jacobin.com/2016/12/richard-spencer-alt-right-dallas-texas.

85. David Dillon, "Safe Havens: Gated Communities Are Appealing to Today's Yearning for Security (June 19, 1994)," in *The Open-Ended City: David Dillon on Texas Architecture*, ed. Kathryn Holliday and Robert Decherd (Austin: University of Texas Press, 2019), 141–46.

CHAPTER 6: COSPLAYING THE NEW MIDDLE AGES

1. This was the Fourth Liberty Fund–Fraser Institute Conference Rating Economic Freedom. Stephen T. Easton and Michael A. Walker, eds., *Rating Global Economic Freedom* (Vancouver, BC: Fraser Institute, 1992), vi.

2. Diana Ketcham, "Sea Ranch, California's Modernist Utopia, Gets an Update," *New York Times*, June 11, 2019, https://www.nytimes.com/2019/06/11/arts/design/sea-ranch-california.html.

3. Martha Tyler, "Sea Ranch Races Toward Build Out: Information from the 2000 U.S. Census," *Soundings* (Spring 2002), https://www.tsra.org/wp-content/uploads/2019/11/Soundings_2002_Census-ID_3595.pdf.

4. Friedman and Friedman, *Two Lucky People: Memoirs*, 562; and "The Sea Ranch Restrictions: A Declaration of Restrictions, Covenants and Conditions," May 10, 1965, https://www.tsra.org/wp-content/uploads/2019/11/Restrictions.pdf.

5. Lawrence Halprin and Bill Platt, "The Sea Ranch as an Intentional Community," *Ridge Review* 3, no. 3 (Fall 1983), http://s3.amazonaws.com

/arena-attachments/2149774/71f003a25682dd4abc2c7aa0b93720b6.pdf
?1525789191.

6. Hadley Meares, "From Russia with Love: Fort Ross and Russia's Failed Attempt to Conquer California," *KCET*, August 2, 2017, https://www.kcet .org/shows/california-coastal-trail/from-russia-with-love-fort-ross-and -russias-failed-attempt-to-conquer-california.

7. Edward J. Blakely and Mary Gail Snyder, *Fortress America: Gated Communities in the United States* (Washington, DC: Brookings Institution Press, 1997), 7. For many it has remained so. Geoff Eley writes about "gatedness" as an "emerging societal paradigm." Geoff Eley, "Liberalism in Crisis: What Is Fascism and Where Does It Come From?," in *Fascism in America: Past and Present*, ed. Gavriel Rosenfeld and Janet Ward (New York: Cambridge University Press, forthcoming).

8. Gernot Köhler, "The Three Meanings of Global Apartheid: Empirical, Normative, Existential," *Alternatives: Global, Local, Political* 20, no. 3 (July–September 1995): 403–13.

9. Roger K. Lewis, "'Gated' Areas: Start of New Middle Ages," *Washington Post*, September 9, 1995, ProQuest Historical Newspapers. See Graham and Marvin, *Splintering Urbanism: Networked Infrastructures, Technological Mobilities and the Urban Condition*, 228.

10. Lewis, "Start of New Middle Ages."

11. Quoted in Natalie Y. Moore, *The South Side: A Portrait of Chicago and American Segregation* (New York: St. Martin's, 2016), 46.

12. Friedman, *Capitalism and Freedom*, 118. See also Nancy MacLean, "How Milton Friedman Aided and Abetted Segregationists in His Quest to Privatize Public Education," *Institute for New Economic Thinking*, September 27, 2021, https://www.ineteconomics.org/perspectives/blog/how -milton-friedman-aided-and-abetted-segregationists-in-his-quest-to -privatize-public-education.

13. He wrote for and helped edit the *Harvard Conservative* and was the university representative for the *New Individualist Review*, for which his father sat on the editorial board along with Friedrich Hayek. *New Individualist Review* 2, no. 2 (Summer 1962); and Friedman and Friedman, *Two Lucky People: Memoirs*, 372.

14. David Friedman, "The Radical: Figs from Thistles," *New Guard* (Summer 1969): 19.

15. Stan Lehr and Louis Rossetto Jr., "The New Right Credo-Libertarianism," *New York Times Magazine*, January 10, 1971, https://www.nytimes.com /1971/01/10/archives/the-new-right-credo-libertarianism.html.

16. David Friedman, "Problems with Libertarianism" (1981), http://www .daviddfriedman.com/Ideas%20I/Libertarianism/Problems.pdf.

17. Friedman, *Capitalism and Freedom*, 32.

18. David Friedman, *The Machinery of Freedom: Guide to a Radical Capitalism* (New York: Harper Colophon, 1973).

19. Patrick M. Flynn, Letter to the Editor, *New Guard*, April 1970, 25.

20. Michael A. Cramer, *Medieval Fantasy as Performance: The Society for Creative Anachronism and the Current Middle Ages* (Lanham, MD: Scarecrow Press, 2010), 1.

21. "Some Tricks," 185, http://www.daviddfriedman.com/Medieval/miscellany _pdf/Articles_about_Persona.pdf.

22. "Pennsic War History," http://www.pennsicwar.org/History.

23. David Friedman, "A Theory of the Size and Shape of Nations," *Journal of Political Economy* 85, no. 1 (February 1977): 59–77. David boasted of being a professional economist without having ever taken an economics course for credit. Friedman, "Problems with Libertarianism."

24. David Friedman, "Private Creation and Enforcement of Law: A Historical Case," *Journal of Legal Studies* 8, no. 2 (March 1979): 400.

25. For inspiration, Friedman credited the work of Gary Becker and George Stigler from earlier in the decade when they proposed "free competition" among enforcers. Gary Becker and George J. Stigler, "Law Enforcement, Malfeasance, and Compensation of Enforcers," *Journal of Legal Studies* 3, no. 1 (January 1974): 14; and Friedman, "Private Creation and Enforcement of Law: A Historical Case," 400.

26. David Friedman, "Legal Systems Very Different from Ours" (2nd Seasteading Institute Conference, 2009), https://www.seasteading.org/david-d -friedman-legal-systems-very-different-from-ours/. For a recent reprisal of the theme see Vincent Geloso and Peter T. Leeson, "Are Anarcho-Capitalists Insane? Medieval Icelandic Conflict Institutions in Comparative Perspective," *Revue d'économie politique* 6, no. 130 (2020): 957–74.

27. Benson's personal web page, accessed January 2021, https://myweb.fsu.edu /bbenson/.

28. Bruce L. Benson, *The Enterprise of Law: Justice Without the State* (Oakland, CA: Independent Institute, 2011), 22.

29. Benson, *Enterprise of Law*, 23.

30. Benson, 28, 46.

31. Benson, 62.

32. Benson, 51.

33. Benson, 71.

34. Benson, 73.

35. Benson, 45.

36. Benson, 182.

37. Benson, 186.

38. William Gibson, *Virtual Light* (New York: Bantam Spectra, 1993).

39. *Battle Angel*, episode 1, "Ruty Angel," directed by Hiroshi Fukutomi, written by Akinori Endō, original video animation, 1993.

40. Bruce Benson, *To Serve and Protect: Privatization and Community in Criminal Justice* (New York: New York University Press, 1998), 91.

41. Benson, *The Enterprise of Law*, 211.

42. Benson, *To Serve and Protect: Privatization and Community in Criminal Justice*, 5.

43. See also Rothbard, *For a New Liberty: The Libertarian Manifesto (1973)*, 108; and Murray N. Rothbard, *The Ethics of Liberty*, 2nd ed. (New York: New York University Press, 1998), 87.

44. Libertarian Forum offices were at 1620 Montgomery St. *Libertarian Review*, April 1979, 3; and Doherty, *Radicals for Capitalism*, 413.

45. Gerald Frost, *Antony Fisher: Champion of Liberty*, condensed and ed. David Moller (London: Institute of Economic Affairs, 2008).

46. David Boaz, "Gates of Wrath," *Washington Post*, January 7, 1996, ProQuest Historical Newspapers.

47. Alexander Tabarrok, "Market Challenges and Government Failure: Lessons from the Voluntary City," in *The Voluntary City: Choice, Community, and Civil Society*, ed. David T. Beito, Peter Gordon, and Alexander Tabarrok (Ann Arbor: University of Michigan Press, 2002), 428.

48. Donald J. Boudreaux and Randall G. Holcombe, "Government by Contract," *Public Finance Quarterly* 17, no. 3 (1989): 266.

49. Boudreaux and Holcombe, "Government by Contract," 276.

50. Gordon Tullock, *Efficient Government Through Decentralization*, BEPA Economic Papers (Pretoria: Bureau for Economic Policy and Analysis, 5 September 1979), 1.

51. Tullock, *Efficient Government Through Decentralization*, 12.

52. Gordon Tullock, "A New Proposal for Decentralizing Government Activity," in *Rationale Wirtschaftspolitik in komplexen Gesellschaften: Gérard Gäfgen zum 60. Geburtstag*, ed. Hellmuth Milde and Hans G. Monissen (Stuttgart: W. Kohlhammer, 1985), 146.

53. Gordon Tullock, *The New Federalist* (Vancouver, BC: Fraser Institute, 1994), xvi.

54. Retiring from George Mason University in 1987, he took a new job at the University of Arizona only to return to GMU from 1999 to 2008. What Tullock wrote about as the Sunshine Mountain Ridge HOA was almost certainly the Sunrise Mountain Ridge HOA in the Catalina Foothills, still active today.

55. Tullock, *The New Federalist*, 11.

56. Tullock, 14.

57. David Boaz, "Opting Out of Government Failure," *Washington Post*, September 10, 1996, ProQuest Historical Newspapers.

58. Friedman, *The Machinery of Freedom: Guide to a Radical Capitalism*, 219.

59. Hans-Hermann Hoppe, "The Libertarian Quest for a Grand Historical Narrative," *Mises Institute*, November 5, 2018, https://mises.org/print/44602.

60. Hoppe, *Democracy: The God That Failed*, 291.

61. David Friedman, "Concerning a Dream," *Tournaments Illuminated*, no. 42 (1977), http://www.daviddfriedman.com/Medieval/miscellany_pdf/Articles_about_Persona.pdf.

62. Patri Friedman, "Ephemerisle," Seasteading Institute Conference, September 29, 2009, San Francisco, CA, video, 31:46, https://vimeo.com/10912197.

63. Philip E. Steinberg, Elizabeth Nyman, and Mauro J. Caraccioli, "Atlas Swam: Freedom, Capital, and Floating Sovereignties in the Seasteading Vision," *Antipode* 44, no. 4 (2012): 1532–50.

64. Friedman, *The Machinery of Freedom: Guide to a Radical Capitalism*, 156.

65. Graham and Marvin, *Splintering Urbanism: Networked Infrastructures, Technological Mobilities and the Urban Condition*, 272; and Keith C. Veal, "The Gating of America: The Political and Social Consequences of Gated Communities on the Body Politic" (PhD diss., Michigan, 2013), 8.

66. Heath Brown, *Homeschooling the Right: How Conservative Education Activism Erodes the State* (New York: Columbia University Press, 2021), 5.

67. Brown, *Homeschooling the Right: How Conservative Education Activism Erodes the State*, 72.

68. David Friedman, "Secession," *Daviddfriedman.com*, April 9, 2013, http://www.daviddfriedman.com/Academic/Secession.html.

69. I take these points from Evan McKenzie, *Beyond Privatopia: Rethinking Residential Private Government* (Washington, DC: Urban Institute, 2012), 55.

70. Evan McKenzie, *Privatopia: Homeowners Associations and the Rise of Residential Private Government* (New Haven, CT: Yale University Press, 1994), 15–17.

71. Friedman, *The Machinery of Freedom: Guide to a Radical Capitalism*, 173.

72. Linda Carlson, *Company Towns of the Pacific Northwest* (Seattle: University of Washington Press, 2003), 193.

73. Carlson, *Company Towns of the Pacific Northwest*, 12.

CHAPTER 7: YOUR OWN PRIVATE LIECHTENSTEIN

1. Peggy Durdin, "Life in Shangri-Liechtenstein," *New York Times*, October 17, 1954, https://www.nytimes.com/1954/10/17/archives/life-in-shangriliechtenstein-the-tiny-nation-has-the-lowest-taxes.html.

2. William McGurn, "Liechtenstein, the Supply-Siders' Lilliputian Lab," *Wall Street Journal*, July 10, 1985, ProQuest Historical Newspapers.

3. Louw and Kendall, *South Africa: The Solution*, 141.

4. "Aufruf zur sofortigen Abschaffung aller Sozialleistungen für Migranten," *Eigentümlich Frei*, April 21, 2017, https://ef-magazin.de/2017/04/21/10876 -massenmigration-wohlfahrtsstaat-und-grenzsicherung-aufruf-zur -sofortigen-abschaffung-aller-sozialleistungen-fuer-migranten; and Titus Gebel, "What We Can Learn from Liechtenstein," *Mises Wire*, September 3, 2019, https://mises.org/wire/what-we-can-learn-liechtenstein.

5. "Sorry, Savers, We've Gone Legit," *Economist*, April 13, 2002, Economist Historical Archive.

6. Andrew Young, "Freedom and Prosperity in Liechtenstein: A Hoppean Analysis," *Journal of Libertarian Studies* 22 (2010): 278.

7. Today, Liechtenstein and Saudi Arabia are the only two countries whose names incorporate the surnames of their rulers.

8. Rudolf Bachthold et al., *Eine Adresse in Liechtenstein: Finanzdrehscheibe und Steuerparadies* (Wiesbaden: Gabler, 1979), 13.

9. David Beattie, *Liechtenstein: A Modern History*, 2nd ed. (Triesen: Van Eck, 2012), 37.

10. George E. Glos, "The Analysis of a Tax Haven: The Liechtenstein Anstalt," *International Lawyer* 18, no. 4 (Fall 1984): 929.

11. Beattie, *Liechtenstein*, 68.

12. Beattie, 75.

13. Brooke Harrington, *Capital Without Borders: Wealth Managers and the One Percent* (Cambridge, MA: Harvard University Press, 2016), 37–39.

14. Vanessa Ogle, "'Funk Money': The End of Empires, the Expansion of Tax Havens, and Decolonization as an Economic and Financial Event," *Past & Present* 249, no. 1 (2020): 218.

15. Beattie, *Liechtenstein*, 75.

16. Bachthold et al., *Eine Adresse in Liechtenstein*, 15.

17. Ferdinand Tuohy, "Booming Capital for Capital in Flight," *New York Times*, January 15, 1933, ProQuest Historical Newspapers.

18. Glos, "The Analysis of a Tax Haven: The Liechtenstein Anstalt," 954.

19. Ronen Palan, Richard Murphy, and Christian Chavagneux, *Tax Havens: How Globalization Really Works* (Ithaca, NY: Cornell University Press, 2010), 117.

20. Vladimir Pozner, "Liechtenstein, the World's Biggest Safe," *Harper's*, October 31, 1938): 604.

21. "A Well-Fixed State," *New York Times*, March 21, 1938, ProQuest Historical Newspapers; and "Citizenship by Investment," https://nomadcapitalist .com/citizenship-by-investment/. See also Atossa Abrahamian, *The Cosmopolites: The Coming of the Global Citizen* (New York: Columbia Global Reports, 2015).

22. "A Well-Fixed State"; Tuohy, "Booming Capital for Capital in Flight."

23. "Nazis in Cabinet in Liechtenstein," *New York Times*, April 1, 1938, Pro-Quest Historical Newspapers.

24. "Nazi Crimes Taint Liechtenstein," BBC News, April 14, 2005, http://news.bbc.co.uk/2/hi/europe/4443809.stm.

25. "Liechtenstein Mecca for Nervous Capital," *New York Times*, July 10, 1932, ProQuest Historical Newspapers.

26. Mitchell Gordon, "Tax Haven: Little Liechtenstein Lures Army of U.S. and Foreign Subsidiaries," *Wall Street Journal*, July 7, 1954, ProQuest Historical Newspapers.

27. Felix Kessler, "Little Liechtenstein Still Draws Tourists—and a Lot of Money," *Wall Street Journal*, October 3, 1975, ProQuest Historical Newspapers.

28. Gordon, "Tax Haven."

29. Matthew Engel, "Lying Low Is Risky for Liechtenstein," *Financial Times*, February 7, 2009, Financial Times Historical Archive, Gale.

30. Palan, Murphy, and Chavagneux, *Tax Havens: How Globalization Really Works*, 108.

31. Paul Hofmann, "For Little Liechtenstein (Population: 25,000) This Is the Golden Age," *New York Times*, August 7, 1978, ProQuest Historical Newspapers.

32. Georges Nzongola-Ntalaja, *The Congo from Leopold to Kabila: A People's History* (London: Zed Books, 2002), 137.

33. "South African Firms Avoid Sanctions, Union Charges," *Wall Street Journal*, June 23, 1989, ProQuest Historical Newspapers.

34. Gordon, "Tax Haven"; and Geoffrey Tweedale and Laurie Flynn, "Piercing the Corporate Veil: Cape Industries and Multinational Corporate Liability for a Toxic Hazard, 1950–2004," *Enterprise and Society* 8, no. 2 (June 2007): 286. See also Jocelyn A. Bell, "The Influence on the South African Economy of the Gold Mining Industry 1925–2000," *South African Journal of Economic History* 16, no. 1–2 (2001): 43.

35. Camillus Eboh, "Nigeria to Recover $228 Million of Abacha Loot After 16-Year Fight," Reuters, June 19, 2014, https://www.reuters.com/article/us-nigeria-liechtenstein-idUSKBN0EU1ZQ20140619; and Edward Luce, "The Prince Knows Everyone," *Gazette* (Montreal), December 4, 1994, Newspapers.com.

36. Andrew Osborn, "Country for Hire: Low Rates, All Amenities," *Guardian* (UK Version), February 14, 2003, ProQuest Historical Newspapers.

37. Walter Wright, "Marcos Used Code to Juggle Fortune, Documents Show," *Toronto Star*, August 23, 1986, Newspapers.com; William C. Rempel, "U.S. Officials Weighing Indictment of Marcos Inquiry in Final Stages," *Los Angeles Times*, June 16, 1988 ProQuest Historical Newspapers.

38. Bullough, *Moneyland: Why Thieves and Crooks Now Rule the World and How to Take it Back*, 10.

39. Beattie, *Liechtenstein*, 151, 157.

40. Beattie, 191.

41. Geoffrey Atkins, "Europe's Blue Bloods Flock to Wedding of Fairy-Tale Prince," *Sacramento Bee*, July 30, 1967.

42. Margaret Studer, "Tiny Medieval Principality Melds Past with the Future," *Calgary Herald*, July 3, 1984, Newspapers.com; and Hans-Adam II, *The State in the Third Millennium* (Schan: van Eck, 2009), 84.

43. Hans-Adam II, *Third Millennium*, 142.

44. Marcia Berss, "The Prince That Roared," *Forbes*, April 29, 1985, Gale Academic OneFile.

45. John Russell, "Royal Treasures Glow at the Met," *New York Times*, October 6, 1985, ProQuest Historical Newspapers.

46. Head of State of the Principality of Liechtenstein, Forty-Sixth Session, General Assembly, Provisional Verbatim Record of the 10th Meeting, September 26, 1991, UN Documents A/46/PV.10, October 1, 1991, 6.

47. Barry Bartmann, "From the Wings to the Footlights: The International Relations of Europe's Smallest States," *Commonwealth & Comparative Politics* 50, no. 4 (November 2012): 536.

48. Hans-Adam II, *Third Millennium*, 7.

49. Hans-Adam II, 117.

50. Hans-Adam II, 81.

51. Rothbard, "Nations by Consent: Decomposing the Nation-State."

52. Beattie, *Liechtenstein*, 222.

53. Eric Gwinn, "Liechtenstein's Prince Gains Power, Absolutely," *Chicago Tribune*, March 28, 2003.

54. Beattie, *Liechtenstein*, 289.

55. Fiona Fleck, "Prince to People: 'I'll Sell Up to Bill Gates,'" *Sunday Telegraph*, February 11, 2001, Westlaw. He claimed later that this was a joke. Sarah Lyall, "In Liechtenstein, a Princely Power Grab," *New York Times*, March 15, 2003, ProQuest Historical Newspapers.

56. "Q&A / Prince Hans-Adam II: Liechtenstein's Future as a 'Clean Tax Haven,'" *New York Times*, August 31, 2000, ProQuest Historical Newspapers.

57. Audrey Gillan, "Liechtenstein Monarchy Tops List of Richest Royals," *Guardian*, June 4, 1999, ProQuest Historical Newspapers.

58. Gwinn, "Liechtenstein's Prince Gains Power, Absolutely."

59. "Among other things, the prince's proposals would allow him to dissolve the government unilaterally and to be impervious to the authority of Liechtenstein's Constitutional Court." Lyall, "In Liechtenstein, a Princely Power Grab."

60. "Sorry, Savers, We've Gone Legit."

61. "Democratic Feudalism," *Economist*, March 22, 2003, Gale in Context: Global Issues.

62. John Blundell, "Enclaves Punch Above Their Weight with the EU," *Sunday Business* (London, UK), September 24, 2006, ProQuest.

63. This included the European Constitutional Group, which included primarily German and Swiss economists. Slobodian and Plehwe, "Neoliberals Against Europe," 97; and Detmar Doering, *Friedlicher Austritt: Braucht die Europäische Union ein Sezessionsrecht?* (Brussels: Centre for the New Europe, June 2002), 41.

64. Paul Johnson, "Foreword," in *The Voluntary City: Choice, Community, and Civil Society*, ed. David T. Beito, Peter Gordon, and Alexander Tabarrok (Ann Arbor: University of Michigan Press, 2002), viii.

65. Johnson, "Foreword," viii.

66. Wolfram Engels from 1989 quoted in Roland Baader, *Die Euro-Katastrophe* (Böblingen: Antia Tykve Verlag, 2017), 31.

67. Gerard Radnitzky, "Towards a Europe of Free Societies: Evolutionary Competition or Constructivistic Design," *Ordo* 42 (1991): 162.

68. Daniel Hannan, "Successful Countries Think Small," *Telegraph Online*, April 11, 2007, Westlaw.

69. Alan Sked founded the UK Independence Party (UKIP). Alan Sked, "Myths of European Unity," *National Interest* (Winter 1990/1): 73. This perspective was especially inspired by Eric Jones, *The European Miracle: Environments, Economies and Geopolitics in the History of Europe and Asia* (New York: Cambridge University Press, 1981).

70. Beattie, *Liechtenstein*, 182. Other states in this position included Iceland and Norway, positive points of comparison for Brexit advocates. Daniel Hannan, "Blue-Eyed Sheikhs," *Spectator*, October 9, 2004, Gale.

71. Göttingen Hayek-Tage, June 21–22, 2013, program.

72. Katja Riedel and Sebastian Pittelkow, "Die Hayek-Gesellschaft-'Mistbeet der AfD?,'" *Süddeutsche Zeitung*, July 14, 2017, https://www.sueddeutsche.de/wirtschaft/hayek-gesellschaft-mistbeet-der-afd-1.3589049.

73. European Center for Austrian Economics Foundation publications, accessed March 22, 2022, https://ecaef.org/epublications/. Prince Michael is also the cofounder of the International Institute of Longevity and Longevity Center, https://l-institute.com/.

74. Ludwig Mises, *Liberalism (1927)*, 3 ed. (Irvington-on-Hudson, NY: Foundation for Economic Education, 1985), 109.

75. See J. C. Sharman, *Havens in a Storm: The Struggle for Global Tax Regulation* (Ithaca, NY: Cornell University Press, 2006).

76. Beattie, *Liechtenstein*, 355.

77. Palan, Murphy, and Chavagneux, *Tax Havens: How Globalization Really Works*, 5.

78. Lynnley Browning, "Liechtenstein to Share Some Secrets of Its Bank," *New York Times*, December 4, 2008, ProQuest.

79. Conal Walsh, "Trouble in Banking Paradise as Uncle Sam's Sheriffs Ride In," *Observer*, October 27, 2002, Gale OneFile.

80. Summarized in Beattie, *Liechtenstein*, 372.

81. Palan, Murphy, and Chavagneux, *Tax Havens: How Globalization Really Works*, 107; and "Is Liechtenstein a Libertarian Utopia?," *ReasonTV*, March 21, 2016, https://www.youtube.com/watch?v=RGeOGnsSayc.

82. Peter Ford, "Trouble in Fairy-Tale Kingdom: Liechtenstein Bows to International Pressure, Moves to Curb Money Laundering," *Christian Science Monitor*, July 3, 2000, Gale In Context: Global Issues.

83. Haig Simonian and Gerrit Wiesmann, "'Fourth Reich' Remarks Take Relations to New Low," *Financial Times*, September 12, 2008, Financial Times Historical Archive, Gale.

84. Richard Rahn, "Attack on the Free," *Washington Times*, February 12, 2013, https://m.washingtontimes.com/news/2013/feb/12/attack-on-the-free/.

85. "Discussion Q&A—Salin, Stone, Malice, Kinsella, Deist (PFS 2018)," https://www.youtube.com/watch?v=ZptziXSxpx0.

86. Daniel Mitchell, "Is Secession a Good Idea?," *Cato at Liberty*, October 17, 2011, https://www.cato.org/blog/secession-good-idea.

87. Stephanie Hess, "The Swiss Village That's Home to an Imaginary State," *swissinfo.ch*, April 13, 2018, https://www.swissinfo.ch/eng/fantasy-democracy_the-swiss-village-that-s-home-to-an-imaginary-state/44040380; and https://modelhof.com/uploads/1/3/5/0/135061344/ich_als_souver%C3%A4n_en.pdf.

88. Titus Gebel, "Is Liberty in Our Lifetime Achievable?," *Free Private Cities*, November 1, 2021, https://www.youtube.com/watch?v=m0gQKvPOIJ8.

CHAPTER 8: A WHITE MAN'S BUSINESS CLAN IN SOMALIA

1. Bruce Sterling, *Islands in the Net* (New York: Arbor House, 1988), 386.

2. Sterling, *Islands in the Net*, 388.

3. Sterling, 261.

4. Yumi Kim, "Stateless in Somalia, and Loving It," *Mises Institute*, February 21, 2006, https://mises.org/library/stateless-somalia-and-loving-it.

5. Biographical details in Michael van Notten, *The Law of the Somalis* (Trenton, NJ: Red Sea Press, 2005), 239–40. Prominent ordoliberals were involved in the articulation and enactment of the laws, which placed the authority of the European Court of Justice above domestic courts. On competition policy see Antoine Vauchez, *Brokering Europe: Euro-Lawyers and the Making of a Transnational Polity* (New York: Cambridge University Press, 2015); and David J. Gerber, "Constitutionalizing the Economy: German Neoliberalism, Competition Law and the 'New' Europe," *American Journal of Comparative Law* 42, no. 1 (Winter 1994): 25–84.

6. NRC quoted in Rudie Kagie, "Bemiddelaar in staatsgrepen," *Argus* 1, no. 7 (May 30, 2017): 14.

7. New member list, 1977, Stanford University, Hoover Institution Archives, Mont Pelerin Society Papers, Box 19, folder 4. The same year, he hosted a special meeting of the MPS in Amsterdam attended by former German chancellor and fellow MPS member Ludwig Erhard where F. A. Hayek presented on his proposal to denationalize money. Van Notten to Hayek, February 9, 1977, Hoover Institution Archives, Hayek Papers, Box 78, Folder 19; F. A. Hayek, *De weg naar moderne slavernij*, trans. Michael van Notten and Boudewijn Bouckaert (Brussels: Acropolis, 1980); and Milton Friedman and Rose Friedman, *Aan ons de keus*, trans. Michael van Notten (Brussels: Acropolis, 1981).

8. Michael van Notten, "Europe: Free-Market Ideas Sprout in Brussels," *Wall Street Journal*, February 29, 1984, ProQuest Historical Newspapers.

9. Alain Siaens, "Les zones franches," Hoover Institution Archives, Mont Pelerin Society Papers, Box 25, Folder 7.

10. Michael van Notten, *De tewerkstellingszone als politiek breekijzer* (Sint Genesius Rode: Institutum Europaeum, 1982).

11. "Wie gelooft in het Wonder van de Deregulieringszone?," *Provinciale Zeeuwse Courant*, July 30, 1983, Krantenbank Zeeland.

12. Michael van Notten, "Make Governments Compete for People," *Economic Affairs* (April–June 1984): 13–17.

13. Michael van Notten, "Politische Beweggründe für Freizonen in Europa," *Zeitschrift für Wirtschaftspolitik*, no. 32 (1983): 199.

14. Van Notten, "Politische Beweggründe für Freizonen in Europa," 205.

15. Van Notten, "Make Governments Compete for People," 13–17.

16. Michael van Notten, "Encouraging Enterprise—the Belgian Experience," *Economic Affairs* (July 1983): 282–85.

17. Van Notten, "Politische Beweggründe für Freizonen in Europa," 206.

18. Aurelia van Maalen, *Dag, ik ga vrijheid halen* (Amsterdam: Prometheus, 2016), 144; and M. M. Notten, *De Arubaanse grondwet: vriend of vijand van de samenleving?* (Brussels: Institutum Europaeum, 1984). This chapter relies in part on the above memoir written by van Notten's daughter under a pseudonym.

19. Kagie, "Bemiddelaar in staatsgrepen," 15.

20. Allegedly, the plan was to have Angolan guerrillas to help in the coup and to be compensated later with weaponry. To make the plan more baroque, van Notten claimed publicly that Libya was using Suriname as a staging area for operations in the region. Kagie, "Bemiddelaar in staatsgrepen," 16; Vicki Rivera, "Libya Reported Drilling Terrorists in Suriname," *Washington Times*, October 24, 1985, Newsbank.

21. Van Maalen, *Dag, ik ga vrijheid halen*, 147.

22. n.a., "Free Trade Zone in the Yukon," *Whitehorse Star*, July 4, 1984, Newspapers.com.

23. Van Maalen, *Dag, ik ga vrijheid halen*, 130.

24. Van Maalen, 155.

25. Van Maalen, 43.

26. Van Notten was influenced by Belgian libertarian philosopher Frank Van Dun's idea of natural law and natural rights. Van Dun wrote the afterword to van Notten, *The Law of the Somalis*, 121. See Frank Van Dun, "Against Libertarian Legalism: A Comment on Kinsella and Block," *Journal of Libertarian Studies* 17, no. 3 (2003): 63–90.

27. See, e.g., E. E. Evans-Pritchard, *The Nuer: A Description of the Modes of Livelihood and Political Institutions of a Nilotic People* (Oxford: Clarendon, 1940). His student I. M. Lewis was the first to codify the Somali clan system in a book called *A Pastoral Democracy* that, as one scholar points out, would be better titled *A Pastoral Anarchy*. Gérard Prunier, *The Country That Does Not Exist: A History of Somaliland* (London: Hurst, 2021), 219. See I. M. Lewis, *A Pastoral Democracy: A Study of Pastoralism and Politics Among the Northern Somali of the Horn of Africa* (Oxford: Oxford University Press, 1961). The technical term for the clan system is "patrilineal segmentary lineage." Alex de Waal, *The Real Politics of the Horn of Africa: Money, War and the Business of Power* (Cambridge: Polity, 2015), 110.

28. Hans-Hermann Hoppe, "Reply to Benegas Lynch," in *Values and the Social Order*, ed. Gerard Radnitzky (Aldershot: Avebury, 1997); and Günther Schlee, "Customary Law and the Joys of Statelessness: Idealised Traditions Versus Somali Realities," *Journal of Eastern African Studies* 7, no. 2 (2013): 258.

29. "Somalië toneel van Afrika's gruwelijkste geweld," *NRC Handelsblad*, December 14, 1991, https://www.nrc.nl/nieuws/1991/12/14/somalie-toneel -van-afrikas-gruwelijkste-geweld-6990603-a1042137.

30. Van Maalen, *Dag, ik ga vrijheid halen*, 36.

31. Van Notten, *The Law of the Somalis*, 121.

32. M. M. Notten, "Somalische Xeer is het meest geschikt voor Somalia," *de Vrijbrief*, no. 166 (March 1992): 11, 16.

33. Van Notten, *From Nation-State to Stateless Nation: The Somali Experience* (2000), draft, Wayback Machine capture August 16, 2020, http://www.awdal .com/awdalp13.html.

34. Van Notten, *Law of the Somalis*, 56.

35. Van Notten, 70.

36. Van Notten, 116.

37. Michael van Notten, "From Nation-State to Stateless Nation: The Somali Experience," *Africa* 58, no. 2 (June 2003): 150.

38. Van Notten, *Law of the Somalis*, 117–18.

39. Van Notten, 137.

40. Van Notten, *Nation-State to Stateless Nation*, (2000), capture August 16, 2000, http://www.awdal.com/awdalp13.html.

41. Van Notten, *Law of the Somalis*, 138.

42. Hoppe, "The Economic and Political Rationale for European Secessionism," 212.

43. Van Notten, *Law of the Somalis*, 143.

44. Spencer Heath MacCallum, "A Peaceful Ferment in Somalia," *Foundation for Economic Education*, June 1, 1998, https://fee.org/articles/a-peaceful-ferment-in-somalia/.

45. MacCallum, "A Peaceful Ferment in Somalia."

46. Spencer Heath MacCallum, "Looking Back and Forward," in *I Chose Liberty: Autobiographies of Contemporary Libertarians*, ed. Walter Block (Auburn, AL: Ludwig von Mises Institute, 2010), 206.

47. Spencer Heath, *Citadel, Market and Altar: Emerging Society* (Baltimore: Science of Society Foundation, 1957), 79.

48. Heath, *Citadel, Market and Altar*, 91.

49. Heath, 82.

50. MacCallum, "Looking Back and Forward," 208.

51. Heath, *Citadel, Market and Altar*, 94.

52. MacCallum, "Looking Back and Forward," 208.

53. Introduction in van Notten, *Law of the Somalis*, xii.

54. Spencer Heath MacCallum, "Werner K. Stiefel's Pursuit of a Practicum of Freedom," *LewRockwell.com*, June 19, 2006, https://www.lewrockwell.com/2006/06/spencer-heath-maccallum/werner-k-stiefels-pursuit-of-a-practicumoffreedom/. For the best account see Isabelle Simpson, "Operation Atlantis: A Case-Study in Libertarian Island Micronationality," *Shima* 10, no. 2 (2016): 18–35.

55. MacCallum, "Looking Back and Forward," 211.

56. Roy Halliday, "Operation Atlantis and the Radical Libertarian Alliance: Observations of a Fly on the Wall," (2002), https://ad-store.sgp1.digitaloceanspaces.com/LUA/Documents/royhalliday%20operation%20atlantis.pdf.

57. Spencer Heath MacCallum, "A Model Lease for Orbis," October 15, 1995, http://freenation.org/a/f33m1.html.

58. MacCallum, "Werner K. Stiefel's Pursuit of a Practicum of Freedom"; and MacCallum, "The Freeport-Clan."

59. MacCallum, "The Freeport-Clan," 170.

60. Heath, *Citadel, Market and Altar: Emerging Society*, 85.

61. Not to be confused with William Rees-Mogg's coauthor of the same name.

62. "Freedonia—The Cabinet," capture August 29, 2000, http://www.freedonia.org/cabinet.html.

63. "What Is the Principality of Freedonia?," capture May 7, 1999, http://www.freedonia.org/whatis.html.

64. "Kyle to Ryan, 3 October 1999," capture April 8, 2000, http://www.freedonia.org/dialogue.html.

65. "Principality of Freedonia Sovereignty Plans," capture October 28, 2000, http://www.freedonia.org/sovereignty2.html.

66. "Recent events have complicated our situation in Awdal," capture February 11, 2001, http://www.freedonia.org/sovereignty2.html.

67. "Somaliland Protest Leaves 25 in Jail," *BBC Monitoring Newsfile*, January 12, 2001, ProQuest.

68. Ken Menkhaus, "Governance Without Government in Somalia: Spoilers, State Building, and the Politics of Coping," *International Security* 31, no. 3 (Winter 2006/2007): 74–106; and Nicole Stremlau, "Governance Without Government in the Somali Territories," *Journal of International Affairs* 71, no. 2 (Spring/Summer 2018): 73–89.

69. Peter D. Little, *Somalia: Economy Without State* (Bloomington: Indiana University Press, 2003), 13.

70. De Waal, *The Real Politics of the Horn of Africa: Money, War and the Business of Power*, 115.

71. Ersun N. Kurtulus, "Exploring the Paradoxical Consequences of State Collapse: The Cases of Somalia 1991–2006 and Lebanon 1975–82," *Third World Quarterly* 33, no. 7 (2012): 1287.

72. Benjamin Powell, Ryan Ford, and Alex Nowrasteh, "Somalia After State Collapse: Chaos or Improvement?," *Journal of Economic Behavior & Organization*, no. 67 (2008): 662.

73. Alex Tabarrok, "Somalia and the Theory of Anarchy," *Marginal Revolution*, April 21, 2004, https://marginalrevolution.com/marginalrevolution/2004/04/somalia_and_the.html.

74. Christopher J. Coyne, "Reconstructing Weak and Failed States: Foreign Intervention and the Nirvana Fallacy," *Foreign Policy Analysis*, no. 2 (2006): 345.

75. William J. Luther, "Money Without a State" (PhD diss., George Mason University, 2012). See also William J. Luther, "The Monetary Mechanism of Stateless Somalia," *Public Choice*, no. 165 (2015): 45–58. In addition to a university position, Luther directs the American Institute of Economic Research's Sound Money Project and is an adjunct research scholar with the Cato Institute's Center for Monetary and Financial Alternatives, accessed March 31, 2022, https://www.cato.org/people/william-j-luther.

76. On the initial research that inspired many libertarians see Little, *Somalia: Economy Without State*, 139–46.

77. Björn Tscheridse, "Der gescheiterte Staat," *Eigentümlich Frei*, no. 60 (March 2006): 23. Libertarians of a less radical persuasion disagreed. "It is difficult to picture people in the United States saying, 'Let's make our nation more like Somalia,'" wrote one. Randall Holcombe, "Is Government Inevitable? Reply to Leeson and Stringham," *Independent Review* 9, no. 4 (Spring 2005): 551.

78. Peter T. Leeson, "Better Off Stateless: Somalia Before and After Government Collapse," *Journal of Comparative Economics* 35 (2007): 689–710.

79. Peter T. Leeson and Claudia R. Williamson, "Anarchy and Development: An Application of the Theory of Second Best," *Law and Development Review* 2, no. 1 (2009): 91.

80. Peter T. Leeson, "Coordination Without Command: Stretching the Scope of Spontaneous Order," *Public Choice*, no. 135 (2008): 73–74.

81. D. K. Leonard and M. S. Samantar, "What Does the Somali Experience Teach Us About the Social Contract and the State?," *Development and Change* 42, no. 2 (2011): 564.

82. Alex de Waal, "Somalia's Disassembled State: Clan Unit Formation and the Political Marketplace," *Conflict, Security & Development* 20, no. 5 (2020): 562.

83. Ken Menkhaus and John Prendergast, "The Stateless State," *Africa Report* (May 1995): 232. See also Rebecca Richards, "Fragility Within Stability: The State, the Clan and Political Resilience in Somaliland," *Third World Quarterly* 41, no. 6 (2020): 1067–83.

84. De Waal, *The Real Politics of the Horn of Africa: Money, War and the Business of Power*, 113.

85. Schlee, "Customary Law and the Joys of Statelessness: Idealised Traditions Versus Somali Realities," 270.

86. Little, *Somalia: Economy Without State*, 132.

87. Henry Srebrnik, "Can Clans Form Nations?: Somaliland in the Making," in *De Facto States: The Quest for Sovereignty*, ed. Tozun Bahcheli, Barry Bartmann, and Henry Srebrnik (London: Routledge, 2004), 214.

88. Srebrnik, "Can Clans Form Nations?" 219.

89. Prunier, *The Country That Does Not Exist: A History of Somaliland*.

90. Harvey Morris, "'Republic' Wants Recognition on the World Stage," *Financial Times*, August 15, 2000, Financial Times Historical Archive, Gale.

91. Srebrnik, "Can Clans Form Nations?," 222.

92. Mark Bradbury, Adan Yusuf Abokor, and Haroon Ahmed Yusuf, "Somaliland: Choosing Politics over Violence," *Review of African Political Economy* 30, no. 97 (September 2003): 455; and Van Notten, *Law of the Somalis*, 142.

93. De Waal, *The Real Politics of the Horn of Africa*, 130.

94. Jeffrey Gettleman, "Somaliland Is an Overlooked African Success Story," *New York Times*, March 7, 2007, https://www.nytimes.com/2007/03/06/world/africa/06iht-somalia.4818753.html. After the establishment of the nationwide Federal Government of Somalia in 2012, Somaliland remained a "semi-autonomous region" actively seeking full independence. Robbie Gramer and Mary Yang, "Somaliland Courts U.S. for Independence Recognition," *Foreign Policy*, March 21, 2022, https://foreignpolicy.com/2022/03/21/somaliland-united-states-independence-recognition/.

95. Finn Stepputat and Tobias Hagmann, "Politics of Circulation: The Makings

of the Berbera Corridor in Somali East Africa," *Environment & Planning D: Society and Space* 37, no. 5 (2019): 798–99.

96. Markus Virgil Hoehne, "The Rupture of Territoriality and the Diminishing Relevance of Cross-cutting Ties in Somalia After 1990," *Development and Change* 47, no. 6 (2016): 1390.

97. Jamil A. Mubarak, "The 'Hidden Hand' Behind the Resilience of the Stateless Economy of Somalia," *World Development* 25, no. 12 (1997): 2032.

98. Andres Schipani, "Somaliland Gears Up for 'Healthy' Battle of Ports," *Financial Times*, September 3, 2021, Global Newsstream.

99. Robert Clyde Mogielnicki, *A Political Economy of Free Zones in Gulf Arab States* (Cham, Switzerland: Springer, 2021), 218.

100. Tatiana Nenova and Tim Harford, "Anarchy and Invention," *World Bank Public Policy Note*, no. 280 (November 2004): 2, http://documents.worldbank .org/curated/en/774771468781541848/Anarchy-and-invention.

CHAPTER 9: THE LEGAL BUBBLE-DOMES OF DUBAI

1. Anthony Shadid, "The Towering Dream of Dubai," *Washington Post*, April 30, 2006, Global Newsstream.

2. Rory Miller, *Desert Kingdoms to Global Powers: The Rise of the Arab Gulf* (New Haven, CT: Yale University Press, 2016), 173.

3. Miller, *Desert Kingdoms to Global Powers: The Rise of the Arab Gulf*, 172.

4. Ellen Knickmeyer, "In U.A.E., Weakened Dollar Slows Dubai Tower's Race to the Skies," *Washington Post*, December 7, 2007, Global Newsstream.

5. Daniel Brook, *A History of Future Cities* (New York: Norton, 2013), 357.

6. Nick Cook, "Gazeley's Guy in Dubai," *Property Week* (February 2010), https:// www.propertyweek.com/industrial/gazeleys-guy-in-dubai/3158663.article.

7. Arch Puddington et al., eds., *Freedom in the World* (Lanham, MD: Rowman & Littlefield, 2007), 845–49.

8. Directorate of Intelligence, *Near East and South Asia Review*, March 29, 1985, https://www.cia.gov/readingroom/docs/CIA-RDP85T01184R 000301390002-9.pdf.

9. Brook, *A History of Future Cities*, 372.

10. Philip Kennicott, "Arabian Heights," *Washington Post*, October 28, 2007, Global Newsstream.

11. Mike Davis, "Fear and Money in Dubai," *New Left Review*, no. 41 (September/October 2006): 60.

12. Davis, "Fear and Money in Dubai," 60.

13. Steve Negus, "An American Style Emirate? Dubai Sees a Future as Ally," *Financial Times*, March 8, 2006, Financial Times Historical Archive, Gale.

14. Björn Tscheridse, "Der kapitalistische Flaschengeist," *Eigentümlich Frei* 8, no. 54 (August 2005): 24.

15. Frank Karsten and Karel Beckman, *Beyond Democracy* (n.p.: CreateSpace Independent Publishing, 2012), 54.

16. Although Yarvin claims not to be a libertarian, many of his writings conform closely to the right-wing anarcho-capitalist tradition described in this book. Curtis Yarvin, "Why I Am Not a Libertarian," *Unqualified Reservations*, December 13, 2007, https://www.unqualified-reservations.org/2007/12/why-i-am-not-libertarian/.

17. Emphasis in the original. "Mediocracy: Definition, Etiology and Treatment," September 8, 2007, https://www.unqualified-reservations.org/2007/09/mediocracy-definition-etiology-and/.

18. In fact, many migrant workers did not receive what was promised in their contract.

19. Brook, *A History of Future Cities*, 370.

20. Curtis Yarvin, "Neocameralism and the Escalator of Massarchy," *Unqualified Reservations*, December 20, 2007, https://www.unqualified-reservations.org/2007/12/neocameralism-and-escalator-of/.

21. Curtis Yarvin, "Patchwork: A Political System for the 21st Century," *Unqualified Reservations*, November 13, 2008, https://www.unqualified-reservations.org/2008/11/patchwork-positive-vision-part-1/.

22. Laleh Khalili, *Sinews of War and Trade: Shipping and Capitalism in the Arabian Peninsula* (New York: Verso, 2020), 110.

23. Abdul Khaleq Abdulla quoted in Ahmed Kanna, *Dubai: The City as Corporation* (Minneapolis: University of Minnesota Press, 2011), 34.

24. John Andrews, "Oasis of Royal Diplomacy in a Troubled Region," *Guardian*, March 3, 1979, ProQuest Historical Newspapers.

25. The company was Halcrow. Rafiq Zakaria, "British Queen's Visit to Gulf," *Times of India*, February 24, 1979, ProQuest Historical Newspapers.

26. "Rivals in Splendour of Gifts," *Guardian*, February 26, 1979, ProQuest Historical Newspapers.

27. Todd Reisz, *Showpiece City: How Architecture Made Dubai* (Stanford, CA: Stanford University Press, 2021), 22.

28. William Tuohy, "Dubai: Where Gold Smuggling Is a Way of Life," *Los Angeles Times*, January 13, 1971, ProQuest Historical Newspapers.

29. William Tuohy, "Dubai's Golden Fleece," *Guardian*, January 13, 1971, ProQuest Historical Newspapers.

30. "India Hacks at Smugglers' Tentacles," *Los Angeles Times*, November 18, 1976, ProQuest Historical Newspapers.

31. Walter Schwarz and Inder Malhotra, "Dethronement of the Kings of Smuggling," *Guardian*, September 19, 1974, ProQuest Historical Newspapers.

32. The Economist Intelligence Unit, "The Arabian Peninsula and Jordan," *Quarterly Economic Review*, no. 3 (1970): 12.

33. Shohei Sato, *Britain and the Formation of the Gulf States: Embers of Empire* (Manchester, UK: Manchester University Press, 2016), 74.

34. Miller, *Desert Kingdoms to Global Powers: The Rise of the Arab Gulf*, 6.

35. The Economist Intelligence Unit, "The Arabian Peninsula and Jordan," *Quarterly Economic Review*, no. 4 (1969): 17; and Paul Maubec, "Arab Sheiks Go It Alone," *Washington Post*, July 26, 1970, ProQuest Historical Newspapers.

36. Stephen J. Ramos, *Dubai Amplified: The Engineering of a Port Geography* (London: Routledge, 2010), 74.

37. Reisz, *Showpiece City: How Architecture Made Dubai*, 308–9.

38. Valerie J. Pelton, "Jebel Ali: Open for Business," *Transnational Law & Contemporary Problems* 27 (2018): 386–87; and "Mina Jebel Ali Free Trade Zone (advertisement)," *Times* (London), February 23, 1981, The Times Digital Archive, Gale.

39. Stewart Dalby, "Yet to Make Its Mark-Jebel Ali Free Zone," *Financial Times*, March 29, 1989, Financial Times Historical Archive, Gale. The fact that foreigners had full ownership inside of the zone gave it the edge over the other emirates, which, for years, offered no such opportunities. Mark Nicholson, "Bahrain Makes Policy Switch to Rebuild Economy," *Financial Times*, July 3, 1991, Financial Times Historical Archive, Gale.

40. Syed Ali, *Dubai: Gilded Cage* (New Haven, CT: Yale University Press, 2010), 86.

41. Ali, *Dubai: Gilded Cage*, 91.

42. Brook, *A History of Future Cities*, 359.

43. Davis, "Fear and Money in Dubai," 63.

44. Christopher M. Davidson, *Dubai: The Vulnerability of Success* (New York: Columbia University Press, 2008), 18.

45. "Fantasy Islands," *Financial Times*, May 28, 2005, Financial Times Historical Archive, Gale.

46. Adam Nicholson, "Boom Town," *Guardian*, February 13, 2006, ProQuest Historical Newspapers.

47. Brook, *A History of Future Cities*, 359.

48. Robert Vitalis, *America's Kingdom: Mythmaking on the Saudi Oil Frontier* (Stanford, CA: Stanford University Press, 2006), 88–92.

49. "Fantasy Islands."

50. Salem Saif, "Blade Runner in the Gulf," *Jacobin*, November 2, 2017, https://jacobin.com/2017/11/gulf-states-oil-capital-ecological-disaster.

51. Nicholson, "Boom Town."

52. Brook, *A History of Future Cities*, 357.

53. Therborn, *Cities of Power: The Urban, the National, the Popular, the Global*, 288.

54. Soules, *Icebergs, Zombies, and the Ultra-Thin: Architecture and Capitalism in the 21st Century*, chap. 2.

55. Deborah Cowen, *The Deadly Life of Logistics: Mapping Violence in Global Trade* (Minneapolis: University of Minnesota Press, 2014), 168. For a similar metaphor see Davis, "Fear and Money in Dubai," 51.

56. Negus, "An American Style Emirate? Dubai Sees a Future as Ally."

57. Kennicott, "Arabian Heights."

58. Ramos, *Dubai Amplified*, 137.

59. Ramos, 133.

60. "Rwandan Government Signs a Feasibility Study with 'Jafza International' to Set Up a Free Zone in Kigali," *Middle East Company News*, September 6, 2005, Global Newsstream.

61. "Rwandan Government Signs a Feasibility Study."

62. Presenna Nambiar, "Jafza Quits Managing Port Klang Free Zone," *New Straits Times* (Malaysia), July 19, 2007, Gale OneFile.

63. "Jafza Manages Tangier Med," *Middle East Financial News*, June 21, 2005, Global Newsstream.

64. "Ready for a Leap from the Desert," *Financial Times*, May 23, 2005, Financial Times Historical Archive, Gale.

65. "TRIL Forms JV with Jafza for Seven Logistic Parks in India," *PTI—The Press Trust of India*, October 30, 2007, Global Newsstream.

66. "Jafza International Offers to Extend Full Support to Russia in Developing Sezs," *Middle East Company News*, March 18, 2007, Global Newsstream; and "Jafza, MFZ Sign MOU on Development of Misurata Economic Zone in Libya," *Middle East Company News*, October 3, 2007, Global Newsstream.

67. "Dubai World to Invest US$800M in Senegalese Economic Zone," *National Post*, January 22, 2008, Newspapers.com.

68. "Romania Shows Interest in Jafza's Unique Business Model," *Middle East Company News*, August 18, 2007, Global Newsstream.

69. Khalili, *Sinews of War and Trade*, 108.

70. Stephen Williams, "DP World Makes Giant Acquisition," *The Middle East* (January 2006), Global Newsstream.

71. Oliver Wainwright, "Inside the London Megaport You Didn't Know Existed," *Guardian*, September 15, 2015, ProQuest.

72. "Somali Pirates Risk Choking Key World Trade Route," Reuters, April 15, 2009, https://www.reuters.com/article/us-somalia-piracy-shipping-factbox-idUSTRE53E2JR20090415.

73. David S. Fick, *Africa: Continent of Economic Opportunity* (Johannesburg, South Africa: STE Publishers, 2006), 285.

74. "JI Project Opens New Vista for Djibouti," *Gulf Industry Online*, August 1, 2007, http://www.gulfindustryonline.com/news/5728_JI-project-opens-new-vista-for-Djibouti.html.

75. Diery Seck and Amie Gaye, "The Impact of the Global Financial Crisis on Arab States and Sub-Saharan Africa: An Agenda for Growth-Inducing Collaboration," in *Regional Economic Integration in West Africa*, ed. Diery Seck (Cham, Switzerland: Springer, 2013), 17.

76. Arang Keshavarzian, "Geopolitics and the Genealogy of Free Trade Zones in the Persian Gulf," *Geopolitics* 15 (2010): 276.

77. Davidson, *Dubai: The Vulnerability of Success*, 116.

78. Fick, *Africa: Continent of Economic Opportunity*, 286.

79. Cowen, *The Deadly Life of Logistics: Mapping Violence in Global Trade*, 123.

80. Gene Zaleski, "Mission to Dubai," *The Times and Democrat* (Orangeburg, SC), March 30, 2008, https://thetandd.com/news/mission-to-dubai/article_a44fa0c4-7148-52b4-b527-fc923e3ecbfc.html.

81. Harvey Morris, "Dubai's $600m Hub in US 'Corridor of Shame,'" *Financial Times*, January 12, 2008, Financial Times Historical Archive, Gale.

82. Kristian Coates Ulrichsen, "The Political Economy of Dubai," in *Dubai's Role in Facilitating Corruption and Global Financial Flows*, ed. Matthew T. Page and Jodi Vittori (Washington, DC: Carnegie Endowment for International Peace, 2020), 17.

83. Greg Lindsay, "From Dubai to Chongqing to Honduras, the Silk Road of the Future Is Taking Shape in Urban Developments Based on Airport Hubs," *Wall Street Journal Asia*, March 4, 2011, ProQuest.

84. Jean-Paul Rodrigue, *The Geography of Transport Systems*, 5th ed. (London: Routledge, 2020), 236.

85. Stephen Yiu-wai Chu, "Brand Hong Kong: Asia's World City as Method?," *Visual Anthropology* 24, no. 1–2 (2011): 48.

86. For a study of these dynamics in India see Ravinder Kaur, *Brand New Nation: Capitalist Dreams and Nationalist Designs in Twenty-First-Century India* (Stanford, CA: Stanford University Press, 2020).

87. Cornelia Zeineddine, "Nation Branding in the Middle East—United Arab Emirates (UAE) vs. Qatar," *Proceedings of the International Conference on Business Excellence* 11, no. 1 (2017): 592.

88. Simon Anholt, "'Nation Branding' in Asia," *Place Branding and Public Diplomacy* 4, no. 265–269 (2008): 268.

89. Ramos, *Dubai Amplified: The Engineering of a Port Geography*, 117, 29.

90. Curtis Yarvin, "UR's Plan to Fix Iraq," *Unqualified Reservations*, May 16, 2007, https://www.unqualified-reservations.org/2007/05/urs-plan-to-fix-iraq/.

91. Heidi M. Peters, "Department of Defense Contractor and Troop Levels in Afghanistan and Iraq: 2007–2020," *Congressional Research Service*, February 22, 2021, 6, 12.

92. Anna Fifield, "Contractors Reap $138bn from Iraq War," *Financial Times*, March 18, 2013, Financial Times Historical Archive, Gale.

93. Curtis Yarvin, "A Formalist Manifesto," *Unqualified Reservations*, April 23, 2007, https://www.unqualified-reservations.org/2007/04/formalist-manifesto-originally-posted/.

94. Curtis Yarvin, "Against Political Freedom," *Unqualified Reservations*, May 25, 2007, https://www.unqualified-reservations.org/2007/08/against-political-freedom/.

95. Yarvin, "A Formalist Manifesto."

CHAPTER 10: SILICON VALLEY COLONIALISM

1. Paul Romer, "A Theory of History, with an Application," *The Long Now Foundation*, May 18, 2009, https://longnow.org/seminars/02009/may/18/theory-history-application/.

2. Paul Romer, "Escape from the Great Distress," *Issues in Science and Technology* (Fall 2012): 65.

3. Romer, "A Theory of History, with an Application."

4. See Evgeny Morozov, *To Save Everything, Click Here: The Folly of Technological Solutionism* (New York: PublicAffairs, 2013).

5. Pauline Lipman, "Obama's Education Policy: More Markets, More Inequality, New Urban Contestations," in *Urban Policy in the Time of Obama*, ed. James DeFilippis (Minneapolis: University of Minnesota Press, 2016), 143.

6. David Wessel, "A Plan to Turn Honduras into the Next Hong Kong," *Wall Street Journal*, February 3, 2011, ProQuest.

7. Song Jung-a, Christian Oliver, and Tom Burgis, "Daewoo to Cultivate Madagascar Land for Free," *Financial Times*, November 19, 2008, Financial Times Historical Archive, Gale.

8. Renée Vellvé and Mamy Rakotondrainibe, "The Daewoo-Madagascar Land Grab: Ten Years On," *Thomson Reuters Foundation News*, November 16, 2018, https://news.trust.org/item/20181116144408-pdi0a. See also Daniel Shepard and Anuradha Mittal, *(Mis)investment in Agriculture: The Role of the International Finance Corporation in Global Land Grabs* (Oakland, CA: Oakland Institute, 2008).

9. Sebastian Mallaby, "The Politically Incorrect Guide to Ending Poverty," *Atlantic*, June 8, 2010, Gale OneFile.

10. Venusia Vinciguerra, "How the Daewoo Attempted Land Acquisition Contributed to Madagascar's Political Crisis in 2009," in *Contest for Land in Madagascar: Environment, Ancestors and Development*, ed. Sandra Evers, Gwyn Campbell, and Michael Lambek (Leiden: Brill, 2013), 242. See also Tom Burgis, "Madagascar Leader Cancels Daewoo Farm Deal," *FT.com*, March 18, 2009, Financial Times Historical Archive, Gale.

11. In the 1980s, the country was a rear operating base for the Reagan administration's contra offensive against Sandinista-governed Nicaragua.

12. Michael Engman, "Success and Stasis in Honduras' Free Zones," in *Special Economic Zones: Progress, Emerging Challenges, and Future Directions*, ed. Thomas Farole and Gokhan Akinci (Washington, DC: World Bank, 2011), 49. The domestic term is ZIPs (Zonas Industriales de Procesamiento).

13. This paragraph draws from Todd Gordon and Jeffery R. Webber, "Post-Coup Honduras: Latin America's Corridor of Reaction," *Historical Materialism* 21, no. 3 (2013): 16–56.

14. Engman, "Success and Stasis in Honduras' Free Zones," 62.

15. Wessel, "A Plan to Turn Honduras into the Next Hong Kong."

16. Adam Davidson, "Who Wants to Buy Honduras?," *New York Times*, May 8, 2012, ProQuest.

17. Congress approved a constitutional amendment creating REDs with a vote of 124–1. Tom W. Bell, "No Exit: Are Honduran Free Cities DOA?," *Freeman* (December 2012): 10; and Wessel, "A Plan to Turn Honduras into the Next Hong Kong."

18. Paul Romer and Octavio Sanchez, "Urban Prosperity in the RED," *Globe and Mail*, April 25, 2012, ProQuest.

19. Michael R. Castle Miller, "The Ciudades Modelo Project: Testing the Legality of Paul Romer's Charter Cities Concept by Analyzing the Constitutionality of the Honduran Zones for Employment and Economic Development," *Willamette Journal of International Law & Dispute Resolution* 22 (2014): 280.

20. For a thorough legal analysis see Miller, "The Ciudades Modelo Project: Testing the Legality of Paul Romer's Charter Cities Concept by Analyzing the Constitutionality of the Honduran Zones for Employment and Economic Development," 271–312.

21. Davidson, "Who Wants to Buy Honduras?"

22. Lindsay, "From Dubai to Chongqing to Honduras, the Silk Road of the Future Is Taking Shape in Urban Developments Based on Airport Hubs."

23. "Hong Kong in Honduras," *Economist*, December 10, 2011, Gale in Context: Global Issues.

24. Eli Sugarman, "Should Struggling Countries Let Investors Run Their Cities?," *Atlantic*, July 11, 2013, Gale OneFile.

25. Bell, "No Exit: Are Honduran Free Cities DOA?," 10.

26. Tom W. Bell, "Principles of Contracts for Governance Services," *Griffith Law Review* 21, no. 2 (2012): 494.

27. Graham Brown, "Honduran ZEDEs: The New Frontier," *PanAm Post*, February 8, 2014, http://blog.panampost.com/graham-brown/2014/02/08/honduran-zedes-new-frontier/.

28. Paul Romer, "Why the World Needs Charter Cities," TED Global (Oxford, UK), July 2009, https://www.youtube.com/watch?v=mSHBma0Ithk.

29. Romer and Sanchez, "Urban Prosperity in the RED."

30. Engman, "Success and Stasis in Honduras' Free Zones," 51, 54.

31. Brian Hutchison, "Opportunity in 'Charter City,'" *National Post*, December 27, 2012, Global Newsstream.

32. Brandon Fuller and Paul Romer, *Success and the City: How Charter Cities Could Transform the Developing World* (Ottawa: MacDonald Laurier Institute, April 2012), 15.

33. Fuller and Romer, *Success and the City: How Charter Cities Could Transform the Developing World*, 16.

34. Stanford Institute for Economic Policy, "SIEPR Economic Summit 2009," March 13, 2009, Wayback Machine capture September 11, 2016, https://siepr.stanford.edu/events/siepr-economic-summit-2009.

35. Paul Romer, "Governance in Developing Countries," *SIEPR Economic Summit*, March 13, 2009, https://www.youtube.com/watch?v=v7fSvDLvkaw.

36. Michael Ignatieff, "The American Empire," *New York Times Magazine*, January 5, 2003; Niall Ferguson, *Empire: The Rise and Demise of the British World Order and the Lessons for Global Power* (New York: Basic Books, 2004); and Deepak Lal, *In Praise of Empires: Globalization and Order* (New York: Palgrave Macmillan, 2004).

37. Niall Ferguson, "The Empire Slinks Back," *New York Times Magazine*, April 27, 2003, https://www.nytimes.com/2003/04/27/magazine/the-empire-slinks-back.html.

38. Keri Vacanti Brondo, *Land Grab: Green Neoliberalism, Gender, and Garifuna Resistance in Honduras* (Tucson: University of Arizona Press, 2013), 168.

39. Keane Bhatt, "Reporting on Romer's Charter Cities: How the Media Sanitize Honduras's Brutal Regime," *NACLA Report on the Americas*, February 19, 2013, https://nacla.org/news/2013/2/19/reporting-romer%E2%80%99s-charter-cities-how-media-sanitize-honduras%E2%80%99s-brutal-regime.

40. Curtis Yarvin, "From Cromer to Romer and Back Again: Colonialism for the 21st Century," *Unqualified Reservations*, August 20, 2009, https://www.unqualified-reservations.org/2009/08/from-cromer-to-romer-and-back-again/.

41. Patri Friedman, "Theory: Competitive Government, Practice: Seasteading," *The Future of Free Cities*, April 4, 2011, https://newmedia.ufm.edu/coleccion/the-future-of-free-cities/theory-of-free-cities-and-seasteading/.

42. Friedman, "Theory: Competitive Government, Practice: Seasteading."

43. Future Cities Development, Wayback Machine capture, September 11, 2012, http://futurecitiesdev.com/about-us/; and "Honduras Shrugged," *Economist*, December 10, 2011, Gale OneFile. South Korean investors were also involved. For details see Bridget Martin and Beth Geglia, "Korean Tigers in Honduras: Urban Economic Zones as Spatial Ideology

in International Policy Transfer Networks," *Political Geography* 74 (October 2019): 1–12.

44. He used the abbreviation "ancap." Michael Strong, "Marketing Free Cities as a Mainstream Solution to Global Poverty," *Future of Free Cities*, April 3, 2011, https://newmedia.ufm.edu/coleccion/the-future-of-free-cities/theory-of-free-cities-and-seasteading/.

45. Michael Strong, "Free Zones: An Additional Option for the Cambrian Explosion in Government," *Seasteading Institute Conference* (2009), https://vimeo.com/7577391. https://vimeo.com/7577391. For details on Strong and other libertarians involved with the Honduras enterprise see Craib, *Adventure Capitalism: A History of Libertarian Exit from Decolonization to the Digital Age*, 227–31.

46. Titus Gebel, "Welchen Staat würden Sie kaufen?," *Schweizer Monat* 94 (February 2014): 36.

47. Titus Gebel, "Markt des Zusammenlebens," *Schweizer Monat* (October 2018), https://schweizermonat.ch/markt-des-zusammenlebens/.

48. Titus Gebel, "'In der Politik findet Man heute eher blender als echte Problemlöser,'" *Mises.de*, October 14, 2019, https://www.misesde.org/2019/10/in-der-politik-findet-man-heute-eher-blender-als-echte-problemloeser.

49. Erick Brimen, "The Startup Society: Political Innovations That Give Rise to Flourishing," *Voice & Exit Festival*, December 14, 2017, https://www.youtube.com/watch?v=Pa5WzcZAsco.

50. Lizette Chapman, "The Hottest New Thing in Seasteading Is Land," *Bloomberg Businessweek*, December 20, 2019, https://www.bloomberg.com/news/articles/2019-12-20/silicon-valley-seasteaders-go-looking-for-low-tax-sites-on-land; Joshua Brustein, "A Private Tech City Opens for Business in Honduras," *Bloomberg*, March 27, 2021, https://www.bloomberg.com/news/articles/2021-03-27/prospera-in-honduras-a-private-tech-city-now-open-for-business; and Mario Aguero and Gissel Zalavarria, "Prospera: the First Charter City Approved by the Honduran Government," *Arias*, June 30, 2021, https://www.lexology.com/library/detail.aspx?g=1ceb727f-364e-4d50–9018–803744f3c88c.

51. The second ZEDE was "Ciudad Morazán" in Choloma. Beth Geglia and Andrea Nuila, "A Private Government in Honduras Moves Forward," *NACLA Report on the Americas*, February 15, 2021, https://nacla.org/news/2021/02/12/private-government-honduras-zede-prospera.

52. Breaking with Romer's vision, the ZEDE was no longer envisioned as a city. Instead, it moved more to the Dubai model with specialized districts for finance, media, education, etc. The list of possible ZEDEs allowed by the law was long, including "International Financial Centers, International Logistics Centers, Autonomous Cities, International Commercial Courts,

Special Investment Districts, Renewable Energy Districts, Special Economic Zones . . . Special Agricultural Zones, Special Tourism Zones, Social Mining Zones, [and] Social Forest Zones." An additional change came in the zone's governance. The governor and Transparency Commission of the RED was replaced by a Technical Secretary and Committee for the Implementation of Best Practices (CAMP) of the ZEDE. Whereas in the RED, the appointed officers slowly gave way to an elected council, in the ZEDE, the Technical Secretary and the CAMP were unelected and retained permanent veto power. Other policies were locked in, including a ceiling of 12 percent tax on individual income, a 16 percent tax on business income, and a 5 percent sales or value-added tax in the ZEDE. Miller, "The Ciudades Modelo Project: Testing the Legality of Paul Romer's Charter Cities Concept by Analyzing the Constitutionality of the Honduran Zones for Employment and Economic Development," 290–96. The CAMP was a who's who of global neoliberals. One-third were members of the Mont Pelerin Society. See Nina Ebner and Jamie Peck, "Fantasy Island: Paul Romer and the Multiplication of Hong Kong," *International Journal of Urban and Regional Research* 46, no. 1 (January 2022): 40, https://doi.org/10.1111/1468-2427 .13060.

53. Oliver Porter, "Prospera," *Startup Societies Foundation*, December 7, 2021, https://www.youtube.com/watch?v=IPKYyD9UuUc.

54. Mark Klugmann, "Interview," *Tabula* (Georgia), May 6, 2012, https://www .youtube.com/watch?v=DHzZp4sx8UE.

55. Katharina Pistor, *The Code of Capital: How the Law Creates Wealth and Inequality* (Princeton, NJ: Princeton University Press, 2019), 168.

56. Pistor, *The Code of Capital: How the Law Creates Wealth and Inequality*, 221.

57. Open Corporates, https://opencorporates.com/companies/us_wy/2017–000763896.

58. "Honduras Prospera LLC," https://sec.report/CIK/0001794703.

59. Bullough, *Moneyland: Why Thieves and Crooks Now Rule the World and How to Take It Back*, 25.

60. Nathan Heller, "Estonia, The Digital Republic," *New Yorker*, December 11, 2017, https://www.newyorker.com/magazine/2017/12/18/estonia-the-digital -republic.

61. Piia Tammpuu and Anu Masso, "'Welcome to the Virtual State': Estonian E-residency and the Digitalised State as a Commodity," *European Journal of Cultural Studies* 21, no. 5 (2018): 552.

62. Brustein, "A Private Tech City Opens for Business in Honduras." The board of advisors also included the former CEO of the Dubai International Finance Center and the chief international trade advisor to the hard Brexit faction of the UK Conservative Party. https://prospera.hn/about/.

63. J. Neil Schulman, *Alongside Night* (New York: Ace, 1979), 106.

64. Schulman, *Alongside Night*, 87–90.

65. "Charter Cities Podcast Episode 12: Erick Brimen on Próspera and the Birth of the First Charter City in Honduras," *Charter Cities Institute*, September 8, 2020, https://chartercitiesinstitute.org/podcast/charter-cities-podcast-episode-12-erick-brimen/.

66. Prospera Arbitration Center, https://pac.hn/, June 3, 2022.

67. Schumacher, ArchAgenda Debates 1: Cyber Urban Incubators in the Blockchain Metaverse-Chicago Architecture Biennial, October 16, 2021.

68. Graham Brown, "The ZEDEs as a Sudden Change," *PanAm Post*, February 22, 2014, http://blog.panampost.com/graham-brown/2014/02/22/zedes-sudden-change/.

69. Ismael Moreno, "A Model City for a Society in Tatters," *Envio* (April 2011), https://www.envio.org.ni/articulo/4330.

70. Wessel, "A Plan to Turn Honduras into the Next Hong Kong"; on Walker see Michel Gobat, *Empire by Invitation: William Walker and Manifest Destiny in Central America* (Cambridge, MA: Harvard University Press, 2018).

71. Maya Kroth, "Under New Management," *Foreign Policy*, September 1, 2014, https://foreignpolicy.com/2014/09/01/under-new-management/.

72. Brondo, *Land Grab: Green Neoliberalism, Gender, and Garifuna Resistance in Honduras*, 168.

73. Craib, *Adventure Capitalism: A History of Libertarian Exit from Decolonization to the Digital Age*, 223.

74. Knut Henkel, "Honduras: Widerstand gegen die Sonderwirtschaftszonen," *BlickpunktLateinamerika*, June 29, 2021, https://www.blickpunkt-lateinamerika.de/artikel/honduras-widerstand-gegen-die-sonderwirtschaftszonen/.

75. Marlon González, "Honduras Economic Development Zones Worry Residents, Experts," AP News, September 3, 2021, https://apnews.com/article/business-honduras-caribbean-d0496aa49fa1ae75547b56ad5476d790.

76. Ian MacDougall and Isabelle Simpson, "A Libertarian 'Startup City' in Honduras Faces Its Biggest Hurdle: The Locals," *Rest of World*, October 5, 2021, https://restofworld.org/2021/honduran-islanders-push-back-libertarian-startup/. See also Jeff Ernst, "Foreign Investors Are Building a 'Hong Kong of the Caribbean' on a Remote Honduran Island," *Vice*, December 2, 2020, https://www.vice.com/en/article/k7a7ae/foreign-investors-are-building-a-hong-kong-of-the-caribbean-on-a-remote-honduran-island; Geglia and Nuila, "A Private Government in Honduras Moves Forward."; and Beth Geglia, "As Private Cities Advance in Honduras, Hondurans Renew Their Opposition," *CEPR*, December 3, 2020, https://cepr.net/as-private-cities-advance-in-honduras-hondurans-renew-their-opposition/.

77. Bay Islands Entertainment TV, https://fb.watch/a96do32miK/. Broadcast is undated but followed the incident in September 2020.

78. Erick Brimen, "Free Trade, Not Aid, Is How to Eliminate Poverty," *Newsweek*, September 29, 2021, https://www.newsweek.com/free-trade-not-aid-how-eliminate-poverty-opinion-1633458.

79. Romer, "Escape from the Great Distress," 63.

80. Gwartney, Lawson, and Block, *Economic Freedom of the World, 1975–1995*, 63.

81. Quoted in Danielle Marie Mackey, "'I've Seen All Sorts of Horrific Things in My Time. But None as Detrimental to the Country as This,'" *New Republic*, December 14, 2014, https://newrepublic.com/article/120559/ive-seen-sorts-horrific-things-time-none-detrimental-country-this.

82. "Incoming Honduran President Wants UN Help to Battle Corruption," *France24*, December 4, 2021, https://www.france24.com/en/live-news/20211204-incoming-honduran-president-wants-un-help-to-battle-corruption; and Ana María Rovelo, "Zelaya: Gobierno de Xiomara derogará las ZEDE con un plebiscito," *Tiempo*, December 8, 2021, https://tiempo.hn/xiomara-derogara-zede-con-plebiscito/.

83. Mark Lutter, "Honduras and the Future of Charter Cities," *Charter Cities Institute*, December 2, 2021, https://www.chartercitiesinstitute.org/post/honduras-and-the-future-of-charter-cities.

84. Michael Strong, *Startup Cities*, podcast, Startup Societies Foundation, April 19, 2017, https://www.youtube.com/watch?v=DRZtFdagJuc.

85. Benjamin Weiser and Joan Suazo, "Ex-Honduran President Extradited to United States to Face Drug Charges," *New York Times*, April 21, 2022, ProQuest.

86. Gustavo Palencia, "Honduran Congress Unanimously Nixes Special Economic Zones," *Reuters*, April 21, 2022, https://www.reuters.com/world/americas/honduran-congress-unanimously-nixes-special-economic-zones-2022-04-21/.

87. Naomi Klein, "Disaster Capitalism: The New Economy of Catastrophe," *Harpers* (October 2007): 55.

88. John Ruch, "Sandy Springs to Bring Most Government Services In-House, Ending Much of Landmark Privatization," *Reporter Newspapers* (Atlanta), May 14, 2019, https://reporternewspapers.net/2019/05/14/sandy-springs-to-bring-most-government-services-in-house-ending-much-of-landmark-privatization/.

89. Laurie Clarke, "Crypto Millionaires Are Pouring Money into Central America to Build Their Own Cities," *MIT Technology Review*, April 20, 2022, https://www.technologyreview.com/2022/04/20/1049384/crypto-cities-central-america/.

90. "Adopting Bitcoin," capture April 26, 2022, https://adoptingbitcoin.org/speaker/VeronikaKuett/.

91. "Free Private Cities: Brazil's New Libertarian Dystopia," *Brasil Wire*, February 24, 2021, https://www.brasilwire.com/free-private-cities-brazils-new-libertarian-dystopia/.

CHAPTER 11: A CLOUD COUNTRY IN THE METAVERSE

1. Stephenson, *Snow Crash*, 40.

2. "Everything Facebook Revealed About the Metaverse in 11 Minutes," *CNET*, October 28, 2021, https://www.youtube.com/watch?v=gElfIo6uw4g.

3. "Investing in the Online Property Boom," *CNN Money*, October 20, 2006; "Making Real Money in Virtual Worlds," *Forbes*, August 7, 2006.

4. Jake Swearingen, "Steve Bannon Saw the 'Monster Power' of Angry Gamers While Farming Gold in World of Warcraft," *New York*, July 18, 2017, https://nymag.com/intelligencer/2017/07/steve-bannon-world-of-warcraft-gold-farming.html.

5. James Dale Davidson and William Rees-Mogg, *The Sovereign Individual: How to Survive and Thrive During the Collapse of the Welfare State* (London: Macmillan, 1997). Page references that follow are from the most recent edition. James Dale Davidson and William Rees-Mogg, *The Sovereign Individual: Mastering the Transition to the Information Age* (New York: Touchstone, 2020).

6. Davidson was a longtime libertarian. He started the magazine *The Individualist* in 1970 and lobbied Washington as the executive director of the National Taxpayers Union (NTU) with Murray Rothbard on its executive committee. "Against Taxation," *Libertarian Forum*, January 15, 1970. *The Sovereign Individual* was Davidson and Rees-Mogg's third collaboration after *Blood in the Streets: Investment Profits in a World Gone Mad* (1987) and *The Great Reckoning: How the World Will Change in the Depression of the 1990s* (1991).

7. Preface in James D. Davidson and William Rees-Mogg, *The Great Reckoning: How the World Will Change in the Depression of the 1990s* (London: Sidgwick & Jackson, 1991).

8. Davidson and Rees-Mogg, *The Great Reckoning*, 13, 69.

9. Davidson and Rees-Mogg, *The Sovereign Individual*, 388.

10. Davidson and Rees-Mogg, 291.

11. Davidson and Rees-Mogg, 31.

12. Davidson and Rees-Mogg, 301.

13. Patrick McKenzie, "AMA with Marc Andreessen," *Stripe* (n.d.), https://stripe.com/atlas/guides/ama-marc-andreessen.

14. George Packer, *The Unwinding: An Inner History of the New America* (New York: Farrar Straus Giroux, 2013), 133. For an insightful reading of the book and Thiel see Mark O'Connell, *Notes from an Apocalypse: A Personal Journey to the End of the World* (New York: Doubleday, 2020), 77–80.

15. Caroline Howard, "Peter Thiel: 'Don't Wait to Start Something New,'" *Forbes*, September 10, 2014, https://www.forbes.com/sites/carolinehoward /2014/09/10/peter-thiel-dont-wait-to-start-something-new/?sh =2b27fd571e69.

16. Another related story line links the web to Burning Man, the gathering in the desert where a makeshift city emerged once a year. Paul Romer and Patri Friedman both promoted the idea that their start-up societies were extensions of the spirit of Burning Man. Craib, *Adventure Capitalism: A History of Libertarian Exit from Decolonization to the Digital Age*, 186–88.

17. Fred Turner, *From Counterculture to Cyberculture: Stewart Brand, the Whole Earth Network, and the Rise of Digital Utopianism* (Chicago: University of Chicago Press, 2006).

18. Jathan Sadowski, "The Internet of Landlords: Digital Platforms and New Mechanisms of Rentier Capitalism," *Antipode* 52, no. 2 (March 2020): 562–80.

19. "Innovators Under 35," *MIT Technology Review* (2013), https://www .technologyreview.com/innovators-under-35/2013/.

20. Balaji Srinivasan, "Silicon Valley's Ultimate Exit," *Y Combinator Startup School*, October 25, 2013, https://www.youtube.com/watch?v=cOubCHLXT6A.

21. Drew Olanoff, "Google CEO Larry Page Shares His Philosophy at I/O: 'We Should Be Building Great Things That Don't Exist,'" *TechCrunch*, May 15, 2013, https://techcrunch.com/2013/05/15/google-ceo-larry-page-takes-the -stage-at-ceo-to-wrap-up-the-io-keynote/.

22. Max Chafkin, *The Contrarian: Peter Thiel and Silicon Valley's Pursuit of Power* (New York: Penguin, 2022), 209. On Tlon and its primary project, Urbit, see Harrison Smith and Roger Burrows, "Software, Sovereignty and the Post-Neoliberal Politics of Exit," *Theory, Culture & Society* 38, no. 6 (2021): 153–57.

23. Balaji Srinivasan, "Software Is Reorganizing the World," *Wired*, November 22, 2013, https://www.wired.com/2013/11/software-is-reorganizing-the -world-and-cloud-formations-could-lead-to-physical-nations/.

24. Srinivasan, "Software Is Reorganizing the World."

25. Marshall Kosloff and Balaji Srinivasan, "#3 Network State with Balaji Srinivasan, former CTO of Coinbase and Founder of 1729," *The Deep End*, podcast, May 26, 2021.

26. Herbert Marcuse, *One-Dimensional Man: Studies in the Ideology of Advanced Industrial Society* (Boston: Beacon Press, 1964); and Naomi Klein, *No Logo: Taking Aim at the Brand Bullies* (New York: Picador, 1999).

27. For an influential pioneering example see Manuel Castells, *The Rise of the Network Society* (Malden, MA: Blackwell Publishers, 1996). Hundreds of similar books followed.

28. Balaji Srinivasan, "How to Start a New Country," *1729.com*, April 9, 2021, https://1729.com/how-to-start-a-new-country/.

29. Srinivasan, "How to Start a New Country."

30. Balaji Srinivasan, "The Network State," *1729.com* (n.d.), 12.

31. Srinivasan, "The Network State," 6.

32. Srinivasan, "How to Start a New Country."

33. Balaji Srinivasan, Twitter post, December 28, 2020, http://twitter.com/balajis.

34. Kosloff and Srinivasan, "#3 Network State with Balaji Srinivasan, former CTO of Coinbase and Founder of 1729."

35. See Matthew Hongoltz-Hetling, *A Libertarian Walks into a Bear: The Utopian Plot to Liberate an American Town (And Some Bears)* (New York: PublicAffairs, 2020).

36. Belew, *Bring the War Home: The White Power Movement and Paramilitary America*.

37. O'Connell, *Notes from an Apocalypse: A Personal Journey to the End of the World*.

38. "The Rise of Cloud Cities & Citizen Journalism with Balaji Srinivasan," *The Paradox Podcast*, July 29, 2020, https://podcastnotes.org/paradox-podcast/balaji-srinivasan-on-the-paradox-podcast/.

39. Kosloff and Srinivasan, "#3 Network State with Balaji Srinivasan, former CTO of Coinbase and Founder of 1729."

40. Srinivasan, "The Network State," 9.

41. Balaji Srinivasan, "Bitcoin, China, the 'Woke' Mob, and the Future of the Internet," *Joe Lonsdale: American Optimist*, August 11, 2021, https://www.youtube.com/watch?v=MMuIyspn7s0.

42. "The Rise of Cloud Cities & Citizen Journalism with Balaji Srinivasan."

43. Balaji Srinivasan, Twitter post, August 28, 2020, http://twitter.com/balajis. See Anna Verena Eireiner, "Promises of Urbanism: New Songdo City and the Power of Infrastructure," *Space and Culture* (2021): 1–11, https://doi.org/10.1177/12063312211038716.

44. F. A. Hayek, *Denationalisation of Money: An Analysis of the Theory and Practice of Concurrent Currencies* (London: Institute of Economic Affairs, 1976). On the earlier history see Eric Helleiner, "Denationalizing Money?: Economic Liberalism and the 'National Question' in Currency Affairs," in *International Financial History in the Twentieth Century: System and Anarchy*, ed. Marc Flandreau, Carl-Ludwig Holtfrerich, and Harold James (New York: Cambridge University Press, 2003).

45. It was called 21, no doubt after the maximum number of million bitcoin that could be mined.

46. Srinivasan, "The Network State," 32. The origin story of bitcoin has been told elsewhere. See, e.g., Stefan Eich, "Old Utopias, New Tax Havens: The Politics of Bitcoin in Historical Perspective," in *Regulating Blockchain* (Oxford: Oxford University Press, 2019), 85–98.

47. Balaji Srinivasan, "The Network State: How Every Country Becomes a Software Country," *Startup Societies Summit*, September 15, 2017, https://www.youtube.com/watch?v=KiLUPvUsdXg&t=3s.

48. Srinivasan, "The Network State: How Every Country Becomes a Software Country."

49. E. J. Hobsbawm and T. O. Ranger, eds., *The Invention of Tradition* (New York: Cambridge University Press, 1983).

50. Aris Komporozos-Athanasiou, *Speculative Communities: Living with Uncertainty in a Financialized World* (Chicago: University of Chicago Press, 2022).

51. "The Rise of Cloud Cities & Citizen Journalism with Balaji Srinivasan."

52. Tarnoff, *Internet for the People: The Fight for Our Digital Future*, 36.

53. Quinn Slobodian, "Cryptocurrencies' Dream of Escaping the Global Financial System Is Crumbling," *Guardian*, July 5, 2021, Global Newsstream.

54. Katie Martin and Billy Nauman, "Bitcoin's Growing Energy Problem: 'It's a Dirty Currency,'" *Financial Times*, May 20, 2021, Global Newsstream.

55. On the frontier myth see Greg Grandin, *The End of the Myth: From the Frontier to the Border Wall in the Mind of America* (New York: Metropolitan, 2019).

56. "The Rise of Cloud Cities & Citizen Journalism with Balaji Srinivasan."

57. On the place they ended up see Justin Gaudet, "Paddle Prairie Metis Settlement," *Canadian Encyclopedia*, August 3, 2021, https://www.thecanadianencyclopedia.ca/en/article/paddle-prairie-metis-settlement. My great-grandmother Emily Houle is in the photograph.

58. See Brenna Bhandar, *Colonial Lives of Property: Law, Land, and Racial Regimes of Ownership* (Durham, NC: Duke University Press, 2018); and Eyal Weizman, *Hollow Land: Israel's Architecture of Occupation*, new ed. (New York: Verso, 2017).

59. Dan Senor and Saul Singer, *Start-up Nation: The Story of Israel's Economic Miracle* (New York: Twelve, 2009).

60. Balaji Srinivasan, Twitter post, May 13, 2021, http://twitter.com/balajis.

61. Quoted in Henley & Partners, "Record-Breaking Global Mobility Grounded by COVID-19 Pandemic," *PR Newswire*, April 7, 2020, https://www.prnewswire.com/ae/news-releases/record-breaking-global-mobility-grounded-by-covid-19-pandemic-301034963.html.

62. Quinn Slobodian, "How the Libertarian Right Plans to Profit from the Pandemic," *Guardian*, June 1, 2020, Global Newsstream.

63. Virtual SSF Summit: Startup Societies in a Post-Covid World, May 1–2, 2020. Streamed online.

64. Balaji Srinivasan, Twitter post, January 13, 2020, http://twitter.com/balajis.

65. Balaji Srinivasan, Twitter post, January 13, 2020, http://twitter.com/balajis.

66. Balaji Srinivasan, Twitter post, January 13, 2020, http://twitter.com/balajis.

67. Joel Stein, "Bienvenidos a Miami," *Financial Times*, February 5, 2022, Global Newsstream.

68. Katie Warren and Mary Meisenzahl, "Peter Thiel Bought This Miami Compound on an Exclusive Manmade Island for $18 Million," *Insider*, January 20, 2021, https://www.businessinsider.com/miami-real-estate-ford-ceo-compound-photos-2020–10.

69. Stein, "Bienvenidos a Miami"; and Chafkin, *The Contrarian: Peter Thiel and Silicon Valley's Pursuit of Power*, 34.

70. Balaji Srinivasan, "The Start of Startup Cities," *1729.com*, May 3, 2021, https://1729.com/miami.

71. Dick Simpson, Marco Rosaire Rossi, and Thomas J. Gradel, "Corruption Spikes in Illinois," Anti-Corruption Report #13, February 20, 2021, https://pols.uic.edu/wp-content/uploads/sites/273/2021/02/Corruption-Spikes-in-IL-Anti-Corruption-Rpt-13-final2.-1.pdf.

72. Thomas Burton, "Donald Trump Looking Beyond Traditional Medical Experts for FDA Commissioner," *Wall Street Journal*, January 13, 2017, ProQuest.

73. Balaji Srinivasan, Twitter post, March 16, 2021, http:/twitter.com/balajis, called the project *1729*, a reference to the lowest number that can be created by adding two cubes in two different ways—called Ramanujan's number after a prodigious Indian mathematician. Srinivasan thought about his project as, in part, a talent finding to the world beyond the industrial core. Like the Hubble Telescope that sought dark matter, he said mobile phones would help find what he called "dark talent." Kosloff and Srinivasan, "#3 Network State with Balaji Srinivasan, former CTO of Coinbase and Founder of 1729."

74. Parag Khanna and Balaji Srinivasan, "Great Protocol Politics," *Foreign Policy*, December 11, 2021, https://foreignpolicy.com/2021/12/11/bitcoin-ethereum-cryptocurrency-web3-great-protocol-politics/.

75. COVID-19 National Preparedness Collaborators, "Pandemic Preparedness and COVID-19: An Exploratory Analysis of Infection and Fatality Rates, and Contextual Factors Associated with Preparedness in 177 Countries, from Jan 1, 2020, to Sept 30, 2021," *Lancet*, February 1, 2022, https://doi.org/https://doi.org/10.1016/S0140–6736(22)00172–6.

76. Ben Tarnoff, "The Metaverse Is a Cubicle," *Metal Machine Music*, November 30, 2021, https://bentarnoff.substack.com/p/the-metaverse-is-a-cubicle?s=r.

77. Richard Barbrook and Andy Cameron, "The Californian Ideology," *Mute* 1, no. 3 (September 1, 1995), https://www.metamute.org/editorial/articles /californian-ideology.

78. See Phil Jones, *Work Without the Worker: Labour in the Age of Platform Capitalism* (New York: Verso, 2021).

CONCLUSION

1. Lizzie Crook, "Zaha Hadid Architects Releases Visuals of Amorphous OPPO Shenzhen Headquarters," *Dezeen*, January 31, 2020, https://www.dezeen .com/2020/01/31/zaha-hadid-architects-oppo-headquarters-shenzhen -china-architecture/; Lizzie Crook, "Zaha Hadid Architects Unveils Pebble-Shaped Science Museum for Shenzhen," *Dezeen*, December 1, 2020, https: //www.dezeen.com/2020/12/01/zaha-hadid-architects-shenzhen-science -technology-museum/; and Lizzie Crook, "Supertall Skyscrapers Linked by Planted Terraces to Be Built in Shenzhen by Zaha Hadid Architects," *Dezeen*, January 13, 2021, https://www.dezeen.com/2021/01/13/tower-c-supertall -skyscrapers-zaha-hadid-architects-shenzhen/.

2. "The First Building of Zaha Hadid's 'Unicorn Island' Nears Completion in Chengdu, China," *Designboom*, January 15, 2020, https://www.designboom .com/architecture/zaha-hadid-architects-unicorn-island-chengdu-china -01–15–2020/.

3. "Unicorn Island Will Be Built in Chengdu, China," https://partners.wsj .com/xinhua/chengdu/unicorn-island-will-be-built-in-chengdu-china/.

4. Kanna, *Dubai: The City as Corporation*, 91.

5. Patrik Schumacher and Rahim Taghizadegan, "The Failure of Urban Planning and the Future of Cities," June 11, 2021, https://www.youtube.com /watch?v=4ZppWV6w4XA.

6. Tom Ravenscroft, "Zaha Hadid Architects Reveals Design for Skyscraper on World's Most Expensive Site," *Dezeen*, September 26, 2020, https://www .dezeen.com/2020/09/26/2-murray-road-skyscraper-zaha-hadid-worlds -most-expensive-site-hong-kong/.

7. Patrik Schumacher and Martti Kalliala, "Total Freedom," *After Us*, November 14, 2016, https://medium.com/after-us/total-freedom-5ee930676b65.

8. Patrik Schumacher and Arno Brandlhuber, "Land of the Free Forces," *ARCH+* (2018): 97.

9. Schumacher and Taghizadegan, "The Failure of Urban Planning and the Future of Cities."

10. Patrik Schumacher, "Increasing Freedom and Prosperity by Means of Private Cities," *Liberland Press*, July 25, 2020, https://liberlandpress.com /2020/07/25/increasing-freedom-and-prosperity-by-means-of-private -cities/.

11. Schumacher and Kalliala, "Total Freedom."

12. Patrik Schumacher, "Liberland's Prospective Urban Planning Regime," *Liberland Press*, February 19, 2020, https://liberlandpress.com/2020/02/19 /liberlands-prospective-urban-planning-regime/.

13. Edward Ongweso Jr., "Inside Liberland, a Crypto-Libertarian Micronation in Eastern Europe," *Vice*, April 29, 2022, https://www.vice.com/en/article /xgdj9k/inside-liberland-a-crypto-libertarian-micronation-in-eastern -europe.

14. Patrik Schumacher, "Politics After the Libertarian Revolution, Interview at LibertyCon, Madrid," March 14, 2020, https://www.youtube.com/watch?v =Oh_3yhcxCeY.

15. Hoppe, Stone, Kinsella, Dürr: Discussion, Q&A (PFS 2017), https://www .youtube.com/watch?v=T4-negu-E0E.

16. Schumacher, "After the Libertarian Revolution."

17. Schumacher and Taghizadegan, "The Failure of Urban Planning and the Future of Cities."

18. Mertha, "'Fragmented Authoritarianism 2.0': Political Pluralization in the Chinese Policy Process."

19. Will Doig, *High-Speed Empire: Chinese Expansion and the Future of Southeast Asia* (New York: Columbia Global Reports, 2018).

20. David Pilling, "Djibouti Row with DP World Embodies Horn of Africa Power Struggle," *FT.com*, October 30, 2018, Global Newsstream.

21. Degang Sun and Yahia H. Zoubir, "Securing China's 'Latent Power': The Dragon's Anchorage in Djibouti," *Journal of Contemporary China* 30, no. 130 (2021): 683.

22. Jonathan E. Hillman, *The Emperor's New Road: China and the Project of the Century* (New Haven, CT: Yale University Press, 2020), 157.

23. Kathrin Hille, "The Chinese Companies Trying to Buy Strategic Islands," *FT.com*, April 11, 2022, Global Newsstream.

24. Carrai, "China's Malleable Sovereignty Along the Belt and Road Initiative: The Case of the 99-Year Chinese Lease of Hambantota Port."

25. Hille, "Strategic Islands"; and Hung, *City on the Edge*, 37.

26. Maximilian Mayer and Xin Zhang, "Theorizing China-World Integration: Sociospatial Reconfigurations and the Modern Silk Roads," *Review of International Political Economy* 28, no. 4 (2021): 988.

27. See Umut Özsu, "The Ottoman Empire, the Origins of Extraterritoriality, and International Legal Theory," in *The Oxford Handbook of the Theory of International Law*, ed. Anne Orford and Florian Hoffmann (Oxford: Oxford University Press, 2016), 124–37.

28. For the connection to earlier Ottoman practice see Moritz Anselm Mihatsch and Michael Mulligan, "The Longue Durée of Extraterritoriality and Global Capital," *Culture, Theory and Critique* 62, no. 1–2 (2021): 1.

29. Vivian Nereim, "Saudi Arabia Is Planning the Largest Buildings Ever Constructed," *Bloomberg*, May 31, 2022, https://www.bloomberg.com/news/articles/2022-05-31/saudi-arabia-is-planning-the-largest-buildings-ever-constructed.

30. Ian Palmer, "Is Saudi Arabia's New Climate City 'Neom' Future or Fantasy?," *Forbes*, February 28, 2022, https://www.forbes.com/sites/ianpalmer/2022/02/28/a-new-climate-city-in-a-big-oil-state—saudi-arabia—is-it-future-or-fantasy.

31. Simon Robinson, Samia Nakhoul, and Stephen Kalin, "Exclusive: New Saudi Mega-City Will Be Listed Publicly, Crown Prince Says," *Reuters*, October 26, 2017, https://www.reuters.com/article/us-saudi-economy-mbs-interview-exclusive-idUSKBN1CV0ZM.

32. Merlyn Thomas and Vibeke Venema, "Neom: What's the Green Truth Behind a Planned Eco-City in the Saudi Desert?," *BBC News*, February 22, 2022, https://www.bbc.com/news/blogs-trending-59601335.

33. Bill Bostock, "Saudi Arabia Announced a Wild Plan to Build a Floating, 8-sided City," *Business Insider*, November 18, 2021, https://www.businessinsider.com/saudi-arabia-oxagon-floating-eight-sided-city-2021-11; Reem Walid, "MENA Project Tracker: Contractors Prepare for Two Libyan Drilling Projects; Bids Invited for $500bn Saudi Oxagon Project and Alinma HQ," *Arab News*, May 9, 2021, https://arab.news/5m3ty; Vivian Nereim, "Saudi Prince's 'Neom' to Expand Port to Rival Region's Biggest," *Bloomberg*, November 24, 2021, https://www.bloomberg.com/news/articles/2021-11-25/saudi-prince-s-neom-to-expand-port-to-rival-region-s-biggest?sref=apOkUyd1; and Osama Habib, "NEOM Project Has Been Fast Tracked to Meet Deadline, Says Top Executive," *Arab News*, February 19, 2022, https://www.arabnews.com/node/2027996/business-economy.

34. Tracy Alloway, "Saudi Arabia Gives Citizenship to a Robot," *Bloomberg*, October 26, 2017, https://www.bloomberg.com/news/articles/2017-10-26/saudi-arabia-gives-citizenship-to-a-robot-claims-global-first.

35. Richard Partington, "P&O Ferries Owner DP World Loses Status as Partner in Solent Freeport," *Guardian*, April 7, 2022, ProQuest.

36. Richard Partington and Gwyn Topham, "P&O Ferries Owner to Benefit from at Least £50m of UK Freeport Scheme," *Guardian*, March 21, 2022, Global Newsstream.

37. Eamonn Butler, "Freeports Will Be a World-Leading Policy—as Long as the Treasury Isn't Allowed to Water Them Down," *Telegraph.co.uk*, March 3, 2021, Westlaw.

38. Gwyn Topham, "P&O Ferries Boss Admits Firm Broke Law by Sacking Staff Without Consultation," *Guardian*, March 24, 2022, ProQuest.

39. The national living wage in 2022 for people over age twenty-three is £9.50, https://www.gov.uk/national-minimum-wage-rates; Topham,

"P&O Ferries Boss Admits Firm Broke Law by Sacking Staff Without Consultation."

40. Simeon Kerr, "DP World Wins $2.5bn Investor Boost," *Financial Times*, June 7, 2022, Global Newsstream.

41. Jeff Deist and Stephan Livera, "Economic Freedom vs. Personal Freedom," *The Human Action Podcast*, May 13, 2022, https://mises.org/library/economic-freedom-vs-personal-freedom.

42. He Huifeng, "China Bets on Hainan Duty-Free Shopping Mecca to Boost Spending at Home," *South China Morning Post*, July 13, 2020, Global Newsstream; and He Huifeng, "China Creates Hainan Special Health Care Zone to Tap Growing Medical Tourism Market," *South China Morning Post*, July 14, 2020, Global Newsstream.

43. UNCTAD, *Handbook on Special Economic Zones in Africa* (Geneva: UNCTAD, 2021), xvii.

44. Claire W. Herbert and Martin J. Murray, "Building from Scratch: New Cities, Privatized Urbanism and the Spatial Restructuring of Johannesburg After Apartheid," *International Journal of Urban and Regional Research* 39, no. 3 (May 2015): 475. See also Benjamin H. Bradlow, "Weapons of the Strong: Elite Resistance and the Neo-Apartheid City," *City & Community* 20, no. 3 (2021): 191–211.

45. "Steps Announced for SEZs in Budget Will Promote Growth, Boost Exports: EPCES," *Economic Times* (New Delhi, India), February 2, 2022, Global Newsstream.

46. Dorit Geva, "Orbán's Ordonationalism as Post-Neoliberal Hegemony," *Theory, Culture & Society* 38, no. 6 (2021): 77.

47. Joshua Oliver and Philip Stafford, "Why the UK Joined the Race to Woo the Crypto Industry," *Financial Times*, April 28, 2022, Global Newsstream.

48. Edwin Heathcote, "Too Rich and Too Thin? Welcome to Manhattan's Newest 'Skinnyscraper,'" *Financial Times*, May 6, 2022, Global Newsstream.

49. "World's Ultra-Rich Flee to Dubai to Escape Pandemic," *Economic Times* (New Delhi, India), May 6, 2021, Global Newsstream.

50. Mogielnicki, *A Political Economy of Free Zones in Gulf Arab States*, 205.

51. Thibault Serlet, "How Special Economic Zones Are Quietly Advancing State Capitalism," *FEE.org*, February 25, 2022, https://fee.org/articles/how-special-economic-zones-are-quietly-advancing-state-capitalism/.

52. Yi Wu, "Subcounty Administration in Rural Southwest China (1950–2000): Changing State Spatiality, Persistent Village Territoriality and Implications for the Current Urban Transformation," *Culture, Theory and Critique* 62, no. 1–2 (2021): 40.

53. Peter Thiel in James Dale Davidson and William Rees-Mogg, *The Sovereign Individual: Mastering the Transition to the Information Age* (New York: Touchstone, 2020), 6.

54. Max Read, "Peter Thiel's Latest Venture Is the American Government," *New York*, January 21, 2020, https://nymag.com/intelligencer/2020/01/peter-thiel-conservative-political-influence.html.

55. Chafkin, *The Contrarian: Peter Thiel and Silicon Valley's Pursuit of Power*, 290.

56. Madhumita Murgia and Sarah Neville, "Palantir Gears Up to Expand Its Reach into UK's NHS," *Financial Times*, June 9, 2022, Global News-stream.

57. China Miéville, "Floating Utopias," in *Evil Paradises: Dreamworlds of Neoliberalism*, ed. Mike Davis and Daniel Bertrand Monk (New York: New Press, 2007), 255; see Tyler Cowen's influential idea of "state capacity libertarianism." Tyler Cowen, "What Libertarianism Has Become and Will Become—State Capacity Libertarianism," *Marginal Revolution*, January 1, 2020, https://marginalrevolution.com/marginalrevolution/2020/01/what-libertarianism-has-become-and-will-become-state-capacity-libertarianism.html.

58. Read, "Peter Thiel's Latest Venture Is the American Government."

59. Damian Shepherd, "World's Top Enabler of Financial Secrecy Is the United States," *Bloomberg*, May 16, 2022, https://www.bloomberg.com/news/articles/2022–05–16/world-s-top-enabler-of-financial-secrecy-is-the-united-states?sref=apOkUyd1.

60. The indicator is created by the Polity Project. Rebecca Best, "Why Risk for Violence in U.S. Rises Without Roe," *Washington Post*, May 10, 2022, https://www.washingtonpost.com/politics/2022/05/10/roe-civil-conflict-military-democracy-gender/.

61. Craib, *Adventure Capitalism: A History of Libertarian Exit from Decolonization to the Digital Age*, 247.

62. Richard Kreitner, *Break It Up: Secession, Division, and the Secret History of America's Imperfect Union* (New York: Little, Brown and Company, 2020), 371.

63. Rich Lowry, "A Surprising Share of Americans Wants to Break Up the Country. Here's Why They're Wrong," *Politico*, October 6, 2021, https://www.politico.com/news/magazine/2021/10/06/americans-national-divorse-theyre-wrong-515443.

64. Joan Faus, "Catalan Leader Says to Freeze Parliamentary Support to Spanish PM over Spying Row," *Reuters*, April 21, 2022, https://www.reuters.com/world/europe/catalan-leader-says-freeze-parliamentary-support-spanish-pm-over-spying-row-2022-04-21/.

65. Alastair Bonnett, *Else Where: A Journey into Our Age of Islands* (Chicago: University of Chicago Press, 2020), 225–30.

66. Neil Munshi and William Clowes, "Mega-Consulate Ties U.S. to Convicted Billionaire in Nigeria," *Bloomberg*, May 9, 2022, https://www.bloomberg

.com/news/articles/2022–05–10/mega-consulate-ties-u-s-to-convicted -billionaire-in-nigeria.

67. Caline Malek, "Middle East Hospitality Project Pushes the Boundaries of Sustainable Construction," *Arab News*, November 20, 2021, https://www .arabnews.com/node/1977791/middle-east; and "How Dubai's Heart of Europe Mega Project Aims to Be Kind to the Planet," April 16, 2020, https://thoe.com /how-dubais-heart-of-europe-mega-project-aims-to-be-kind-to-the-planet/.

68. Becky Ferreira, "We Need to Talk About a Planned Retreat from Climate Disaster Zones Now," *Vice*, September 20, 2019, https://www.vice.com/en /article/3kxv73/we-need-to-talk-about-a-planned-retreat-from-climate -disaster-zones-now. See also Liz Koslov, "The Case for Retreat," *Public Culture* 28, no. 2 (2016): 359–87.

69. On this episode see Isabelle Simpson, "Cultural Political Economy of the Start-Up Societies Imaginary" (PhD diss., McGill University, 2021), chap. 6.

70. Rowland Atkinson and Sarah Blandy, "A Picture of the Floating World: Grounding the Secessionary Affluence of the Residential Cruise Liner," *Antipode* 41, no. 1 (2009).

71. Bell, *Your Next Government?: From the Nation State to Stateless Nations*, 56.

72. Madeline Berg, "Coronavirus: Even the World's Largest Luxury Yacht Has Now Stopped Sailing," *Forbes*, March 16, 2020, https://www.forbes.com /sites/maddieberg/2020/03/16/the-worlds-largest-luxury-yacht-suspends -operations-amid-coronavirus/?sh=6d497e7d5f78. For a similar observa- tion see Simpson, "Cultural Political Economy of the Start-Up Societies Imaginary." For an extraordinary story of another failed libertarian cruise ship venture see Sophie Elmhirst, "The Disastrous Voyage of Satoshi, the World's First Cryptocurrency Cruise Ship," *Guardian*, September 7, 2021, Global Newsstream.

73. Benjamin Haas, "Hong Kong Government Seeks to Bar Four More MPs," *Guardian*, December 2, 2016, Global Newsstream.

74. Antony Dapiran, *City on Fire: The Fight for Hong Kong* (Melbourne: Scribe, 2020), 254.

75. Hannes Gissurarson, *Spending Other People's Money: A Critique of Rawls, Piketty and Other Redistributionists* (Brussels, Belgium: New Direction, 2018), 8.

76. M. Ackbar Abbas, *Hong Kong: Culture and the Politics of Disappearance* (Minneapolis: University of Minnesota Press, 1997).

77. Summers, *China's Hong Kong*, 68. See also Jamie Peck, "On Capitalism's Cusp," *Area Development and Policy* 6, no. 1 (2021): 1–30.

78. "The JOC Top 50 World Container Ports," *Journal of Commerce* (August 20–27, 2012): 24, https://www.joc.com/sites/default/files/u48783/pdf/Top50 -container-2012.pdf; and World Shipping Council, "The Top 50 Container Ships," accessed January 31, 2022, https://www.worldshipping.org/top-50-ports.

79. Edwin J. Feulner, "Hong Kong Is No Longer What It Was," *The Heritage Foundation*, April 5, 2021, https://www.heritage.org/asia/commentary/hong-kong-no-longer-what-it-was.

80. Hung, *City on the Edge: Hong Kong Under Chinese Rule*, 8.

81. Hung, 209–16.

82. Mark Lutter, *Charter Cities Podcast*, episode 8, "Building a New Hong Kong with Ivan Ko," July 13, 2020, https://www.chartercitiesinstitute.org/post/charter-cities-podcast-episode-9-ivan-ko.

ACKNOWLEDGMENTS

I am filled with gratitude to the people who have lent their support, ideas, and friendship in the years it's taken to write this book. Thank you to Atossa Araxia Abrahamian, Hadji Bakara, Tim Barker, Grace Blakeley, Mark Blyth, William Callison, Will Davies, Daniel Denvir, Kristin Fabbe, Katrina Forrester, Heinrich Geiselberger, Ryan S. Jeffery, Ana Isabel Keilson, Alexander Kentikelenis, Aaron Kerner, Kojo Koram, Mathew Lawrence, Jamie Martin, Thomas Meaney, Dieter Plehwe, Justin Reynolds, Thea Riofrancos, Pavlos Roufos, Stuart Schrader, Hank Silver, Ben Tarnoff, Christy Thornton, Alberto Toscano, Isabella Weber, Moira Weigel, Kirsten Weld, and a special one to Boaz Levin for reading an early vision of the whole thing. Thank you to Mel Flashman for your intellectual camaraderie and advocacy and to Sara Bershtel and Grigory Tovbis for helping rebuild the book at sea and guide it into port. Thank you also to Marion Kadi for the maps and, at the presses, to Tim Duggan, Anita Sheih, and Clarissa Long at Holt and Thomas Penn, Matthew Hutchison, Eva Hodgkin, and Julie Woon at Penguin. Thanks to Cameron Abadi at *Foreign Policy*, Hettie O'Brien and Jonathan Shainin at the *Guardian*, Gavin Jacobson at *New Statesman*, and John Guida at Suein Hwang at the *New York Times* for helping me try out parts of the argument in public. The Harvard Book Store, Munro's, and Raven provided many of the books needed to write this book. NTS provided much of the music. Emotional molten core provided by my parents and siblings and family penumbra in the pandemic years and always. And, most of all, endless thanks to my love and fellow traveler Michelle and our son, Yann, with whom I am lucky enough to wake up in the same home every blessed morning.

INDEX